Radical Media

Radical Media

The Political Experience
Of Alternative Communication
By John Downing

South End Press

ISBN 0-89608-191-5 Paper
       0-89608-192-3 Cloth
Library of Congress Number: 83-061475
Typeset at South End Press
Cover by Jeanette Brown

Foreword and Acknowledgements

I have attempted to carve out entirely new territory in this study. So far as I know it is the firt comparative treatment in detail of the political experiences of organizing "self-managed" media.[1] Thus the media surveyed are not merely radical in their political communication, but also in their very organization. Self-managed factories have had a considerable literature devoted to them,[2] but the experiences of self-managed media is scattered over numerous countries and continents, often not written down, and living solely in their organizers' memories. Many times in the course of research for this book such individuals have told me I was the first person ever to ask them systematically about their experiences. At the very least, then, I have acted as historian/chronicler, and as a contributor to the growing literature on self-management. My intention, however, has been larger. I have hoped that by collecting together these accounts, I would provide materials for media activists now and in the future to use as they begin to develop media projects in their own, no doubt quite specific, circumstances. Those in power can afford to employ an army of intellectuals to reflect in think-tanks on their experiences and problems. Those outside the power-structure too often spend time simply reinventing the wheel.

There are gaps in the book which should be noted. There is no material on Third World experiences in organizing popular media (apart from the few pages devoted to Puerto Rico), although that experience is rich and instructive.[3] Nor is there any material on the increasingly important question of popular utilization of computer communications.[4] Both are fertile ares for future study. Nor is this a technical, legal or financial primer for organizing alternative media: it is an examination of their political experience.

Self-management of media or any other aspect of society is not a topic normally calculated to appeal to the power-vertices of East or West (unless within a rigidly circumscribed environment, such as a rural commune). Media moguls display a calm dismissiveness for the subject, whenever they fail to keep it off the public agenda altogether. Yet the topic persists in resurfacing, whether in Solidarity, or the Prague Spring, or Chile during the Popular Unity period, or the other countries in ths book, or in many other countries never mentioned here at all. The examples of self-management in action may be relatively small, even rather short-lived in some cases. Yet the ship from which the Boston rebels tipped those tea-chests at the beginning of the American revolution was minute by present-day standards, barely imaginable as a vessel in which to cross the Atlantic Ocean. Measuring political significance by size alone is a chancy undertaking for the powers that be. We shall see below that they rarely risk it. For those of us who wish to see substantive social change, it is a foolish, needless counsel of fatalism. The record of the media studied in this book should help to irradicate such despair. With William Blake, "Were we not slaves till we rebelled?"[5]

For this work a whole host of voluntary respondents and helpers have been essential. I hope I have written a book worthy of their efforts, even if they still spot matters of continuing disagreement. For these, I ask their indulgence.

For the U.S. case studies, I should like to thank the following. *The National Guardian/ The Guardian:* Jim Aronson, Cedric Belfrage, John Trinkl, Karen Geller, Bill Ryan. *KPFA, Berkeley*: David Selniker, Vera Hopkins, Bari Scott, Ginny Berson, Eve Mathews. *Union Wage:* Joyce Maupin. *Akwesasne Notes*: Ismaelillo, Carol Mohawk. *NACLA Report on the Americas*: Judy Butler. *Third World Newsreel*: Christine Choy, Allan Siegal, Pearl Bowser. *California Newsreel*: Larry Deressa, Cornelius Moore. *Puerto Rican* sources preferred not to be listed.

For the Portuguese case studies, I should like to thank the following. *Rádio Renasença*: Fernando da Sousa, Gabriel Ferreira, Joao Alferes Goncalves. *República*: Jorge Almeida Fernandes, Raul Rego, Fernanda Barao, Jose Salvador, Fernando Cascais. *Rádio Clube Português*: Adelino Gomes; Jaime Fernandes. In general, for their helpfulness on many fronts, I should like to thank Alvaro Miranda, Jean Seaton, Manuel Vilaverde Cabral, Phil Mailer, Bruno Ponte.

For the Italian case studies, I should like to thank the following. *Il Manifesto*: Gianni Riotta, Guido Moltedo, Rina Gagliardi, Angela Pascucci. *Lotta Continua*: Michele Buracchio, Luisa Guarderi, Marie DesCousts, and two *compagni* whose names I have mislaid. *Controradio*: Paolo, the director, Massimo Smuraglia, Stefano Fabbri. *Radio Popolare:* Federico Pedrocchi, Biagio Longo, Paolo Hutter, Manuela Barbieri. In general, for their helpfulness on many fronts, I should like to thank Vito Conteduca, Bruno Cartosio, Livio Sansone and his family, and Gabriella Camilotto.

For the section on Czechoslavakia, I should like to thank A. J. Liehm, Jiri Hochmann and Paul Bernstein. For the section on Poland, I should like to thank especially Tadek Walendowski, Witek Sulkowski, Piotr Naimski, Ryszard Knauff, Wojciech Ostrowski, Aria Mages, and Martin Burchardt.

I should like to extend my thanks to the British Social Science Research Council for their grant which made the first studies in Portugal and Italy possible. I should also like to thank the Sociology Department at the University of Massachusetts in Amherst for providing me with an untrammeled year in 1980-81 in which to begin to write up this material; and the Communications Department at Hunter College, City University of New York, for providing a superbly stimulating environment in which to clarify my thinking on alternative media and communication in general. Translations from French, German, Italian, Portuguese at intervals through the text are my responsibility.

South End Press is a media institution itself collectively run, a fine example of the mushrooming of radical media to which this book is directed. It too proves that self-management works, and its list of publications proves that collective responsibility, whatever the hassles, can issue in excellence. I should like to thank Ellen Herman, John Schall and Michael Albert for their labor as midwives in helping produce this book, and for their encouragement and prodding along the way.

Last but not least, thanks to Corinna and Anneli, who hung in there; to Juanita, who kept my eyes open to what's going on; to Jamal, may he triumph; to Stansil Lamb, who lived through much of it and whom some peasants in the Picos de Europa won't forget in a hurry. And to my own dear love, mia compagna dappertutto, Ashi mou, I dedicate this book. For she represents what it strives to bring about.

John Downing

Footnotes

1. Kathy Lowe's study (*Opening Eyes and Ears*, Geneva: World Council of Churches 1983) is valuable, especially in its inclusion of Third World material, but is not especially detailed. Otherwise there are only single-nation studies. There is Bertrude Joch Robinson's study of Yugoslav self-managed media, *Tito's Maverick Media,* Urbana, Ill.: University of Illinois Press 1977, and F.M. Samuelson, *Il Etait Une Fois Libe...* (Once there was Libe), Paris: Le Seuil 1978, an account of the French self-managed daily *Liberation.* In chapters 8 and 9 of my *The Media Machine*, London: Pluto Press 1980, I gave a brief account of Lenin's, Gramsci's, Brecht's and Mao's thinking about socialist communication, a critique of the British socialist press, and an account of a socialist radio station in Rome. A. Mattelart's and S. Siegelaub's second volume of their *Communication and Class Struggle* reader (Paris and New York, International General/IMMRC 1983), gives some valuable sources.

2. G. Hunnius (and others), *Workers' Control,* New York: Vintage Books 1973; K. Coates & T. Topham (eds.), *Workers' Control,* London: Panther Books 1970; J. Vanek (ed.), *Self-Management,* London: Penguin Books 1975; I. Clegg, *Workers' Self-Management in Algeria,* New York: Monthly Review Press 1971; E. Mandel (ed.), *Controle Ouvrier, Conseils Ouvriers, Autogestion* (Workers' control, workers' councils, self-management), Paris: Maspero 1970; Michael Albert and Robin Hahnel, *Socialism Today and Tomorrow*, Boston: South End Press 1982; Steven Shalom, ed., *Socialist Visions*, Boston: South End Press 1983.

3. See for instance the journals *Chasqui* (Centro Internacional de Estudios Superiores de Communicacion para America Latina, Apartado 584, Quit, Ecuador); *Cuadernos de Communicacion Alternative,* (Apartado 20-617, Delegacion A. Obregon, 01000 Mexico, D.F., Mexico); *Communicacao e Politica, (Centro Brasileiro de Estudos Latin-Americanos, Rua do Rosario, 104/3⁰ andar, CEP 20041, Rio de Janeiro, Brasil).* Also the present author's *Film, Politics and the Third World,* New York: Praeger/Autonomedia 1984, a Third World cinema reader.

4. See for example the journal *Reset,* edited by Mike McCullough, Apt. 3A, 90 East 7th Street, New York, NY 10009.

5. William Blake, "Tiriel," in his *Complete Poems* (ed. A. Ostriker), London: Penguin Books 1977, p. 85.

Table Of Contents

Foreword

General Introduction   1

The meaning of media—the West—the East—
alternatives in principle—alternatives in practice

Section One: The United States   **33**

1. Political Context of Alternative Media in the U.S.   35
   The structural characteristics of U.S. Media—the
   curious offensiveness of alternative media in the U.S.
   —a map of continuity and change, fragmentation and
   connection—the 60s movements: achievements and
   difficulties—conclusions

2. The National Guardian / Guardian   55
   History up to 1967—internal organization—the
   split—the Guardian since 1967—revisions in internal
   organization—conclusions

3. KPFA, Berkeley   74
   Introduction—a mini-history—power and the division of labor—KPFA, third world minorities, and the
   women's movement—conclusions

4. Union Wage   96
   An organizing paper for women—problems
   with labor unions—organizational history—
   financial base—internal democracy

5. Akwesasne Notes and ERIN Bulletin   104
   A history—communal democracy—changes in focus
   —the demands of land-based peoples

6. NACLA: Report on the Americas   115
   A brief history—internal organization—threats
   from outside—the changing face of South America

7. Third World Newsreel   125
   From 1967-74: Newsreel becomes Third World Newsreel—the collective from 1974—struggling against
   racism and sexism—the politics of film exhibition—
   organizing film production

8. California Newsreel   139
The politics and practicalities of independent film
distribution—focussing on labor's strategies for
alternative economic policies—developing national
debate around Southern Africa

9. Independent Film-making in Puerto Rico   146
Challenging colonial culture—finance and
organization outside the metropolis—developing a
national consciousness—conclusions

10. Conclusions   152
Political potential for alternative media in the U.S.

Section Two: Portugal and Italy   **159**

11. Introduction   161
The geopolitics of power in the Mediterranean—its
impact on Portugal and Italy

12. The Portuguese Explosion   167
General political economy—the nature of official
mass media—the character of the popular movement

13. Radio Renascenca   181
The build-up to self-managment—struggle with the
hierarchy—popular support—internal processes

14. Republica   195
Sole opposition newspaper in fascist regime—clashes
with its management after April 1974—the printers'
strike of May 1975—self-management—reporting the
squatters' movements and military mutinies

15. Radio Clube Portugues   208
Balanced reporting of the revolutionary process—
financial success—effectively functioning workers'
control—nationalization

16. The Italian Ferment   215
North and South in Italy—the experience of
fascism—the continuing weight of the Catholic Church
—the character of the Italian Communist Party—
official mass media—political upsurges in the 60s—
the impact of terrorism

17. Il Manifesto   237
Creating an independent marxist debate—experience
of self-management—women and the newspaper—
financial turmoil—acclaimed throughout Italy

18. Lotta Continua   255
Movement politics—its separation from its
parent body—to be a "transmission belt" or not—
—women in the paper—change in structure of
democracy—forging a fresh language on the left

19. Controradio   273
The search for a "fourth way"—the development
of a professional identity—training people to
use radio—preparing for the long haul

20. Radio Popolare   283
Bringing the rank and file together—open access
versus instant access—the problems of immediacy—
creating a lingua franca—negotiating with political
parties of the left—developing imaginative
dimensions of media work

21. Conclusion   303

Section Three: Eastern Europe   **305**

22. Introduction   307
A few specifics—the significance of samizdat—
contrasts in Eastern Europe

23. Czechoslovakia: The Prague Spring   310
The slow build-up—the role of writers—the dizzying
speed of 1968—how self-management emerged out of
nowhere—the decisive role of independent media
after the Soviet invasion

24. Poland 1976-1980   322
What censorship meant to the culture—the role of
the Catholic Church—the struggle for new media
—five instances of autonomous media—workers,
intellectuals, and farmers develop their own
communications networks

25. Conclusions   347
Atomization, East and West—the vulnerability of
Soviet bloc regimes to lateral communication

26. General Conclusions   349
Fogarasi and Enzensberger on radical media—the
disproportionate impact of small-scale media—
problems of aesthetics—interconnections between major
media and alternative media—does internal democracy
work in media?—radical media and political movements
—radical media and autonomous political action

GENERAL INTRODUCTION

One of the most familiar claims of the late 20th century—but on reflection one of the oddest—is that industrially advanced countries are revelling in an abundance of media. Whether we read of the achievements of satellite transmission, cable TV, electronic shopping, computerized newspaper editing and printing (typical Western themes), or in soviet bloc countries of the cultural and informational heights scaled by triumphant socialist construction, the general message is identical. The "leisure society" is upon us, the "information society" has dawned. A third of the planet's people is luxuriating in a near orgy of media recreation and information. The only question which seems to remain is, when will these people reach saturation point? How culture-rich, entertained and informed can they become before their circuits snap?

A chilly reinterpretation of this abundance of media is available, however. In novels such as Eugene Zamyatin's *We,* George Orwell's *1984,* Ray Bradbury's *Fahrenheit 451,*[1] we see the worker ants atomized by a polystyrene culture, and the few rebels singled out for relentless surveillance and destruction. Here, media abundance is employed to suppress all independent thinking or action. On the one hand, for the mass, there is canned TV laughter, one-minute radio news bulletins, tabloid newspaper sex-sationalism and "Son of..." movies. For the dissident minority, there is telephone tapping, infra-red photography, computer cross-checking, microbugs. This second scenario defines the media as offering mindlessness plus mind control.

1

Neither scenario represents pure fantasy. Media technologies undreamt of a hundred years ago proliferate. Many
contemporary regimes less oppressive than Hitler's have
indeed been quietly arming themselves with a mass of electronic surveillance techniques since the sixties and before.[2] Yet
the media universe we inhabit is a good deal untidier than
allowed by either the optimistic or the pessimistic scenario.
This study, for example, reports on the experiences of a whole
array of dissonant media, dissonant in the sense that they
have posed a genuine alternative to the media patterns of both
West and East. These media have articulated and amplified
popular challenges to power structures; they have enabled
people fighting injustice to communicate with each other; they
have empowered communities and classes and women and
ethnic minorities. The optimistic scenario—West and East—
would claim these upsurges do not need to exist when "everything is for the best in the best of all possible worlds."[3] The
pessimistic scenario would deny that rebellion is possible.
These media prove that both scenarios are lies.

Democratic, popular power and the media are the focus of
this book. Not as an ideal, but as that power has been
experienced in everyday situations within media that are "self-
managed," owned neither by a corporation, nor by the state, a
church, political party or labor union. Rather than examine
challenges that from time to time erupt within the major
media, rather than explore the gap between media pap and
audience obduracy—and both are real problems for the one-
way scenarios outlined above—this book focusses on how
newspapers, radio-stations, film, magazines and publishing
have been organized from below since the second World War.
The cases chosen are from the United States (a liberal democracy), Portugal (immediately following the collapse of fascism), Italy (from the "hot autumn" of 1969 onward), and eastern European periods of revolt against soviet-style socialism.

For the importance of self-managed media to be context-
ualized, we need first to understand the hollowness of official
media rhetoric, both West and East. Subsequent to this, we
need to identify the elements of political theory, emanating
from feminism, dissident east European Marxism, and socialist
anarchism, which underlie the effort to construct media communication along radically different lines to either the Eastern

or Western models. Finally, we need to observe how rapidly these new media are multiplying, just in case the examples cited in this study should be thought of as the only instances which could be discovered!

Western Media Rhetoric: Freedom, Objectivity, and Access

Certain themes are constant: press freedom, balance and objectivity, public accountability, social responsibility, pluralism, public access. These are the standard catchphrases that celebrate the media status quo, and apparently honor the public's right to know. They co-exist uneasily with a covert but tenacious contempt for the public common among media executives. This contradiction beween private opinions and public glosses expresses itself at its sharpest in First Amendment discussions in the USA. Because of the historical importance of the First Amendment, promising citizens freedom of opinion and self-expression, and because the press is usually seen as the most virtuous of the media, the closest in practice to the rhetoric, let us begin at this point.

U.S. media comentators have never been slow to take pride in the fact that the freedom to communicate was the subject of the very first amendment of the U.S. Constitution. Insofar as, historically, that amendment has spurred people in and out of the United States to communicate in defiance of power structures, such pride is justified. But from the start, with its assumption that women, Afro-Americans and Native Americans (at the least) were not to be actors in the public realm, the Constitution was crucially flawed. Distrust of the civic competence of the "lower orders" has been a constant in American life, existing cheek-by-jowl with an official commitment to equality and to media freedom.

A contemporary illustration of these historically interlocked viewpoints can be found in *New York Times* columnist James Reston's Elihu Root lectures, published in 1967 by the Council on Foreign Relations.[4] Reston took pains to cite the insufferably pompous Matthew Arnold complimenting the United States on its "excellent stock" and its "excellent Puritan discipline" which had produced, Arnold pronounced, a peculiarly sound governing class. "Like Plato and the Hebrew prophets," Reston added for good measure, "Arnold had little confidence in the judgement of the mass of the people, but he believed in the growing power of the "intelligent minority."

Thus a Victorian Englishman, an ancient Greek philosopher and some even more ancient Hebrew prophets are
yanked into service—I cannot digress on how unfair Reston is
to the prophets—in order to justify Reston's ingrained elitism.
How oddly this seems to sit with his earlier remarks in his
lectures, celebrating the American press:

> The American press was telling the country and the
> world where to get off before there was a State
> Department. The eighteenth century pamphleteers...
> believed that government power was potentially if not
> inevitably wicked and had to be watched...and they
> wrote the rules so that the press would be among the
> watchers. The Founding Fathers were quite dogmatic
> about this...and something of this same pugnacious
> spirit remains in our newspaper offices today.

In fact this contrast only jars once we forget how deeply rooted
Reston is in American traditions and realities. As stated a
moment ago, the Founding Fathers had not a shred of serious
respect for the civil or communicative rights of a majority of
the inhabitants of the U.S.A.: slaves on plantations, women,
Native Americans, even white males below a certain level of
affluence. Class, racism and sexism were integral pillars of the
"new" society. The Founding Fathers were insisting on *their*
rights, not everyone's rights.

Thus mass culture in the United States is, as it always has
been, an arena of political contest. The rights to literacy, to the
vote, to political influence, to political self-expression, have
had to be fought for on that level, and still have to be fought for.
Culture is not de-politicized leisure activity, let alone just art
and music consumed by the well-to-do. It is the wide-ranging,
complex expression of social and political relationships. It is
historically formed but in constant movement. The right to
know, for example, is a historical demand, a cultural theme,
and an ongoing battle in the nuclear era. Anti-nuclear films are
culture, as are pro-nuclear obfuscations by two generations of
official spokespeople. From both superpowers.

What are we to make then of Reston's assertion that in
practice "the responsible government official and the responsible reporter in the field of foreign affairs are not really in
conflict ninety per cent of the time"?[6] Is this independence,

pluralism, public access, balance, and objectivity? Or is it a constituent factor in the continuance of government of the people by a relatively cohesive—"ninety per cent of the time"—minority? Power, culture and communication are indissolubly linked, and if their control is located in the ruling class and the forces allied to it (Reston's "intelligent minority"), all the rhetoric about media freedom in the world will not alter the communicative dilemma of the majority.

The everyday operation of this control requires considerable insight into the standard procedures of the media industry to be able to be fathomed with precision in liberal democracies.[7] Its effects, however, are everywhere and readily visible. To take three rapid examples: how often do workers get prime-time, locally or nationally, to explain coherently and effectively how they experience their work and its structural problems? How often do Black or Latin people get prime-time to explain properly their history and their present? How often do women get prime-time to illuminate the mechanisms of their subordination? There is no need to wade through huge tomes of sociological research in order to know the answers to these questions.

"Balance," "objectivity," and "pluralism" (ie many competing voices) are also catchphrases thrown into some confusion once these measures are applied to them. Do you balance Black people's rights with the views on this subject of the Republican Party? What is the objectivity of the average male reporter making a presentation—if he ever does so—on feminist issues? How often do situation comedies or comic strips present office or factory labor? And when they do so, is work presented realistically or as a constant succession of coffee breaks? There is plenty of scope for anti-employer humor, as anyone with work-experience knows; but somehow it is not part of the plurality of media voices.

There are still other defenses of official media which can be made to justify their open nature, their democratic essence. Commercial media conventionally portray themselves as virtual slaves to "the market," and thus—as providing people with exactly what they want! They quietly gloss over the power of major advertisers and corporations to define *poor* people's media wants as irrelevant, compared to those of the more affluent sectors of the market. Compare, for instance, the media attention given in the USA to Black issues and demands, as compared to elegant home decor. But this is almost nitpicking: only the extraordinarily gullible believe in the democratic passions of commercial media executives.

Public broadcasting, by contrast, is often held up as an alternative and desirable model, whether in its U.S. minority version, or in the more balanced western European combination of public and commercial channels. In this model, public influence over the media is argued to be wielded through the broadcasters' accountability to the public. Celia Heller, however, has demonstrated in some detail how flimsy are the mechanisms in Britain for ensuring this accountability.[8] Britain is taken internationally as something of a broadcasting model in terms of quality of output, so that we may take it that weaknesses there will be likely to be still greater elsewhere. Neither Parliament, nor the Board of Governors, nor the General Advisory Council of the British Broadcasting Corporation actually hold any reins of power in their hands for the *public*. Parliament's control is only over the exceedingly crude instrument of level of financial support. And as Heller says of the General Advisory Council, echoing common experience of such committees:

> If an energetic critic penetrates the system, the chances are that the two year term (renewable at the secretariat's decision) will allow him or her to be shuffled off the stage before damage is done or disturbance created. It has also been pointed out by a former member of the BBC that within a group of sixty it takes time to make a coherent criticism felt: the amorphous whole has a capacity to muffle particular parts and cancel out stringent views in the rhubarb of sixty voices engaged in unstructured discussions.

Dents may be made from time to time in BBC policy by outside forces on particular issues, such as the portrayal of sex or of the northern Ireland conflict, but this is far from a requirement that the BBC genuinely mirror general public attitudes.

In the U.S.A., it is argued as well, public broadcasting effectively substitutes the decisions of elitist professionals on media output, for the decisions of advertisers:

> ...programming what people "ought" to see, without regard for audience habits, has been the ruling credo of

public television....Decisions are made by well-educated, typically "establishment" professionals and reflect their world view. It is not surprising that public television, indeed all television, is under increasing attack from the minority groups it ignores.

Much of public television programming represents not just the bias of its professionals but the interests of its elite supporters at the government, foundation and community level.... Financial appeals are directed at affluent viewers and naturally so is the programming.[9]

Thus the less disreputable quality of public broadcasting should not seduce anyone into concluding that its accountability to the overall public is any higher, or its responsiveness to their needs any greater than that of commercial media. It could easily provide a high quality *popular* service, but does not.

In recent years, these fundamental facts of commercial and public media organization have prompted numerous internal and external initiatives in favor of some form of public access to media. However, as the excellent survey by Berrigan and others shows, the gap between promise and performance in public access broadcasting continues to widen.[9] This is so whether we are looking at the U.S.A., Canada (supposedly a pace-setter in this field) or western Europe. The projects surveyed vary between offering participation in making programs, providing access to the airwaves, or making the media available as instruments of lifelong education. So-called "narrowcasting" by cable TV has been widely touted as the incoming answer to the demand for access. The U.S.A. itself offers relatively few instances of any of these, except of course for the phone-in, which can usually take only a few of the many calls that come in (10 to 15 percent at best), and which therefore requires successful callers to hang on the phone for considerable periods of time. As we shall see in the next chapter, community-owned cable TV stations account for less than 3 percent of all cable stations in the U.S.[11] City after city "got cable" in fact, after uncontested business deals promising cable viewers mass-produced entertainment only.

Canada is often cited as the metropolis of community access media. It is then instructive and sobering to learn that "There is no right of access to the broadcast media in Canada."[12] What is more, out of 387 Canadian firms licensed to put out cable programs in 1972, only 139 offered any form of community programming, and very few, open access. The cable operator, once assigned a license, is perpetually anxious that anything unplanned in open access programming will cause the license to be revoked, since legally the operator is responsible for content, not the production team, and certainly not the community. Furthermore, since only one cable station in Canada is allowed to raise revenue by advertising, cable operators are particularly anxious not to offend any subscribers, actual or potential.

This is not to say that valuable experience has not emerged in Canada on the question of access. The need has been found to be paramount for a community development agent to be in place a while before broadcasting equipment arrives, so that people in the community can collectively focus on and define their key issues. It then becomes much more practicable to work out how media may be used to advance particular causes. One station (Wired World, of Kitchener-Waterloo, Ontario) developed a console design for TV production which was suitable for use by non-professionals. These and other gains are worthwhile, but are still a long way from the development of popular power over the media.

The western European instances examined by Berrigan are also worthy of attention, despite being subject to many of the same strictures. Examples of public access she cites include *Open Door* (Britain), *Van Onderen* (Netherlands), and the Danish Film Workship. *Open Door* was a BBC TV program put out late at night on a weeknight, and then repeated on Sunday afternoons, neither time therefore at peak viewing hours. Its channel was BBC-2, the channel with the most upper middle class image, again somewhat reducing its audience. The program crew put their expertise at the disposal of a particular interest group, who might also if they chose be present at and comment on the editing of the film.

However, despite its guidelines, which specify that there shall be "no racialism or attempts to incite racialist feelings," one pressure-group it helped to make a program was the Campaign To Stop Immigration, an avowedly anti-black body whose position was made extremely clear during this program. Even this unique program was capable of being harnessed by the forces of explicit racism. (The role of the major media can be imagined.) The question "access to whom?" was sharply posed by this episode, and underlines the degree to which the term "community" is too vague to act as a discriminant between constructive and destructive forces.

Van Onderen, which in Dutch means both "from the grass roots" and "watch out below!", was perhaps the most interesting advanced case of access broadcasting.[13] The films were made by freelance professionals for showing weekly, and covered ordinary workers' experience of wage-labor and their feelings about it. No official person, not even a labor union official, was allowed to speak. The participants decided the content outlines, and could be present during editing. It went out between two high-rated series, and was watched by about 900,000 people, a significant slice of the Dutch viewing public. This program, despite its rather isolated status in Dutch TV, represents perhaps the closest to genuine public access out of all the cases cited in Berrigan's study.

The Danish Film Workshop gave participants full access to film equipment, some basic instruction in how to use it, and set no deadlines for completion. It was, all in all, a very liberal operation, which had as one of its effects that many more films were started than were completed. To try to check this tendency and to handle a declining budget, participants came to be charged 75 to 80 percent of costs. This immediately turned it into a service for the relatively well-to-do. In 1974 it was closed down. Its experience is mentioned here mainly because it raises some of the budgetary problems of open access media, which are usually intense. The substantial funds immediately available to conventional programming never seem to overflow into this area.

For the present, I hope to have illustrated sufficiently what I mean by the contention that public control of, or influence over, or access to, the official mass media in the West, are all rare phenomena. Whether we are discussing press freedom and objectivity, or commercial media "giving the public what it wants," or public broadcasting's feeble public accountability mechanisms, or the practical realities of access programming, the overall picture is rather similar. Indeed, writing on the question of community cable and video projects. Siliato[14] has argued that it is quite in keeping with a movement toward global telecommunications controlled by the major electronics corporations (General Electric, AT&T, ITT, etc.), that there should be a parallel movement fostered by these same firms to experiment with highly localized community comunication ventures. His position is that this localism is designed to help avoid what might otherwise be a much wider perspective on the national and international forces of the late 20th century, of which GE and the rest are themselves classic examples. People's grievances can be directed onto local issues, and apparent solutions sought out, whereas, increasingly, local problems are rooted in the international system of power.

In the political cultures of the U.S.A. and Canada his argument seems especially plausible, though it clearly has a bearing outside the region as well. In a critical assessment of those moments in western media policy which seem to move toward a vision of mass public involvement, we have to recognize how this involvement is already parcelled out into relatively insulated community units, only capable with difficulty of dovetailing their particular local concerns into a wider political movement.

The often less than spectacular experience of access programming should not be taken glibly to indicate its impracticality however. As the Dutch case cited shows, access is fully feasible. The demand for access is a muted echo of an increasingly widespread weariness and frustration with official media, and of a growing demand for more media democracy. In the final part of this Introduction, I will explore this demand in more detail, but let me re-emphasize one point made at the outset. The thrust of this book goes much beyond simply giving people, as individuals or communities, the right sometimes to broadcast or publish widely. Overcoming class, racism, sexism, other forms of subjugation, are central concerns of this book. It is concerned with how people subjected to these forces can communicate with one another so as to construct an understanding of *how* they are subjected, and still more, of how they can act together to create new social relations unmarred by these wounds.

Presently, the major media are directly or subtly a part of our problem. What are the possibilities people have for constructing their *own* media, independently of capital, the state, the church, and other agencies of oppressive power? This book is then ultimately about power, ours versus the established order's. Media communication is a fundamental element in the battle for power.

Eastern Media Rhetoric: Life on the Transmission Belt

Officially the battle for public control has been won in the East (I refer to the soviet bloc). Let us try to penetrate behind the rhetoric a little. A familiar joke in eastern Europe has it that the working class there is always to be found drinking the very finest French champagne. They drink it, the story goes, through the mouths of their highest representatives in the party and the state. It is a little too easy for people brought up in the West to accept that there is this total gulf between real democracy and the soviet bloc rhetoric of democracy (a gulf they find far harder to recognize at home). Western media harp on the distinction, for obvious reasons.

Social realities in the East, however, are not quite so straightforward.

Just as there are variations in broadcasting structures in the West, so the East is far from completely homogeneous. For example, from the 60s onwards a whole series of finely crafted, imaginative films have come out of Hungary, Czechoslavakia, Poland, and the Soviet Union itself. In 1979 even Leonid Brezhnev himself publicly attacked the boredom of soviet TV.

Take the example of Hungary, especially significant because of its role as pace-setter for reforms within the whole soviet bloc. From a decade after the 1956 revolution, it has been a kind of trial balloon society for the Comecon countries. In Hungary, a daily newspaper is published which gives accurate and detailed information about world and domestic affairs. It is called *World Economy*. Yet its circulation is absolutely restricted to officials approved by the party at a very high level. A few others are also allowed to read it, but they must pay for it (quite a substantial price) rather than having it donated as part of their work.

At the same time, there is a department of public opinion research within the Centre for Mass Communication Research of Hungarian Radio and TV. It has been in existence since 1968, and does a whole series of public opinion polls on general attitudes to everyday problems, economic issues, the government, and so on. Its operation completely sidesteps the party's mechanisms, which in the view of Marx and Lenin were the means for wage-earners and farmers to express their views on social and economic policy within a socialist state. Clearly the Hungarian state does not think the party capable of fulfilling this role, nor does it intend to radicalize it so it can. Instead, it has set up this information-gathering mechanism about public reactions to itself, which is licensed to tell the truth—but only to senior state officials. (Similar institutions have been set up in some other Comecon countries.)

Occasionally, there is greater license. Radio in Hungary, because it is less popular then television, is sometimes allowed to broadcast more critical material than is TV. Critical (not revolutionary) films are produced, even though there is sometimes a delay of years before they are shown, and when their screening takes place it is often at some cinema on the far outskirts of Budapest, unannounced in the press. In the USSR itself, the film studios of the Georgian and Uzbekistan republics have for some time been producing films of far greater integrity than the main Moscow and Leningrad studios, with their interminable literary adaptations and epics of the second world war.

What is often being experimented with at these margins is a familiar western mechanism: self-censorship. That is to say, there is a certain degree of communicative license, yet there are boundaries. Media workers try to work within them, if only not to get any future projects cancelled, let alone this one. No one physically intervenes and checks your work in progress. Only you do, without needing to be prompted.

To pin down the mainstream rhetoric of soviet bloc media, let us venture into an official text on socialist journalism published in East Germany in 1966.[15] The German Democratic Republic is the most economically advanced country in the soviet bloc, with an official standard of living higher than Britain's. At the same time, it has one of the most dogmatic and instinctively pro-soviet political hierarchies in eastern Europe. This is reflected in Budjilawski's text on journalism, which is historically situated at a point when the purest rigidities of stalinism were beginning to be discarded. His treatise is directed toward having the state continue doing the same things as before, but with greater comprehension and involvement on the part of the general population. For example:

> The journalist breaks up complex economic processes into stages...so that his public experiences the process of economic development as it takes place. For this method of presentation, which is the only one with which he can reach his public, the journalist creates for himself new literary journalistic forms and genres.[16]

He does not say in so many words, but the role of the journalist as set out in his text is to try to make state policy plausible and desirable, to put attractive communication flesh on the bare bones of economic decrees from on high.

Thus he attacks the production of masses of figures, a standard feature of stalinist media, and what he terms the "collapse into journalistic bureaucratism."[17] *"The great target of journalistic activity,"* he wrote, *"is effectiveness on a mass scale."* "We must express themes in the press, radio and television which explain the party's policies *in a living way*, and organize their realization."[19] "The socialist journalist is a teacher of the whole people, an educator of the masses in the revolutionary spirit...He becomes a co-worker, a co-creator of the economic construction of our republic."[20]

As Budjilawski makes wearisomely clear, what this means in practice is simply that state economic policy must be made effective. There are one or two references to combatting the revanchist imperialist West Germans, and to storming the heights of culture with the people, but the core of his message is the core of the stalinist definition of socialism in action: economic growth organized by a "socialist" state. Budjilawski echoed this precisely:

> Our major problem (ie. as a socialist state) is the rapid development of the productive forces. Thus the socialist journalist must...delve ever more deeply into the economic laws of socialism, in order to propagate their correct implementation in the press, radio and television.[21]

Or, again:

> On the level of the economy, in the struggle for higher labor productivity, is decided the *decisive* battle with capitalism...press, radio and television cannot make the new machines...they cannot organize the daily factory process...But they can form the *human beings* who produce and use the machines, who guide and direct our factories. On this ground the economic-organizational role of our press cannot be mastered in a technological fashion, *but only through the mobilization of human beings.*[22]

As Stalin himself used to put it, the Soviet Union had to catch up and overtake the West in the shortest possible time. The costs of this violent and protracted mass exploitation of labor-power are well enough known.

Some of Budjilawski's examples of how to do it are unintentionally ironic. He wrote:

> An expert journalist always shows his respect for simple people. In this, he fundamentally distinguishes himself from the bourgeois ideologue and newspaper writer, who sees the masses as an object to influence...

Or, again, having discussed a particular newspaper article on the production problems of a factory turning out screws, he concluded:

> ...even those who are not yet interested in the problems of a particular screw-factory, would certainly like to get a sense for what goes on in the heart and head of a socialist brigade leader, or why a cattleminder on a collective farm has taken on extra duties.

How do you keep them down on the farm?

As regards control over the media, Budjilawski left no doubt in the reader's mind. Early in the treatise he announced:

> The whole history of the proletarian press teaches that a revolutionary socialist press arises only in unbreakable unity with the marxist leninist party, that the party must guide the development of the press, and that socialist journalists first attain the peak of their tasks when they feel themselves to be party functionaries and behave accordingly.

He added, with the conventional stalinist substitution of the party for the working class:

> The journalistic personality is *therefore* firmly bound up with the working class in our situation, and identical with its struggle.[25]

Later in the book he expanded on this theme:

> It is obvious that no one in an editorial position is continually waiting for directions. He must normally be in a position to find his way correctly through the major and minor details of policy on the basis of the general party line. But he should never put himself side by side with his party leadership and make his own policy, so to speak disconnectedly and independently. That is incorrect.[26]

Budjilawski's version of ultimate truth may serve to conclude this brief account of soviet bloc media philosophy. The
journalistic "personality is...so to speak an executor of history
and its laws."[27] Truth consists of objectivity, and objectivity is
facilitated by dialectical materialism.[28] As to the future, the
USSR "is already opening the gates to communism. There we
can in a certain manner study characteristics of the future of
our own journalism."[29] What more need be said, or hoped for?

We can see that media communication, in relation to the
stated objectives of the historical socialist movement, is as
much in a state of crisis in soviet bloc countries as is the
supposedly democratic media pattern in the West. Events in
Czechoslavakia in 1967-69 and in Poland from 1976 forcefully
demonstrate this crisis. The long-standing institution of publishing letters from readers in soviet bloc publications, which
does allow for the frank expression of criticism, nonetheless
serves essentially as a safety-valve for the general public and
early warning system for the power-structure. *In no way does it
enable people to engage in lateral media communication and
dialogue.* Indeed, given the stated aims of Marx and Lenin, the
crisis of the soviet bloc consists more in its communication
policies and patterns than in its level of economic efficiency,
even though this latter is the favorite target of western commentators. (No doubt the two issues are related, but that is
beyond our scope here.)

The main principles of soviet bloc media comunication can
be defined as follows: the media are the "transmission belt" for
party definitions of reality; the foremost aspect of this reality is
economic growth constructed by the state; journalistic creativity is limited to mobilizing the hearts and minds of the
public toward fulfilling their parts in achieving the state's
objectives. To this we must, of course, add a vital fourth principle, never mentioned by Budjilawski: the state's right to censor
media communication.[30] We shall see the crushing impact of
this last principle in the section on Eastern Europe.

Despite the greater complexity of soviet bloc media than
popular images would allow, a search for models of democratic
communication in those countries only yields the counter-
media that their regimes struggle to suppress. Neither East nor
West can actually deliver on their rhetoric. Are there any other
models in existence?

Media Alternatives in Principle

The first set of alternatives we shall examine might be called alternatives in principle, being perspectives relevant to media organizations drawn from libertarian marxism, feminism and socialist anarchism. Sometimes these overlap, as in the cases of feminist anarchist Emma Goldman, or the libertarian Marxist feminist Sheila Rowbotham; sometimes they are distinct. These perspectives are crucial because they simultaneously address the practical failures of marxism to realize its democratic promise and also raise issues central to democratic media communication. In my view, capitalism's failure to realize its own rhetoric and bring authentic media democracy into being is scarcely surprising. The fact that its official alternative in the East is no alternative at all, indeed offers even less media democracy than liberal capitalist regimes, demands explanation. Is a vision of media democracy merely utopian? Are soviet media the predictable product of certain organizational and political imperatives deeply embedded in marxism? Or are they historical products of a specific form of social development inaccurately labelled marxist by its proponents and leading figures?

The view that media democracy is utopian is the standard line of defence of western apologists—their first line of defence being that the West has reached as near to media democracy as is feasible or desirable. The second view, that there is a straight line running from marxism to present-day Comecon countries, is both a familiar bourgeois critique of marxism and the official line of those countries' regimes—give or take a plus or minus sign. It is also a view to be found in anarchism, the great historical antagonist of marxism on the left, as well as in feminism. The reasons are different: for anarchists, the readiness of marxism to continue to operate with any form of state power represents a fatal betrayal, whereas for many feminists, marxism is one more patriarchal theory issuing in one more form of patriarchal society. The other interpretation, that the soviet bloc regimes are in some sense pseudo-marxist, is the position of major currents within marxism itself, whether pro-Chinese or Trotskyist or others.

The argument has not strayed from media democracy. We are simply focussing on its preconditions, and trying to establish why it is that soviet state "socialism" has foreclosed on it.

Let us examine the anarchist angle of vision a little more

closely, both for its critique of marxism in practice, and for what it offers instead. As we proceed, we shall see how certain angles of vision emerging from radical forms of feminism, and critical currents within marxism, often coincide with anarchist perspectives. What follows is not an anarchist or a feminist position as such, but an attempt to draw from all those traditions of analysis certain basic postulates in principle, of media democracy in practice.

We should begin with the recognition that anarchism is not purely a philosophy. In many countries the labor movement has been deeply influenced by it, with Spain being the preeminent example, but others include Italy, Portugal, Mexico and some Latin American countries. Up to 1917 the British labor movement had a considerable anarchist element. Anarchism has been a multifaceted movement, divided not only into its syndicalist wing and its purer wing, rejecting all central organization, but also into many different grouplets. There is no single anarchist view on many questions. This includes the position of women, for surprisingly often in anarchist movements or publications it has been assumed that women will continue to fulfill established women's roles. Furthermore, anarchists have been as capable of vicious sectarian infighting as any other political tendency. Lastly—and importantly for some case studies—the notion is mistaken that all anarchist variants *require* ultra-democratic procedures, namely structures which deny individual skills, and/or demand consensual decisions rather than majority votes, and/or give the part-timer the same weight as the editor. We shall see some media working with these approaches, others developing more formal styles, but these approaches are not necessarily anarchist.

There are points at which anarchist angles of vision seem to bypass some of the standard deficiencies of marxist movements, and focus strongly and positively on issues that have conventionally been defined as non-issues in marxism. Let us examine four in particular which have direct implications for realizing media democracy in the world we live in.

They are the emphasis on multiple realities of oppression beyond the economic; the critique of marxism's blindness on the intelligentsia and the party; the priority accorded to movements over institutions; and the attempt to construct prefigurative politics and a liberating "process."

The continual emphasis on the economy within marxist

thinking, whether the Second International or stalinist regimes—compare Budjilawski—is much rarer within anarchism, though somewhat to be seen in its syndicalist version. When reading Emma Goldman's lectures or autobiography I am not only struck by the breadth of her concerns—the theatre, women's rights, contraceptive education, sexuality, prisons, puritanism, patriotism, the positive intellectual contributions of Freud and Nietzsche—but by the fact that they are valued in their own right, or denounced (prisons, etc.) for their impact on the human personality in its entirety.[31] Marxist writers often seem to have to link everything to political economy for their analysis to be validated; having made the linkage, which is regularly present at some point or points, the analysis is considered complete. No more is needed to clarify the oppressiveness or the revolutionary content of the matter at hand.

Within anarchism, however, there is a recognition as David Wieck has put it:

> that any theory that finds the secret of human liberation in something as specific as the politics of property neglects the interdependence of the many liberations.[32]

Sheila Rowbotham, writing from within a libertarian marxist feminist position, echoes this in a way which also directly raises the question of lateral communication, of media democracy:

> For if every form of oppression has its own defensive suspicions, all the movements in resistance to humiliation and inequality also discover their own wisdoms. We require a socialist movement in which there is freedom for these differences and nurture for these visions. This means that in the making of socialism people can develop positively their own strengths and find ways of communicating to one another what we have gained.[33]

(The communication is not first and foremost a matter of having a printing press or a radio transmitter at hand, but it must surely include that.) In fact, any history of socialist movements and thought which is not absolutely fixated on the marxist contribution, repeatedly turns up this wider angle of vision. Robert Owen's socialism, for example, set women's liberation as one of its main immediate targets, rather than relegating it to later centuries as so many marxist movements have done.[36]

It is probably true, though we cannot pursue it here, that Toni Negri is dead on target in his work on Marx's *Grundrisse*, in arguing that much of marxism's limitation of vision has arisen from the canonization of *Capital* as Marx's ultimate contribution to socialist analysis and action. Hence the compulsiveness of marxism's attention to the economic dimension, fundamental as it is to human society.[35]

What bearing have these reflections on media democracy and its preconditions? A decisive one. For if we are thinking of organizing democratic media, we cannot imagine them as liberating forces unless they are open to lateral communication between social beings, with their *multiple* experiences and concerns. Once we reduce humans to economic agents, we are back in Budjilawski's visions of media bliss, and a very long way from liberation.

This is first base. The second point at which anarchism raises vital issues bypassed by marxism, with once more a direct bearing on media democracy, is the question, or related questions rather, of intellectuals, culture, education and the marxist political party. Rudolf Bahro, in his marxist critique of soviet bloc society, *The Alternative*, cites Bakunin writing in 1873 about the results of marxist theory if put into political practice. The result will be, said Bakunin:

> a despotism of the *governing minority*...But this minority, say the Marxists, will consist of workers. Certainly...of former workers, who however as soon as they have become representatives or governors of the people, *cease to be workers* and look down on the whole common workers' world from the height of the state. They will no longer represent the people, but themselves and their pretensions to people's government... [The Marxists plan to establish] a single state bank concentrating in its hands all commercial-industrial, agricultural and even scientific production, and to divide the mass of the people into two armies, one industrial and one agricultural, under the direct command of state engineers, who will form a new privileged scientific-political class.[36]

By any account this was an extraordinarily prescient understanding of marxism's potential to be harnessed as an ideology of a new ruling class. Bahro emphasises Marx's and marxism's refusal to recognize the political implications of its own intellectuals' culture in the shaping of new societal forms, pre-eminently in the institution of the revolutionary party as the nucleus of the new state. The cultural dimension of the capitalist division of labor was no casual fact, but one which came to determine the power structure of soviet bloc states, with the intelligentsia enthroned in a position of ever greater influence within them. In particular, vaunted knowledge-supremacy of the leaders of marxist parties over the majority of their members and followers has constituted their right to lead, the "transcendent correctness which leninism implies" as Rowbotham puts it.[37]

Central to Bahro's own vision of the necessity for drastic change within soviet bloc societies is the overthrow of this continuing cultural-political division of labor. Specifically, this means the democratization of their media:

> ...the essence of bureaucratic domination consists in its power of disposal over the social nervous system, the hierarchy of information processing. It is in this way that the corporation of functionaries appropriates the wealth of society. Socialization of the process of social knowledge, therefore...is both the means and ends of the cultural revolution...As a general rule, the "decisive instances" have no greater knowledge in their decision-making than any ordinary citizen would have *if he was fully informed of the alternatives*...In a bureaucratised society, however, the downward flow of command and instructions rolls ahead with exceptional force down the pyramid's cascades...At the bottom, the various particular interests find themselves systematically isolated, so that they have no prospect of being directly taken into account in the synthesis...It would only need public access to more generalised information, with the entire society having an elementary right to this and the use of the mass media to discuss the various possible solutions...What is decisive is that...individual participation in the formation of the general will can regain, by way of an appropriate organization of mass communication, something of the directness it had in simple communities that were immediately susceptible to general comprehension.[38]

Notably, it is in the organization of communication that soviet bloc societies can retain their political structures, or liberate themselves. In pre-and post-revolutionary societies, communication, education, culture, knowledge, power, the single correct marxist-leninist party, are completely interwoven, and represent a crucial blind spot in marxist socialism. Not, it must be said, the only one; I am not trying to reduce the problem to this question. But the organization of mass communication is neglected as a central issue in many leftist analyses of soviet bloc societies. Bahro, perhaps because of his long first-hand experience of the German Democratic Republic, does not make that mistake.

To the definition of the economy in marxism (as often practiced), we therefore have to add the definition of the party's claim to superior knowledge and encompassing wisdom as a source of the media patterns of soviet bloc societies.

Conversely, democratic socialist media must expunge this definition from their own forms of organization, not merely because the claim is arrogant in principle, but because the overwhelming priority in our practice in the late twentieth century must be the *linkage* of various movements against oppression and inequality. This is only possible by developing infinitely better lateral media comunication between us than exists at present. It cannot be achieved by relying on a superior entity—the "Party"—to define what has to be done and achieve it for us. Bahro was careful to note the systematic isolation of particular groups at the bottom of society from each other in soviet bloc regimes—familiar enough in the West as well—so that they have no prospect of being taken into account in the synthesis worked out for them by the "Party." Rowbotham puts it forcefully and insightfully:

> There remains then no effective guarantee within Leninism that the groups who are in a dominant position within capitalism won't bring their advantage into "the Party." Worse, there is an effective sleight of hand which conceals this inherent tendency in the assertion of the *ideal* of the Party transcending the interests and visions of its sections.[39]

In other words, the leninist party cannot create liberation. Only unity among the oppressed can be the basis for change, and media can act as a key instrument in the emergence of this unity.

This leads us directly into a third strength of the anarchist angle of vision, the priority of movements over institutions. The possibility of a women's movement in eastern Europe is not only alarming because it challenges patriarchy, but because it is a social *movement*. For anarchism, however, it is deemed essential that revolutions construct themselves on the basis of mass activity, of self-mobilization, of popular movements. Given this emphasis, which once again puts "the Party" in its place, it follows still more clearly that effective comunication among the oppressed is a vital necessity for this self-mobilization to occur and prosper. Self-managed media are not a curious little experiment for revolutionary culture-freaks. Their lynchpin role becomes all the more obvious as we face the *divisions* among movements of the oppressed. These divisions are fostered by racism, imperialism, sexism, ageism, language, unskilled work vs skilled work vs career work vs clerical work, to name only the main ones. Lateral communication is a first, essential and very difficult step, if we are not to be forever pitted one against the other. Our *shared* understanding of the dynamics of exploitation and humiliation has to grow enormously in order to form any movement powerful enough to shake the power structure.

An example of what movement-building with self-managed media to aid us would actually be like could be taken from the women's movement's development of sensitivity to the daily immediacies of oppression. This is a gain, not only for the women's movement itself, but for the rest of us. To cite Sheila Rowbotham once more:

> When women on the left began to criticize this language (ie Fraternity, Chairman, Brothers) we were told we were just being petty. But the ideas and politics of women's liberation emerged out of precisely *these small everyday moments of dismissive encounter*.[40]

Self-managed media can enable people to communicate these and other realities to one another. Not automatically of course. But the potential of media to communicate laterally is contained within their technology, whereas the social structure of "the Party" has been predefined for so long that it could only operate laterally in the ideal, not the real world. Typically, political movements have sprung into being outside the party, and the latter has fallen over itself trying to lead them, or at least keep up with them. And it is from these movements that significant changes have begun to emerge: anti-colonialism, women's rights, feminism, black liberation. There is a very long way still to go, however, and the issue of democratic media faces us squarely in our path.

The final aspect of anarchism's angle of vision that I wish to discuss here is also closely related to the last one, namely prefigurative politics, the attempt to practice socialist principles in the present, not merely to imagine them for the future. Wieck puts it this way:

> ...anarchism proposes the *continuous realization* of freedom in the lives of each and all, both for its intrinsic and immediate values and for its more remote effects, the latter unpredictable because they depend on the unpredictable behavior of persons not known and of non-personal historical processes.[41]

Porter adds to this the following dimension:

> ...any liberated areas, however limited, are a challenge to the capitalist order. The challenge lies in their visceral resistance to and struggle against the system, and in their offering time and space for potentially less sublimated behaviors....Such zones sustain the energies of militants.[42]

The only prefigurative politics taken seriously by marxism, is, once again, the party, the nucleus of the future state. Given the nature of marxism's emphasis on the economy, this means that struggles for political power and factory struggles are the most highly regarded activities, followed sometimes by housing and tenants' committees. Other areas of struggle are relegated to secondary status because they do not appear to bear directly on the economy, the state, or the party. For anarchism, however, it has normally been enough to attempt little islands of prefigurative politics with no attention to how these might ever be expanded into the rest of society. Example has often been considered sufficient. What is needed is a recognition of the many areas which are political (as opposed to conventional marxism's hierarchy), together with attention to how prefigurative politics can expand beyond its islands (as opposed to anarchism). A socialist society "cannot be separated from the process of its making," as Rowbotham puts it, and prefigurative politics must therefore do more than simply prefigure. It must in some measure provide staging posts along the way, moments of transformation, however small.

Liberated communication channels do offer the chance to begin breaking down the divisions among us *now*, not after the conquest of state power. It is precisely in the realm of everyday consciousness in the world of immediate realities, that these media can function at their best. It is plain for all to see that conventional leftism fails in major capitalist societies, not merely because of state repression and the hegemony of bourgeois ideology, though these are real enough, but also because it is generally weak at operating in these realms of the immediate. Leftism is only at home with the high peaks of confrontation between classes, not with what Edward Thompson has described as the forgotten half of people's culture:

> [People] also experience their own experience as *feeling* and they handle their feelings within their culture, as norms, familial and kinship obligations and reciprocity, as values, or (through more elaborate forms) within art or religious beliefs. This half of culture (and it is a full one half) may be described as affective and moral consciousness.[43]

In particular, imagination in media presentations—strongest in left theatre, weakest in conventional left media—is required to relate to this half of popular culture. We shall see in some of the case studies later in this book how this challenge has been taken up. Thus prefigurative politics, imagination, and democratic practice should naturally coincide in the endeavor to achieve lateral communication. The development of fresh political aesthetics is one of the most urgent tasks on the agenda of the socialist movement.

To conclude this section on alternatives in principle: anarchism's historical emphasis on movements, on prefigurative politics, against economism, against the elite party, has been taken up by the feminist movement and applied particularly to the immediacies of the personal, of everyday life. Interestingly, eastern European marxist critics of soviet bloc regimes (not only Bahro), have taken up some of these themes as well in their critiques. Together, these constitute certain basic principles of an alternative media politics to West or East, which we shall see partly in action in the rest of this book. The fundamental conclusion of this section however is that *the social possibilities of media democracy are in no way exhausted by the restrictive experience of East or West.*

Let me turn now to the striking development of movements for autonomous media in the 70s and 80s.

Media Alternatives in Practice

For centuries the press has been utilized by radicals, whether for books, pamphlets, magazines or newspapers. The new development of the 70s was the use of radio. Maybe the first major instance was to be found in the two radio stations which operated during the Popular Unity period in Chile (1970-73), one run by the trade union federation, the other by the Movement of the Revolutionary Left (MIR). During the November 1973 uprising in Greece against the fascist colonels, a radio transmitter was operated by students from Athens Polytechnic. It broadcast information, calls to resistance and news of military and police movements. In 1974-75 in Portugal, two radio stations were taken over by their workers and run by them until forcibly closed in November 1975. From 1975 in Italy autonomous radio stations of the left began broadcasting in defiance of the state's broadcasting monopoly; a year later local broadcasting was deregulated, and today numerous stations, mostly not revolutionary, are broadcasting in Italy. Let us not forget either the role of radio and media under self-management in Czechoslavakia in 1968.

In Britain, France, and West Germany there are also continuing challenges to state broadcasting monopolies. Usually these take the form of clandestine radio-stations, broadcasting for a few hours at a time. Examples from France before the Mitterrand regime changed the law in 1981 included Radio Coeur d'Acier (Heart of Steel), a station which broadcast continuously for some months from Longwy in Lorraine province during the long 1979 steelworkers' strike. Others at various times have been Radio Quinquin, Canal 75, Radio Moyenne, Radio Mélun, Fréquence Nord, Radio-Bleue, Radio 7, Radio Corsica International, Radio Lille 80, Radio Gilda. In 1981 there were also Ici et Maintenant (Here and Now) broadcasting from Paris; a Communist Party union federation station at Annécy, Radio Ondes Pures (pure waves); Radio Ploganoff in Brittany, an anti-nuclear station close to a major projected nuclear power-station; and, not least, the extremely well-equipped and professional Radio K, broadcasting into France 24 hours a day from San Remo in Italy. Surveys indicated that about two-thirds of the French population are in favor of free radio, and despite the constant closures of stations by the then French government, the law continued to be flouted.

After legalization in 1981, the problems shifted for free

radio. They were not allowed to have transmitters of more than 300 watts, with a broadcasting range of less than 15 miles. The airwaves became extremely congested. And last but not least, they were not allowed to raise revenue by advertizing. Those that did, were jammed. Nonetheless, the situation has clearly advanced somewhat.[44]

The fact that Italy permits free local broadcasting clearly set a major precedent for other western European countries, even though the Swiss government succeeded in getting the Italian government to close down one station (Radio 24) which had been transmitting from Italy to German-speaking Switzerland. The statutes of the International Telecommunications Union, however, offer little aid to governments trying to maintain their control on broadcasting, since they are designed to ensure the best possible reception, not with preventing broadcasting happening. (What would happen to Voice of America and Radio Free Europe if they did?)

West Germany and Britain offer fewer examples than France. In Bremen there is one station (Radio Zebra) which has succeeded in broadcasting at the same time each week on the same wavelength for some years. This is despite the heavy fines and prison sentences the West German state can hand out to offenders. West Germany also boasted Radio Jessica in Hamburg, Radio Fledermaus (Bat) in Münster, Radio Radikalinski in Hamburg, Radio Klabautermann—a ghostly apparition in German legend which haunted ships doomed to be wrecked—also in Hamburg, and others. Austria had stations in Graz and Vienna; Zürich had Radio Schwarze Katz (Black Cat); Belgium, Holland and Sweden also had autonomous radio stations.[45]

Another station in West Germany of particular note was Radio Verte Fessenheim (Green Fessenheim),[46] in the far southwestern corner of the country at the borders with France and Switzerland. Known locally as "Three Corner Land," the area has common problems (remoteness from central government, attempts to build nuclear power plants there on the Rhine), as well as a common dialect. National frontiers are particularly irrelevant to its inhabitants. Radio Verte Fessenheim was an attempt to expand the mobilization of the local populations, already underway for five years, against combined neglect by their governments and the threat of a nuclear power plant. The local media were rather unresponsive to people's grievances, so that the need for a new station was widely felt. In 1977 transmission began, usually of twelve to forty minutes' duration. The West German and the French police made repeated attempts to capture the equipment and arrest the collective but were never successful, largely due to local support for the project.

In case their sole transmitter fell into police hands, the collective decided fairly soon on to start a radical decentralization of the station. They set up six low frequency (16 miles) transmitters in different places, and thirty five booster aerials. They broadened the content of their programming from purely ecological issues to cover various labor conflicts and cultural themes, and set up an overground group called "Friends of RVF-Dreyeckland." The decentralization created severe problems of coordination, and did not solve the problem of getting non-activists to take part in the project.

The news at the time of writing was that RVF was still functioning and had been formally permitted to broadcast. It is one more indication of the bubbling up of autonomous radio stations in western Europe. There are several such short-broadcast British stations. It is clear that popular demand to communicate exists; indeed, within the European section of the USSR, pirate ham-radio broadcasting is a significant phenomenon. Exactly what the outcome will be—deregulation in some form or not—is completely unclear at this time. Yet one thing is absolutely plain; the issue is very much alive and will not simply vanish.

The desire for popular communication goes hand in hand with a growing desire among print journalists to organize their own self-managed collectives to run their newspapers, rather than work for a press baron or giant corporation. The most famous case of this is the leading French newspaper *Le Monde*, which has been organized this way for several years. British journalists on *The Sunday Times* tried unsuccessfully to realize this objective during the 1980 takeover bid by press baron Rupert Murdoch. In 1981 many Québec journalists went on strike to lend force to their demand to run their own newspapers themselves. The conspicuous success of *Le Monde* has been a great encouragement in this direction. To a lesser extent, the example of Yugoslav media, which are self-managed, has also stimulated interest in these possibilities.[47]

To be sure, these forms of media autonomy vary considerably in structure and purpose. Collectively run enterprises have no necessity to act as revolutionary organizations. Indeed, the whole notion of workers' participation, even the notion of self-management, are very wide. They can easily stretch from the rightwing weekly *O Tempo* in Lisbon, through to the London Newsreel film collective who have written:

...we recognize different capacities as skills which go entirely unrecognized in the bourgeois media; the ability to relate to people; to express feelings directly; to recognize and express differences and personal needs; to take care of one another. These skills are also often unrecognized on the left.[48]

Self-management can also embrace newspaper collectives which have emerged out of a strike, like the *Scottish Daily Express*[49] or the Madison Wisconsin *Press Connection*.[50] In these, however, many journalists continue to work with the standard professional codes of conventional journalism, what is news, what is balance, where news should be sought.

There is in the 1980s a growing movement internationally for the democratization of media. The continuing life of *Libération* in France, the emergence of *Tageszeitung* in 1979 in West Germany, the formation of the Union of Democratic Communication and of the Media Alliance in the U.S.A., are further cases in point. An increasing politicization of journalists' and writers' unions against state censorship, against newspaper control by giant monopolies, the demand for open access broadcasting, are all part of the same movement. It is a predictable response to press barons, paper corporations, electronics transnationals, the increasingly secretive branches of government. Media democracy is firmly on the political map and processes are underway which can be used to open up media communications at certain points to control from underneath. The models of West and East are not our duolithic fate.

It therefore becomes peculiarly important for socialists, feminists and radicals in general, to reflect both on the principles which should govern alternative media, and on the historical experience of self-managed media. These are exactly the focuses of this book. We have already briefly surveyed some general alternative principles of media work. We will turn in the body of the book to a series of actual cases of self-managed media, drawn from the U.S.A., Portugal, Italy and eastern Europe—these latter because there the experience of self-managed media has been the richest and most detailed. This experience deserves recording in any case, as a historical high water mark in creativity in media organization from below. From the political experience of organizing these media, it will be possible at the end of the book to draw more specific conclusions about the problems of self-managed media.

Certain problems will not be addressed. Difficulties in fund raising are recognized, but methods of doing it are not discussed. Nor are the practicalities of handling and repairing equipment, or the details of legal sanctions over broadcasting, and many other such perfectly real problems. What will be addressed here are issues in political analysis. What is the relation between mass political upsurges and self-managed media? How does internal democracy in the media relate to the wider democracy of social movements, and indeed of the society as a whole? What roles do women play in these democratic structures? What place do Black people have in them? How do these media handle political or financial or morale crises in their own organization? What are the standard financial problems they face? What happens when the novelty of organizing media communication has worn off? How are commitment and discipline maintained? How do they relate to other political forces on the left? How do they relate to official media? How do they organize imaginative material and presentations?

Many of these issues are raised in chapter 9 of my *The Media Machine*,[51] where I dealt in a preliminary way with the Italian experience, and one station in particular, Radio Città Futura (City of the Future) in Rome, up to 1979. In this book, the case studies are more numerous, the detail richer, and a thorough overview consequently far more feasible. A simpler introduction has been supplied for the Portuguese, Italian, and East European cases than for the U.S., in order to enable readers unfamiliar with those societies to place the case-studies, to understand the full range of problems of political movements and self-managed media there. But first let us turn to the U.S.A.

Footnotes

1. E. Zamytin, *We,* New York: Dutton 1952; George Orwell, *1984,* London: Penguin Books 1975; R. Bradbury, *Fahrenheit 451,* London: Rupart Hart-Davis 1972.
2. C. Ackroyd (and others), *The Technology of Political Control,* London: Penguin Books 1977, chs. 13-14; F. Donner, *The Age of Surveillance,* New York: Vintage Books 1981; J Wicklein, *Electronic Nightmare,* New York: Viking 1981; also the British journal *State Research* and the American journal *Covert Action Information Bulletin.*
3. The favorite assertion of the incurably optimistic philosopher Pangloss in Voltaire's *Candide.* His unflinching reiteration of the claim in the face of successive disasters like the Lisbon earthquake, provides one of the main satirical messages of the book.
4. J. B. Reston, *The Artillery of the Press,* New York: Harper and Row, for the Council on Foreign Relations 1967, p. 105.
5. *op. cit.* p. 5.
6. *op. cit.* p. 108.
7. See the fine work of Phiip Schlesinger, *Putting 'Reality' Together,* London: Constable 1977; also J. Tunstall, *The Westminster Lobby Correspondents,* London: Constable 1970; A. McBarnett, "Disciplining the journalist," *Media Culture and Society* vol. 1 1979; H. Gans, *Deciding What's News,* New York: Oxford University Press 1979. J.W. Freiberg, *The French Press,* New York: Praeger 1981; J.L. Curry & J. Dassin (eds.), *Press Control Around the World,* New York: Praeger 1982, Part I; D. Prokop, *Massenkommunikation und Spontaneitat,* Frankfurt: Suhrkamp Verlag 1977; D. Prokop, *Medien—Wirkungen,* Frankfurt: Suhrkamp Verlag 1981.
8. G. Heller, *Broadcasting and Accountability,* London: British Film Institute 1978 (BFI Television Monograph 7). The quotation below is from p. 43.
9. R. Kletter (and others), "Access and the social environment in the United States of America," in F. J. Berrigan (ed), *Access: some western models of community media,* Paris: UNESCO 1977, pp. 27-83. The quotation is taken from p. 34.
10. *op. cit.*
11. See footnote 15 to the chapter on the political context of alternative media in the United States.

General Introduction   31

12. E. Rosen (and others), "The community use of the media for lifelong learning in Canada," in F. J. Berrigan, *op. cit.* n. 9, pp. 85-143. This quotation is taken from p. 87. The figures quoted are from the same page; the information on Wired World is taken from pp. 108-09.

13. F. J. Berrigan, *op. cit.* pp. 145-211. The information about *Van Onderen* comes from pp. 152-54.

14. F. Siliato, *L'Antenna Dei Padroni, (The Bosses' Aerial),* Milan: Mazzotta 1977.

15. H. Budjilawski, *Sozialistische Journalistik: eine wissenschaftliche Einfuhrung (Socialist Journalism: a Scientific Introduction),* Leipzig: VEB Bibliographisches Institut 1966.

16. *op. cit.* p. 56.

17. *op. cit.* p. 189.

18. *op. cit.* p. 156.

19. *op. cit.* p. 151.

20. *op. cit.* pp. 19-20.

21. *op. cit.* p. 31.

22. *op. cit.* p. 117.

23. *op. cit.* p. 38.

24. *op. cit.* p. 51.

25. *op. cit.* p. 17.

26. *op. cit.* p. 104.

27. *op. cit.* p. 14.

28. *op. cit.* p. 61.

29. *op. cit.* p. 69.

30. See J. L. Curry and J. Bassin, *op. cit.* n. 7, Part II; A. Brumberg (ed), *Poland: genesis of a revolution,* New York: Vintage Books 1983, pp. 241-262; and for the dismal situation in 1980s Czechoslavakia, see *Index on Censorship* 12.2 (April 1983).

31. Emma Goldman, *Living My Life,* New York: Dover 1970, 2 vols; *Anarchism and other essays,* New York: Dover 1974.

32. D.T. Wieck, "The negativity of anarchism," in W.J. Ehrlich (and others), *Reinventing Anarchy,* London: Routledge Kegan Paul 1979, pp. 138-55. This quotation is from p. 143.

33. S. Rowbotham, *Beyond the Fragments,* London: Islington Community Press 1979, pp. 46-47.

34. Barbara Taylor, "Robert Owen and women's liberation," *Radical America* 14.4 (July-August 1980).

35. A. Negri, *Marx Oltre Marx, (Marx beyond Marx),* Milan: Peltinelli Editore 1979 (Materiali Marxisti 14).

36. R. Bahro, *The Alternative,* London: New Left Books 1978, pp. 40-41.
37. *op. cit.* p. 47.
38. Bahro, *op. cit.* pp. 300-303.
39. *op. cit.* p. 46.
40. *op. cit.* p. 27.
41. *op. cit.* p. 32, 144.
42. D. Porter, "Revolutionary realization: the motivational energy," in Enrlich, *op. cit.* n. 32, pp. 214-228. This quotation is from pp. 223-224.
43. E. P. Thompson, *The Poverty of Theory,* London: Merlin Press 1979, p. 352.
44. The material before the change in the law is drawn from *Le Monde* March 31 1981, p. 20 and April 1 1981, p. 20; afterwards from Peter Inserra, "Breaking the sound barrier," *Passion* (Paris), Nov. 26-Dec. 9, 1981, pp. 6-8.
45. Christoph Busch, *Was Die schon immer uber Freie Radios wissen wollten...aber nie zu fragen wagten!* (What you always wanted to know about free radios...but never dared to ask!), Munster: 1981, self-published.
46. Serge Bischoff, Radio Verte Fessenheim," *Ikon* I-2 (September 1978), pp. 192-200; Busch, *op. cit.* n. 45, pp. 143-155.
47. G J. Robinson, *Tito's Maverick Media,* Urbana Ill.: University of Illinois Press 1977; F. J. Berrigan, "Yugoslavia: a different model," *op. cit.* n. 9, pp. 223-234.
48. Cited in Rowbotham, *op. cit.* n. 33, p. 41.
49. R. McKay & S. Barr, *The Scottish Daily Express,* Edinburgh: Canongate Press 1976.
50. D. Wagner & P. Buhle, "Worker's control and the news," *Radical America* 14.4 (July-August 1980), pp. 7-21.
51. J. Downing, *The Media Machine,* London: Pluto Press 1980.

SECTION ONE
THE UNITED STATES

1

THE POLITICAL CONTEXT OF ALTERNATIVE MEDIA

The Structural Character of U.S. Media

One thing is plain: alternative media flourish in the wastelands left by official media. Later in the book we shall see how this happened in Portugal against the fascist background up to 1974, and within the sterilities of established media in Italy. The briefer account of self-managed media in the soviet bloc in section III will illuminate the process still further. In the U.S., the post-World War II alternative media are no exception; in the selection of cases that follows this introduction, we see women, Afro-Americans, Native Americans, Puerto Ricans, workers, marxists, opponents of U.S. dominance in Latin America and peace activists giving voice to the issues that concern them. These issues are shut out of the established media or are so distorted that the original voices are lost, or are so fleetingly present as to be effectively absent.

Sometimes, as in the case of *Rolling Stone* or the *Village Voice*, a commercially viable audience is discovered and alternative media become specialized additions to the established media. This only happens, however, when the newcomers are also within the general spectrum of established politics. There is space for radical columnists within them, just as there is sometimes space in big media for critical voices. There is a kind of continuum, ranging from a minority of perceptive journalists in the major media who are allowed a degree of latitude by their editors and publishers, to radical columnists in some rather more specialized established media, through to alternative media. Such people working in the major media deserve a great deal of credit for their activity, but it represents only a fraction of the main flow, even if sometimes a politically sensitive fraction (e.g. dissonant reporting from Vietnam or Central America).

In their normal reporting of the brutalities, chicanery and underlying rationales of U.S. foreign policy, the established media have repeatedly sold the American public a massive patriotic snow job.[1] In their presentation of women, they have repeatedly reinforced the sexist themes of woman as domestic consumer, as sex-object, and as object of violence.[2] They have always ridiculed and misrepresented the women's movement.[3] In their rare presentation of ethnic minorities, standard racist stereotypes have prevailed.[4] In their handling of the student anti-war movement in the 60s, and its serious questioning of American priorities at home as well as abroad, they served to trivialize and negate the issues raised: of war, peace, neo-colonialism, consumerism, careerism.[5] On the nuclear issue which threatens to destroy us all, and future generations as well, the U.S. media have been discreet to the point of absurdity, shrouding its key aspects in a fog of incoherent technicalities, denials of danger, and accusations of pro-Kremlin naivete.[6]

The media, as we saw in the General Introduction, have their own mythology of their critical power. Ed Murrow's *See It Now* attack on McCarthy, the *New York Times'* publication of part of the Pentagon Papers, the *Washington Post's* Watergate exposure, public TV's broadcasting of the Watergate hearings, the revulsion against the war in South East Asia "caused" by its full-color horrors on the livingroom TV screen: these are the legendary heroic feats. One has only to ask why they are so legendary, however, to be reminded of their rarity.

Patterns of ownership and control of the major media demonstrate their distance from being an independent "Fourth Estate" in the U.S. Advertising is the basic source of support for television, radio and the press, and ad agencies are only retained to represent the best interests of their corporate clients. Barnouw[7] has cited many instances of what this has meant in practice for the potential freedom and openness of that potential service. Newspapers depend between 60-80% on advertising for their revenue.[8] A few magazines scarcely use it, usually with financial instability as a consequence; many others depend on it 100%.

The concentration and centralization of power in the media world is as considerable, in some cases even more so, than in other branches of industry, commerce, and banking. In 1978, 5% of firms producing newspapers accounted for 48% of daily circulation. This has remained fairly constant since the 20s: in 1923, for example, 5% of firms accounted for 50% of circulation.[9] Since 1948, less than half of the U.S. population has lived in a city with a daily paper. [10] In 1978 just 35 cities enjoyed more than one daily paper (2.3% of the total). Back in 1923, 502 cities boasted more than one;[11] clearly it is not a profitable activity in most places. In mass market paperbacks, the top eight firms in 1976 accounted for 81% of total sales.[12] In television, the most recent figures available (for 1972) indicate that the network affiliate stations spent 63% of their time on network programs; the so-called "independents" spent 67% of their time on films, films made for TV or syndicated videotaped programs.[13] In other words, program content was remarkably centralized. TV is, of course, particularly important, with a national average of 45 hours' viewing per person per week.[14]

The new development of cable TV reflects the same concentrated pattern: in 1978, 30% of cable TV stations were owned by broadcasting corporations, 13% by magazine or book publishers, 12% by newspapers—and just 3% by communities or subscribers.[15] In 1977 one third of local media establishments (radio, TV, newspaper) were owned by conglomerates, defined as a firm owning at least three radio stations, or at least two papers, or at least two TV stations, or a newspaper and a radio station.[16] The pattern is also to be seen in the film industry, where 0.2% of firms in 1972 received 53% of the receipts.[17]The pattern of multiple sector involvement by media corporations is very clear in the case of the film industry, as three examples indicate.[18] The Avco Corporation, a major film presence, only has 1% of its action tied up in film; the rest is in consumer finance, insurance, credit cards, space research, aircraft and farm machinery manufacture, medical products and real estate. Gulf & Western has 19% of its action tied up in films; the rest is in financial services, consumer and agricultural products, apparel, building products and automotive replacement parts. Transamerica has 15% of its action in films; the rest is in consumer lending, insurance, manufacturing, aircraft operation, data processing, real estate, and moving and storage. Film involvement includes, of course, distribution and exhibition as well as production.

Within these gigantic empires, the perspectives of the majority are usually only present insofar as they have to be advertised to. A demonstration of this is the virtual invisibility of women and minorities in journalism.[19] Inside the news media, the forms of control over journalists and the definitions of what constitutes professional newsgathering combine to hamstring dissidents.[20]

Although the U.S. media have an official ethic of balance, of objectivity, of reproducing "all the news that's fit to print" as the *New York Times'* masthead would have it, the reality is different and quite beyond popular control. There follows, as naturally as night to day, an explosion of small attempts at mass communication. Here, we shall deal only with these attempts since World War II, although there is a long history of these media stretching back to the Revolution and before.

The Curious Offensiveness of Alternative Media in the U.S.

It could easily appear that de Tocqueville's characterization of the U.S. in the early 19th century still holds true, namely that little associations proliferate at all levels throughout the society, amongst them little media. According to this view, alternative media can be straightforwardly encompassed within the U.S. polity, and are furthermore a demonstration of its innately democratic and altogether superior qualities.

The problem with this reading of the situation is that it omits one major feature of life in the alternative media surveyed in this book: the extraordinary lengths employed to close and repress them. What in the world, in de Tocqueville's vision, could explain the mail interference, the telephone tapping, the harassment of street vendors by the police, the raids for non-existent drugs by police squads who carry off files and subscription lists, the obscenity trials whilst pornographic magazines are openly on sale, the Internal Revenue Service political audits, the FBI pressure on landlords to evict alternative media or to refuse to lease to them or to raise their rents? To say nothing of physical intimidation by neo-fascist groups, infiltration by plain-clothes policemen, payment of informers.[21]

So if a Tocquevillean perspective fails to capture this harsher reality, how is the situation to be understood in which the most powerful state in the world has felt impelled, despite its democratic ethos, to try to squash these mosquitoes, and—it would seem—has only been held back by its desire to sustain the mythology of its own restraint?

Indeed, in the McCarthy era at the nadir of the first Cold War, the state came to define its own "restraint" as precisely the virtue of American life which it had to forego—in order to preserve! In a curious parallel to the marxist notion of the dictatorship of the proletariat, which argues that after a socialist revolution the rights of capitalists must be restrained in order to protect the rights of the majority, McCarthy and his allies argued that the freedom of dissent had to be withdrawn in order to protect the freedom of the majority. "Extremism in defense of liberty is no vice," insisted Senator Barry Goldwater a decade after McCarthy's disgrace, in his 1964 bid for the presidency.

Such sentiments are very firmly embedded in the U.S. ruling classes. One of the most influential statements of this philosophy is to be found in George F. Kennan's seminal presentation of the doctrine that the USSR had to be "contained" in the journal *Foreign Affairs,* three years before McCarthy's ascendancy. It has direct implications for critical media:

> "...exhibitions of indecision, disunity and internal disintegration within this country have an exhilarating effect on the whole Communist movement. At *each* evidence of these *tendencies,* a thrill of hope and excitement goes through the Communist world; a new jauntiness can be noted in the Moscow tread; new groups of foreign supporters climb on to what they can only view as the bandwagon of international politics; and Russian pressure increases all along the line in international affairs."(my emphasis)[22]

When it is a question of *each* evidence just of "tendencies," we can easily see how a small critical organ of opinion can be defined as giving aid and comfort to the global foe, even unintentionally.

The history of this pressure from on high stretches back before the foundation of the Soviet Union, of course, as a reading of Emma Goldman's autobiography *Living My Life*[23] amply demonstrates. Her revolutionary career in the U.S. began in the 1890s and ended with the Palmer raids of 1919-20. It is in those decades that the genesis of state harassment of radical expression must be sought. There was then, as is well known, a high-level (as well as a popular) nativist suspicion of the foreign-born immigrant workers of 1880-1920. In particular, their supposed propensity to marxist and anarchist convictions, combined with the multitudinous languages and dialects they spoke, which made their intentions and activities utterly opaque to decent anglophone policemen, certainly had a major impact on developing the schools as agents of Americanization, and—it was devoutly hoped—pacification.[24] Popular films at the nickelodeon at the beginning of the century were another thrust in the same direction.[25] This strategy was helped to maturity by the profound reverberations of Upton Sinclair's *The Jungle,* published in 1906, with its threat of a *domestically* produced socialist movement composed of embittered, previously apolitical immigrant workers who might link up with native radicals.

For the few, the "outside agitators" who have seemingly been the sole flies in the ointment in every otherwise happy polity throughout the history of capitalist industrialization, there was a different strategy: coercion. Its target has been variously described: "troublemaker," "wreckers," the "Red Menace," "mindless militants," "godless communists," "commie perverts," and most recently, the "terrorist network."[26]

The strategy was always to impose a strict ceiling on the organized expression of significant dissent, without usually going to the point of officially closing media down and jailing their staff. The procedures listed a little earlier have often been sufficient, combined with the considerable organizational, financial and morale problems of organizing alternative media, to keep the institutions tiny, or push them into oblivion. The liberal niceties could be preserved: who could really see something excessive in an IRS audit or in the police keeping street-corners clear of vendors so passers-by could walk freely? Or in some citizen urging the Federal Communications Commission to look again at its decision to grant a license to broadcast to a small radio station? If it were not for files obtained under the Freedom of Information Act, who would believe landlords had been pressured to raise alternative media rents?

It has been as though blips on the authorities' radar-screen were presumed to be growing larger and moving closer, at very high speed, so that only resolute action could save spaceship America. Maybe the blips would have disappeared anyway, sinking off the screen from their own lack of sustained momentum; but that risk was not going to be entertained. Just as the wealthy are often characterized by their obsessive concern with the minutest details of their finances, so perhaps the most powerful state in the world has programmed itself to keep all political movements and the media meticulously below a certain threshold. Certainly since the Palmer raids, with the consolidation and extension of the FBI through Hoover's protracted reign, with the growth of CIA involvement in domestic affairs, with the emergence of the National Security Agency, with the continuance of urban "Red Squads" in the police, with the involvement of military intelligence and the Pentagon in domestic affairs, this mood has been bureaucratized, institutionalized and dyed into the political life of the nation.[27] Thus, the seeming overkill in repression of small alternative media has its origins in these historical developments, culminating in the Cold War.

A complementary paradox of alternative media in the U.S. is that the outside world—not just Moscow, as in Kennan's superpower-style formulation—is as keenly interested in them, albeit for very different reasons, as are the repressive departments of the state. For U.S. readers, therefore, who may sometimes wonder whether the enormous personal effort that is put into organizing alternative media communication is worthwhile, this longer view of the situation may help to restore a sense of political significance to an otherwise lonely trek. For much of the rest of the world, the question as to whether the U.S. is a monolith is a very real one. Movements of dissent, media of dissent, are welcome evidence that the U.S. is not simply an imperial machine. At the very least, such media are seen as bulwarks of resistance against the reconstitution of the U.S. in a still more reactionary direction than has been seen in Korea, Vietnam, Iran, Chile and southern Africa, to name a few. Their work is important on a national scale, and therefore on a global scale.

However, this David and Goliath perspective on alternative media in the U.S. is only one dimension, however important. We need to have an overview of political and social change within the country in order to contextualize these media properly, for they have certainly not existed in a vacuum otherwise only inhabited by the FBI and its rivals. To carry this out is potentially a mammoth task. David Armstrong's survey of alternative media in the 60s, *A Trumpt To Arms*,[28] is insightfully written, but provides in essence a wealth of descriptive detail about a great variety of media and their motivations. The objective here is rather different, namely to examine the problems of organizing those alternative media that pose fundamental challenges to the given order; and to examine them across different countries and social movements. Thus the task at this point is to offer a more theoretical overview of their context in the U.S. during the period 1945-83 than is provided in Armstrong's otherwise valuable account.

A Map of Continuity and Change, Fragmentation and Connection, 1945-83

Looking at the development of the U.S. over four decades, the first observation to make is that the continuities are certainly as noteworthy as the undoubtedly important changes. In particular, the United States is only to be understood, and will only develop in the close future, as a socio-political "Micronesia."

The changes have been considerable. Just consider the following. Afro-Americans in the South are now actually allowed to vote. By 1980, only 20% of the U.S. labor force worked in factories—a major change in social experience for Americans.[29] By that year, about 40% of the overall labor force was composed of women, as against 28% in the late 40s.[30] Because of its isolation in world opinion, the U.S. had been forced to withdraw from Vietnam in 1975. In the same year, with President Ford's endorsement, New York City was declared bankrupt, and a drastic austerity regime was imposed on its poorer citizens. One president had been forced to resign or face impeachment proceedings, another had been shot dead. A major recomposition of labor has gathered momentum, swinging employment away from the unionized North and Northeast (e.g., Detroit) to the barely unionized South (e.g., Houston).[31] Major black rebellions in the North in the 60s and 70s had in turn sparked explosions in Chicano, Puerto Rican, Native American and women's awareness: social movements proliferated. Many participants felt they were on the edge of turning the world upside down, in a great international eruption touching France, Italy, Poland, Czechoslovakia, Vietnam, Japan, China, Brazil, Mexico, West Germany and many other countries.

In the face of these upheavals and reversals, it seems odd to speak of continuities. Yet first and foremost is the continuity of social struggle, by which I mean that the roots of the 60s explosions lay in the much lonelier battles of the 40s and 50s, and that the "Sixties" in actuality lasted well into the 70s. There is a tendency on both Left and Right to isolate the 60s (nostalgically or with relief) as a miraculous decade, with 1968 equivalent to, say 1848, as the year of international magic. And you can see why. The temptation is to be resisted though. The roots of the Berkeley "Free Speech" movement, as of the anti-draft and anti-war movement, lay in the southern civil rights struggles overwhelmingly conducted by Afro-Americans in the 50s and early 60s.[32] These in turn were given heart by the Supreme Court's reversal in 1954 of its 1896 endorsement of school segregation. That reversal itself was not spontaneous. It was brought about by two previous, interlocking developments. One was slow, patient legal work by the NAACP in the South since 1949 in challenging segregation through the court system. The second was the U.S. regime's need to avert criticism, as "leader of the Free World," from the USSR and the Third World, regarding the shackled condition of its own black citizens. Finally, the leadership of many of those early anti-segregation battles in the South was most often in the hands of black World War II veterans who, for the second time this century, had ventured their lives for the U.S. in a segregated military. (And these, plainly, are only some chapters in the history of black struggle.)

The roots of the war in Southeast Asia are to be located in another aspect of class relations inside the U.S. that was one element in the new plan for world order hammered out in its essentials by U.S. policy-makers toward the end of World War II. Their thinking pivoted to a great extent on the conviction that capitalism could not politically survive another 30s— could not quell the rage that would explode if the 30s were to resume after the hardships and privations of the war itself. Hence, they had to secure markets, minerals and political compliance throughout the world, in order to secure the growth of the U.S. economy.[33] (See the Introduction to the Geopolitics of the Mediterranean for a more specific commentary on this development.) "We have nothing to fear but fear itself," Roosevelt had warned at the depth of the Depression; it was the resumption of that fear that U.S. policy-makers were dedicated to avert. What many 60s activists initially saw as new, separate and horrifying developments—the Bay of Pigs, the Dominican invasion, Vietnam, Cambodia—were in actuality closely bound up with each other at the time, and over time. An overview of their interconnections is a vital corrective to that fragmented perspective.

The women's movement developed, as Sara Evans has demonstrated,[34] out of the civil rights and anti-war struggles. It did so in two senses. First, a number of leading activists in both these movements, whose names and work were in danger of being lost from view until she published her research, were women. Negatively, the forms of sexism evinced by many of the male activists in both movements galvanized a number of these women into deep reflection on the significance of sexism in politics and social life. (The parallel is close with the origins of the women's suffrage movement in the 19th century abolitionist movement.) What Evans also emphasizes is the growing impact of waged employment and college education among women since World War II in developing a mass sense of the contradictions of patriarchy, and so a widely responsive mood among women to women's liberation activists. She also notes how there had been no parallels on the Old Left, for which male chauvinism and women's rights were always issues to be taken with great seriousness, to the aggressive sexism of much of the New Left student movement leadership. Finally, and absorbingly, she has observed what a large proportion of activists of both genders in the civil rights and anti-war movements, came from families with a strongly dissident or leftist outlook. Often this outlook had been concealed outside the home in the McCarthy era, for fear of job loss or imprisonment, but had nonetheless persisted in private. Women from these homes had often been nurtured on the assumption of female equality in principle if not always in practice.

Thus the ferments of the 60s had firm roots in what had gone before. They did not, despite their apparent suddenness, spring up out of a vacuum. Nor did they peacefully extinguish themselves on or about December 31st 1969. The major media gave the *impression*, for instance, that the last serious black revolt was in Washington D.C. following the liquidation of Martin Luther King, when in actuality black urban riots and revolts continued well into the 70s in smaller cities not normally covered by the networks or the quality dailies.

Springfield, Mass., for example, is much less likely ever to be in the national news than Washington.[35] It was as a result of mainly black and Latin effectiveness in getting welfare and municipal wages raised that New York was singled out for exemplary punishment by the banks and President Ford in 1975. Many other cities were then and have remained on the brink of the same fiscal crisis. Since 1975, with the major exception of Black Christmas in New York in 1977[36] the high peaks of movement activity have subsided. However, the conditions that create unrest have developed, and there is a certain subterranean experience of lessons from the previous cycle of struggle. *Thus, the continuities of four decades are vitally important to understand; and within them, the continuities in certain struggles rightly claim our attention first of all.*

There is a second area of continuity, however, which demands our attention. With a new Cold War and a "New" right in the 80s, it is evident that the policy options of at least one wing of the U.S. ruling class have not succumbed to the assaults of previous decades. The extractive aggressive relation with the rest of the planet, of which the Cold War (old or new) is but one ideological strategy, has continued in full force. ("Trilateralism" is effectively an alternative strategy to the same imperial ends.)[37] Its concomitants—control over labor, relegation of women to domestic subordination, extrusion of black people from the labor process, exploitation of Indian nations' lands for minerals—mesh easily with militarism overseas. The sheer recital of these examples evokes the continuities of U.S. history. Goliath has not been felled.

Aided somewhat by geography, but created by the specific development of "its" capitalism, the U.S. continues to consist—in socio-political, not economic terms—of a bewildering variety of communities. In some cases they are indeed a very long way from each other, in the small towns and settlements of 25,000 or less which in 1980 accounted for almost 55% of the U.S. population.[38] But even in the huge population centers of New York, Los Angeles, Chicago, Boston and elsewhere, ethnic community neighborhoods constitute islands as diverse, as communally distant from each other, as the specks of land in the Pacific that make up Micronesia. These communities exist side by side geographically; but individuals' contact is almost always tightly limited to the workplace. White racism always

lends a predictable and vicious twist to this ethnic checker-
board (it is evidently a unifying factor for whites of some
importance). But ethnic rivalries inside black and Latin communities are also strong.

It is damaging, but not surprising, that the struggles of
undocumented workers in the Southwest, of Haitian refugees,
of Indian communities in the Dakotas, of unemployed Ken-
tucky miners, go largely unrecorded in the major media; and
that no opposition media have a widespread circulation to
remedy this state of affairs. The same is, unfortunately, true of
countries other than the U.S.

But what is peculiar to the U.S., Katznelson has argued,[39]
is a long-term formation of class resistance. Beyond the
language differences, beyond the cultural and religious differences, beyond racism—though they all combine to provide
material underpinning—lies the political organization of
urban-industrial life since the 1850s. Seen in its most classical
version in machine politics, but evident in more simply organized forms elsewhere, the pattern has been for each urban
neighborhood to receive whatever services it enjoyed on the
basis of its ethnic identity. This made for whatever urban
political strength it had, large or small. Churches or syna-
gogues, ethnic associations, sometimes religious or supple-
mentary schools, political clubs and bars, were the knots in the
neighborhood network. (Peter Lloyd has described a very
similar version of urban political life in the cities of West Africa
since World War II.[40]) On the basis of negotiating with the
leading figures in these ethnic associations, urban politicians
have exchanged votes for the subsequent delivery of favors
(municipal jobs, better services). It was, still is, a marriage of
local self-help and cultural organizations with the patronage
possible from city hall. Even when ethnic communities split on
the merits of particular urban politicians they were still
unfailingly appealed to as ethnics. It may not always have
worked well, but nothing else worked at all.

Katznelson's analysis of this pattern, highly familiar in
itself to most readers, is that it has shaped the whole direction
of class politics in urban-industrial America. Workplace struggles, persistent, intense and often bloody as they have been
have nonetheless been divorced from the community concerns
of the working class. To get what it wanted in that realm,
entirely ethnic tactics have been as normal as trade union

tactics at work. The successes of the Wobblies in uniting linguistically fragmented workers in strikes, the success of the CIO in the 30s and 40s in unionizing black workers, the considerable ethnic diversity of present day union membership, have none of them reached noticeably into political cooperation beyond the workplace. Katznelson's book is in large part a discussion of how in this *accepted* mutual insulation of the two realms lay the Achilles' heel of the urban community control movements of the 60s and 70s.

There have been moments, perhaps the high water marks of the 60s and 70s, when there were serious bids to overcome this fragmentation of political struggle. Many black movements, most notably in Detroit,[41] mounted a critique of U.S. society as a whole. Many women's movements raised connections between the immediate and the general, the home, the school and the factory, and subjected them to an inter-related analysis. Many Native Americans posed the relation of human society to the earth in a manner both ancient and integral. These were the major *anti*-fragmentation achievements of the period. Despite them, the divorce pinpointed by Katznelson, the structural reinforcement of America as Micronesia, persisted and prospered.

The 60s Movements: Achievements and Difficulties

I have reviewed the long, interconnected sequence of opposition movements inside the U.S. since World War II (though some I have virtually or entirely overlooked[42]). I have noted the continuities in U.S. foreign policy, with its variations in strategy. And I have explored the character of the U.S. as a socio-political Micronesia. The task now is to examine the movements of the 60s and 70s as they bear upon the alternative media studied in this section of the book. Very often such media are assumed to belong lock, stock and barrel to popular movements. We can see why, in their extraordinary proliferation in the 60s when those movements were at the height of their activity, and in the rapid disappearance of the majority of them as those movements began to subside. Also, not one of the examples we examine was untouched by those movements. Yet two of them, the *National Guardian* and KPFA, Berkeley, originated in the 40s, not the 60s. Furthermore, as I have emphasized, the 60s movements were not just a flash of lightning on a clear day. Many alternative media died in the 70s: but many remain. And a number began in the 70s.

I am going to argue that the 60s movements had two faces. One was highly positive. Black movements demanded and won black leadership. A massive alliance developed against U.S. military action in Southeast Asia, including members of the armed forces themselves, where many alternative papers were produced.[43] Women put their concerns on the political agenda in ways not previously registered, especially in the assertion that "the personal is political." A whole series of political insights began, if not to intertwine with one another, then at least to jostle one another for attention.

The other face was negative, though nowhere near as deeply negative as the first was positive. This other face was indelibly stamped with a reaction against the frozen 50s, the "dark ages" as Jezer has called them.[44] The two most salient internal repressions of that period as they bore down on the bulk of the domestic population were McCarthyism and sexual puritanism.

The first halted the development of socialist politics in its tracks for the best part of a generation. Normal political development, based on argument and debate and prior experiences of various struggles, was quite simply wiped off the map. Naked physical repression was admittedly fairly rare (unlike the everyday experience of minorities), but the mechanisms of the McCarthy era sufficed to intimidate and silence people nonetheless. The Rosenbergs' execution (in the end, as W.E.B. DuBois said, for refusing to lie that they had been Soviet agents), was an exemplary one, and intended to be. Their Jewish origins, the substantial Jewish presence on the U.S. left, and the timing of the judicial murder coming so soon after the Holocaust, were factors that were not lost on the organizers of the electric chair any more than on their opposition. It felt to many on the left as though fascism was once more around the corner. Although people still talked politics in the privacy of their own homes, a public socialist arena was absent. Even concern with black civil rights was evidence of Moscow-orchestrated subversion.

A result of this in the 60s was that SNCC, the paramount civil rights (and then Black Power) body, and following it SDS, the main white student body, often defined good political organization according to a simplified version of anarchism. Instant action, immediacy of feelings, primacy of moral revulsion over political or economic analysis, hostility to structure, abolition of leaders: these were the moods and even watchwords that dominated political discourse. "Don't trust anyone over thirty!" They constituted the response of what was for the most part a generation newly exposed to socialist or anti-imperialist or black nationalist or radical perspectives. Even the political tumults in Portugal after forty-eight years of fascism in 1974 were—as we shall see later—more conditioned by previous socialist and anti-colonialist experience than were the 60s in the U.S.

The experience of working within these strictures—though to most people they *felt* like the absence of strictures—gradually developed a widespread sense that other, tighter forms of political organization should be attempted. The most famous expression of this was the paper "The Tyranny of Structurelessness,"[45] which emerged out of the women's movement, itself stamped strongly with the impulses described above. Some people began examining the marxist classics on party organization at this point and seized on them with the same uncritical fervor that had been in evidence previously for a principled absence of structures. A number of new sects came into being after the collapse of SDS in 1969, mostly looking toward a simplified image of the Cultural Revolution in China as their examplar. The CPUSA, the SWP and other Old Left splinters, were dismissed as sub- or counter-revolutionary, but without any sustained analysis of their history and problems. It was a relief to have Cuba with Che, China with Mao— neither of them getting on with the other, but that could be overlooked—and neither of them apparently contaminated with the Soviet model which, in a kind of unison with the McCarthy of their earlier childhood years, they could lambast with an excellent conscience. Their own past, the crippling influence of Soviet marxism on marxist thinking since the 30s, the reasons behind Soviet marxism's atrophy: all these were swept into a trashbag and dumped. The immediate future was the thing.

There followed a series of frantic attempts by sects through the 70s either to promote themselves into being the authentic revolutionary party, guaranteed by the apostolic succession of Marx, Engels, Lenin, Stalin, Mao (yes, Stalin); or, more flexibly and less arrogantly, to have protracted debates with other sects to see whether they could federate or even unite. The career of the christian ecumenical movement could have illuminated their deliberations at a number of points, but so far as is known, this parallel was never introduced into the discussions.

By the end of the 70s a greater feeling for the realities of the situation was asserting itself. But it had taken about as long as the period of the first Cold War and McCarthyism for many people on the left to regain the experiential ground which had been lost. By that time the intensity with which these matters had been pursued had burned many of them out altogether.

The other repression of the 50s, sexual puritanism, can be dealt with more briefly. A problem of sexual repression in a male-dominated society is always likely to be that when the rules relax, macho values will be everywhere. The role of Elvis Presley in exploding sexual restraint toward the end of the 50s is well enough known. The manner in which he did it precisely foreshadowed and influenced the male arrogance and sexism of the 60s movements. The assumptions that only men should get into dangerous confrontations with southern sheriffs, that AWOL soldiers should be "solaced" by movement women, that militant male activists had the right to sleep with movement women, that women were inappropriate as political leaders or thinkers: all these were facets of a macho-dominated reaction against sexual puritanism. Not a pleasant face of the 60s movements, but it is one which has to be recognized for what it was.

No political movements of the left are unflawed, any more than political parties or labor unions. It is still crucial to be honest about their flaws, while respecting their achievements.

Conclusion

The overview just presented has emphasized the dialectic between history, political structures, social movements and alternative media in the U.S. over two generations. Only thus can we hope to understand the conflicts and currents which animated radical media, or the political lessons to be drawn from them for future media work.

Undoubtedly, for every media instance I have chosen in the pages that follow, some readers would have thought another one more appropriate. My selection principles were as follows. Each case had to be of media posing a fundamental political challenge to the status quo. Examples had to be selected across newspapers, magazines, radio and film. Each instance had to have a fairly long organizational history (which is not to downplay the political impact of ephemera).[46] Lastly, I have tried to ensure a certain political and geographical spread.

Footnotes

1. J. Aronson, *The Press and the Cold War*, Boston: Beacon Press 1970; I.F. Stone, *The Hidden History of the Korean War*, New York: Monthly Review Press 1969 (2nd ed); N. Chomsky & Ed Herman, *The Political Economy of Human Rights*, Boston: South End Press 1980 (2 vols); E. Said, *Covering Islam*, New York: Pantheon Books 1981; L. Wolf, "The Pentagon's Other Option," *Covert Action Information Bulletin* 17 (Summer 1982), pp. 8-24.

2. M. Haskell, *From Reverence to Rape*, New York: Harper & Row 1974; J. Dispenza, *Advertizing the American Woman*, Dayton, Ohio: Pflaum Publishing Co., 1975; G. Tuchman (ed), *Hearth and Home*, New York: Oxford University Press 1978; S. Ewen, *Captains of Consciousness*, New York: McGraw Hill 1976; E. Goffman, *Gender Advertizements*, London: Penguin Books 1980.

3. M. Morris, "Newspapers and the New Feminists," *Journalism Quarterly*, vol. 50 (1973); M. Morris, "The Public Definition of a Social Movement," *Sociology and Social Research*, vol. 57 (1973).

4. D. Leab, *From Sambo to Superspade*, London: Secker & Warburg 1975; T. Engelhardt, "Racism and the Media," *Bulletin of Concerned Asian Scholars* 3.1 (Winter-Spring 1971); *Kerner Commission Report, 1968*, New York: Bantam Books 1968, ch. 15; R.C. Toll, *Blacking Up*, New York: OUP 1974.

5. T. Gitlin, *The Whole World Was Watching*, Berkeley: University of California Press 1980.

6. E. Barnouw, *The Sponsor*, New York: OUP 1978, section III; S. Hilgartner (and others), *Nukespeak: The Selling of Nuclear Technology in America*, New York: Penguin Books 1983; J. Prados, *The Soviet Estimate*, New York: The Dial Press 1982.

7. *Op. cit.*

8. J.N. Rosse & J.N. Dertouzas, "Economic Issues in Mass Communication Industries," paper for the Federal Trade Commission, December 14-15 1978, Studies in Industry Economics 99, Economics Department, Stanford University, p. 29. See also A. Smith, *Goodbye Gutenberg*, New York: Oxford University Press 1980, Section II, chs. 2-4.
9. Rosse & Dertouzas, cited paper, Table II.A.5, p. 51.
10. *Idem.*, Table II.A.6, p. 52.
11. J.N. Rosse, "The Evolution of One Newspaper Cities," Federal Trade Commission paper, December 14-15 1978, Studies in Industry Economics 95, Economics Department, Stanford University, Table 2, p. 4.
12. Rosse & Dertouzas, cited paper, Table II.C.13, p. 130.
13. *Idem.*, Table II.B.3, p. 85.
14. *Idem.*, Table II.B.2, p. 79.
15. Rosse & Dertouzas, "Media Conglomerates: Chains, Groups and Cross-Ownership," Federal Trade Commission paper, December 14-15 1978, Studies in Industry Economics 96, Economics Department, Stanford University, Table 12, p. 28.
16. *Idem.*, Table II, p. 26.
17. T. Guback, "Theatrical Film," in B.M. Compaine (ed), *Who Owns the Media?*, New York: Harmony Books 1979, Table 5.27, p. 229.
18. *Idem.*, Up From the Footnote, New York: Seabury Press 1978; N. Kotz, "The Minority Struggle for a Place in the Newsroom," *Columbia Journalism Review* XVII.6 (March-April 1979), pp. 23-31.
20. A. McBarnet, "Disciplining the Journalist," *Media, Culture and Society* vol.1 (1979); E. Epstein, *News From Nowhere*, New York: Vintage Books 1973; H. Gans, *Deciding What's News*, New York: Oxford University Press 1979.
21. See Geoffrey Rips, *The Campaign Against the Underground Press*, San Francisco: City Lights 1981; J. Aronson, *Deadline for the Media*, New York: Bobbs-Merrill Inc. 1972; D. Armstrong, *A Trumpet to Arms*, Boston: South End Press, 1984, ch.5.
22. G. Kennan, "The Sources of Soviet Conduct," excerpted in R. Hofstadter (ed), *Great Issues in American History, From Reconstruction to the Present Day*, New York: Vintage Books 1969. Quotation from pp. 426-7.
23. Dover Publications Inc., New York, 1970, 2 vols.
24. J. Spring, *Education and the Rise of the Corporate State*, Boston: Beacon Press 1972, chs. 4-6.

25. L. May, *Screening Out the Past*, New York: Oxford University Press 1980, chs. 3, 5, 6. For a contrary view, see D. Czitrom, *The Media and the American Mind*, Chapel Hill, NC: University of North Carolina Press 1982, pp. 48-59.

26. See E. Herman, *The Real Terror Network*, Boston: South End Press 1982, chs. 1, 4.

27. F.J. Donner, *The Age of Surveillance*, New York: Vintage Books 1981; Center for Research on Criminal Justice, *The Iron Fist and the Velvet Glove*, Berkeley: Center for Research on Criminal Justice 1975.

28. Cited n. 21.

29. *Handbook on Basic Economic Statistics* (March 1983), vol. 37.3, pp. 16-17. This figure is for February 1983. It contrasts with 41% of the workforce in manufacturing in 1943.

30. U.S. Bureau of the Census, *Statistical Abstract of the United States 1982-83*, Washington D.C.: 1982, Table 627, p. 377; *Statistical Abstract of the United States 1976*, Table 569, p. 355.

31. There have been several accounts of this move; the best overviews, regrettably, are in other languages. See Bruno Cartosio (ed) *Dentro L'America in Crisi: saggi sulle lotte sociali negli Stati Uniti degli anni Settanta* (Inside America in Crisis: Essays on the Social Struggles in the USA during the 70s), Bari, Italy: De Donato 1980 (Movimento Operaio series, no. 62); *Le Monde Deplomatique* 336 (March 1982), pp. 12-14: "Les travailleurs americains victimes de la restructuration" (American Workers as Victims of Restructuring). Such overviews would be most valuable in English.

32. See especially "The Borning Struggle: The Civil Rights Movement," interviews with John Lewis, Jean Smith, Bernice Reagon, in D. Cluster (ed), *They Should Have Served That Cup of Coffee*, Boston: South End Press 1979, pp. 1-40. See also Mario Savio's famous speach at Berkeley in M. Teodori (ed), *The New Left*, Indianapolis: Bobbs Merrill 1969, pp. ??? The other essays in Cluster's book reinforce this continuity. See to W. Strickland, "The Road Since *Brown*," *The Black Scholar* 11.1 (September-October 1979), pp. 2-8; and D. Bell, "Learning from the *Brown* Experience," the same, pp. 9-16.

33. See the essays by Eakins and by Gardner in D. Horowitz (ed), *Corporations and the Cold War*, New York: Monthly Review Press 1968; L. Shoup & W. Minter, "Shaping a New World Order," in H. Sklar (ed), *Trilateralism*, Boston: South End Press 1980, pp. 135-57; M. Jezer, *The Dark Ages*, Boston: South End Press 1982, chs. 1-4.

34. S. Evans, *Personal Politics*, New York: Knopf 1979.

35. E.J. Epstein, *News From Nowhere*, New York: Vintage Books 1973, ch. 3.

36. P. Mattera, "Hot Child in the City," *Radical America* 13.5 (September-October 1979), pp. 49-60.

37. H. Sklar (ed), *Trilateralism* (n. 33), especially Sections IV, VI, VII.

38. U.S. Bureau of the Census, *Statistical Abstract of the United States* 1982-83 (103rd edition), Washington D.C. 1982, Table 23, p. 21.

39. I. Katznelson, *City Trenches*, New York: Pantheon Books 1981.

40. P. Lloyd, *Africa in Social Change*, London: Penguin Books 1965, ch. 8.

41. Ernie Allen, "Dying from the Inside: The Decline of the League of Revolutionary Black Workers," in D. Cluster, *op. cit.*, n. 32; D. Georgakas & M. Surkin, *Detroit: I Do Mind Dying*, New York: St. Martin's Press 1975; J. Geschwender, *Class, Race and Worker Insurgency*, New York: Cambridge University Press 1977.

42. Gay and lesbian movements are a conspicuous case in point.

43. J. Aronson, *Deadline for the Media*, Indianapolis: Bobbs-Merrill 1972, ch. 11.

44. M. Jezer, *op. cit.*, n. 33.

45. J. Freeman, "The Tyranny of Structurelessness," *Berkeley Journal of Sociology* XVII (1972-73).

2

THE NATIONAL GUARDIAN AND THE GUARDIAN

We made our position on Marxism sufficiently obvious
(we liked it) but our wavelength was America.[1]
Cedric Belfrage
co-founder of the *National Guardian*

...we're confident, too. Confident that our political line
will continue to develop to meet not only the needs of
the broad progressive forces and the revolutionary
movement but the needs of the millions who will
acquire class consciousness as our decadent, capitalist
society plunges to its doom.[2]
Jack Smith
Editor of the *Guardian* from 1967-82

National Guardian

Location: New York
Began: 1948
Staff: ten full-time (1948)
Appeared: weekly
Circulation: 35,000 (1948); 75,000 (1949); 45,000 (1953)
Finance: sales; subscriptions; individual donations;
working wives and husbands; mail-order *'Guardian
Market';* some advertising; events; sustainers

The Guardian

Began: 1967
Location; New York

Staff: 23 full-time (1982)
Appears: weekly
Circulation: 20,000
Finance: sales; sustaining subscriptions; some adver-
tising; individual donations.

The Guardian, despite the major 1967 split after which its original name was altered, is the longest running non-party paper in the history of the U.S. left. For this reason alone, it demands attention in this survey. It has survived through McCarthyism, through the silent 50s (in the North, that is), through the social movements of the 60s and 70s, and into the period of the New Right and a new Cold War in the 1980s. Its form, contents and personnel have changed, and attitudes are still sharply expressed on whether it should have changed in the ways it has, but the paper has managed to maintain a consistent, noticeable place within radical movements in the U.S. In particular, its international correspondents have often been the only ones to transmit news from the other side in major conflicts: Korea, Vietnam, China, Angola, the Polisario Front.

History up to 1967

What follows is based on the history of the *National Guardian, Something To Guard*[3] published by Aronson and Belfrage, two of the original three co-founders. (The third, Jack McManus, died in 1961.) I also had the benefit of personal discussions with Aronson and Belfrage.

The driving force that launched the paper was shock in the late 1940s at the rapid reversal in U.S. policies at home and abroad, following Roosevelt's death. The second world war, on one level, seemed to many to be an anti-fascist crusade which had succeeded in breaking down the pariah-status of the Soviet Union, and thus in opening up the traditional non-question of marxist socialism inside the U.S. The sharp upturn in the economy during the war, the consequent employment of women and Afro-Americans in large numbers, the rise of labor unions to a position of some established power, the militant strike-wave that swept the country for fifteen months immed-iately after the wartime no-strike pledge was lifted: all these seemed to indicate that while progress might not be invincible, it could at least be expected to maintain at some level. I.F. Stone has vividly evoked the sense of almost heady excitement that progressive intellectuals experienced during the latter phases of the New Deal period.[4]

However, for those with eyes to see, the writing on the wall was clearer by the day following the war. A major crusade to return both the Soviet Union and domestic ferment to the *status quo ante* was in full evidence, horrifyingly expressed by dropping atomic bombs on Japan in August 1945 as an assertion of U.S. supremacy, and explicitly announced in Winston Churchill's "Iron curtain" speech in Missouri in March 1946. Belfrage and Aronson themselves had seen at first hand the hasty rehabilitation of second-tier Nazis in U.S.-occupied postwar Germany. The formal declaration of the external Cold War came in 1947 with President Truman's request for major financial aid to quell the popular communist insurrection in Greece[5]; and of the internal Cold War, with the passage of the Taft-Hartley Act in the same year, aimed at subduing labor's strike power.

Overseas, the USSR openly denounced Yugoslavia's independent socialism in 1948, and—more personally for the *National Guardian*—Anna Louise Strong, their Moscow correspondent, was denounced by the Kremlin as an American agent. This last blow came after the paper had begun publishing, but served to solidify its own independent socialist convictions.

The times were exceedingly somber. Rather than cave in, however, the *National Guardian*'s nucleus decided to fight back by starting an independent radical newsweekly. Their position was both negative and positive. They rejected militarism and the Cold War; the notion of a single marxist center (e.g., in Moscow), and consequently their own subordination to the U.S. Communist Party; and yet also opposed any attempt to harass or constrain the Communist Party's freedom to operate ("we were the voice of anti-anticommunism," as Belfrage put it). As the Cold War extended its grip inside and outside the U.S. even these positions became the object of considerable hostility from the government. In a time when such positions are much easier to hold, their contribution to the sustenance of an open-minded left in the U.S. deserves considerable respect.

Positively, they supported labor, Afro-Americans, women, peace groups, when to do so was to court definition as supporting Soviet subversion (or in the case of women, to be absurdly shouting in favor of victories already long achieved...).

Positively, too, they maintained a list of correspondents at home and overseas of exceptional caliber (for example W.E.B. DuBois and Wilfred Burchett), who provided *National Guardian* readers with a rare taste of informed political journalism while papers like the *New York Times* were self-censoring themselves to the tune of the Dulles brothers and even of Senator McCarthy.[6]

During the late 40s and 50s, the *National Guardian* was identified with a whole series of national and international political issues and campaigns of considerable dimensions. It was the unofficial press supporter of Henry Wallace's Progressive Party. It was the only newspaper to support the Rosenbergs, and single-handedly set in motion a huge international campaign against their execution (which culminated in Pope Pius XII, hardly a sturdy defender of Jews or leftists, publicly urging clemency on Eisenhower). It threw most of what it had into the campaigns of New York Congressman Vito Marcantonio, the lone, unabashed radical in the House of Representatives. It published news about U.S. prisoners-of-war in North Korea, at at time when their families could get no information about them (because of State Department suppression to foment war antagonism). It single-handedly took on McCarthy as well, without any of the "ifs and buts" that dominated the few major papers that ever criticized him. It presented evidence of anti-Semitism in the USSR and condemned it forthrightly. It attacked U.S. involvement in Vietnam early on, long before the anti-war movement. It supported the overthrow of Batista in Cuba and the new *fidelista* government. Its attempt to alert international as well as national opinion against the racism of courts and established power in the South led on one occasion to the French parliament's standing for a minute's silence in honor of a southern black victim of U.S. "justice." In the years of the Freedom Rides in the early 60s, the *National Guardian* was passed from hand to hand by the riders.

Its stands did not go unnoticed from on high. McCarthy's Senate Committee on Government Operations hauled Aronson and Belfrage before itself, forcing them to take the Fifth Amendment or face having to supply the Committee with its subscribers' names and addresses. As an extra, McCarthy ensured the presence of an Immigration and Naturalization Service official at the hearing, and Belfrage's deportation proceedings—he was a British resident alien of nearly thirty years' standing—followed shortly thereafter. The loss of Belfrage was a major blow the paper suffered in that period. Harassment was extensive; threatening telephone calls were received; staff were telephoned at home in the middle of the night by callers who said nothing; a piece of metal was discovered in the printing press, and it had to be meticulously checked for foreign bodies every time thereafter before use; FBI agents would visit subscribers' homes and put them under heavy pressure to stop subscribing to the paper. News vendors were told by some distributors that they could stock the *National Guardian* or the major press, but not both. Last but not least, the great democratic press of the freest country in the world raised not a single cry at McCarthy's inquisitions or the INS deportation of Belfrage (for no crime).

The lesson was plain. It was not enough to be non-aligned socialists, not enough to criticize and condemn the show-trials in eastern Europe in the late 40s and early 50s, not enough to call attention to racist judicial frame-ups, not enough to be in favor of peace and international dialogue. All these positions sapped the Cold War rationale that marxism is monolithic and brutal (even more brutal than U.S. military and police might). The *National Guardian*'s position could only be compared to an anti-Zionist newspaper in Israel, surrounded by the screeching forces of super-patriotism on the boil.

People often think of alternative media as functioning within the context of major political upsurges of the left. Certainly many of the media examined in this book began within that context. In a sense, too, even the *National Guardian* and KPFA, Berkeley, emerged from the final wave of New Deal optimism, though their first fifteen years were set against a very different national mood. In 1983, however, when this book is being written, the alternative media in virtually all countries face a period of repression whose duration can only be surmised. This may take a course quite different from the period of the first Cold War, evidenced by the New Right, a reactionary populism, apparently enthusiastically backed by ordinary, "sensible" people. There is a battle in many countries between a confident, aggressive, well-financed far right and a fragmented, confused and listless left. The role of alternative media, as I shall argue in the conclusions to this book, becomes *more* vital, not less so, in such a period. Attention to the *National Guardian*'s experience in ploughing a lonely and—at the time—seemingly purposeless furrow, is directly relevant to the times that appear to be upon us. Keeping certain flames alight, providing a network of people with fresh information and perspectives, is an essential contribution to constructing the next upsurges. In the U.S. today there are far more progressive publications than could have been dreamt of in 1955. But without persistent efforts at that time such as the *National Guardian*, or *Monthly Review*, or *I.F. Stone's Weekly*, or KPFA, the picture could easily be distinctly different. Arguably, the task now is to resist and persist in alternative media communication until the next political ripening enables a qualitatively new advance.

Internal Organization 1948-67

The *National Guardian*'s organization was predicated on three major principles: democratic discussion by the staff; final editorial authority clearly defined; and the attempt to achieve maximum professional thoroughness in writing and presentation. The commitment to democracy was not merely formal. Everyone sat in on the weekly meeting. The general manager, McManus, wrote many of the editorials. The circulation manager regularly contributed editorial ideas. There was also a close working relationship between the manager of the progressive printers upstairs (Trade Union Service) and McManus, who spent long hours together in slack periods discussing how the paper could be improved.

Furthermore, the paper made extensive use of stringers, the three most famous having been named already: DuBois, Strong, Burchett. These were only a few, numerically speaking, of the total. But the practice made for a consistent opening of the paper's columns to people outside its full-time staff, which obviously extended its democracy in an important fashion. There was a conscious effort to involve women and black correspondents in the writing of the paper, an acid test of the meaningfulness of democratic institutions in a sexist, racist society. From the start, there were several women, and one or two people of color, on the full-time staff.

As regards editorial authority, there was general agreement that the paper would never come out unless this was clearly defined, and unless a time limit could be set to discussion. Naturally enough, anyone still in disagreement could raise the issue in subsequent meetings and hope to reverse the error, as they saw it, for the future. But the experiences of *Lotta Continua* (see the section on Italy), and *Union Wage*, demonstrate all to clearly the difficulties associated with implicit editorial authority and apparent total democracy. The "ultra-democratic" wave of the 60s and early 70s, which we shall see at work in many of the cases examined here, was never a phenomenon within the *National Guardian* until 1967 and for a while thereafter. The explicit delineation of editorial authority is an aspect of "Old Left" experience that the "New Left" has come gradually to make its own.

Professional quality was also highly valued. Everyone in the original nucleus had had at least freelance journalistic experience. Everyone, however was subjected to editing, with Aronson and Belfrage editing each other, and with the latter particularly committed to crisp, punchy stories and articles. He claimed to have trimmed virtually every piece ever handed to him, the exception being DuBois, whose prose was so excellent the that there was never any need to do so. Instructively, DuBois always attached a note permitting them to use or alter his work as they saw fit, a modesty often in short supply amongst other contributors. Their emphasis on professional quality and brevity was not just a bow toward established journalistic canons, but came from a conviction that sloppiness detracted from their arguments, and that sectarian leftists' jargon was utterly counter-productive in U.S. culture, or anywhere.

The paper was financed only partly out of subscriptions and sales. Other sources of revenue included the Guardian Buying Service, a list of artifacts from a scattering of countries, that were made available on a mail-order basis; donors both small, medium and large (only one substantial, and she shortlived); an annual fundraising dinner and other events; and to a small extent advertisements. The other, undocumented source of revenue was working wives or husbands of *National Guardian* staffers. The pay, though equal for everyone, was not always to be found. In those cases, everyone went without (and "with" was hardly princely!) Only the financial support of domestic partners was able to keep staff afloat at such times: compare the Italian case-studies in particular for similar experiences.

A major contributing cause of financial problems on the paper—beyond harassment by the state—lay in the difficulty of finding people able and willing to handle the business side competently. One particular person, a black woman, worked excellently at this, but she could not solve these problems alone. This dimension of alternative media is one I shall mention throughout this survey. In this instance, it used to force the immensely sympathetic head of the printing firm to come down at intervals and threaten not to print unless the paper paid up.

How did the *National Guardian's* internal organization work out in practice? Until the major upheaval in 1967, the structure operated remarkably well, surviving the death and deportation of two of its three founders, the inroads of McCarthy and his minions, and intermittent financial crises. Its staff increased gradually to about twenty people. There were, naturally enough, problems, some of which have been indicated already. One in particular should be mentioned, the damaging hiatus caused in 1965 by the then general manager's bid for power in the paper. The staff voted against his request to be assigned half-ownership of the paper, he resigned in June, but then immediately sought to withdraw his resignation. The result was to pay him until September, but for him to fulfill no function within the paper. He utilized the intervening period to inform the subscribers of what was happening, and to persuade some of the staff to change their minds. The messiness of the situation needs no underlining. Together with the comparable experience of *Union Wage*, the episode suggests that alternative media may not be best served by being "nicer" than the occasion will allow. If marriages can rupture, then why not political relationships?

Other problems included an attempt on the part of some staff, shortly after Belfrage's departure, to put Aronson and McManus against each other. It failed resoundingly. Another included sending a black staff member to cover the historic Bandoeng conference of Third World peoples in Indonesia in 1955, at great expense for a paper the size of the *National Guardian*, only to have him produce copy that was unutilizable because of its virtual incoherence. None of these or other difficulties wrecked the paper, partly because of the staff's strong sense of common adversity, partly because of a commitment within it to working through difficulties. None of this, however, was to prove sufficient to avoid a major split in 1967.

The Split

Splits are hard to write about, especially when you have met and warmed to people on both sides. Perhaps the distance of fifteen years from the event and my status as a total outsider to the clash will enable me to offend just about everybody.

The outline of what happened is that younger staff taken on in the 60s began to express increasing discontent with the paper's contents and line. Aronson, who had extended half the ownership of the paper to the staff, feeling he did not wish to be sole owner following Belfrage's departure and McManus' death, eventually ceded his own half-ownership to the staff and left the paper altogether.

Accounts have been published in several places of the reasons for, and circumstances of, the rupture.[7] The easiest conclusion to draw is that, personalities aside, the paper was swept into the larger maelstrom of left politics at the time. A whole mass of the younger generation had lost contact with direct experience of socialist ideas or organizing as a result of McCarthyism in particular, and of the powerful tendency toward historical amnesia in the U.S.A. in general. Their rediscovery of the reality of imperialist war (in South East Asia), and later on of marxism, was a heady moment, untempered in the first instance by the possibility of mature reflection based on experience. These points have been made in the introduction to this collection of U.S. case-studies, and so will not be reiterated here. The essential point, however, is that political disagreements in the *National Guardian* in the face of a changing political control would have been much more amenable to patient discussion had the customary arrogance of youth not been compounded in this instance by its political inexperience. In my view, this aspect of the generational clash was chiefly responsible for the feeling among the inheritors of the paper that the rupture was self-evidently a sign of progressive currents.

They seem to have seen themselves as having the opportunity, even the vocation, to lead "the movement," to be its intellectual political mentors. An editorial in 1968 said:

Today's crisis in America is a fantastic opportunity for our movement, but only if we fully and without illusion understand both the crisis and our (i.e. *The Guardian's*) role as a revolutionary force...

...it is not at all clear whether those engaged in discussing tactics for the radical left understand that tactical confusion is a direct derivative of strategic confusion...

...we believe the radical left in general has gained enough experience and understanding *in the last few years* to begin thinking in terms of long-run strategic methods and goals. (my emphasis)[8]

A month later one of the staff wrote, having roundly criticized the Old Left for its failure to grasp either history or theory:

...a new, young movement came into being in this decade. The key to the future of an independent radical paper is whether it can become so important to that movement, merge so well with its needs, that it in effect becomes the paper of the movement.[9]

Today, *The Guardian* collective would be a good deal more cautious in its estimation of the situation and of its own role within it. In 1968, it *felt* to many as though the world was turning upside down. Urgency was the order of the day. To turn the *National Guardian* round in its tracks and lead it off toward the sunrise seemed to be making the revolution (and was a more practical proposition than doing the same to the *New York Times*). Aronson's greater caution, and sense for the enduring dynamics of U.S. society as a whole, probably appeared as stick-in-the-mud obduracy and pessimism. For him, without the daily stimulation and support of Belfrage and MacManus, there was a wearisome, cumulative onus always to be on top of all situations.

Hence the split, with personalities as normal playing a strong role in its details. They have been omitted here, not because they are irrelevant to this or any other medium. Their particular contribution would take too long to rehearse, and because in any event their role was shaped by the wider forces at work in the late 60s. How has the *Guardian* developed since then, and what is its internal structure now?

The Guardian Since 1967

The staff that inherited the paper, and those that joined it within the succeeding year or so, were less than totally united among themselves. In rejecting the paper's former line, and in their basic enthusiasm for radical change, they were indeed at one. But their notion of how radical change was to be achieved in the U.S. left something to be desired in many instances. As one of their number wrote in *Radical America*:

> The signs are that the new staff favors "mucho Vetnams" abroad and "mucho Detroits" at home *as tactics for the Movement*.[10]

The implications are alternately irritating and amusing: that the overwhelmingly white (and male chauvinist[11]) student movement was in a position to create such struggles (while being unlikely to do much of the dying); and that *The Guardian* collective could have played verbal games with Spanish as a slick index of its awareness of Che Guevara ("one, two, three, many Vietnams") and Latin American struggles.

By 1970 some of these internal contradictions came to maturity, effectively polarized around advocates of an electoral structure for full-time staffers, and advocates of a much more open structure, embracing part-timers with full voting rights. The former won the day, but not before a concerted attempt was made by the other side to seize the building. They destroyed files and equipment, and were left in virtual control of access to the offices because no one was prepared to call the police. That week the paper was produced elsewhere, and eventually the attackers desisted, going off to produce their own *Liberated Guardian* for a while.

From this point, having shed its ultra-democratic members, the paper took on a systematically marxist-leninist orientation, supporting China to the hilt, and defining the Soviet Union as a social-imperialist power. Its language often echoed official Chinese discourse of the period, though normally stopping short at the animal-analogies favored by *Peking Review (Beijing Review)* in those days: "tigers and ghosts," "wolves," "running dogs," and the like. Cuba was effectively defined as outside the soviet orbit—except for its economic ties. Although not linked to any particular political formation in the U.S., much of its contents read like one of the "maoist" sects. Indeed, it then had a mutually respectful relationship with one of them, the October League, which supplied it with some of its most experienced members to work on its staff.

There came a point, however, in 1975, when a majority of the staff grew increasingly ill at ease with China's foreign policy. What were they to make of the declaration that the USSR was the leading threat to the world, that the U.S.A. was temporarily a neutral force, and that certain movements for liberation were not to be supported because of their Soviet connections, notably in Chile and Angola? Tension became acute when a minority on the staff took the opposite view, and argued—for instance—that the 1974 Portuguese revolution was a depressing victory for the USSR and its "social-fascist" Communist Party of Portugal. With some exceptions, this minority consisted of October League members. The annual elections came up for the co-ordinating committee (see below on the paper's internal structure), and the October League candidates lost in a close vote. They withdrew from the paper, which meant finding a new labor editor, a new women's editor, and not long afterwards a new foreign editor as well. Two others stayed with the paper despite their disagreement on this score.

From this point onward, the *Guardian* began to grow increasingly confident in its independence from any particular political grouping. It lost the financially and politically valuable right to conduct tours to China, then a unique service for anyone except academics, but learned "a healthy lesson about hitching its star to a foreign revolution." This independence, a strong feature of the paper in its pre-1968 days, was especially emphasized as a strength of the paper by its leading personnel in 1982. They were convinced that the paper's commitment to anti-capitalist, anti-nuclear, feminist, Third World, gay, and ecological struggles, its involvement in coalitions, including with Church and pacifist groups, was a much more important contribution than they could make through being a "transmission belt" for a particular line evolved outside the collective itself, at least in the absence of a revolutionary political party that was clearly going places. As the new (1982) editor, Bill Ryan, put it:

> We want to be a marxist paper without sounding like
> it, to bring marxists and these forces together for their
> mutual advantage.

Internal Organization

In 1982 the paper's structure was what its members described as modified democratic centralism. A five-person co-ordinating committee was elected annually to be in charge of the papers's political leadership, its editorials, and its financial affairs. The posts of managing editor and of general manager formally accounted for two of the five places. In practice, but not by statute, two places went to people from the business side, three to the editorial side. The committee appointed the news editor and the foreign editor. However, the highest decision-making body was the staff as a whole. Any major political issue would be discussed first in the Monday evening staff meeting, at which there was also a permanent agenda item for criticism and self-criticism, to allow problems to be vented quickly before they festered (though it was rarely utilized). At this meeting the previous week's edition would be taken apart page by page. On top of this, there were weekly editorial meetings, weekly business meetings, plus almost daily editorial meetings. On Friday mornings there was a mandatory political discussion session, based on assigned study.

It was a heavy load, given that everyone was only paid a hundred and twenty dollars a week (including medical and dental insurance and a child-allowance of sixty dollars a month), and was expected to work about fifty hours a week before study-time. Working hours for the editorial side were eight on Mondays plus the 2-hour evening meeting; Tuesdays 10am-midnight; Wednesdays 10am-anywhere between 8:30 and 11:30 at night; and another eight hours a day on Thursdays and Fridays. Business staff had rather more regular hours, but were equally short-staffed. None of this takes in the added, cumulative strains of always working against the political tide. As we shall often have cause to observe in these case studies, self-management generally means harder work than in the average capitalist analogue!

Let us now probe a little more deeply into four particular areas of the paper's organization: the place of women; the place of Afro-Americans and other Third World groups; the paper's relation to its printers; and to the role of its business side. All four topics have a close bearing on the paper's internal democracy: a democratic stucture with space only for white males is a mockery; the division of labor in democratic newspaper production often leaves its printers out entirely; and democracy is often assumed to be utterly inimical to business efficiency, or—the other side of the coin—magically able to do away with something so grubbily bourgeois as accounts and financial procedures.

The paper's record as regards women's employment improved steadily in the later 70s and into the 80s. In 1974 there was only one woman on the paper. By 1982 the ratio was about half and half, and both the news editor and the foreign editor were women. Nor was it unprecedented for women to occupy such positions, even though the paper's three chief editors since 1948 had been men.

The quality of life had improved for women in the paper as well. The foreign editor recalled how in 1970 when she was expecting a child, the choice was simple: would it be she or her husband who would continue working there? By 1982 the office had become geared to a degree of collective care of very small children, and meetings would wait to begin until the father or mother had finished feeding their child. The word "child" may be important: a large number might well have stretched the organization beyond its capacity. Nonetheless, there had clearly been movement in a positive direction.

(It should be recognized that *The Guardian's* coverage of women's issues and movements, and of Third World issues in and out of the U.S.A., is extremely good. The topic here is its internal organization not its coverage.)

The position of Third World people inside the paper was not so advanced. They had better representation on the business side than in editorial work. The Third World group was entirely Afro-American in composition. Since the split, the paper had been almost exclusively white, working on the basis that any black people who were genuinely interested would turn up, and be as welcome as anyone else with ability and political maturity. (Up to 1967, active searches had been made, but without much success.) From about 1980, however, contacts were being once more energetically sought with black and other Third World organizations to solicit applications. The four Afro-Americans on the staff had formed a black caucus, and this had been one of their major demands.

The result has been distinctly to the paper's advantage, and very far from a token advance. The caucus began to point out in no uncertain terms that the paper's business habits on many levels were an offense to Third World people. Slowness in answering letters and requests, they made plain, was such a typical experience for Third World people at the hands of white organizations that *The Guardian* would easily become identified as just another one, even if it was plain inefficiency that had been the cause. Massively detailed interviews of applicants were a common experience they explained, often leading to the applicant's metaphorically stripping himself or herself naked to a stranger, only to be then told they could not have what they were requesting. Once again, for *The Guardian* to interview in this manner, in the interests of ensuring itself of someone's political experience, was to be similar to a whole mass of white establishment bodies. A failure to offer adequate on-the-job training for vacant posts was also pinponted as a standard excuse for the high turnover of Third World people once hired, and *The Guardian* was remiss in organizing this kind of training in specific procedures. By the end of this process of political debate within the paper, the counter-arguments of some staff-members, that they were not treating anyone any worse than anyone else, had been rather systematically dismantled, and old procedures substantially revised.

The position of *The Guardian's* printers had double dimension. One is very straightforward: they contracted out the printing to a commercial firm. The firm had no involvement in the paper beyond this, unlike the informal relationship on the *National Guardian* when for a long period they shared the same building. However, printing costs were very considerable, because of the collective's principled refusal to use non-union labor.

The more complex issue concerns a period in 1979 when the paper tried to set up its own typesetting operation, not only for the paper itself, but also to take in contract work from outside to help the paper's finances and contribute to various campaigns. Once again, they paid union rates to the typesetters, an amount about three times their own salaries. The venture proved a disastrous failure, however, quite the opposite of the money-spinner they hoped it would become. Spiralling costs drove them eventually to close it down, laying off about seven part-time typographers in the process. The crunch came over the typesetters' demand for better benefits, which *The Guardian* granted at once in principle but could not act upon financially.

Already depressing, the dispute became particularly so when three weekly papers, the *Village Voice* and two sectarian organs, gleefully announced that *The Guardian* was involved in a labor struggle as an employer. It is not hard to visualize the coverage. *The Guardian* collective tried repeatedly to contact the *Village Voice* journalist, a well-known radical commentator, to explain its case, but neither beforehand nor afterwards did he deign to talk to them. The episode is instructive in a number of ways, not least the substantial practical problems of trying to overcome the division of labor between journalists and printers. The cases of *República* in Portugal, and of *Lotta Continua* and *Il Manifesto* in Italy, also shed light on this problem.

The business operation of the paper is the last aspect of its purely internal operation under review. It is not altogether surprising that for a long time *The Guardian* described it as its "administrative department," anxiously shunning the very word "business." To work on the business side was effectively to be a second-class citizen within the collective, doing the shitwork that was beneath the high and serious *politics* of the paper. We shall meet this attitude repeatedly, though not universally, in the course of these case-studies; it has created a mass of problems for the effectiveness of alternative media.

Over time, however, attitudes about the business side of the paper began to change within the collective. The business people objected strenuously to never being chosen to represent *The Guardian* at political gatherings, and to the dismissive demeanor of some editorial people toward the importance of their contribution. A concession was experimented with, that they could also write some articles for the paper, but they found after a time that combining this with business work proved impossibly taxing, and the practice disappeared. In 1982, the paper's new managing editor and foreign editor had both come from the business side, although the latter had had to threaten to resign from the paper altogether because she realized she was not going to be allowed to make the transfer otherwise.

The net effect of all these processes, taken together with the arrival of able newcomers to the business side of the paper, was to rescue the business operation and re-establish it as a fully important dimension of work that had to be done. The need to move away from the business side to make a political impact more or less disappeared. People from throughout the paper were chosen to represent it in public meetings and political coalitions. The stressfulness of the business operation had not declined however. Its demands, together with the feeling that everyone's job and the paper's future sometimes seemed to be hanging on a knife-edge, had literally given some staff ulcers.

The last area of *The Guardian* to be examined is its relationship to political forces and movements outside its walls. As mentioned already, its long-established use of stringers supplied it with voices and perspectives from outside. At other times, though, the paper operated with regional news bureaus and even with *"Guardian* clubs" in order to try to develop its work outside New York City. These experiences are important to evaluate, because there are a number of other alternative media which have also experimented in these directions (the Pacifica Foundation, *Union Wage, Libération* in France, *Tageszeitung* in West Germany).

The bureaus flourished briefly during the mid-70s, although small informal ones existed in Chicago and Los Angeles from the late 60s. In 1973 the collective began to feel that the paper's coverage ought to be as good nationally as internationally, and this debate spurred the growth of new bureaus in Detroit and the Bay Area, joined not long afterwards by Boston and Washington D.C. At one time, the Boston bureau was exceptionally large, numbering about 25 people (all part-time).

Normally, bureaus worked voluntarily, except for fees paid for articles. Occasionally the paper not only appointed, but also paid a part-time co-ordinator for such bureaus. It was this person's task to phone in once a week and discuss what the central office and the bureau together felt should be covered. Stories were rarely if ever rejected, though obviously they were subject to editing. Five or six might be presented for publication each week, and they could usually be put into a subsequent edition if there was no space for them straightaway. There was, then, only slight friction, if any, between the bureaus and the collective—not a situation unfortunately, that could be paralleled in all the other cases studied. The bureaus also worked on improving circulation. Their operation certainly contributed to the paper's contents.

Out of these bureaus, and out of the strong anticipation on the sectarian left in the late 70s that the situation was rapidly becoming ripe for the formation of a new Leninist party, the collective decided to institute *Guardian* clubs. These would be bodies where leftists could meet each other, plan political work together, participate in the party-building movement, socialize, and no doubt discuss *The Guardian*. The idea was highly attractive, but unfortunately fell rapidly by the wayside. The paper was in no financial or staffing position to support these clubs, whose membership usually substantially overlapped with bureau membership. For these reasons the clubs were a "dismal failure," as a *Guardian* staffer put it. They could set them up, but neither sustain, service, nor guide them. The then executive editor appears to have tried to utilize his role vis-a-vis the clubs to build a new revolutionary party (which eventually emerged as "Line of March"). This experience capped the general dissatisfaction in the paper with the clubs' ineffectiveness, as it seemed, in advancing party-building, and they were cut adrift. The collective resolved to go back to building up its stringers, numbering one hundred in 1982, inside and outside the country. The paper had obviously over-reached itself, and the lesson was clear: However nationally desireable this expansion might have been, it was not grounded. It is curious how often marxists, of all people, dismiss the necessity of some material basis for their own activities, whether in this kind of premature expansion, or in the business side of their work.

Conclusions

This short account of a thirty-four year development has tried to single out the major points in that history which are necessary to make sense of it, and which are instructive within our general considerations of alternative media. It has endeavored not to gloss over conflict, inefficiency, short-sightedness and other failings, not because these are the sum total of this experience, or even its most distinctive trait, but because honesty is a necessary preliminary to clarity. The left does not need to embrace this honesty as a form of punitive self-flagellation for its missed opportunities, but in order to mature from its own experience. Then, and only then, can we enjoy contemplating the things we have managed to build for a better world.

Footnotes

1. C. Belfrage and J. Aronson, *Something to Guard*, New York: Columbia University Press, 1978, p. 77.
2. *The Guardian,* November 1, 1978, Editorial, p. 2.
3. *Op. cit.*
4. I.F. Stone, *The Truman Era*, New York: Random House 1972, pp. xx-xxi.
5. See the introduction to the sections on Portugal and Italy.
6. See the account by James Aronson, *The Press and the Cold War*, Boston: Beacon Press, 1970.
7. See Belfrage and Aronson, *op. cit.*, chs. 16-17; Irving Beinin, *"Guardian* History: Late 50s to Date," part 2, *The Guardian,* Dec. 14, 1968, p. 9; Michael Munk, *"The Guardian,* From Old to New Left," *Radical America*, vol. II. 2 (March-April 1968), pp. 19-28.
8. Cited in Massimo Teodori (ed.), *The New Left,* Indianapolis: Bobbs Merrill Co., 1967, p. 467.
9. Beinin, *art. cit.*
10. Munk, *art. cit.* p. 27.
11. Sara Evans, *Personal Politics,* New York: Alfred A. Knopf, 1979, chs. 5-9; Ann Popkin, "The Personal is Political: The Women's Liberation Movement," in Dick Cluster (ed.), *They Should Have Served That Cup Of Coffee*, Boston: South End Press, 1979, ch. 7.

3

KPFA, BERKELEY

"My friend who went from here to work in ABC was bored, even though there was a lot more money it it. Here at KPFA you can change things by yelling. You never could at CBS. Here we *can* argue."

Bari Scott
Head of Third World department, KPFA
June 1982

Basic Information

Location: Berkeley, California
Broadcasts: 24 hours a day on FM
Paid full-time staff: around 20
Unpaid staff: over 100 (i.e., working over 20 hours a month for four consecutive months).
Volunteers: 50-60
Began: April 1949
Programs include: 51% music of all varieties; 37 hours a week public affairs and news.
Finance: No advertisements; listener-supported; corporate support refused.
Institutional links: with Pacifica Foundation, which is the licensee.[1]

Introduction

KPFA is the oldest of the listener-supported independent stations in the U.S. Except for one break from August 1950 to May 1951, it has broadcast every day since April 15, 1949.

Continuity however, is only one of the features which distinguishes it from other local radio stations in the U.S. In its early days when the first Cold War, and its ultimate expression, McCarthyism, were placing a rigid clamp on political criticism and independent thought, KPFA struck out in the opposite direction. It was in a sense an echo from the Roosevelt era, and—without seeking to glamourize that period—the hopes and optimism it inspired in many politically committed and internationally minded U.S. intellectuals. The little cluster of half a dozen people who founded the station did so with a philosophy of broadcasting and communication strongly marked with sincere liberalism (as contrasted with its corporate version), and a Quaker variety of pacifism. Some had been conscientious objectors during World War II, like the principal founder, Lewis Hill. One or two had even been imprisoned for their beliefs.

In general, their broadcasting philosophy could be interpreted at first glance as not especially adventurous or radical; indeed, to be rather reminiscent of the British Broadcasting Corporation:

> He [Lewis Hill] believed radio and press should not be run by entrepreneurs motivated by profits, but by journalists and artists whose motive would be the most objective and enlightening programming possible.[2]

In fact he and his co-founders were prepared to take advertisements for an initial period, simply to gather the necessary financial support to bridge the period between what they realized would be minimal listener support, and what they trusted would be adequate listener support. As it happened, they never broadcast ads at all, but their view of advertising in U.S. broadcasting was nonetheless hardly equivocal:

> Sale of time on KPFA will be...governed strictly by an advertising code which eliminates the intrusive, repetitious and in other ways offensive commercialism common in American radio.[3]

This critical broadcasting philosophy and practice do not of themselves seem much more than high-minded. But as the not so dissimilar instance of Rádio Clube Português shows (see below), the context is everything. In 1949 that context was the continued dominance of rampant commercialism throughout the U.S. airwaves, with the exception of military and police channels, combined with the deadening fear associated with McCarthy's ascendancy. It should be realized, too, that KPFA's internal structure was highly radical: everyone was paid the same wage, and decisions were made collectively on all major matters. In addition, KPFA's stated aims were to develop:

> Peace, social justice, promotion of the labor movement, and support of the arts.[3]

Interestingly, its definition of how to promote the labor movement was not tied to any particular political line on the left. Hill observed:

> Unfortunately, the only press and radio sources of consistent and comprehensive labor reporting are either controlled by the Communist party or Stalinist in orientation.[5]

However, this did not prevent the station from allowing CPUSA members from joining their voices to the numerous other perspectives given air time. KPFA's position was determinedly liberal, in the classical sense of the term.

Such a view, however, in those years, was officially interpreted as active sympathy for "Communism"! The paradox of KPFA's origins is that in another place and time it might have been unusual to refuse advertising sponsorship, but not radical. At the time, however, the station was a small beacon of political sanity in a climate of rightist hysteria.

Not surprisingly, therefore, it soon attracted to itself the organized reaction of the far right in the manner so characteristic of the official exponents of liberal freedoms when taken at their word. Repeatedly, the sledgehammer was heaved up on high by official Federal Communications Commission inquiries in response to "listener" complaints and once by the Senate Internal Security Subcommittee—in order to pulverise this small challenge to the American way of political communication. Nor were these threats confined to the McCarthy period. As I write in June 1982, the chair of the American Legal Foundation, a body whose conservatism is renowned, has petitioned to deny FCC license renewal to a sister station of KPFA in Washington DC. The costs of defending itself for that station will be around $10,000-$15,000, a fact assuredly not lost on the wealthy complainant. The ALF has promised, if successful, to go after the licenses of the other four stations in the Pacifica chain, including KPFA. With such valiant seekers-after-truth is the U.S. political establishment adorned.

The fact of these attacks figures at the outset of this account of KPFA. Rather like the legal and police attacks on the underground press of the 1960s and 1970s[6], the extraordinary concentration of effort to uproot these media in the name of freedom is one of the crucial paradoxes of their history. Why were they, are they, deemed so important and threatening when they form such a tiny, fragile element in national media? The paradoxes do not end here, however; equally amazing is their tenacity and survival despite these assaults, despite their minority role in national life, despite their usually acute financial constraints, and despite the organizational crises which have intermittently wracked their internal life. These are certainly not the only issues which will concern us in this and the other case-studies of this book, but they are worth early mention.

Having set out this overall view, let me now proceed to a more orderly account of how KPFA has organized itself. I shall present first a greatly abbreviated history of the station, and then focus on a number of issues central to its present-day organization: the question of power and the division of labor inside the station; its relation to popular political forces and movements outside its walls; the problem of finances. This sounds rather dry, almost like an exercise in the sociology of organizations. The flesh on these dry bones, however, consists of key political problems. Is it feasible to organize media democratically? What are the practical hazards in doing so? Are they surmountable? Furthermore, democracy itself is not just an abstract virtue in this case. What are the practical possibilities for women and Third World minorities not simply to broadcast, but to broadcast what they want to communicate, both within their own ranks, and to a wider audience? Can advertising sponsorship be avoided without financial chaos? Is a chain of such radio stations a viable enterprise? Can such small media stand up to organized onslaughts from the far right? What are the costs, on all levels? These problems are among those to be examined.

A Mini-History[7]

KPFA's founders had originally intended to broadcast on AM from the town of Richmond in California. When both proved impossible, they switched to broadcasting on FM in the mainly university town of Berkeley. They began with a revamped 250-watt transmitter that could function at 550 watts, with their antenna poised on the roof of the building which housed their studio. When KPFA-Interim, as it was first called, went off the air in August 1950, it owed $2000 in bills and nearly $7000 more in back salaries; a considerable sum of money for the time. In its 16 months of operation, however, it had involved over 2000 individuals locally in making programs, often on topics or in areas not addressed by other media, spanning the range from news to music, drama and other cultural programming. This involvement was to repay handsomely in restarting the station. When it came back on the air nine months later, its supporters had helped to get it a new transmitter and frequency, and a solid financial reserve, the latter supplied in part by the Adult Education division of the Ford Foundation.

Unfortunately, no sooner had these financial problems been put in some order than another trend began to interfere with KPFA's efficacy. The national production of FM radios declined from over a million a year in 1947 to 131,000 a year in 1954.[8] By 1954 the only station broacasting solely on FM in the area was KPFA. In desperation, two volunteers put together 500 FM sets, priced at thirty dollars rather than the usual fifty at that time, and got them sold in the district. After these had gone, KPFA sold inexpensive models to subscribers. But with the decline in FM, newspapers and weeklies began to cease printing FM program details. KPFA was destined for a lengthy period of arrested growth.

Hill worked feverishly on other related projects for expansion (a literary magazine, for example), none of which were ever to be properly realized during his lifetime. He appears to have been an anxious, intense, but physically frail man, whose energy and vision were vital to realizing the radio project. His perspective is perhaps best summed up by his own summary of it, from the KPFA *Folio* of August 1952:

> If KPFA is 'with' anything, it is clearly on the side of those who believe in the mind and who endeavor to make responsible mentality more socially effective.

A whole series of internal wrangles and upsets, combined with the intellectually and politically hostile times in which he was living, and the acute difficulty therefore of realizing a whole range of fine projects, bore in upon him and were amongst the forces that, tragically, pushed him to take his own life in 1957. It was the heaviest blow of all to the station; and it is a tribute to Hill himself as well as the others, that despite staffers' acute differences at times, the station was sufficiently stable to survive.

Indeed, in 1959, just two years after Hill's death, KPFA was joined by its first sister station, KPFK in Los Angeles, and in 1960 by WBAI in New York. In March 1970, KPFT Houston went on the air, only to have its transmitter bombed by the Ku Klux Klan in March and October of that year. It continues, nonetheless. In 1977 another station opened in Washington, DC, after a license battle that had ground on since 1968! The Pacifica National News Bureau also began to function on a small scale in Washington, DC, during the 70s. Expansion did take place, despite the apparently endless blockages on growth in 1957.

During this period, as noted already, the FCC responded many times to listener complaints, often aimed at denying licenses to the Pacifica stations, and at one point the Senate Internal Security Subcommittee hauled KPFA over the coals. The attacks were usually concerned with obscenity—compare the experience of the underground press[9]—or with lack of political "balance." Obscenity charges usually centered on the use of particular four-letter words in poetry or drama programs, since such terms were not liberally interspersed into public affairs programming. Mores change, and what was once considered abhorrent is now far less likely to be so viewed. A single four-letter word as part of a half-hour of poetry is hardly likely to stir much controversy in the 1980s, outside "Moral" Majority supporters. In the 50s it could and did.

The political charges against KPFA revolved around its willingness to broadcast CPUSA members. (As is not widely known, the FCC interpretation of the "Fairness" doctrine always explicitly excluded the "communist viewpoint" from those perspectives which need to be given adequate time on the air.) The accusation was accurate, as KPFA regularly allowed CPUSA spokespeople to broadcast. It was a politically warped accusation, however, as the overwhelming majority of people broadcasting did not take the CPUSA view, and at least 98% of programs were given over to that majority.[10] Indeed, when the Senate Subcommittee asked why three CPUSA members had been allowed to broadcast, the station manager pointed out to it that in the same month KPFA had also given the microphone to a Los Angeles broker, an academic from the Center for the Study of Democratic Institutions, a Unitarian minister, the former chair of a Democratic Party club, a public relations specialist, the president of the Los Angeles chapter of the American Federation of Scientists, and Caspar Weinberger, then chair of the Central California Republican Party committee, later to be Secretary of Defense in the Reagan administration. They might have added that other conservatives, such as William Buckley, had been regular contributors at an earlier time.

These details are recorded in order to emphasize the committed liberalism of the station. It was not self-defined as a revolutionary radio station in the sense espoused by the Portuguese and Italian stations examined later on in this book. However, in certain ways the station did begin to move in a more radical direction in response to the upheavals in the U.S., beginning with the civil rights and anti-war movements, the black rebellions in Harlem in 1964 and Watts in 1965, and the emergence of the women's and gay movements. In 1949 the term "minorities" inside KPFA had meant minority opinions. By 1969, it had come to refer to the explosion in political, ethnic and gender consciousness that had taken place in the younger generation. The very notion of taking a loyalty oath, on which the FCC had formally required information from KPFA in October 1963, would have been patently ludicrous by 1969.

Let us turn now to KPFA's recent organization, and then to the impact of these new political movements on its functioning.

Power and the Division of Labor

The experimental policy of paying all members equally and of having majority votes on programming policy after open discussion, was the most nearly revolutionary feature of the early KPFA. It was a policy framed in conscious rejection of the undemocratic structures of national media in the U.S., and it is of special concern to this book. How did it work?

It was not that long in the development of the station before a number of people began to observe, if not complain, that the project was effectively being run by a triumvirate of Hill and two close associates. This situation led gradually to a maze of resignations and counter-resignations at intervals between 1951 and 1953. Hill wrote in exasperation on July 15, 1953:[11]

The rejection and choice of leadership by part of the group had, in my own mind, grievously demonstrated that the organizational theory of the Pacifica Foundation is unsound...Knowing that most of the individuals concerned are intensely sincere, I am forced to the conclusion others have reached before me: that an impossible task confronts these individuals; that the organizational theory is false which requires that engineer, announcer, stenographer, producer, must also be reponsible for the decisions of leadership.

This is quoted in order to underline the difficulty, not the impossibility, of making any change in traditional authority patterns or the division of labor in the media. As we shall see, one of the most persistent problems in such attempts has arisen precisely from the view that these structures can simply be wished out of existence by politically determined and dedicated people. That at one point both sides in the wrangle were writing to the Ford Foundation to ask it respectively to cancel or to continue its support, is a measure of the passions involved and the seriousness of the argument.

From 1954 to 1957 the disputes seemed and probably were largely resolved. However, in April 1957, Hill, prompted by a budget crisis, chose to fire three staff members, two of them belonging to the California Federation of Teachers, which was soon threatening a strike. Hill insisted there be no internal inquiry into his decision, as he had authority, being Pacifica's President, to hire and fire. He was, however, overruled by the Committee of Directors, whose reasoning was that whatever the formal realities, KPFA's commitment to the labor movement could not justify such a dismissive response to the situation.[12]

Some of what had happened in the station over these first years of its life was perhaps predictable. It had, after all, shifted from being a tightly knit group of co-founders to a larger structure of more disparate individuals. The kind of group culture and history which enables spontaneous, participatory debate on policy and programming is not something which can instantly be transposed onto a large group of people who have not all worked together and grown together over a period of time. This is a real dimension of democratic functioning, and it is ignored at peril.

Today, the structure of authority at KPFA is in certain respects much more traditional. Technically, the Pacifica Foundation has control over all its stations, from Los Angeles to Houston to New York. In practice, they run themselves. They have to. KPFA has a manager responsible for the overall running of the station. There are three assistant managers, namely the chief engineer, the program director and the assistant to the station manager. They are defined as management, and do not belong to UE, the union first established there in the course of a dispute that dragged on through 1964-65. Below the management are department heads (Engineering, Production, Music, Drama and Literature, News, Public Affairs, Women's, Third World.) Each head is paid, mostly full-time; each department has two votes in major decision-making. There are about another eight full-timers in addition to the people mentioned.

Below them there is a large body of part-timers, defined as people working unpaid for twenty hours a month for a few consecutive months. A further corps of volunteers works on a more occasional basis, for example on fund-raising drives. The part-timers, but not the volunteers, are—unusually and perhaps uniquely—covered by the UE contract in certain respects. For example, they have the right to first preference for any paid position that opens up for 60 days or less, and they have the right to participate in the selection of a manager, enjoying collectively 50% of that vote. Departments also have an important say in the selection of all department heads. There is, however, no formal right of recall of heads or management.

It can readily be seen that the station retains a strong dose of democracy even given its formal hierarchical structure. How does it work in practice? This means looking at the role of the unpaid workers in the station, at the technical division of labor, the union, and the role of Third World and women's groups.

Despite the unusual concessions made to unpaid workers, there is still a great potential for strife inherent in their position in the station. For one thing, their understanding of what goes on in other departments of KPFA, let alone in the Pacifica chain, is slight. Their slot is their slot. As David Salniker, station manager in 1982, ruefully remarked about the station in general:

> I have yet to have the experience of someone coming to
> me and urging that their program should be taken off

the air. And rarely, of someone coming to me and saying they want to cede their time to give space to a key issue.

He described the position in the station during his tenure as "bureaucratically regulated individualism".

By this, he meant that virtually everyone in the station, paid or unpaid, had powerful commitments to their particular contributions. General priorities could always be agreed upon; their specific implementation was another matter, especially if it came to a reduction of time for any given program. The people in the music program and cultural programs, for instance, though generally progressive, were usually wrapped up in their particular projects, and had little detailed sense of contemporary political developments. When push came to shove in this situation, there is no doubt that the unpaid, despite their larger numbers, were able to exert far less influence than the paid. This was so, despite their protracted struggle in the past to get themselves a voice in decision-making.

For example, Wednesday evening meetings were open to all workers in the station, and were chaired by the Program Director. This person could either make decisions, in the absence of anything approaching consensus, or defer them for further consideration and debate. This meeting clearly could have acted as a forum for the expression of debate over programming policy, and of political differences. In practice, they were usually concerned solely with practicalities or the most general issues. Controversial issues were generally avoided.

Similarly, department heads were supposed to confer on a regular meeting basis with their unpaid staff, though this was more honored in principle than practice in some departments. In the week I was interviewing KPFA staff, the unpaid staff had called a special meeting to protest the loss of some early evening weekday hours for a new program instituted by the Program Director. They perceived this as symptomatic of their lack of voice in decision-making, as well as having the effect of cancelling their own programs in some cases. Some were calling, apparently for the fourth time, for a programmers' bill of rights.

Clearly, the structure did not lead to perfect harmony, even though this was partly due to the individualistic way many staff, paid and unpaid, used the facility of the station. The structure did, however, offer mechanisms for working democratically on a number of problems. It was certainly not a straitjacket.

Some full-timers felt that the major dissatisfactions of the unpaid staff revolved around two issues, though these were not always recognized as such. One was the lack of overall resources to do everything that was desirable; the other was the individualism referred to, which meant that formal procedures often seemed to be bypassed. Certainly a number of the practices familiar from conventional broadcasting institutions were not in force, such as minutes and agendas for departmental or programming meetings, or house-rules on terms to avoid in broadcasting. This had not always been true of KPFA, nor was it fated to continue forever. It is, however, one more indication of the confusion that can emerge from impatient neglect of routine procedures, a confusion that may not be any more liberating than their pedantic observance.

The technical division of labor was also part of the station's structure, though in a somewhat muted form. There was no formal rotation of work, for instance, between members of the engineering department and the programmers. On the other hand, being small and the kind of station it is, people got "hands-on" experience in a way they would not in a larger or more formal operation. Similarly, engineers and technicians are not precluded from involvement in program design. The result is that almost all the technicians in KPFA are capable producers, and many programmers are well informed technically. Training classes are organized from time to time on how to operate the board, and in a variety of types of production. (Further on we shall return to the question of training.) For reasons as much practical as political, therefore, the technical division of labor is less heavily entrenched in KPFA than is customary.

Unionization has been a very hot potato in KPFA's history. Mentioned above was the role of the California Federation of Teachers in one dispute. The reasons for not having a union structure at the very outset are probably obvious, but it was a 1964 management decision to fire—or as it later turned out, to attempt to fire—one of the founding KPFA members, that crystallized the issue. Previous sporadic efforts to organize a union in the station were interpreted by the National Association of Broadcast Employees and Technicians (now a part of UE) as attempts which had been systematically thwarted by management, and the firings as victimizations. It called a strike and half the station (including over half its full-timers) came out. The strike lasted seven weeks, though the station was only off the air for three hours the very first day. It was eventually settled, though not to the taste of the principals on either side of the dispute. There were highly personal investments in the attempt to form the union, which went beyond the obvious case for having them. Despite this personal diversion, it was clearly coming to be time to have such an alternative center of power and redress in the station.

Since this time, the union has been a regular part of KPFA. We have already noted its unusual mode of incorporating unpaid staff into the contract, though not without an extensive struggle by them in the past to this end. Today, it functions well, and particularly so when its elected officers are effective individuals. It has one chief steward and four stewards. Its present grievance procedures (1982) date from 1978, and it has organized a twice-yearly raise for its paid members. Pay-levels in 1982 stood at about 1200 dollars a month with everyone paid at more or less the same rate.

The structure of authority and the technical division of labor were certainly key parts of KPFA's operation. Nonetheless, the formal opportunities for the unpaid staff, the largest single category of station workers, were quite extensive, far more so than would be imaginable in a conventional station. The fact they originated in a series of sometimes bitter conflicts, and that conflicts, overt or latent, still persist, does not reflect adversely on these structures. If conflicts did not exist there would be no call for such mechanisms, to try to work through them and resolve them.

KPFA and external political forces

Any examination of democratic media structures must go beyond the organization of the medium and survey the inter-relation between internal democracy and the access rights of varying interests and groups in the politicized public. To take an obvious example, it is one thing to have a democratic internal structure, but quite another to have one which is resistant to access demands by women or Third World minorities, or which has no members of those sectors of society in power positions in its structure. (Compare the early history of Third World Newsreel.) An issue which directly arises out of this is how to handle political fissures within these or other groups, since no social group is a homogeneous political entity. How are decisions made to broadcast one position on gay rights, say, as against another? KPFA, as contrasted to conventional radio-stations, has always been singularly sensitive to external political forces of this nature. All the same, its awareness has not protected it from a series of confrontations.

In this section I propose to review four examples which illustrate these issues. They are the creation of a Third World department; the creation of a Women's department; the station's response to a split in a local political group; and the station's response to criticism of its reporting of the Zionist annexation of south Lebanon in 1982.

The question of Third World minority participation, and the significance of the creation of a Third World department, require a little prior clarification, which will also serve in understanding the later emergence of a Women's department. Firstly, out of all the departments in KPFA, News dominates: it has the most paid staff, the largest budget, the most listeners, and it is the best known and organized department. Secondly, the cultural programmers, especially in music, have their own highly specialized but dedicated audiences. Some have been in KPFA, like its jazz programmer, virtually since the station started. Many are crucial to fund-raising drives because of this. Yet, as noted above, they are wedded to hewing their own paths. News and the cultural sections therefore *are* the station for many listeners. Yet within the station, to be a major interest and not to have a department, is to be condemned to marginality. Hence the significance of the Third World and Women's departments. To be a department gives two votes in major decisions; other departments and interests are forced to negotiate with you.

Even in the early 70s, there were still only two or three regular workers in KPFA who belonged to Third World minorities. The station had no clearly defined policy regarding them, except that slots were made available to them on an ad hoc basis. When one full-timer was retired in 1972, her position was split into two half-time positions to develop the station's programming on women. One appointed was white; the other was a Latina. The Latina sensed as time went on that there was insufficient real interest in the station in Third World issues, so she left to work in a Latin women's collective. Before leaving, however, she argued strongly in favor of her half-post being allocated to a specialist in Third World issues. The half-position was left vacant for a long time.

In 1973, and stretching into 1974, there was a strike in the station, mostly arising from a generalized dissatisfaction with the station manager. The various Third World collectives working in and around KPFA considered the moment opportune to press for a Third World department, and for the half-time position to be allocated to paying its head. This demand was met with the argument that Third World people should integrate into all departments, which in turn was countered with the position that integration would mean their power would be dispersed and dissipated, since there were fairly few of them at that time. One group in the course of this struggle marched into the main studio, locked it, and broadcast their demands for a department and a paid position over the air!

Eventually the concession was made, and a Latin brother and sister team became co-founders of the Third World department in 1975. Before the strike, she had been program director, and he production director. He quickly organized a very good corps of white males to join in programming on Third World issues. The department also began political work within the station, challenging for instance the appropriateness of white reporters covering black events, and white assumptions about news priorities.

The storms were only beginning though. The brother and sister team were late fired, a major reason given being their failure to organize volunteers for the department. The firing sparked a hot response from quite a number of people. A new manager failed to resolve the issue, and left after losing a confidence vote two months later. The Pacifica Foundation became closely embroiled in the dispute. It identified two Third World members as major troublemakers (not the brother and sister), and tried to impose a more intensively hierarchical power-structure on its then four stations, declaring pompously that "we anoint" the station managers. (This move came to nothing, not surprisingly, given the many feisty individuals involved in the Pacifica stations.)

Another storm developed over the opening of a news bureau in East Oakland, the largely black industrial city (but with Asian and Native American communities) next to Berkeley. (The merits of establishing firmer links with a working class base for the station hardly need underlining.) The Third World department was very closely involved in this project, and helped to raise $5000 to start it. The senior members of KPFA interpreted this as an attempt by the Third World department to cut loose from the station, and voted to freeze spending the money. The Third World department promptly wrote to the foundation concerned and urged them not to send the grant. The management then proclaimed that anyone working for the Oakland bureau could no longer be considered a KPFA member, and consequently voted seven or eight of the most experienced Third World members out of the station. Of those remaining, a number also began to leave, including individuals who had had direct involvement in struggles in Nicaragua and Argentina.

Meanwhile the News department decided to try to open a news bureau in the Mission district of San Francisco, in the heart of a Chicano barrio. Local residents quickly asked what they thought they were doing there. The News department instantly assumed, incorrectly, that the Third World department had put them up to it! The Third World department, however, was incensed that the East Oakland project was treated so poorly at the same time that a second bureau was being permitted to establish itself by the News department in a Third World neighborhood.

The situation eventually resolved itself in favor of the East Oakland bureau, which proceeded to broadcast a daily news and issues fifteen minute slot of KPFA (*Talking Drum*) which continued for some years. This episode demonstrates once more how a progressive medium is liable to be more prone to the political upheavals and cleavages in the world at large, than is a conventional one. Democracy is different, and preferable, but is not an instant chemical solution to complex social and political issues. Indeed, within the Third World department itself, there were quite often views expressed by Afro-Americans, black Hispanics, and Native Americans, that white South Americans were settlers' offspring and not "really" Third World people. These debates are also part of the real world, especially with the rise of assertiveness by Indians throughout the Americas in recent years. Neither the department nor the station was immune from them, unlike the established media.

A part of the history of Bari Scott, the present head of the Third World department, is an appropriate note on which to conclude this presentation of the role of Third World people inside the station. She had had her full share of the department's tumults, having been fired twice in the past—each time on New Year's Eve! The first time the union successfully defended her; the second time there was no need for this, since she was instantly supported by a majority of her colleagues in the station. Her own history in KPFA is a tribute to the merits of staying inside to fight issues within an institution at least partially open to change. Unromantic, no doubt; but once again, a very different story from the big media.

The Women's Department was started much more recently, in 1981. Women's programs had been a regular feature of KPFA, and programs conveying the rebirth of the women's movement had been in continual evidence for ten years before the formal announcement of a Women's department in 1978. The declaration remained formal, however, until mid-1981, when its first head was appointed, half-paid out of a Third World department post. In 1982, the department was responsible for only six hours' programming a week, three of them during midnight hours, as contrasted with the thirty hours assigned to the Third World department (though there was some prospect of expanding on this allocation). Nonetheless, the Women's department was there, one of the very few in any branch of U.S. broadcasting. The long delay between its announcement and the appointment of its head, which had angered many women to the point of leaving KPFA, seemed to be receding in significance by summer 1982 as many were now coming back, with considerable energy for new projects.

Women's department members considered its quality of life to be much more supportive and caring than was customary in other departments. The department, however, had not moved to differentiate itself from the other departments by becoming a formal collective. Its head was committed to seeking out and listening to her members' feelings, but in the final analysis she did have the power to act as she thought fit. We see here once more, not the dissolution of power, but its softening in a progressive direction. For example, controversial issues in the women's movement would be talked through before programs were put together, and the programs were then discussed before being aired.

The purpose of the Women's department, according to Ginny Berson, its head, was exactly the same as that of the women's movement at large. Within KPFA it constituted firstly a *place* to which women in the station, or new to it, could go. Secondly, as already noted, it constituted a power base. From this base it was possible to begin to have an effect on the rest of the station, to encourage feminist programming in general, from sensitivity to masochistic "love" lyrics, through awareness of women's presence, issues and perspectives in news, public affairs, and cultural programming. Their other major activity was to do programs on "standard" women's issues, such as domestic violence, abortion, rape, and on the feminist dimension of a whole range of other issues.

Not every woman in the station was involved with the Women's department; some men, moreover, according to Ginny Berson, were genuinely trying to change their programming in more feminist directions. But without the base and without the departmental vote, this would have been more difficult. Even though the tendency was still well in evidence at KPFA to say "Oh, that's a women's issue: pass it on to the Women's department," the department was still there to counterattack and insist issues be dealt with properly, not ghettoized. Without this base, the whole debate would have been one step further back, with women's issues dealt with or rejected haphazardly.

Furthermore, having a half-time paid person meant that someone had the time to get an overview of how women's issues were presented in general, and of the spectrum needed in women's programming. Ginny Berson found that going through Public Service Announcements (up to 100 a week) had given her a valuable check-list of events and issues to assign the women in her department by their area of interest. The result was a very large number of women involved in their programs.

Attitudes to women within KPFA were not, of course, magically different from those in society in general, with the single exception of gross, unrepentant male chauvinism. The overall culture was one of condemnation of sexism. Expressions of sexism within the station tended to be evidenced largely, by all accounts, in interpersonal one-to-one encounters, not in formal rules or gatherings. Able, experienced women would find their coments not taken as seriously as men's; would find themselves not considered for particular assignments on grounds of their gender; and would encounter a patronizing attitude when proposing new directions. The view that feminism was reducible to lesbianism plus the Equal Rights Amendment was not too hard to find at KPFA.

Beyond these issues, there had been something of a history of women and Third World people finding themselves pitted against each other, all the more easily because there were relatively few Third World women in the station. Indeed, the Third World department had been opposed for some time to the formation of a Women's department, because it felt that women and women's perspectives were already well-represented inside KPFA (in 1982 for example, two of the four managers and one department head were women). However, the first person to be appointed head of the Women's department was sensitive to Third World issues, and relations between the two departments seemed pretty good in 1982. As with other problems, so too this one is mentioned in the interests of realism: it is hardly unusual for white women and Third World people to find themselves told to divide the crumbs harmoniously between themselves in the contemporary U.S.

As noted above in connection with the public meetings in KPFA, these and other strains and stresses tended to be addressed for the most part in private conversation rather than in public. As Ginny Berson remarked, the station contained within it lesbians, homophobes, liberals, anarchists, marxists, Zionists and anti-Zionists. Public debates around these subjects, while unlikely to resolve them, could have split the whole project into multiple factions and destroyed the broadly based coalition it represented. Feminists were not alone in thinking that at least in KPFA you could talk to people individually about these things, and that in this respect it was much better than in the outside world.

Training is the other main point to touch upon in connection with the Women's department. It is a key topic, because a crippling dimension of technology for women in a patriarchal capitalist society, is that it is defined in many, many ways as a male domain. Women have often found themselves awed by it, even overwhelmed with a sense of their own inability to confront it. Their tiny numbers in math, science and engineering careers are partly attributable to the inculcation of this belief into their own thinking from their earliest years. Learning to use radio technology successfully can thus be a problematic process for women, at least at the outset. Training is therefore a particularly important political commitment of the Women's department.

The amount of time consumed in training is, however, considerable. At one point the Women's department was discouraging inexperienced applicants just because of this. In the 1980s, a period of declining employment and welfare payments, the pressures were very strong on people to drop everything in KPFA if they could just get a regular wage. This might well have been one reason why so few Third World women worked in KPFA, given labor market trends toward the employment of much cheaper female labor power as opposed to male labor power. In practice, KPFA trained people partly by formal instruction, and partly by resigning itself to their making some technical blunders on the air. There was no other way.

In 1982, however, the California Arts Council had given KPFA a grant to do outreach work to women and ethnic minorities, in order to begin to train them in radio. Two summer concerts were planned to draw attention to the program. As one person observed, though, while KPFA work remains largely unpaid, training will be a particular problem for these groups. Even though the union contract provides for some money for day care, and even though no mother has actually told the Women's department she needs help with her children to make programs, it is still highly probable that class factors are invisibly at work, manifest in the low number of Third World women working in KPFA.

The other examples of the interface between KPFA and outside political currents I will deal with much more briefly, simply as illustrations of how the station processed certain conflicts during the period of this survey. Two events were fresh in the mind of David Salniker, station manager. The first was a political split that had occured in the local Peace and Freedom party, by 1982 an explicitly socialist grouping. He had come back from vacation to find a picket waiting outside the station at 8:00 a.m. Having invited them in, he discovered that one faction in Peace and Freedom had become convinced of the urgency of working with progressive members of the two major parties, such as Ron Dellums, rather than pursuing its purely individual political line (as argued by the other faction). The second faction was the one picketing the station.

A member of the station's advisory board, who occasionally substituted for one of its regular public affairs programmers, was also a leading exponent of the first position and on its new slate for local elections. In the ten days before the elections she had been on the air three times, without referring to her own candidacy, the split, or other candidates. But she had expounded the position of the John Brown Club, another political splinter with which her faction had united, and had broadcast its telephone number. When her opponents in Peace and Freedom asked for equal time, they were refused it by the programmers, themselves unaware of the split, but knowing that this woman had usually spoken for Peace and Freedom in the past. Hence the picket.

This was a run of the mill type of incident, but one which still had to be dealt with by KPFA. The department involved was rather defensive, but eventually willingly—and that was vital, in Salniker's view—acquiesced in the excluded faction's being allocated a ten-minute interview.

The other recent issue was a good deal more serious. For over two years up to 1982, the News department had been criticized for handling the Palestinian issue differently from other liberation movements. Not that it was accused of being pro-Zionist, but rather of a liberal Zionist perspective, Israeli-based, and focussing much more on the Israeli peace movement than on the Palestinians' struggles. It was argued that South Africa, El Salvador and Poland were handled very differently. The critics were mainly people with a series of disputes with news policy, but included some unpaid staff.

The difficulty, as the station manager saw it, was that Middle East reporting was not organized, and certainly could not be paid for, by KPFA. It was provided by the News Bureau in Washington D.C., which serviced all the Pacifica stations. However, the issue was clearly a critical one, and on his own initiative, without consulting the News department, the manager asked a member of KPFA's advisory board to put him in touch with people living locally who represented a spectrum of opinion on the Middle East. One of the names she suggested was of a member of the Committee for Academic Freedom in Israeli-Occupied Territories. Before the meeting could take place with the people she had also suggested, a large number of the Committee turned up spontaneously at the station.

The manager talked with them, and then asked three or four to stay on to discuss the issues with members of the News department, which agreed to this, albeit with some reluctance. Before this fact-to-face encounter, the manager had requested that the committee members not raise specific past instances, to avoid provoking defensiveness in the News department, and instead to focus on how they could together promote better communication between information sources on the Arab world, and KPFA, and on how the station could develop greater sensitivity on this issue. He hoped the meeting would bring useful results, though it was too early to say whether it had.

Reviewing the station's relations with the outside world, which are after all the acid test of its effective democratic functioning, it is safe to conclude that there is a startling degree of openness in KPFA. This is true both in contrast with conventional media, and with the tiny presses of many leftwing sects. The possibility of dialogue within a very broad spectrum on the left, the potential of alternative media to open up a whole variety of progressive views for debate and consideration is— even taking account of its many problems past and present— strikingly demonstrated by KPFA. One member said, "We chose to work in KPFA, but not with each other." Nevertheless, the working experience of coalition and cooperation within a left so often paralyzed by its own entrenched positions and intrigues is highly positive and constructive. The ruling class, after all, has no idealism (except in the mouths of its campus and media ideologues), no future vision except its own en-trenchment. It can afford to buy off many of its own human traumas. Its passions and commitments exist, but are far more easily realizable than the often searing visions—with their fumbling practical approximations—within progressive move-ments. If we do not learn to work together within those movements, we leave the field amazingly clear to the powers that be. KPFA is a living reminder that, despite huge dif-ficulties inside and out, past and present, such cooperation is viable and creative.

Footnotes
1. The relation between KPFA and the Pacifica Foundation
has been through a series of phases, one or two of which are
alluded to in the pages that follow. Presently, the Foundation
acts as a trouble-shooter for stations in difficulties, and as a
central accounting agency for foundation and other grants. It
is also the repository of the tape record of all Pacifica stations.
2. G.R. Stebbins, *Listener-Sponsored Radio: the Pacifica Stations*. Ph.D. thesis in Mass Communications, Ohio State University, 1969. University Microfilms, Inc., Ann Arbor, Michigan.
No. 70-14, 102. P. 41.
3. Idem., p. 61.
4. Idem., p. 38.
5. Hill, cited in idem., p. 40.
6. See G. Rips, *The Campaign Against the Underground Press*,
San Francisco: City Lights, 1981.
7. My thanks are due to Vera Hopkins, Historian of KPFA,
whose assistance was generous and unfailing; and my debt is
clear to Professor Stebbins' thesis.
8. Stebbins, p. 130.
9. Rips, p. 92.
10. Stebbins, p. 218.
11. Idem., p. 167.
12. This proved, most sadly, to be the final blow for Lewis Hill;
the next day he took his own life.

4

UNION WAGE

Basic Information

Contents: varied, but strong emphasis on labor news and aspects of ongoing struggles by women workers; mostly an organizing newspaper
Location: Mission District, San Francisco
History: 1971-82
Personnel: paid office co-ordinator; token payments for office work; one year's experiment with a paid editor
Finance: subscriptions; waged and unwaged memberships; monthly pledges; annual and semi-annual donations
Appeared: bi-monthly
Social base: women wage-workers, both employed and unemployed
Related activities: pamphlets on union organizing, women's labor history, bilingual English and Spanish leaflets, etc.

Union Wage, short for Union Women's Alliance to Gain Equality, is the only one of the U.S. alternative media surveyed in this book which will no longer be in existence when it is published. It had, however, a particular place in the experience of those media, being the only one to be run by women wage-workers for women wage-workers. Thus, its importance cannot be discounted simply because it was forced to close. Like the three Portuguese examples surveyed later on, like *Lotta Continua* in Italy, it is because the experience was so important and would otherwise be likely to be lost, that it is especially urgent to record it. Why alternative media collapse, which they quite often do, may be instructive, if depressing. We need to learn from failures just as much as from successes.

96

Union Wage was primarily forced to close for financial reasons beyond its control. What those reasons were will be made plain further on, but it needs to be clear from the outset that the paper consistently had a living relationship with women wage-workers' struggles, especially but not exclusively in the Bay Area. Its political usefulness, while obviously not functioning at a continuous level of intensity, was never in doubt.

From the start, *Union Wage* was off with a bang. The issue that sparked the paper into life was anxiety among women labor activists that legislation protecting women and children at work might be swept away if the Equal Rights Amendment were to be passed. The position taken by *Union Wage* was that protective legislation should be extended to men, not that only women's rights were to be guarded. The media, not expecting a women's group to be publicly arguing for men's rights, gave them a great deal of early coverage. "Official" spokespeople for the women's movement in the Bay Area pronounced themselves against the protective legislation, perhaps because of its history of use to exclude women from better paid jobs; but *Union Wage* attacked this argument as promoting "negative equality" in current conditions.

The dispute is illuminating, because it shows at once the distinctive fusion between labor politics and women's movement politics that characterized the paper. At several other points we will observe this perspective, fiercely independent, but very much the result of this particular cross-influence. How often, in the history of women wage-workers, have their interests as women been squelched by the official labor movement, or their concerns as workers been put on the back burner by the leadership of the women's movement! *Union Wage*, usually, pointed beyond this dichotomy, not only in its content, but also in the form of its organization.

Union Wage also needs to be distinguished from the other main women wage-workers' organization, the Coalition of Labor Union Women (CLUW). From *Union Wage's* vantage point, CLUW was far too closely tied into the labor movement hierarchy, and seemed only interested in the single theme of sexual divisions at work, rather than the whole process of labor struggle. The result was that, at least in public, CLUW never criticized union leaders, even if the latter were plainly failing to support their rank and file in an eminently legitimate industrial action (such as a strike at the *Bay Guardian* newspaper).

Similarly, CLUW insisted in point 14 of its charter that it would never get involved in union jurisdictional disputes. In California, for example, this meant neutrality between the Teamsters Union and Cesar Chavez' United Farmworkers. Yet CLUW chose to be bound by its constitution, rather than amend it to deal with this conflict. Although *Union Wage* and others got point 14 changed in the end, they still did not succeed in getting positive support from CLUW for the Farmworkers. A consequence of *Union Wage's* stand was, not surprisingly, that it never enjoyed financial backing from any union.

A further point at odds between the two organizations was that CLUW would only accept women as members if they held union cards. The *Union Wage* view was that this was ridiculous. With only 10% of U.S. women wage-workers unionized, and with women massively over-represented in low-wage, non-unionized industries and firms, the CLUW policy seemed self-defeating as a strategy for organizing and empowering women workers. Given the high proportion of Third World women in these jobs, its effect could easily be to exclude them en masse. *Union Wage*, by contrast, was always open to any woman to join, including the wageless. This openness held its own problems, as we shall see when we consider the internal organization of the paper. Nonetheless, it represented once more that balance between labor politics and women's movement politics that CLUW failed to achieve.

One of the unions with which the paper most closely involved itself was the hotel and restaurant workers' union, the largest single union in San Francisco. On two occasions, radical caucuses managed to form a temporarily united front and took control of Local 2. The first time this toppled a thirty year leadership, quite a signal achievement. Regrettably, the unity did not persist very long past the elections, but *Union Wage's* involvement and support for the new slates undoubtedly helped the change into being. At least the union hierarchy thought so: following the second election, its president sat next to Joyce Maupin—a leading *Union Wage* organizer—at the housewarming for a Chicano Labor Institute, and berated her for an hour. He was particularly aggrieved, he said, because he had not been personally invited to *Union Wage's* support party for his striking members. "Brother," Joyce said to him at the end of the harangue, "you are always welcome at our parties."

Another key group with whom *Union Wage* involved itself was household workers, who were totally un-unionized. The largest concentration of such workers in the world is in Southern California, where many of them are Latinas. It was imaginable that they could combine in certain ways to take action against their agencies, and thus overcome their isolation from one another. Thus *Union Wage's* politics were firmly with rank and file workers, not with union members alone— and certainly not with union bureaucrats.

The internal organization of *Union Wage* was highly democratic. As Joyce Maupin remarked when referring to numerous attempts by sectarian groups to take the paper over:

> They never really understood our democracy. They would usually stay for about a year, offering to do all sorts of administrative chores, and then give up. Once only I was forced to use my experience of meeting-rules and procedures, as a long-time labor unionist, to confuse a group that wanted to take us over. One of these people once told me that getting a grip on *Union Wage's* organization was like trying to seize a bowl of jello!

The first constitution was modelled on a simplified trade union model, a fact which greatly confused foundations on the few occasions *Union Wage* sought money from them. "What do you mean, you don't have a director?" asked one foundation attorney in bewilderment. Throughout the paper's life, however, the constitution was perpetually under review and being revised. The basic electoral structure was the formation of an Executive Board by postal ballot every one to two years.

This structure was not without its difficulties. The numerical strength of *Union Wage* lay primarily in its San Francisco and East Bay chapters, with a membership running into several hundred on the West Coast at large. But there were chapters elsewhere, one in Indiana, another in New York; people wrote in from Philadelphia, Texas and other places seeking to start chapters. The paper normally had about fifteen hundred subscriptions from all over the country. The constitution allowed any seven women to start a chapter. Yet ensuring real representation for these chapters, and equally, striving to service them properly, proved a constant headache. *Union*

Wage constantly tried to give all the chapters a measure of power, and experimented with proportional representation, but found it was practically unrealizable. (Other bodies, such as CLUW, and NOW, did not even try.) The most it could do was to print news stories from the various chapters in the paper.

Similar headaches had plagued newspapers like *Libé-ration* in Paris, and *Tageszeitung* in Berlin, not to mention *The Guardian* and *Newsreel* in the U.S., in their efforts to create a national structure whose regional units would have a real measure of power in decision-making. Perhaps the major lesson to be learned is that local chapters need to be told they are on their own from the start, so that they do not develop unfulfillable expectations.

In any event, for those in the Bay Area who constituted the bulk of *Union Wage's* activists, the structure was very open. Anyone could be present, without voting, at Executive Board meetings. Each chapter had a structure parallel to the national organization structure, with its own Executive Board. For a long period, the politics of consensus decision-making dominated meetings. Majority voting was perceived as a concession to male power structures, and an attempt was made to pursue debates until there was general agreement. As time passed, however, many members grew increasingly frustrated with this procedure. In one campaign in coalition with a section of the Teamsters, over the rights of women working late to be given their taxifare home by their employers, one women's group was unable to achieve consensus in time to produce a flyer, and so could not formally join the coalition. Although it was not *Union Wage* itself that suffered this setback, the experience was sufficiently close to its own to give members pause for thought.

Out of this and other experiences, *Union Wage* moved back to majority votes as its normal procedure. If it were ever to function as an organizing instrument, this decision made sense. Employers very often have the power to impose time-tables on negotiations, and an organization which cannot operate in these circumstances is hog-tied.

However, its characteristic openness to differing view-points persisted. For instance, the only restriction placed upon a Catholic woman worker who joined was that she could not declare herself a member of *Union Wage* if she was campaigning against abortion rights (her only anti-feminist position, admittedly). For an organization whose position on abortion was "Free abortion on demand!," and which vigorously contested CLUW's more cautious call to "Defend Abortion Rights" as hopelessly short-sighted, such openness was rather striking.

Meetings were quite often stormy, if stimulating. From the perspective of most leading members of *Union Wage*, this was one of its great pluses, bringing a whole variety of women wage-workers together to begin to work through the issues confronting them. At the same time, it did not magically solve problems, as a couple of instances will illustrate. One concerned the invitation to a Polish woman to speak on the Polish situation in the period of Solidarity. The meeting was packed, but one CPUSA woman left in protest after five years' work with the paper, although another CPUSA member agreed the paper had every right to create a public forum for these topics. The other instance concerned the capacity of the Executive Board to argue on occasion about trivia, such as whether they should buy more chairs for the office. This second instance is not included to imply that such time-wasting was frequent, but merely to emphasize there is no simple route to avoid these distractions. (They are certainly not absent from the supposedly rational, goal-oriented, efficient corporate world!)

In the course of its history, most of the central issues of the labor and women's movements were talked through in *Union Wage*: the question of superseniority in lay-offs (i.e. is seniority not effectively harmful to women's rights at work?); the question of unions outside the AFL—CIO; the question of women's spontaneous consciousness as women, and the value of their various attempts at poetry and highly personal communication; the question of sexuality. And many, many more issues, not least the particular experiences of Latinas and of Afro-American women, to whom *Union Wage* was always very open.

There were intermittent journalistic / political rows about a number of topics. One major one was around an issue of the paper devoted to women in prison. Letters had been received from Sarah Jane Moore, the ex-FBI agent who had tried to kill President Ford, and Betty Lou Harris, of the Symbionese Liberation Army. Some felt that to put their letters in would make the paper look as though it was favoring what they had done, and that it would at best be sensationalistic. The letters did go in, however, as the information they contained about events in their prisons was corroborated from other quarters.

The one occasion when *Union Wage* experimented with a full-time paid editor deserves some comment. The woman who filled this role worked unpaid for a year, and then worked a second year paid. She was also paid to act as the paper's book-keeper. The experience of the second year appears to have been a rather traumatic one, ending with a messy six-month tussle between herself and the Executive Board who were and remained overwhelmingly in favor of terminating her contract.

The Board's decision revolved around her autocratic personal style in the office, which included changing articles' wording just to suit her whims of style. They also judged her to overemphasize the "consciousness-raising" elements of the women's movement to the point where at one stage four pages of each issue were given over entirely to rather nondescript poetry (written by people she termed "poor" and "really oppressed" women). They also found her morally arrogant about her anti-racism, often claiming to be the only "real" non-racist in the office (she lived at the time with an Afro-American). And finally, her writing was felt to be often over-ready to condemn, as in one article when she violently attacked social security officials in the office booths dealing with clients. They too are often women workers, and the way they are used to absorb clients' rage by their better-paid office supervisors behind the scenes, also demands attention.

In the end, she did leave, but not without having clung tenaciously to her editorship for as long as she could, packing meetings with her friends, who hotly accused the paper of "throwing her out onto the street." It was a curious situation, because it would have been impossible for her to function as an editor given people's negative feelings about her. But the open structure of *Union Wage* permitted the issue to drag on almost endlessly, in a way which could not possibly have helped the paper to achieve its aims. (Compare The *National Guardian's* difficulties with its general manager in 1965.) The episode coincided with a major decline in labor activism in the area, and effectively heralded the paper's closure. It is to these reasons for its closure that I lastly turn.

They were essentially financial. Postal subsidies for non-profit organizations' mailings were removed, with the effect of trebling this cost. The numbers of subscribers changing their subscription level from employed to unemployed ($15 to $7.50) nearly quadrupled. The rent for the office had risen 25% for 1982, and would rise another 10% in 1983. To these already crippling financial exigencies we must add the fact that money and book-keeping had, as so often is the case in these media, never been a preferred topic at Executive Board meetings. Essentially, they had not wanted to think about the foundation of their future operation. The public meetings they had, like the one on Poland, were completely free, so that no income was raised from that source. Their approaches to foundations were few and far between, probably wisely, for when they and the Women's Labor Project sent in drafts of booklets on women's labor organizing to the Ms. Foundation, they were told that one was too simple, the other too complex. Their rapid sales when they did manage to get them printed told a lot about foundations' political preferences.

They depended for at least 80% of their income on subscriptions. An occasional donation might come in, once for as much as $500, but they were very unpredictable and small-scale. Unions, as noted, did not rush to assist them. Their basic crime was to be involved in communicating *as part of organizing*. That was, more than any of the other factors, why they would always have been dependent on subscriptions. That was where their media project bit. Capitalist recession and slump damage many aspects of society; amongst the casualties will always be numbered projects like *Union Wage*.

Looking back over the experience of the paper, the verdict must be that its demise dealt a serious blow to women and to the labor movement. Its unique fusion of the political experience and demands of both movements, its commitment to mass communication as an empowering activity for women wage-workers, are not commonly found. Among its roles it included training women workers and giving them experience in writing, graphics, lay-out, newspaper production, all in the context of a very open political debate. On occasion the contents could have been more polished than this allowed them to be, but the price was well worth paying. Its leading members were certainly not giving up with the paper's demise, but were transferring their energies into other areas of struggle, notably supporting the organization of household workers. Nevertheless, papers with this focus are badly needed, and sadly missed.

5

AKWESASNE NOTES AND ERIN BULLETIN

"We don't get paid much. If the work gets too much, or the bills seem impossible, or we want to spend more time with our families, then we think about what is happening to Indians in Guatemala, or about a 78-year-old Cheyenne man in Montana who is struggling to stop ARCO from drilling on his land. Then what we have to do doesn't seem so much in comparison."

—Carol Mohawk
Akwesasne Notes

Akwesasne Notes

Began: 1968
Circulation: toward 20,000 (1982); many copies seen by 30-40 people
Location: Mohawk Nation, via Rooseveltown, New York State
Staff: 9 full-time
Appears: bi-monthly
Financial base: mostly subscriptions and private donations; sales from books, posters and local crafts; some foundation money; governmental and corporate support rejected

Erin Bulletin

Began: 1979
Circulation: 2000 (1982)
Staff: three
Appears: monthly
Financial base: subscriptions

A History

Akwesasne Notes and the *Erin Bulletin* which we shall examine below, are produced from within the Mohawk nation. They represent a different "case" from all the others in the book, in that they are based neither on a socialist politics, nor on a "liberal forum" politics (like KPFA, Berkeley) which offers substantial space to liberatory and socialist viewpoints. Instead, their liberation philosophy is derived from traditional Native American culture and from the historical experience of near-genocide and "ecocide" at the hands of Europeans. They explicitly disavow the label "marxist," although, beginning in 1980, *Akwesasne Notes* seriously engaged in a dialogue with marxist socialist thought and practice, giving space to a variety of views from both camps in its columns. Native peoples' perspectives on human existence and their struggles for land, justice and sovereignty are so significant—not only in North America, but in Brazil, Guatemala, Australia, and many other places—that democratic media independently communicating these realities are of the greatest interest to this study.

What cannot be done here is to review this historical and present oppression of Native peoples inside North America.[1] That is no footnote to real history, however, as even supposedly humane observers have been content to define it, but a narrative that poses fundamental questions about the present direction of the planet's development. The logic of industrial advance, and its ultimate expression in "nuclear progress," can be seen from the first European explorers' and settlers' violence against the indigenous peoples of the Americas. A coherent line can be drawn between the point of Puritan extirpation of fellow farmers in the 16th century, and the iron pursuit of competitive advantage in uranium mining or oil extraction on Indian reservations in the late 20th century[2] (to say nothing of the death and destruction meted out in building the Trans-Amazonian highway in Brazil). The practice of a number of states claiming the mantle of Marxism—notably the USSR—is no more encouraging as regards either environmental destruction or the treatment of Native minorities.[3] The future of Miskito Indians in Sandinista Nicaragua has particularly preoccupied *Akwesasne Notes*: were they being trapped in a vice between the new government's need to protect itself and maybe develop resources on their land, and the United States' military subversion of the Sandinistas?

Thus the significance of Indian struggles cannot be relegated to the sidelines, either politically or ethically. Although these movements have persisted through the centuries of European occupation, the most recent cycle of struggles, beginning in 1968, has perhaps been the most far-reaching this century in the U.S. Within the Mohawk nation itself, which is cut in half by the U.S.-Canadian border, border guards were making free passage increasingly difficult during 1968. Family visits, and the collection of black ash trees to weave baskets (an important revenue source and cultural expression), became almost impossible. The Canadian border guards, in particular, were levying import duty on black ash. All this, needless to say, was in violation of a treaty (the Jay Treaty) with the Mohawk nation, guaranteeing them free passage across the border.

In protest, the bridge linking the U.S. and Canada was blockaded by Indians, and fifty were arrested. They were, however, successful in getting their demands met, at least for a time. This was when *Akwesasne Notes* came to birth, simply taking the form of a series of xeroxed news sheets reproducing clippings from the local press on their struggle. (Initially it was called Notes from Akwesasne).

Although they did not realize it at that moment, similar struggles were simultaneously bubbling to the surface elsewhere in North America. In Minneapolis, Native American meetings were called to protest police violence at about this time. The American Indian Movement, armed with CB radios, began to follow police cars, to try to patrol the patrolmen. In autumn 1968, a 50-year-old dispute blew up once more in Northern California over fishing rights. Somehow, odd copies of the *Notes* reached these and other areas, and the three or four people involved in the *Notes* began to get letters, often including clippings, from people who wanted to hear more about the Mohawks' situation, and to communicate information about their own struggles and achievements. These came to be reproduced in the xeroxed news sheet, expanding its coverage considerably.

Meanwhile, a caravan movement began from the Mohawk nation with the objective of hearing the situations, and also the religious perspectives, of different Indian peoples across the U.S. The caravan went first to the Hopis of the Southwest, as the cultural "grandparents" of all Indian peoples in North America. The caravan grew in size in its subsequent travels, and eventually culminated in the 1969 seizure of Alcatraz Island, a potent symbol of Indian land rights.

At that point, *Akwesasne Notes'* circulation leapt from under 600 to about 10,000. Two or three more individuals joined the paper, numerous Indian peoples (Sioux, Navahos and others) began feeding it with information, while boxes of tapes and documents arrived, often without author or sender being named, covering numerous aspects of Indian life across the continent.

The editorial group began its own process of outreach both to reservations and to universities, visiting perhaps 20 to 30 of the former and 50 to 60 of the latter to talk, to lecture, to discuss. They they would come back and put together the next issue of *Notes*. The paper appeared quite irregularly in those days, from five to ten times a year. During this period many individuals joined the paper for a time, and then went off to start their own newsletters and papers elsewhere. The development of *Akwesasne Notes* and the fast growth of the movements of Indian struggle in the early 70s were absolutely part and parcel of each other.

Two important developments in these movements emerged in 1972-73, both sharply expanding the paper's circulation. During 1972, the American Indian Movement began to organize against racist killings in the small towns of the Dakotas. One killing particularly spurred this action, when Raymond Yellow Thunder was forced by whites at gunpoint to strip himself naked in the winter snow, swallow an entire bottle of whiskey, dance naked in a bar for the amusement of its clients, and then was taken outside and stabbed to death by two of the whites. The horror and outrage felt at this and many other instances of white barbarism expressed itself in the Trail of Broken Treaties caravan in 1972, which travelled through the Midwest to Oklahoma holding large meetings in every reservation along the way. A 20 point set of demands was put to the Bureau of Indian Affairs, Washington's agency to manage Native peoples, and when they were not conceded, the Bureau headquarters were occupied.

The *Notes* jumped to a circulation of 20,000, and began to print a number of the documents seized in the BIA takeover, many of them detailing government and corporate plans to "develop" Indian territories for minerals and other purposes. As a result, Native activists were put in a position of knowing what was in the pipeline, and could begin to organize against it in advance.

The second climactic moment was the 1973 occupation of Wounded Knee, site of the notorious 1890 massacre of hundreds of unarmed Indian men, women and children by the U.S. cavalry.[4] The occupation protested the exceptionally brutal and corrupt "neo-colonial" tribal administration that governed the Pine Ridge reservation where Wounded Knee is located. Appointed from above, disregarding most rules, procedures and laws, the chair, Richard Wilson, ran the reservation in a manner generally reminiscent of Somoza or the Shah. Every complaint was neglected, all resistance was punished, sometimes viciously by his goon squad. The AIM takeover of the village, a story which is a classic of its own in revealing Washington's duplicity and media management,[5] was fully supported by the villagers. It lasted from February 27th to May 8th through snowstorms, firefights, a blockade of food and medical supplies and two deaths on the Indian side from sniper fire. The U.S. Army was dispatched there in the first few days, and surrounded the village right up to the end. In the course of this struggle, *Akwesasne Notes* shot up to its highest ever circulation at 53,000 copies.

The virtual fusion between the paper and these movements, which makes it strongly reminiscent of the three Portuguese cases examined later in the book, is obvious. From 1974, the relationship continued in force, but given the expansion of the movements, the paper began to devote itself to longer term strategic concerns and philosophical issues as its most distinctive contribution to the movements. At the time, and subsequently, this focus involved two areas of work in particular. One was the attempt to bypass the U.S. courts' refusal to deal seriously with Indian sovereignty rights, by trying to get these rights redefined in international law. This strategy had the secondary effect of bringing the issues involved before an international audience. The other area of work also involved the internationalization of Indian struggles, linking with the movements of land-based Native peoples throughout the world. Connections were built with Central and South America, in Australia, with Kurds, Berbers, Basques, Romanis, Ainos and many other peoples.

A high point in these developments was the 1977 Geneva conference on discrimination against Indians in the western hemisphere. With the exception of Brazil, which would only allow Indians to attend if chaperoned by non-Indian Brazilians, all major groups were represented. The sense of unity, of being part of a much wider movement, was palpable. It confirmed the direction of *Akwesasne Notes* toward producing thinkpieces, almost toward magazine format, as a greater priority then immediate news items. Other Indian media were doing the latter pretty effectively by then, so the need for *Notes* to do so was lessened.

By 1982 however, the pendulum had begun to swing back little, with the late summer issue focussing more closely on elements of autonomous community-building, with a commitment to produce more of this practically-oriented material in the future. The point is not that *Notes* had "gone theoretical" and needed rescuing from abstraction, like a set of European left wing gurus! The birth of the *Erin Bulletin*, as we shall see, gives the lie to that. Nonetheless, the advent of a larger number of women into the paper in the 80s than had been present hitherto, served to re-emphasize the importance of everyday life, issues such as health and education, which previously had taken rather a back seat.

Internal Organization

Like most of the other media in this book, *Akwesasne Notes* is a collective. In 1982, everyone received subsistence enough to buy groceries and help survive. The payment of subsistence came relatively late in the paper's history (1980), as did the switch to subscription sales from free distribution. This was necessitated by the decline in campus funds for speaking tours and the decision to bring the paper out regularly five times a year (in 1982, six times a year).

Since 1977, the editor-in-chief has been appointed by the Council of Chiefs of the Mohawk Nation, which also has the ultimate authority over the paper, acting as the "spiritual grandparents" of the collective. All day-to-day matters are handled within the collective. There, in its members' view, traditional cultural commitment to consensual decision-making, and the particular, tolerant personalities involved, had managed to combine together to produce a very united working group. The process of discussion they regarded as an essential ingredient in their success, even though it involved many meetings. Sometimes there would be half-day meetings among the editors for a whole week on end and when a production deadline was nearing, the whole weekend and even all night might be taken up in producing the paper. Obviously this is more feasible given a bi-monthly production schedule than a weekly, let alone daily, routine. Nonetheless, the commitment to discussion is not a luxury of time for the *Notes* collective. Experience has shown them that without this the project starts to go downhill, with hurt feelings generated by non-consensual decisions.

It is important to realize that the *Notes* collective also lives very much as a community; most members are married with children, and they organize communal childcare for one another. There is a very close relationship with the adjoining Akwesasne Freedom School, which offers an alternative education to Indian children of all ages. Both institutions are part of a concerted drive to re-establish centers of cultural and political autonomy within the Indian nations of North America, and to overcome the destructive inroads made into that autonomy by the U.S. over the centuries. In the Akwesasne community, these efforts also include a 20-watt radio station broadcasting daily between 6 and 10pm, and at other times; a medical emergency service; and a birth-delivery service. All are part of an effort to be as self-sufficient as possible, predicated on a position not too far from—but much older than—a variety of western anarchism, namely the necessity of creating communities sufficiently small and decentralized for democracy to function easily. To this position the community brings the added commitment, central in Indian culture, to a scaled-down economy without the ecological disruption of mining, deforestation and other forms of environmental blight.

For the *Notes* people, these firm community links were the essential basis for their work, as was their attempt to take care of each other's personal needs. The function attempted by the Women's Department at KPFA for women, was here attempted for the whole group. They readily admit that as a result their work proceeds far more slowly than in a capitalist project, but view this as a price well worth paying. The authority of the editor-in-chief, for instance, became much more akin to that of an older, more experienced brother than of a central administrator.

There is a division of labor within *Notes* between people working on the business side, and those working on the editorial side. Each is entrusted with doing what has to be done under these headings, but the paper is discussed, and approved or amended as the case may be, by everyone, as are business decisions. Final responsibility lies with the collective as a whole (and beyond them, as stated, with the Council of Chiefs, who in Mohawk culture are chosen by women). During 1982, however, the *Notes* collective was becoming increasingly conscious of their weaknesses in the area of marketing the paper. None of them had any skills or experience in doing this, but were acutely aware of its relevance for their work's success in reaching as many people as possible. Yet again, we see the significance of serious attention to business practicalities in alternative media. Plans were being made to increase the production of pamphlets, for example reproducing debates in *Notes* on marxism and Native peoples, as a means both of stimulating further debate and of adding new sources of revenue for the collective's work. In time, they felt the pamphlets might well be further expanded into books.

The only real history of internal strife within *Akwesasne Notes* dated back to its editor previous to the present one (1982). An adopted Mohawk citizen, he found it increasingly hard to combine collective work with his own impulse to be everywhere, get involved in everything. Even delegation of responsibilities came hard to him. With an increase in Indian activists around the paper in 1976-77, these work patterns became impossible to reconcile with a commitment to collective work. He and they decided to part company, and he left, starting a new paper on Indian subjects and issues in Pennsylvania.

As regarded editorial policy decisions on controversial issues, the practice in the paper was generally to be very open, albeit within certain limits. For example, the paper carefully printed both pro- and anti-Sandinista accounts of the position of Miskito Indians in Nicaragua. When dealing with the American Indian Movement or the International Treaty Council, with both of which they had their differences, they would nonetheless reproduce the range of views fully and fairly. They were distinctly hostile to Christianity as an organized force, and to anthropology as generally practiced, but would still not automatically condemn every anthropologist or—for instance— Guatemalan Indians for being Catholics (though in the latter case, the powerful influence of Mayan culture on traditional Catholicism in Guatemala made their task easier).

Women's roles in the collective had already been touched upon. Mohawk culture has traditionally been quite sensitive to women's rights and concerns, and this has generally been reflected in the *Notes* collective. However, the stronger representation of women was leading in 1982 to an increased emphasis on health and education issues, as we have seen. Without any confrontation, as took place in other cases in this study, women's interests and perspectives had carried through into the paper's content. The worst clashes reported between the men and women amounted to the former accusing the latter of being overly picky at 4am when proof-reading the paper...

Akwesasne Notes had a policy of encouraging self-development in journalism. Thus a new collective member with photographic skills, who as it happened had been with the paper in the earliest days as well, was actively engaged in teaching other members effective use of the camera. Assignment of writing tasks is also evenly shared out; one collective member hates to do Supreme Court and legal issues, but nonetheless accepts doing them; she also found herself suddenly highly competent to talk about Native peoples in Micronesia, through being assigned to write on it, not having known very much at all about the subject beforehand. This attitude toward training is also evident in the Italian media we survey later, and represents an important softening of the division of labor. Another aspect of this division, namely the printing of the paper, had always been farmed out to sympathetic printers, who were extremely patient in waiting for their bills to be paid. Eventually, however, the collective hoped to be able to make use of a second hand printing press they had been offered, which would enable them to carry out the whole operation themselves.

In conclusion, it has to be said that, like so many other media of this kind in the U.S., *Akwesasne Notes* gets its fair share of harassment from the powers that be. Phone interference has ranged from echoes and clicks on the line, to voices interrupting asking who they were calling, to having their lines cut twice by state troopers. Their papers and packages often do not reach their destinations. Philanthropic foundations have had pressure put on them not to allocate *Akwesasne Notes* any grants. In moving now to consider the *ERIN Bulletin*, we shall have reason to see more of these hostile pressures against their work, and how they fight back against them.

The *ERIN Bulletin*

ERIN stands for Emergency Response International Network. It consists of about 2000 individuals in and out of North America who have sufficient commitment to Native peoples' rights to pick up the telephone if they are told of some incident abusing or threatening those rights, and call the police, or whomever might be appropriate, to inquire about the matter. The effect on a racist sheriff in a tiny South Dakota town of being phoned from New York, Zürich, Paris, London, Rome, Hamburg, to ask what he is doing, is at least likely to cause him to ponder his actions a little. To Indians living hundreds of miles from the nearest large city, exposed to the unnoticed persecution of ranchers and police, this system can be a lifeline of support.

The spark for its creation was a police action against an Indian camp in Akwesasne in late August 1979. They circled the camp, armed with high-powered rifles and other weapons, trying to terrorize the camp members into leaving. The Akwesasne community set about telephoning everyone they could, and were pleasantly surprised when the calls their contacts then made to police and local authorities had the effect of cancelling the police action. From this experience, they decided to organize what they had done on a more permanent basis.

Their strategy is to bring international pressure to bear on a single point. To do this, they check with the local community to find out who has the power to pull back the assault: is it a fisheries warden? a police chief? a senator? Once they have this person's address and telephone number, they activate ERIN, calling people and groups in Western Europe and North America, including human rights groups and non-governmental organizations at the UN. It is an attempt to produce an analogue to Amnesty International, but without sharing Amnesty's political perspectives.

In the course of time they hoped to build up teams of people, each including a lawyer, a doctor, a skilled negotiator, who could go and trouble-shoot at short notice. The merit of this strategy is that it can often buy time for a solution to be found; and, as noted already, it is at its most valuable when applied to isolated communities where no oversight exists on abuses that occur all the time.

Thus the communication projects at Akwesasne embrace an exceptionally wide spectrum of activity on behalf of Native nations in North America. The rebuilding of sovereignty is being slowly and painstakingly hammered out here, in ways that constitute something of a beacon in the cultures that have come close at times to being pulverized by the aggression of white settler society. Perhaps the crucial ingredient in the struggle at Akwesasne and elsewhere is the conviction that while western and soviet culture jointly threaten the planet's survival, their own traditions express a respect for the earth that, if given its due internationally, could inform a new, peaceful world order. In the midst of all the urgent defense specifics of ERIN, this strong assertion of the potential of their own past and present illuminates the seemingly gathering dusk.

Footnotes

1. F. Jennings, *Invasion of America,* Chapel Hill: University of North Carolina Press, 1975.
2. E. Stillwaggon, "Anti-Indian agitation and economic interests," *Monthly Review* 33.6 (November 1981), pp. 28-41.
3. B. Komarov, *The Destruction of Nature in the Soviet Union,* London: Pluto Press 1981; A. Nekrich, *The Punished Peoples,* New York: Norton 1978.
4. Dee Brown, *Bury My Heart At Wounded Knee,* New York: Holt Rinehart & Winston 1970.
5. See *Voices From Wounded Knee, 1973,* Akwesasne Notes, via Rooseveltttown, NY 13683, for an extraordinary account of this event by participants.

6

NACLA
REPORT ON THE AMERICAS

Location: New York City
Appears: bi-monthly
Sales: upwards of 5500 subscribers an issue in 1982; a similar number on bookstalls and solidarity tables, and for classroom use.
Began: 1967
Staff: in 1982, ten full time; three part time; some volunteers
Pay: equal

Journalistic flair and clarity, combined with political thrust and academic thoroughness: the NACLA *Report on the Americas* is a prime example of a new breed of committed magazine journalism. *Monthly Review,* the senior radical journal in the U.S. since World War II, has a consciously theoretical stamp to it but the NACLA *Report on the Americas* has served as something of an example for more informationally weighted political magazines, both inside and outside the U.S. Such would include the MERIP *Report* on the Middle East, *Southern Exposure* and *Covert Action Information Bulletin*, and the many magazines and small journals in western Europe, Japan and Australia that focus on ecology, peace, the nuclear issue, the Third World, or the soviet bloc. Out of NACLA have directly emerged other radical information activities: Corporate Data Exchange, the Data Center, and the Information Service on Latin America (the last two in the Bay Area). Not only has the magazine very extensive classroom and back issue sales, beyond its regular subscriptions, but it finds many of its articles resurfacing translated in European and Latin American publications, as well as in books and anthologies on Latin America, and also being used as a basis for pamphlets and leaflets in the U.S.

With the eruption of Nicaragua, Jamaica, Grenada and El Salvador into the news in the late 70s, the *Report* became standard reading for many U.S. journalists, and its staff was highly in demand as resource people for individual journalists, media interviews and addressing public meetings. Thus the political impact of the *Report* has been considerable. Its particular role in exposing conditions in "Uncle Sam's backyard" is reason enough for including it in this survey of alternative media in the U.S., but its status as flagship for a whole new kind of committed magazine journalism is equally valid in this respect. From the outset, it is important to recognize that NACLA is first and foremost an organization, whose principal activity is publishing the *Report*; thus its other activities are not somehow extraneous to it, but an integral aspect of its work.

A Brief History

NACLA's foundation dates back to 1966. The first, cyclostyled issue of the *Newsletter*, as it was then called, appeared in February 1967. This was a period of intense turmoil in the country following the sharp escalation of the Vietnam war, and the decision by President Johnson to put 20,000 Marines into the Dominican Republic to oppose the popular forces attempting to reinstate a liberal president (Juan Bosch). A number of individuals who had lived in South America, and who had a clear sense of the havoc wrought there by U.S. corporate and military involvement, decided that a publication was needed to examine "those elements and relationships of forces in the United States and Latin America which inhibit and frustrate urgently needed profound social and economic change."[1] The initial basis of readership was the growing anti-war movement; this continued until the decline of the movement in the early 70s.

The term North American *Congress* on Latin America (NACLA) was chosen to express the broad base of political opinion the leaders originally canvassed and involved in the work of the organization. Soon NACLA became a small collective, producing its own original research for a variety of uses, including its own *NACLA Newsletter*. Over its life the name of the publication was changed twice, first to NACLA *Latin America and Empire Report* (1971) and then to the present NACLA *Report on the Americas* (1977). NACLA's focus has

also changed a number of times. In the earliest days it conducted what came to be called "power structure research,"
namely, a highly empirical detailing of the links between U.S.
corporations and Latin American countries, or of links between the corporations, the military and the U.S. government.
The appearance and format of the publication were rather
makeshift and somewhat strident in tone, not least in the
graphics and illustrations.

The coups in Uruguay in 1972, in Chile in 1973 and in
Argentina in 1976, all three being countries with a well organized left, broke many of NACLA's personal links with the
continent. NACLA continued its focus on Latin America: the
question of *abertura* in Brazil, capital restructuring in Chile,
and so on. But in response to questions about what repression
in Latin America had to do with struggles inside the U.S. the
Report began to examine the political economy of U.S. involvement in Latin America, with the goal of understanding
common working class interests internationally. Thus it carried a number of industry studies on apparel, steel, cars and so
on, which examined the linkages between corporate strategy in
the U.S. and Latin America, of which a classic case is/was the
"runaway shop" (compare California Newsreel's film *Controlling Interest*). Journalistically speaking, the adoption of a
more thorough marxist political economy orientation in the
Report's analyses took time to work through, and for a while
the magazine became somewhat indigestible. The theoretical
advance was, however, translated through in due course into a
clearer writing style, an important breakthrough for marxist
magazine journalism in the U.S.

At the end of the 70s, the relation between the U.S. economy and South America, and analyses based on marxist political economy, had become consolidated in the magazine. Two
other developments should be noted which also coalesced
around that time, although quite different from each other.
One was the growing significance of NACLA's Central American connections: the *Report* was the first to detail the Sandinistas' organized resistance to the Somoza dictatorship. As that
and other struggles gathered momentum to overthrow the violent dictatorships of the region, so the *Report* found its readership substantially expanding. The other development was that
the collective came to devote much more serious attention to
the "look" of the magazine and its promotion. These highly

practical dimensions of media work had long been neglected in favor of apparently more radical concerns. Two appointments helped in this crystallization. One was the present editor, who had a background in graphics and advertizing, who stressed that, for instance, decent paper was needed if only to keep back-copies legible, and to enable good photographic reproduction. The other was a full-timer specializing in promotion and distribution, who was able to emphasize the pointlessness of working so hard to produce the magazine if only relatively few people were ever going to see it.

Paradoxically, the success the *Report* had was beginning to produce its own difficulties by 1982, with overwhelming demands on staff energy and time for public speaking and debating.

Internal Oganization

Five major aspects of the *Report*'s way of organizing itself require attention. They are its internal democracy; the continuing dilemma of integrating research work and activist work; the relationship between the business side and the research side; the role of volunteers; and the period when there were two NACLA offices, in California and New York (1971-1978). In line with one of the basic concerns of this book, namely the relation between internal and external democracy in alternative media, we shall also examine the *Report*'s relation to its constituencies in the Americas.

As the editor, Judy Butler, put it in another interview,[2] the original notion of democracy in NACLA in its earlier years was that everyone should "eat from the same fork." All decisions were shared, all activity was parcelled out equally, right down to gumming the labels onto copies for mailing. Pay, of course, was equal. Decisions were not only shared, but arrived at by consensus, not majority vote.

Over many years of working together—for the NACLA team has been quite stable over time considering the low salary—the merits of this definition of democracy, so evident at first, seemed less and less alluring. The equal pay issue has never been disputed, but the advantages of having everyone discuss every single aspect of mailing, for instance, began to seem rather meager in comparison with the time lost for other pressing commitments for the magazine. Meetings became unconscionably long. Very gradually, out of the direct experience of doing it that way, a desire arose on all sides for a shift in organizational structure. By 1979, decisions on such issues were left to the people involved or were assigned to a steering committee of three to consider with just them, rather than with meetings of the entire collective. If the steering committee felt the matter required wider discussion, then it would recommend to that effect.

By 1980, a division of labor had emerged for the first time in the organization, with people hired for skills in special areas. Researchers were relieved of most administrative responsibilities, and given a research director to help provide an overview and a perspective on future directions for the magazine. It is too early to be able to know how the new arrangement will pan out, but in tune with their feeling that issues should be discussed before they became too highly charged, a weekend retreat was being organized in 1982 to discuss, among other issues, the implications of having a business "side" and a research "side." The combination of a stable core of people with this mature commitment to grasping nettles rather than delaying doing so, seemed to bode well for the *Report*'s future.

(While discussing the division of labor, it is appropriate to note that the magazine's printing is contracted out, so that there is no direct printer involvement to discuss in the production process—contrast the experience of *República* in Portugal and of *Lotta Continua* in Italy.)

The internal issue which agitated the collective for this first ten years of life in particular, was the dilemma of doing research and publication work, as opposed to activist solidarity work with Latin America. In the politically intense years around the late 60s, when it seemed to political activists as though almost anything might happen to the U.S. externally in terms of foreign policy defeats (Vietnam, Chile, Angola), and internally as a result of mass political mobilizations—or during the 70s with the horrors perpetrated by new U.S.-sponsored military coups in Latin America—activism often seemed more important political work than providing information and analysis. They had to examine the political role of information, the division of labor within the support movement, and the importance of consistency in the organization of the *Report*. In the final analysis, the collective was forced to ask itself: is our work worthwhile? And if the answer was yes, then it followed logically that the work should be carried through with the maximum commitment and energy. Only so could it be of the best value to people in solidarity groups, to groups in Latin America themselves lacking access to information sources such as transnational corporate reports, and more generally to expanding awareness of the relation between the Americas within the English-speaking world.

The quality of the discussion was usually anguished rather than recriminatory, since everyone genuinely wished to be able to do both types of work effectively. In the end, the consensus that emerged after nearly ten years of veering in first one direction, then the other, was that the activism of informing public opinion was not a second-class or escapist commitment. All the same, the related activities that were undertaken as a result of the explosion of Central America into the news—speaking tours, advisory and consultant roles—were themselves imposing heavy pressure on the organization in 1982, as noted above. Even recognizing the specificity and validity of media work as part of the general struggle would not provide a complete solution to that problem.

The role of the business side of the organization has already been touched upon twice, but it is worth re-emphasising the practical issues of (a) the need to make sure business work is done properly, and (b) making sure that those responsible for it are not ghettoized (compare *The Guardian*'s method of approaching the latter problem). If business is not given sufficient regard, stretched finances will likely snap, the audience will be lost, and even state repression is made easier (see the Internal Revenue Service saga below). If however a specialist business section is simply instituted without very careful discussion and planning of its political relation to the whole project, the chances are high that the capitalist division of labor will impose its own models by default, with destructive implications for the culture of democratic work that collectively owned media have built up so painfully.

The role of volunteers is another aspect of NACLA's organization that demands a moment's reflection. Their place is not the same as that of unpaid workers in KPFA, in Berkeley, because they are often students and thus transient, working with the collective for a period, and then moving on to other things. For those interested in research, the collective has found it hard to divide up the work that has to be done into pieces small and compact enough to allow a volunteer to complete an assignment within a fairly short space of time. A result has been that some volunteers end up feeling a little excluded, a function partly of the problem above, partly of limited staff time to work with them on projects, and partly of the sometimes high expectations volunteers have of what NACLA is and what they can learn from it. Some volunteers during the summer of 1982 offered suggestions as to how to reduce the problem and these were being worked on by the staff. In addition, NACLA was having a series of weekly meetings for everyone in which staff would discuss their recent visits to Latin America, of which there had been quite a number just previously. One objective of these meetings was to make the volunteers feel more involved in the project.

The fifth issue of internal organization concerns the period when there were offices on the two coasts (1971-78). This is important to discuss, given the number of democratic media which have tried to operate in more than one location. We could compare the *Guardian*'s bureaus in other cities, the different chapters of *Union Wage*, the multiple sites of Newsreel, not to mention the headaches of *Libération* in France and of *Tageszeitung* in West Germany around these very issues.[3] The merits of expansion, of having a base or bases outside the cultural metropolis in any country, are self-evident. The problems are also instructive, however, and must not be ducked.

In NACLA's case, the decision to add a California office seemed logical and important, given proximity to Mexico, a large Chicano population on the west coast, and that a sizable slice of NACLA's other constituencies was also near at hand. They decided that the offices would be co-equal, and would produce each issue alternately, with full autonomy, albeit under guidelines established by a joint annual meeting. Resources were divided equally. It seemed both very tidy and quite democratic.

In practice, the marathon annual ten-day meetings they used to have (for lack of funds to meet more often), were a hopelessly clumsy instrument to deal with problems as they arose. There was also insufficient money to communicate through long-distance telephone calls, even if that had been a viable way of proceeding. Financial and administrative requirements were necessarily duplicated, with resulting inefficient use of resources. In the mid-70s the strong focus within the marxist left on party-building also provided a new source of dissension, raising questions about the role of the *Report* in the context of the various attempts to construct new political organizations.

Very painfully, but much less acrimoniously than could easily have been the case, the decision was made in 1978 to close the California office and to concentrate on the New York office. In retrospect, this consolidation, along with the increased attention to promotion and distribution referred to already, seems to have served the *Report* very well.

The relation between NACLA's internal democracy and its responsiveness to its constituencies, has also been raised already in this account (the dilemmas of solidarity work, the use of its material in the U.S. and Latin America). Ideologically at least, this relationship in a project such as NACLA is critical, and utterly different from the marketing policy discussions which regularly take place in a conventional periodical. There the success of a commodity (the periodical) is guaranteed solely by its sales curve; in cases such as NACLA, that is only one dimension of the question, however necessary.

In 1982 the feeling of the collective was that they wanted to stimulate more effective contact and dialogue both with their general readers, and with student and activist users of the publication. The "Readers Respond" section of the magazine had been created to give the collective feedback either on how issues were used, or further comment on analyses presented, but letters were usually just supportive. Under consideration was a questionnaire to tell the staff who their readers were and what needs were or were not being met. They were also beginning to initiate closer pre-research discussions with relevant activist groups for direction on specific projects, as well as re-opening contacts with research institutes in Latin America that have emerged in recent years.

Another aspect of this attempt at outreach was their effort to improve the quality of their library service to the community. Consisting of books, journals, reports, clippings, both from North and South America, the library constituted a most valuable resource to many outside their own staff researchers. Rather than hang on to it for themselves, they were anxious that as many people as possible knew about and used the library. Improving its organization became the chief focus of a summer 1982 volunteer program.

Threats From Outside

The last aspect of the *NACLA Report* to which we shall devote attention is its harassment by the state. The collective has been subjected to intimidating actions by the powers that be, in line with so many other radical media in the pluralist democracy of the U.S. Under the Freedom of Information Act they were able to prove what they had always assumed, the tapping of their phones and the monitoring of their personal bank accounts by the FBI during the late 60s.

More recently, from March 1981, the Internal Revenue Service put the collective through an extended audit whose purpose was plainly to add a major burden to their workload.[4] Their accounts had always been kept carefully and honestly, but that was not enough; they had published and then re-issued a comic book on the Rockefeller dynasty, and the IRS agent regarded this as a particularly blatant example of "partisanship" (impugning the fairest flowers of the corporate world). Legally speaking, his strictures were *ultra vires*, as was laboriously but comprehensively proved by NACLA's lawyers in long consultation with the collective. In this, no doubt, lay the real point of the exercise, namely harassment. (*The Guardian* was to be put through the same mill in 1982.)

During 1981, NACLA was also slated (along with *Mother Jones* and some other publications) to be investigated by the Senate Subcommittee on Security and Terrorism. The collective took it that the wiretaps and surveillance had recommenced. They continued their work, unable to prevent this intrusion into their formal rights as U.S. citizens, but determined not to allow its strategic goal—their disconcertment and self-censorship—to be realized. As of the time of writing, no further developments were in view from this Senate subwatchdog of democracy.

To date, NACLA has managed not only to survive, but actually to expand and consolidate its operation. It has done so despite external attacks, and probably because of the confluence of three factors. These are its longstanding internal stability (not a chemistry easily achieved); its timely attention to sales and business practicalities; and last but certainly not least, the continued ferment in "Uncle Sam's backyard." Possibly the first and last factors have some relationship. It may be that a working political unity is rather easier to achieve on countries outside one's own, where in addition the basic focus is on exploitation, repression and the *fact* of resistance. Once the different strands of opposition have to be evaluated, especially their different strategies for the period following the overthrow of military dictatorship, then political unity becomes harder to maintain. In a discussion session begun in early 1982 on "Democracy and Revolution," in which they planned to look at different theories of democracy and their application in the context of struggle and social transformation, these problems would be more likely to surface. Perhaps also the growing assertiveness of the Indian populations of "Latin" America would raise difficult issues, as would emerging patterns of Soviet involvement with South American regimes. I am optimistic that NACLA would handle these problems illuminatingly; time will tell.[5]

Footnotes

1. Cited in H. Shapiro, "NACLA Reminiscences," *Report on the Americas* XV.5, (Sept.-Oct. 1981), p. 45.
2. Shapiro, p. 54.
3. See for instance F.-M. Samuelson, *Une Fois Il Était Libe* (Paris, Le Seuil, 1978).
4. S. Volk, "NACLA vs. the IRS," *Report on the Americas* XVI.4 (July-Aug. 1982), pp. 39-41.
5. See "Le réveil des Indiens de l'Amérique Latine," *Le Monde Diplomatique* 336 (March 1982), pp. 15-20; and the debate around the Miskito Indians in Nicaragua in *Akwesasne Notes* 14.3 (Early Summer 1982).

7

THIRD WORLD NEWSREEL

> Many film-makers are just like technicians. They
> don't *feel*. They have a colonized attitude toward their
> work, almost like a typist in an office-pool.
>
> Christine Choy
> Third World Newsreel

Location: New York
Activities: produces, distributes and exhibits independent flms
with a particular focus on Third World communities, women
and the working class.
Staff: three paid full-time; some interns and volunteers
Began: 1967, as New York Newsreel
Finance: from film rentals and grants.

From the earliest days of Newsreel to the present operation
of Third World Newsreel, a long, tempestuous saga has
unfolded. Its stormy evolution is very instructive, however, in
understanding the dynamics of democratic media, as well as
the specific problems faced by the progressive wing of the
independent film movement since the 1960s. This account will
summarize the collective's trajectory during its first 15 years,
mostly emphasizing three questions: the way the Third World
issue, in particular, surfaced in the organization; the changes
in organizational structure and priorities over those years; and
the changing definitions of political film-work inside the
project.

From 1967 to 1974: Newsreel becomes Third World Newsreel

The catalyst for Newsreel's formation was the failure of
the established media, especially T.V., to report extensive police
violence against a major anti-war demontration at the Pen-

tagon in late 1967. A number of individuals, overwhelmingly white and male, some with considerable means, some with experience in film-making, decided to form a politically committed film collective to service and expand the anti-war movement. From the start, then, Newsreel had a certain involvement with Third World issues, although its basic constituency was the white student movement and anti-war movement. About 50 people were involved in the project at that point, the leadership being largely from Students for a Democratic Society (SDS) and representing both its wings, cultural radicalism and committed marxism.

Their objectives in production were three, though only the last was actually realized: to get out political newsreels extremely fast, within a week of the event in question; to make films on political organizing; and to develop longer focus political education films.

Distribution was also a dimension of film-work that the organizers thought central from the beginning. Early on they hired a large van, and took their films into the streets of New York City and showed them to passers-by. A memorandum dated January 1968 stated:

> Our principal concern is the creation of what we call the community distribution network. This network is based on individuals and activist groups throughout the country, functioning as distributors at the grassroots level... The films become tools they use in the course of their work, and like any other tools, they help the group in its organizing work, and serve to bring the group into contact with more people...Our experience has been that when a group has films that are wanted, they are often given opportunities to speak to and work with groups that they might never otherwise be in contact with.[1]

Fairly soon the optimism of this statement was replaced with a rather more guarded and cautious position; the next statement dates from April 1968, just three months later:

> When we first started we deluded ourselves into thinking that...across the country there exists a monolithic movement called the "New Left" with hundreds of dedicated organizers starving to death because they

don't have films to organize with. Not only doesn't this group exist but the movement is hardly monolithic; its existence is vague and its direction almost invisible ...we should no longer be working under the impression that we are servicing any one group or organization.[2]

At the conclusion of this account of Newsreel we shall see how a similar concern with exhibition developed later; at this point it was seen as an automatic consequence of distribution, rather than as a moment in the process of film communication which must be analyzed seperately, and which bears directly on the processes of production and distribution. This was in line with Newsreel's belief in the early days that a film validated itself once it moved people; but the how's and why's of this impact went unanalyzed, empirically or theoretically. All the same, their concern with the politics of distribution was important.

The internal organization of Newsreel was ultra-democratic. There was a five-member co-ordinating committee whose decisions were subject to the judgement of the membership as a whole. This scrutiny included decisions on already edited films. Every film was screened, and its distribution in that form was subject to majority approval. Strenuous attempts were made to arrive at a consensus. If the majority, at least, did not approve, the film had to be re-edited or scrapped. (In urgent cases, film production could begin before majority approval was obtained.)

Over and above the question of the coordinating committee's composition—it consisted of white males, some wealthy, which rather accurately mirrored Newsreel's constituency—this democracy had some subterranean flaws. They were in the realms of "ideas" and "finance". There was a strong tendency for the ideas of the coordinating committee to be the ruling ideas. They were highly articulate individuals, well read in history, politics, film theory and marxism. Their analyses were fluent and plausible, as a reading of their published comments evinces.[3] Perhaps as a by-product of their articulate styles, rather than because they set out to achieve hegemony, they tended to appear at times as, in the words of a former Newsreel member, "The theoretical generals for an army of shitworkers."

Financially, too, the basis of Newsreel was opaque to the bulk of its members. Some members of the coordinating committee had trust-funds, others had access to wealthy donors: the wife of one committee member came from a leading distilling family, for example. Once the decision was democratically made to proceed with a particular film project, someone would say "O.K., I'll try to raise the money"; but the sources and the process were never discussed. The very term "business"— compare *The Guardian* at the same period—was shunned. Thus these material realities, so integral to a functioning democracy, were veiled in secrecy, even if partly by the implicit consent of the majority.

Despite these problems, Newsreel was on the crest of a wave. Its films were in very high demand on campuses, a demand made all the higher by the collective's readiness to let them out for free to groups who claimed they could not afford to rent them. Costs were also lowered by neglecting to insure prints on their way to or from their exhibition, truly a sign of the political ferment of the times as well as of a cavalier attitude toward finance. "Newsreels" existed in Boston, San Francisco, Los Angeles, Kingston, Ontario, and even London, England. Not all of them were as active as New York: in Los Angeles , for example, a high level of political theory of film work was developed, but no actual film! Nonetheless, the sense of mushroom expansion was exciting.

It probably served to gloss over some of the tougher realities which were about to obtrude. As the various national minority movements and the women's movement developed during the later 60s, it was inevitable that they should make themselves felt in *Newsreel*. Making films about these movments, like the one about the Puerto Rican Young Lords, was one thing. The internal organization of Newsreel was another. Let us examine two key areas in which these movements impacted on Newsreel itself. The women's movement made the first substantial dent; movements of Third World communities the second.

As we noted in the introduction to the U.S. case-studies, the women's movement was brought to birth in part by women's experiences of male chauvinism in the movements of the 60s. Newsreel was no exception. It could and did happen, that a male in the collective had slept with several of the women in it, according to a definition of free sexuality which required of "politically conscious" women that they demonstrate their emancipation by making themselves sexually available to "revolutionaries"—a common demand levelled at women in the 60s movement in many countries. Yet the subtle and not-so-subtle dynamics of this situation, while often expressed in clashes over political issues in Newsreel, was never openly expressed or placed on the political agenda.

Beginning around 1969, this covert reality began to be "named", as did male dominance of the project, by the women working in Newsreel. After a long series of emotionally charged meetings—themselves only some examples of quite frequent two or three day political marathon meetings—a number of the leading men began to move out. Other men remained, but not automatically in positions of leadership. Those who did move out, took their equipment with them—a pattern that was to be repeated in two years' time, when it had much more serious consequences. This time, some individuals with financial means remained in the organization.

The impact of Third World community movements on Newsreel came next, and very quickly. Two episodes sharply illuminate the dynamics of the impact, one being the reception accorded Christine Choy, the first non-white woman to join Newsreel (in 1971),[4] and the other being the saga of making *Finally Got The News* about the League of Revolutionary Black Workers in Detroit.[5]

On first arriving in Newsreel, Christine Choy found most people pretty unfriendly towards her. No one even showed her how to thread a projector. In line with the view that film content is everything, and that film technique is simply a bourgeois mystique, a movie camera was placed in her hands on May 1 in Washington D.C. and she was told to go ahead and shoot part of the anti-war demonstration! The curious balance between cold nonchalance and ultra-spontaneity in Newsreel at the time could hardly be more graphically illustrated.

However, because of her experience of having grown up in Shanghai after 1949, and thus having had direct experience of living in an (acceptable) communist regime, she achieved an early and meteoric promotion. Newsreel had recently taken to running its affairs through a quasi-leninist central committee, and she found herself jetted onto to it soon afterwards. Once they had realized the legitimacy her presence would supply to the committee, the decision was not long in the making. Her undoubted articulateness and forcefulness would almost certainly have been insufficient to get her there in themselves had it not been for these other factors, including the women's struggle in Newsreel. Her promotion is all the more remarkable when it is recalled that there was then an acute paranoia about infiltration by spies, and that all members had to go through a period of candidacy, followed by a political security vetting. She fulfilled all the categories: a woman, a non-white, background in a socialist country, politically revolutionary. With the best will in the world, it is hard to see that she was responded to other than as a bundle of categories, in a kind of multiple tokenism.

The Detroit film came a little earlier in Newsreel's history, but is also illuminating as an instance of the difficulties Newsreel experienced in moving beyond solidarity with Southeast Asia and anti-war involvement. To understand the significance of the Detroit episode, it is first necessary to recall that San Francisco Newsreel had become virtually the film unit of the Black Panther Party. Their 1968 filmed interview with Huey Newton in jail, at a time when T.V. news would not have dreamt of interviewing him because of his dangerous radicalism, not only had considerable impact—here *was* the revolutionary army's leader—but impelled New York Newsreel to commit itself to the Panther political line, in order to prove its close links with the black struggle. At a time when black militants mostly refused to discuss anything with whites, even with those against the system, San Francisco's "coup" was too exciting to do anything but identify with totally.

Then a number of Newsreel people from New York visited Detroit in 1969 to discover there an authentic, autonomous black revolutionary movement which was organizing a union outside the UAW—the Dodge Revolutionary Union Movement— several of whose leaders officially espoused marxist politics. The complication was that the League of Revolutionary Black Workers, the organizers of DRUM, explicitly and strongly rejected Panther analysis and tactics. Not defining the Black lumpenproletariat as the central revolutionary force, rejecting the Weatherman tactics of clandestinity and armed action with which the Panthers sympathized, the League argued in more conventional marxist terms for the centrality of the Black working class as vanguard of the revolution at that time in U.S. history.

When the Newsreel members proposed making a film about the League to the leading figures in New York the response was less than fully enthusiastic. They began to ask a lot of blocking questions. Who are the League? Are they just a flash in the pan? What are their real class politics? What relation would a film about them have to the anti-war movement? And—this being the nub—what about the Panthers? In the end, faced with these maneuvers, those who wanted to make the film went and raised the money themselves—one even doing so illegally as a large-scale marijuana dealer and ending up in prison.

It can be seen from this episode how Newsreel got itself into a difficult bind through its total immersion in the politics of the moment as they bore on the issue of racial oppression in the U.S. Their thinking appears to have been (at least at the top) that if one bridge could be constructed into a militant black organization, then it had to be hung on to at all costs. Freedom to argue about the direction of progressive politics was perilously close to being thrown away.

One final aspect of this saga is also worth recounting. When the crew was shooting the film in Detroit, there was a major split in the League's leadership over whether the film should be made at all. Its crew had to endure a fair amount of verbal confrontation in the streets because some League members refused to identify themselves with the project, and would not validate the film crew's presence to young Afro-Americans. Even those in the League who wanted it made, wanted it for a black workers' audience, not the white student audience that was Newsreel's base at the time. The crew found itself caught between three lines of fire, two on site and one back home.

As Newsreel expanded, problems of this kind were bound to emerge. At the end of the last section, the observation was made that it is much easier to analyze oppression, especially overseas, than to work out a commitment to one or another strategy for change. The clash within Newsreel on *Finally Got The News* exemplified the difficulty. The clumsy white sincerity of supporting black movements uncritically, because it was the price to be paid for recognition as a genuine ally, was a mood to be lived through; as was the same sincerity, woodenly expressed in the almost instant promotion of Christine Choy to the Central Committee. Such, arguably, was part of the price of the McCarthyite destruction of a political generation, combined with the foully knotted politics of racism in the U.S.

To take the story through to the emergence of Third World Newsreel demands attention to two further aspects of Newreel's development. One is the "leninist" phase it went through; the other, its three-way split in 1972-73 between the Third World group, the poorer whites, and the wealthy whites. Let us take each in turn.

The early 70s were a tense and intense period politically. The FBI was busy persecuting the underground media,[6] Watergate was being perpetrated, and the Nixon-Agnew team was constantly threatening both media and universities. Police repression of Black movements was acute. Newsreel actually organized a clandestine film processing laboratory in Boston, convinced that police might swoop in at any time and carry off their undeveloped film. (Most collective members were kept unaware of its location, and all were strictly urged not to discuss its existence with anyone.) Entry to Newsreel became hedged about with a period of candidacy, followed by a political security check. The formation of the quasi-leninist central committee followed this line of reasoning closely.

Indeed, many felt that the ideal outcome would be for a revolutionary party to emerge, along the lines of Lenin's *What Is To Be Done?* They would then hopefully be adopted as the film arm of the party. They did not seem to recognize that there was no parallel at the time in the U.S. to the Tsarist ban on political activity or trade unions, or to Tsarist censorship. This type of politics could not and did not last very long. People began questioning particular central committee directives. Women continued to question the narrow basis of that kind of politics. And the few Third World members began to insist on the priority of their issues for film-making.

With the emergence of a Third World caucus in 1972, Newsreel once more began to divide internally: the Third World group, the "Have's" (the wealthy whites); and the "Have-not's" (the poorer whites). These were the terms everyone used. In practice, the "Have-not's" tended to line up with the Third World group against the "Have's". Both the first groups lived communally in two separate houses and caucusing was therefore much easier for them than for the "Have's" who lived individually. Nonetheless, the situation became further complicated when some of the "Have" women began sleeping with some Third World men. The reactions of the Third World women were predictable. The conflicts of nationalism were everywhere, and Newsreel reached its maximum point of disunity and confusion.

This situation, too, could not last, anymore than the attempt to impose an unthinking leninism. The "Have's" left, taking their equipment with them, and moved into their own independent film-making. The "Have-not's" joined sects such as the October Legaue, Revolutionary Union, and Harper's Ferry, arguing that political organizing was logically prior to film-making. The disarray is indicated by the fact that no one left knew the lease was up till the realtor told them the day before. Only three of the Third World group turned up the next day to move films and files to new premises. These were promptly burglarized.

It looked like the end. There was no money, no film cata-logue, no rental income. The collective was living off of welfare, which paid their rent and gave them another twenty dollars a week. But tenacity began to have its rewards. They put in a grant proposal for film-making to the New York State Council on the Arts. It was initially turned down, but they rewrote it offering to make three films for $10,000. Perhaps out of surprise at this shoe-string proposal, the money came through. And they made all three films as promised—which put them in a good position for future grant money. Their internal troubles, however, had one more episode to run. They discovered that one of their own members, one of the few who had been stead-fastly loyal and ready to help throughout this troubled period, had been gently siphoning off small amounts from the funds. He was apprehended by the bank in which they deposited the new grant from NYSCA in the process of signing over no less than $4,000 to his own account. He was discovered in time, but the personal trauma was deep.

Looking back over the years of Newsreel, it can be seen how the tumults in the society outside repeatedly surfaced inside, in ways different at points and similar at others to the ways they surfaced in *The Guardian* and KPFA. The expe-rience of learning politics from scratch, which was true of much of the political movement at large, was also true of News-reel. Despite the chaos, the process was fundamentally con-structive, which is why it is particularly important that it be set down.

Third World Newsreel from 1974

To understand the evolution of Third World Newsreel from this time until the early 80s it is necessary to focus on three issues: its developing theoretical awareness both of politics and of film-making; its changing view of how to organize film-work; and its increasing focus on the importance of exhibition and audience development.

Although a number of people who had dominated News-reel were well read in film history and theory, as well as in socialist politics, the dominant view at the time was that film content was everything, and attention to form was bourgeois avant-gardism. To want to make a film was enough; if you made it, and people were moved by it, then that was its final justification. As regarded political analysis, Mao and Che were sufficient for all purposes. The Little Red Book was much in evidence.

As Third World Newsreel consolidated itself after 1974, its members began to move beyond some of these simplicities. For the first time, especially during 1976-78, they settled down to the serious study of marxist classics, such as Lenin's *State and Revolution*, Mao's *Talk at the Yenan Forum on Literature and Art*, Marx's *Critique of the Gotha Program* and parts of *Capital*. This was an advance, in the sense that hitherto much of the U.S. Left reflected the strong anti-intellectualist strain in U.S. culture. It was also a necessary stage along the way, in that only by thorough study was it brought home that whatever the value of marxist classics, their illumination is next to nil in the specifics of revolutionary film-making. Some people joined marxist-leninist sects for a while, in the vain hope that this would somehow invigorate their perceptions of film work.

Toward the end of this period, they began to focus on the more subtle writers on cultural politics, such as Walter Benjamin, and the more personally and psychologically oriented writers such as Wilhelm Reich and R.D. Laing. These writers' location within the marxist tradition was a necessary legitimating bridge for the collective to begin to consider other perspectives on film, neo-marxist or not. They joined a study group on culture and Third World politics at the Center for Puerto Rican Studies, which looked at texts from around the world on this subject. At the same time, the growth of film schools and general media awareness inside the U.S. developed a greater consciousness at large of media and film theory and criticism. All these factors, Third World Newsreel now feels, were very important in its change of direction, enabling it to respond to the present phases of American society more flexibly and effectively.

The second issue, the question of organizing film-work, is equally important. One of the long-standing failures of Third World Newsreel, like Newsreel before it, was to talk perpetually about itself as a "collective" without ever pinpointing what that term might mean. This failure was not peculiar to itself, but in the course of its members' work for the study group at the Center for Puerto Rican Studies, they came to focus at one stage on ICAIC, the film production center of Cuba. Its firmly framed procedures bluntly contradicted many of their previous ultra-democratic assumptions about how revolutionary film-work is organized. (In a sense, the utopian image of Cuba was confronted at the right moment with the actual fact of Cuba.)

From their own experience, and their reflections on other models of organization, Third World Newsreel came to believe that a truly collective film production is only possible within a socialist environment. All film, in reality, is a collective endeavor; but to be a collective activity in the sense of having a directorial committee rather than a director, is—they would argue—impossible in a capitalist environment, for some very practical reasons. To get money to produce films, if you are not wealthy already, is extremely difficult without a clear track record as a film director. In these conditions, a directorial collective will quickly produce cliques, each seeking to stamp their mark on the film; this process can very easily paralyze film-making. Furthermore, to combine fund-raising, film production, and office work, in a swift cancellation of the division of labor, and expect to be able to give any of them the needed concentration, is an absurdity. In their view, co-direction is as far as the system will allow the collective impulse to express itself; and this they have done.

The other dimension of organizing film-work at Third World Newsreel which they have come to emphasize is the reality of personal feelings. In earlier days, pure self-dedication was felt to be sufficient in and of itself to ensure that the organization would function constructively and productively. We have seen how this hope failed to be realized, and how the denial of personal feelings led to emotionally charged confrontations precisely because feelings were off the public agenda. In the old days people were never fired because they were personally incompatible (only purged, as Christine Choy wryly remarked); yet in small organizations, personal compatibilities are central to daily functioning. The greater success of Third World Newsreel since 1980 lay, they felt, in its members' recognition that they constituted a tiny group of individuals with different skills who had learned to get on with one another. Not to be able to do that was no longer "just one of those things"; and mechanical rotation of tasks or mechanical de-centralization of power were regarded as purposeless in such a small setting.

At the same time, the principle of more or less equal pay for members continued to be seen as being as constructive a policy as it has so often elsewhere (see other case-studies from Portugal, Italy and this country). It means that a potentially serious source of resentment and competitiveness is removed from the project. It would, then, be a major inaccuracy to conclude that all the bag and baggage of capitalist business methods had simply resurfaced inside Third World Newsreel as a result of "bitter experience". The overall objectives of the organization have expanded, deepened and become much more realizable over the years, rather than fundamentally altering. What has significantly altered is the group's understanding of how to achieve those objectives.

The last dimension of Third World Newsreel's attempt to remould itself is the increased attention it has given to exhibition. In the mid-70s there was one movie theater which served as outlet for its films. When that closed down, Pearl Bowser, an Afro-American woman with considerable experience as an archivist of Afro-American films, was made a member of the collective. Her task was to promote exhibition of the existing stock of films, to develop their audience, and to bring her particular interest in independent black cinema to bear on the collective's work (a task also undertaken in a major way by the Black Film-Makers' Foundation in New York City.) Sometimes her job involved travelling with the films and lecturing at their showing. Sometimes she acted as writer of the program notes, or selector of a particular package of films. The work might also involve getting local groups to mobilize interested organizations and audiences in their area to turn out for a particular film series.

Her experience in getting independent black films shown (for instance Tom Gunn's *Ganja and Hess*, or Haile Gerima's films), including in the white alternative and "progressive" arena, is instructive. Overwhelmingly, critics and exhibition organizers define black films as something apart, not quite normal, and definitely "less than" white films of whatever genre. Their aesthetic, which is often not the same as the aesthetic of white American films, is covertly or overtly defined as unacceptable. People who would bend double to accomodate themselves to the new aesthetics of a Godard or a Fassbinder or a Jancsó, will not make the slightest effort to do so for Afro-American film aesthetics. Paternalistic comments such as "Even black people wouldn't understand it" are heard. All kinds of excuses will be made for poor Polish or French film-work; none for black film-work. The nuances and allusions of the latter regularly remain unnoticed. Only the affirmative action clauses of federal grants put any real pressure on video and film exhibitors to pay serious attention to black cinema. (With any slackening of these pressures, or any decline in overall funding, it is clear which films will be the first targets for exclusion.) As with other independent films in the U.S., an important route to acceptability is often their acclaim by European critics and television program companies. The American critics are always anxious not to be too far behind the European avant-garde.

These experiences are important, not only in themselves, but because they underline that the barriers to Third World film distribution and exhibition can often include a strong dose of racism. The problems are not limited to distributors' inexperience or a less receptive economic climate. If the U.S. is to mature as a society, one key component of that maturation has to be the growth of general alertness to Afro-American culture and realities, and nowhere is this easier than when expressed in their own terms in the media. For any substantial social change to take place in a revolutionary sense, this development is even more critical.

The overall experience of focusing more closely on film exhibition has given Third World Newsreel a stronger feeling for its own audiences, and this in turn has a useful impact on its values in production. Audiences cease to be an abstract rental-paying entity, and become known. A certain intimacy and respect can develop with them, essential for committed film-making. It become easier to know what kinds of communication are useless. Didacticism, the standard vice of "progressive" films, is avoided more easily. To overcome or at least lessen this communication gap in alternative media work is equally to the point as trying to uproot the division of labor in media production.

Footnotes

1. Cited in M. Teodori (ed), *The New Left*, Indianapolis: Bobbs-Merrill 1969, pp. 388-9.

2. Cited in M. Teodori, *op.cit.*, p. 391.

3. See J.S. Katz (ed), *Perspectives on the Study of Film*, New York: Little Brown, 1971, pp. 234-246; and "New York Newsreel: towards a new definition of propaganda", *Leviathan* 1.6 (October-November 1969) pp. 27-30.

4. Sherry Millner, "Interview with Christine Choy: Third World Newsreel, ten years of left film", *Jump Cut* 27 (1982) pp. 21-22, 39.

5. D. Georgakas & M. Surkin, *Detroit: I Do Mind Dying*, New York: St. Martin's Press 1975, ch. 6.

6. G. Rips, *The Campaign Against the Underground Press*, San Francisco: City Lights 1981.

8

CALIFORNIA NEWSREEL

Location: downtown San Francisco
Activities: mainly distributes films on Southern Africa and on strategies for the U.S. labor movement in the 1980s. Some production. Growing attention to exhibition.
Paid full-time staff: four
Began: 1968 (as San Francisco Newsreel)
Funding: mostly from distribution

In writing about California Newsreel, I shall be more concerned to analyze its experience of distributing films and of producing and exhibiting them, than in its history or internal political problems. As a core group of three from 1975 to 1981, when it was augmented by a fourth, its internal political experience does not raise the organizational problems of larger groups. This is not to say, of course, that its life has always been one of pure harmony, but clearly the continued close cooperation of these three individuals over a period of years has as much if not more to do with the development of their personal adjustment to one another than with any formal division of labor or structure of authority.

They had identical pay-levels (1982, $5.85 an hour), and also very compatible backgrounds, personal styles, types of wit and verbal repartee. These features operated very cohesively. It was indicative of this that one of their members could tell the writer quite frankly that all their major arguments internally were about ego: it bespoke a level of adjustment and self-reflection as a working group that was important to its functioning. The same person was equally candid about the implications of the fact that the three long-serving members were white males, although the new fourth was an Afro-American male. In his judgment, the original triad's culture was male, had built up over an extended period, and would be difficult for a woman to join and feel at ease within, given the few people involved and their close working relationship. He felt the group had a reasonably good sensitization to issues affecting women, without making any exaggerated claims to a feminist consciousness.

These aspects of California Newsreel are not mentioned at the outset because they are its most important feature, but because they present yet another case to readers of how alternative media institutions are organized. Is it the same issue in 1982 to have an all-male membership, as it was to have an all-male leadership in the original Newsreel in New York in 1968? How should the need to have a functioning institution, with an awareness of issues raised by the women's movement, be balanced against the need to institutionalize that awareness within it by the presence of feminists? Is that kind of head-counting appropriate to a tiny organization? Both this and the previous case-study suggest these problems are less easily soluble in small collectives than in large ones.

Let us now pass on to the question of what California Newsreel does politically speaking, within the progressive wing of the independent film movement. Its main activity today is distribution, though it does get involved in production from time to time, and is beginning to pay more and more attention to the question of exhibition. When the shell of San Francisco Newsreel (its original title) was handed over to the three individuals already referred to in 1975, its activity was limited to distributing anti-war and prison support films, together with a few documentaries from or about other countries, especially Vietnam, North Korea and China. The people who handed it over had taken over its running a year or two previously from the maoist Revolutionary Union, but without the slightest practical notion of why they wanted to do so. Receipts from film rentals totalled $16,000 at the point of transfer.

Those who took it over accounted themselves marxists, with a particular anti-imperialist bent. They set to work to regularize and improve distribution, and to begin work on a film about U.S. transnationals in the Third World, eventually to appear as *Controlling Interest* in 1978. Work on the film took an exceptionally long time because of their lack of funds, some of the film being shot in black and white video for that reason.

Then, in 1976, Soweto exploded. Interest in California Newsreel's documentaries on South Africa rose sharply. They found themselves buying a fourth, then a fifth, then a sixth print of their films of South Africa. Both this level of interest in South Africa, and its political centrality within imperialism, suggested to them that they might usefully set themselves up as the media arm of a non-centralized support movement for southern African liberation struggles. They brought out a flier entitled the Southern Africa Media Center, and the project was immediately successful. Demands for films poured in, and it became possible for the first time to pay their own salaries (previously they had been living on unemployment compensation).

They discovered that by concentrating on a single issue they could use pre-existing mailing lists; they could reduce the size of their catalog and so save on printing and postage; and they could become established as a reliable source of film material on that issue. Over time they began to understand much more precisely the mechanics of film distribution: what networks existed that should be tapped, the differing utility of particular mailing lists, in short their own approach to what is often termed "market segmentation." On southern Africa, they had some claim by 1982 to be the largest film resource center in the world, distributing foreign documentaries (eg from British television) as well as more politically committed films. Financially, they were now in a position to survive without grants, though not to expand their work.

Their second major focus as distributors arose partly from the experience of making *Controlling Interest*, a film which defines imperialism as the key political agenda item both for the Third World and the U.S. (in the shape of run-away shops and unemployment). In retrospect, having buried themselves for several years in trying to get it finished, they came to consider their political agenda too narrow in focus, particularly as regards the U.S. They began, therefore, to develop film distribution on the problems facing working people in the U.S., and particularly on how new strategies might be developed by labor for the post-boom era. Their politics on this issue came to be more and more closely identified with those of the British trade union shop stewards in Lucas Aerospace, whose best known exponent is Mike Cooley.[1] Briefly, this group of shop stewards used their understanding of the technical processes of their firm in the British defense industry, to set out a detailed alternative production and investment strategy. Their plan was formulated, as Cooley emphasizes, through a survey of the workers in the firm, designed by the shop stewards. The results were that instead of the machinery of war and destruction, the plant could be developed, they and the workers argued, to manufacture a whole series of humane and constructive products. Examples included kidney machines, a low-cost power generating complex potentially of great use to Third World countries, and energy conservation devices, to mention only a few. (Not surprisingly, perhaps, Cooley was finally fired from his job at Lucas Aerospace in 1981: capitalism's reward for constructive thinking.)

The essence of this approach is that economic and industrial problems have now reached a point at which corporate executives are bankrupt in solutions to them. This is not to say that there is no more money to be made in capitalism. Simply that levels of unemployment, and of wasteful, destructive use of technology and scientific development have now risen to a societally disastrous point, with no visible prospect of reverse. (Compare the position of *Akewesasne Notes*.)

To this capitalist nemesis, the basic answer proposed is workers' democracy: the direct involvement of producers, not in dropping notes into the firm's suggestion box, but in formulating investment plans, production methods, and marketing organization. This "involvement" should not by understated. By it is meant the power of workers to determine the economic future, on the one hand; and on the other hand, the dissolution of corporate economic power, not merely the democratization of management in a capitalist economy. The process is not visualized as taking place on the leninist model of an armed insurrection to overthrow the state, nor is it seen as happening easily, without fierce conflict, but as a process in which, during which, the working class develops its self-understanding as the only class—the majority—capable of planning the future for social needs possessed of a detailed knowledge of production possiblities.

Unlike the newspaper *In These Times*, which pursues a social democratic politics solely within the power structure and the intelligentsia, and unlike Tom Hayden's Campaign for Economic Democracy, which by 1982 was sliding ever more rapidly into the standard political opportunism of the Democratic Party, California Newsreel saw itself as pursuing a democratic socialism at the grassroots, among workers themselves. This expressed itself in their second major project, *Media At Work*, which distributes a series of films on the labor process, and on workers' planning for a new economic strategy. In 1982 they were also hard at work producing a new film on Pittsburgh steelworkers threatened with plant closures. The film was designed as a critique of Reaganomics' claim to be able to revitalize the U.S. economy, and as an exploration of the alternative, workers' democracy. They had deliberately chosen a traditional bastion of well-paid male labor, in order to evoke and yet question the applicability of the "ordinary american worker." (In fact, interestingly, one of the steel workers they were interviewing most intensively in the film, was a woman; another, a black man.)

California Newsreel had also brought out a brochure, *Planning Work*, with the following chapter headings: Planning Work; Shopfloor Employment Monitoring; Counter-Planning; Planning for Investment; Planning for Technology; The Detroit Model. Based very much on the Lucas Aerospace model, it sought to give workers a highly practical guide to developing their own economic counter-strategies to capital, in conjunction with the film possibilities of California Newsreel. Importantly, in connection with this study, the brochure's afterword made it clear to its readers that its contents had been produced on a word-processor and stored in a magnetic disc. This, it emphasized, meant that the experience of using the brochure in different plants could be fed back to California Newsreel, and relatively easily incorporated into an improved version, by way of deletions or additions. This approach underlined the potentially constructive, democratic uses of new technology, including communications technology, that can be grasped by the left if it so chooses.

Thus by 1982, California Newsreel had decided to specialize in these two major areas, southern Africa and alternative strategies for the U.S. economy. If they were to expand at all, their feeling was that the expansion would be in the rest of Africa. As of summer 1982, these remained discussion points only.

The last dimension of California Newsreel's work to be reviewed is its increasing interest in the practicalities of film exhibition. as with the independent film and video movement in general, this is a key issue, especially so once film is defined as an instrument in developing political debate, rather than simply for sharpening aesthetic sensibility. It is not simply whether films are to be seen (distribution) which matters, but in what context. This as we argued earlier, needs to taken very seriously. The person added to the original California Newsreel trio had previously been involved in exhibition work in Philadelphia, and his appointment signalled an intensification of the group's awareness of its importance.

An example of the way the issue expresses itself was to be seen on an occasion in 1979 when the Southern Africa Media Center requested help from a number of black churches in a national drive they were planning to raise awareness of southern Africa. Initially, representatives of 200 black congregations met at the UN. Forty subsequently organized events in their own churches around the question; twenty of these used films. This illustrates the practical possibilities of using films to help develop political awareness, at least in a highly motivated segment of society.

In response to these and similar experiences, California Newsreel has developed brochures which give potential filmusers a whole cluster of practical information about film use. They contain everything from a description of a simple check on the room beforehand for acoustic problems, through a description of each film they distribute and a multiple grading of its utility. The grading is refreshingly frank, and came from an independent evaluation by the African Studies Center of the University of Michigan. One film on Namibia, for instance, is commended for dealing with the liberation movements, but graded only 2 in a scale of 1 to 5 as a film. This kind of honesty in political distribution is directly related to a concern for exhibition. If the people watching the film are simply seen as so many objects who somehow pay for its rental, than the whole purpose of an alternative media institution is lost. If people exist as political actors, they must be treated with respect and concern about their reactions.

There are many other details about exhibition which demand discussion such as the relative utility of trying to get film-makers to come along to discuss their work, compared with having someone from the local group or community lead a discussion. California Newsreel is keenly aware, for instance, of the problems in showing a powerful film about South Africa, and then seeing the shock and anger in people dissipate as they realize the gulf between what they feel and what they can actually do. The organization's experience of exhibition will clearly grow, and hopefully be widely discussed. Its brochures already contain practical advice to film discussion-leaders on how to handle a good debate after a film, what standard problems to avoid, the importance of a good introduction to films, and other issues.

California Newsreel's experience led it to one other practical conviction. It is that educational institutions, from university labor studies centers to community colleges, are the crucial avenues to independent film exhibition in the foreseeable future. Few other bodies or groups have the same continuity, or access to equipment, space and some rental funds. Other bodies often have fewer individuals who will act as informed discussants of films. In other places, there may not exist the same type of audience, already geared to consideration of certain problems. In the U.S. situation, this is much less elitist as a strategy for developing the use of independent film than it might be in many other countries, since in the U.S. about half the population attends college at some point in their lives. California Newsreel's experience in this respect requires serious reflection.

Footnotes

1. Mike Cooley, *Architect or Bee?*, South End Press, Boston, 1982, ch. 4.

9

INDEPENDENT PUERTO RICAN FILM-MAKING

Puerto Rico, on one important level, does not belong in a survey of alternative media in the USA. Colonized by the U.S. government in 1898 ostensibly to liberate it from the Spanish, but actually for its cheap sugar, it enjoys today neither statehood nor independence. Not until after World War II, with the increased assertiveness of the independence movement, were Puerto Ricans allowed to elect their own governor. Not until that time did it cease to be a criminal offense in Puerto Rico to possess a Puerto Rican national flag.

The differences between political life in Puerto Rico and the U.S. reflect this history. Arguments for and against statehood, for and against national independence, are common coin in the island. It is small enough geographically, but large enough demographically (3 million inhabitants, or five times the Alaskan population) for vigorous political movements to coalesce quite readily. Thus political debate is concerned with much more basic issues than is generally the case in the U.S., with the severe economic deprivation of large sections of the population also serving to focus political thought and activity much more intensely than in most of the mainland.

Independent film-making had no existence in Puerto Rico until 1970. The only film-making that took place at all was in advertizing, and even there the field was completely occupied by non-nationals, either from the U.S. or other Latin American countries. In that year, however, a group of Puerto Ricans, from the country itself, or with a New York background, decided it was past time that this situation was remedied.

146

"With no capital, only commitment," as one of them put it, they formed themselves into a group called Sandino Films. It was much more of a verbal than a practical commitment, insofar as only one of them had any experience at all with any aspect of film-making. They had no capital in the sense of technical equipment, either. Their numbers included a history professor who decided to quit his job, and a recently graduated literature student. They were indeed starting from scratch.

It was clear to them from the start that any films they made would have to be commissioned or self-financed, since wealthy donors with an interest in critical films were practically speaking an absent category in Puerto Rico. Self-financed production, given their lack of resources, could only mean their joining the television advertizing industry and seeking to generate enough funds over time by making commercials, to produce the kind of films they really wanted to make. Needless to say, these would be films that attempted to portray aspects of Puerto Rican life almost completely absent from Puerto Rican television screens and film theaters, for the very good reason that neither Washington D.C. nor its Puerto Rican clientele was desirous of seeing them there. For instance, their first completed project was a 30-minute documentary on the islet of Culebra, which was used for bombing practice by U.S. Marines, who repeatedly and flagrantly disregarded the distance limits set by the U.S. government between bomb practice areas and human populations, overflying the islet's villages with live bombs, and sometimes exploding them by accident on the beaches. (To say nothing of the sound pollution involved.)

Their next project was commissioned by U.S. Public Television, following the Young Lords' 1972 invasion of its New York studios to press their demand for proper programming on Puerto Rican affairs. The response was a magazine format program called *Realidades*, and as one item Sandino Films were asked to make a film about Puerto Rican veterans of the Vietnam war. *GI José* was the result. Once it was clear to the Channel 13 authorities that the necessary expertise was available, the group was then in a position to suggest its own program ideas to Public Television with a reasonable chance they would be accepted.

Examples of the films they were allowed to make are interesting for their choice of topics. They included one on the village of Piñones, a black settlement of centuries' standing that the government proposed to relocate in order to "develop" the island. Another was on a Puerto Rican poetess, Julia de Burgos, who had died in New York in the 50s. Another was on a hero of the 1868 Lares insurrection against Spanish rule. Yet another was on the historical adoption of Catholic religious saints and symbols by African slaves, banned from practicing their own religion. The film analyzed how this adoption was actually a concealed adaptation of Catholic emblems, with their content being effectively subverted in favor of the leading figures of the African religions at issue. The group felt itself in some ways to be in an analogous position, operating through the constraints and strictures of official television in order to try to convey its own sense of the Puerto Rican situation.

Organizing the film-making during the earliest days of the collective was ultra-democratic, rather on the pattern of Third World Newsreel. Everyone had the right to speak about everything, to have a voice in everything. As elsewhere, so here, this interpretation of the meaning of collective labor was found to be hopelessly unrealistic. The group's members were of widely differing experience, ages, levels of social awareness. Some could handle the technical side, others could not. Some were able to be businesslike about finance, others were not. Yet discussion presumed everyone to be at exactly the same point of ability on all scores. The result was, once again, interminable discussion that sometimes descended into personalities because it was simply one person's view against another's, without there being any recognized basis for decisions. The personal irritations engendered by these endless arguments would then play their part in subsequent discussions, muddying the water still further.

One feature of this type of organizing which often plagues it was notably absent from this group: lack of discipline. Everyone was always agreed on the importance of being on time, of deadlines, of budgets. The sense of practical purpose in the group was strong.

Out of this experience, Sandino Films decided to restructure their operation, assigning authority over the selection of topics, deployment of personnel, allocation of budgets, fundraising and finance decisions, to two individuals. Debate, often intense, still took place among the entire production team through the shooting and editing process, but there is now a known, explicit authority which can take action when further discussion would hinder the project (compare *Lotta Continua*).

Almost all the individuals involved have known and worked with each other over a long period of time, with the result that their working relationships have matured in a way quite uncharacteristic of even independent film-making in the U.S. and elsewhere. The situation never arose, although familiar enough in other places, where an unknown cameraperson could be hired in to form "part of the team," while having no basic sympathy with the project at stake. On this and other grounds, as we shall see below, the group felt that its own work—despite its limitations—was a much different and preferable form of independent film-making than the customary models of even critical or radical film-making in the U.S.

The most difficult internal problem the group faced was the frustration of wanting to make meaningful documentaries while being tied to producing an interminable stream of commercials in whose purposes they had little interest. Their feeling is not unique in the advertizing industry, but that scarcely makes it easier to bear. For some, the combination of alienation and frustration became so intolerable after a while that they felt impelled to leave the group, some going to do media work elsewhere, others leaving the field altogether. For those who remained, the conviction grew that one step should be taken at a time, and also that the time to reflect carefully in advance on future projects was probably a good deal more useful than charging into half-baked ventures at a gallop. Nonetheless, the frustration of being bound up in work which was just that and nothing else, never left them.

Their worst period financially speaking was 1977-78. It ws a period when their documentaries had become quite widely known in Puerto Rico. They had done two episodes in 1975 for a TV series called *Caribe* produced by Quinn Martin (otherwise best known for *The Streets of San Francisco* and *The Untouchables*) and a large-budget film for a Mexican company. They had also, however, produced a play which created many waves in the Puerto Rican establishment, about a New York Puerto Rican junkie in jail whose perspectives are drastically altered through meeting Puerto Rican nationalists imprisoned there since the 1950s. For raising the tender subjects of national life, they became labelled by furious, intellectually sclerotic, but influential figures on the island as communists, whose talents as TV advertising producers should not be contracted by responsible business clients. In the small society which is Puerto Rico, this amounted to an attempt to declare them anathema.

Gradually, however, their fortunes revived, thanks mainly to the fact that their work in advertizing had developed an excellent reputation for professionalism and honesty (not a dominant trait in the industry). And because as individuals they hardly fit the image of sour-faced Kremlin-governed robots! Individuals at a number of points in the advertizing industry, who did not suffer from the "blinkered vision" of their senior directors, were not swayed from using their professional services.

More recent films have focussed on women workers; on the Cuban ballerina Alicia Alonso; on the development of sports in Puerto Rico; and on civil rights and community organizing. A further word on each of these last two is in order. Sports have a role in Puerto Rico not readily appreciated by outsiders. Over and above their usual popularity in any country, in Puerto Rico they have an added significance. The only point at which the country participates in international events *as* a country is in the Olympic Games. Thus this represents the only avenue presently legitimated for national identity and aspiration. This dimension could be seen also in their 1982 film on the Central American Games, which had been scheduled to be played in Puerto Rico. Because of the political animosity between the Puerto Rican Olympic Committee's president, formerly an active nationalist, and the pro-statehood governor, the latter refused permission for the Games to be held in Puerto Rico. The Olympic Committee president promptly switched the venue to Cuba! And this film's making was financed by a wealthy Cuban exile living in Puerto Rico. It was the first documentary ever distributed commercially throughout the island, and was countrywide the fifth most successful film of the year.

The film on civil rights raises a different issue, one which repeatedly comes up in our other case studies; the involvement of the wider community in film-making, and—as an acid test of that—the involvement of women in the process. From the perspective of the group, the trap to be avoided was having token, symbolic women—or for that matter, black people, or "workers"—in order to validate their films. The reality of the social movements in Puerto Rico was that women were highly salient in them, not as feminists who had decided on that basis to get involved in a particular campaign, but as people directly affected by the conflict who felt impelled to do something about it. They were often at the forefront becaue they were the most articulate and strategically clear individuals in their communities. Thus in the film on civil rights and community organizing, women were prominent in providing information and in acting as consultants during shooting, over and above their speaking on camera. For the group, this indicated a living involvement of women, even though its core members (presently five, with another fifteen free-lancing) were overwhelmingly male. Certainly the civil rights film had been shown all over the island, with almost certain reinforcement of women's activism and leadership. (The situation in this respect is reminiscent of Portugal, as will become obvious in the next section).

Other films made in the 1980s included *Puerto Rico Libre* and *Puerto Rico: A Colony in the American Way*. Both raised the hot issues of nationalism and colonialism. As a prod to meaningful public debate around a variety of key problems of the society, the group—although it dissolved as Sandino Films in 1982 in favor of a much looser structure of occasional involvement in film-making—had clearly continued to make a serious contribution to culture and public debate in Puerto Rican society.

We should conclude by noting the main differences between independent film-making in Puerto Rico and the U.S. Some have been commented on already: the fact that the group in Puerto Rico is composed of individuals who have worked over a long period of time together (rather than the situation of the independent director with a "name" and revolving film-crew personnel); the fact that money for independent film-making is simply not a feature of Puerto Rico (with the single exception of the Central American Games film mentioned). But perhaps the most critical difference is that independent films inside the U.S., even critical ones, are not a vital component in national debate—with the possible exception of anti-nuclear films in the late 70s and into the 80s. In Puerto Rico, the political context of independent films acts as a catalyst of widespread reflection and analysis in Puerto Rico to a markedly higher degree than in the U.S. They are elements in a continuing ferment.

10

CONCLUSIONS

What potential impact on national politics do these media have for the remainder of this century? They have not so far hit the spectacular heights of radical media in the 1974-75 Portuguese explosion or the 1968 Prague Spring, but does this mean they are destined to play only a tangential part in future developments?

To answer this question, we have to settle in our minds what we think would be a significant impact for them to achieve. Judging their role by their size alone is the kind of fallacy which used to be unkindly thought of as typically Texan (a fallacy the FBI has carefully eschewed).

As against such instant empiricism, we need to bear in mind some easily overlooked dimensions of the issue. For example: organizing media, under the conditions we have observed, requires great stores of energy and determination. Some of the most dynamic and imaginative elements in the U.S. are those engaged in the struggle for change—and of those, the most aware of the texture of everyday problems are often media activists (though there are dreadful exceptions, not least in the sectarian press). At their best, these media carry this provocative grip, this fire, this dissonance, and spread its ferment into everyday conversation. Rethinking begins there. Slowly, patiently—but in this task, that is the secret of success. To expect instant impact is to demand a rootless revolution, and the twentieth century has its warnings on that score.

However, these media are developing fast in the U.S., partly as a spinoff from its notable affluence. I have in mind here especially the independent film and video movement, which has long roots in this country,[1] and which has gained considerable ground in recent years. That movement has its radical wing, as we can see in the rapid growth of anti-nuclear films, as well as in the increasing number of films by or in support of Native Americans. The emergence in 1983 of two digests of the alternative press—*The Utne Reader* of St. Paul, Minnesota, and *The Left Index* of Santa Cruz, California, the second being devoted to magazines only—offers more evidence of this growth pattern. The development of an alternative computer movement is another case in point.[2] These are movements in the capillaries of North America, and *all the more strongly based for that fact.* Arguably, they are part of the slow maturation of a specifically North American alternative consciousness, not just a transposition from European socialist culture.[3] And, despite the disappearance of many 60s media, these and others not studied here are the tough ones who have kept developing alongside newer arrivals of the 70s and 80s.

So, it is important to be clear in our own minds what kind of impact, over what time span, we expect of radical media. They may well be stronger today in reality, because more rooted, than they were in the headier 60s.

A key problem, however, is to interpret the growth of media activism in relation to the political alienation of many U.S. citizens. Nowhere is this alienation more evident than in the declining proportion of voters taking part in presidential elections (despite the major media hype of 1972 and 1980 as major landslides for Nixon and Reagan).

1960: 62.8%	1972: 55.5%
1964: 61.9%	1976: 54.3%
1968: 60.9%	1980: 53.2%[4]

Alan Wolfe has summarized supporting evidence[5] that this weak involvement does originate in a distanced and cynical view towards official political processes. He is rightly at pains to point out however that this alienation has an ambivalent character. Such detachment could conceivably tolerate highly authoritarian government, at least in periods of crisis, just as easily as it could favor radical challenges to the status quo. It is hard too, to imagine that non-voters are unanimous in their reasons for distancing themselves from the political process. Nonetheless, within this vast mass of Americans, and *not least among some voters*, there is a sizable constituency open to a genuine alternative democracy. Such an alternative has not yet been developed in a series of practical forms, but the role of alternative media could be and should be precisely to fill that gap, both by their own experience of organizing, and by providing a series of public spaces for us to grapple with the issues collectively, in neighborhood circles and eventually as a nation. Gradually, a new mass culture of political involvement may come to be activated, of a totally different kind to the dollar-drenched media spectaculars which currently pass themselves off as political participation. In the nuclear era, we are fools not to try.

This leads to two last observations, both on divisions in U.S. society. In the General Introduction, I quoted Sheila Rowbotham as urging different segments of the oppressed to "learn from each other's wisdoms" in resisting oppression and humiliation.[6] In the Micronesian structure of the U.S., this advice is especially to the point. Laterally communicating media are in a unique position to foster such a process.

Indeed, the cases studied are rather strong examples of this linkage-politics. *The Guardian* and KPFA have tried to staff their operation accordingly, over and above voicing a variety of experiences and concerns. *Union Wage* tried to bring together women's concerns as feminists and as wage-workers. *Akwesasne Notes* and California Newsreel are within hailing distance of each other on the logic of industrial "progress." The NACLA *Report* has tried to link the impact of corporate and government decisions on North, Central, and South Americans. Independent film-makers in Puerto Rico focussed on African cultural imagery, on women as community organizers, on U.S. colonialism.

Not all alternative media have achieved this degree of linkage. There have been Black media, labor media, anti-nuclear media, Latin media, anti-imperialist media, lesbian media, gay media, community media. This partly reflects the fact that in the U.S., hard experience shows you rely on your own community, or risk the shaft. At the same time, the focus has to widen, or we will all slide into competing with each other for who will be pushed around a little less than the rest.

At the time of writing, a series of U.S. cities have been electing minority mayors, and one presidential candidate,

Jesse Jackson, was making his campaign slogan the creation of a "rainbow coalition" of the poor, different ethnic groups, women, gays and lesbians, the elderly. Linkage politics was in the air. Yet without its implantation in everyday awareness, in the capillaries of local life, such slogans would stay empty, and even such mayoral victories would remain formal. White racism in particular is so tenaciously, so pervasively rooted in the U.S., and the corresponding reactions it provokes are so visceral, that these victories and slogans at the public level must be matched at the block level or else they will wither away. Radical media, not exempt from these problems themselves, still have a powerfully constructive role to play, if they so choose, in building bridges over the U.S. Micronesian archipelago. Unified resistance cannot be declared: it can only be painfully constructed. Without media, it cannot be constructed at all.

The other aspect of division in U.S. society also sets an important agenda for radical media. I refer to the contradictions within our own consciousness. Gramsci had some interesting, if concentrated observations on this score,[7] but he saw people's consciousness as a complicated battleground in which the status quo and the revolutionary impulse were in frequent transaction with each other. (Arguably the fast-paced incoherence of major media "reality" contributes to this process still further.)

Sennett and Cobb have suggested that this fragmentation expresses itself also in the conversational patterns of many workers in the U.S. (and no doubt elsewhere as well), where topics and attitudes switch and switch back quite often with what seems dizzying speed, at least to the academic observer, trained to be terribly methodical (and so to find Nietzsche "difficult to pin down"!). Especially hard to handle are the rapid switches from radicalism to reaction. Their explanation for these switches is based on their analysis of the humiliations forced on the working class. They argue that:

"One tends to think of fragmentation in a life as a result of some social disorganization in which the person has been ripped apart...(yet) given the fact of being nameless in society, given the ambushes and contradictions of dignity class creates, the more a man's actions are split up in his own mind the less chance he has of being overwhelmed as a whole."[8]

The reason for emphasizing this here in the discussion of radical media ought to be obvious, but may not be. Not only are Sennett and Cobb drawing attention to the vital interaction between structural forces and inner psychic processes, but by implication they are pinpointing exactly that realm of contradictory moods and emotions to which media in principle can be amazingly sensitive. They can allow these to be voiced, they can open up the exchange of partial perspectives, for the disentangling of these tight knots of grudge and anxiety.

If radical media only convey exploitation, brutality, and chicanery, if counter-*information* is their only world, then their appeal is only to the cognitive, orderly, settled dimensions of human existence. They will have no graft onto the multilayered skin of human passion, no imbrication in the turmoil of clashing human feelings and worries, no humor, *no life*. As I quoted Edward Thompson in the General Introduction, "a full half of culture is experienced as *feeling*."[9] The division of labor between art and journalism should not dominate in radical media. The major media, the advertizing industry, play at will in this arena, destructively toying with the cross-currents of our everyday emotions. Until we can do better, constructively better, consistently better, attractively better—and it doesn't require huge funds—only imagination and belonging—these other media will win each day. We will at best be left to semaphore to each other from island to island in our Micronesia. Uncensored...

Footnotes

1. Bill Alexander, *Film on the Left*, Princeton: Princeton University Press, 1981.
2. See the newsletter *Reset* (details in n. 4 for the Forward).
3. Paul Breines, "Germans, Journals and Jews/Madison, Men, Marxism, and Mosse: a tale of Jewish-leftist identity in America," in *New German Critique* 20 (Spring/Summer 1980), pp. 81-103.
4. U.S. Bureau of the Census, *Statistical Abstract of the United States: 1981* (102d ed.) Washington D.C., 1981, Table 824, p. 496.
5. Alan Wolfe, *The Limits of Legitimacy*, New York: Free Press 1977, ch. 10.
6. See p. 18.
7. Antonio Gramsci, *Prison Notebooks*, London: Lawrence & Wishart 1971, pp. 327, 333.
8. Richard Sennett & Jonathan Cobb, *The Hidden Injuries of Class*, Cambridge: Cambridge University Press 1972, p. 214. The whole chapter IV repays reading in this context.
9. See p. 24.

SECTION II
PORTUGAL & ITALY

11

INTRODUCTION

We turn now to consider the experience of alternative media which have played a very conspicuous role in national politics.

To grasp the real significance of the political movements in Italy and Portugal during the seventies, and to understand the self-managed media which were part of them, we have to appreciate the geopolitics of U.S.—Soviet contention in the Mediterranean. What may seem a detour has a direct bearing on the situation, for the range of options open to these movements was quite tightly defined by this major competition between the superpowers, acted out through their Mediterranean supporters.

The first major definition of U.S. state interests in the Mediterranean was the proclamation of the "Truman Doctrine," more popularly known as the "Cold War doctrine," by President Truman on March 12, 1947. Today, many people are unaware that this fundamental definition of American foreign policy in the world at large was originally made to hinge on two Mediterranean countries, Greece and Turkey, which were defined as pivotal both to the Middle East and to western Europe. In 1947, Greek communists controlled about ninety percent of their country, and had massive popular support (quite unlike the situation in East Germany or Bulgaria, for instance.) Turkey, however, had no such political movements in existence. President Truman took the following definition of the situation to a meeting of both houses of Congress; note his emphasis on the oil-producing areas of the Middle East and on the politically unstable countries of postwar western Europe:

> It is necessary only to glance at a map to realize that the survival and integrity of the Greek nation are of grave importance in a much wider situation. If Greece should fall under the control of an armed minority, the effect upon its neighbor, Turkey, would be immediate and serious. Confusion and disorder might well spread throughout the entire Middle East.
>
> Moreover, the disappearance of Greece as an independent state would have a profound effect upon those countries in Europe whose people are struggling against great difficulties to maintain their freedoms and their independence while they repair the damages of war...
>
> Should we fail to aid Greece and Turkey in their fateful hour, the effect will be far-reaching to the west as to the east...
>
> If we falter in our leadership, we may endanger the peace of the world—and we shall surely endanger the welfare of the nation.[1]

Pax Americana indeed! The result of the Truman Doctrine was that Greece, far from remaining an "independent state," became a client-state of the U.S., at least until 1974. Turkey continued to be such up to the time of writing. What was agitating U.S. policy-makers was the turmoil and the accompanying popularity of communist and/or socialist parties, especially in Italy and France, but also in Belgium, the Netherlands, Scandinavia, and even Britain, in the shape of a huge 1945 general election vote for the Labor Party. In Yugoslavia, the socialist partisans were in full control of the country and enjoyed overwhelming support. (Fascist Spain and Portugal were not "struggling to maintain their freedoms," but this did not seem to concern the President unduly.) The inauguration of the huge Marshall Aid Plan fund a few months later to western European countries was designated specifically to shore up the often rickety, but pro-American governments in those countries.

Thus, since 1947, the Mediterranean has been defined by the U.S. as a critically important area, abutting both Arab oil, and the United States' industrially advanced allies in western Europe. The foundation of NATO (North *Atlantic* Treaty Organization) in 1949—including not only Portugal, but also Italy, Greece and Turkey—was also initiated on this assumption. Yet this same Mediterranean has also been a region of deep and continuing instabilities. Without any pretense at being exhaustive, let us list some of them.

The major claim on people's attention has inevitably been made by the Israeli-Arab wars of 1948, 1956, 1967, 1973 and 1982. But we may add many more: the Egyptian revolution of 1953 that brought Nasser to power; the Algerian anti-colonial revolution against the French from 1956 to 1962; the civil wars in Lebanon in 1958, and from 1976; the overthrow of King Idris in Libya in 1969, and his replacement by the Khadafi regime; the increasing Soviet presence in Syria from 1966 onwards; the continuing Palestinian insurgency; the several attempts to overthrow the Moroccan monarchy; the departure of France from NATO in 1966; the continuing instability of Italian governments ever since World War II; the developing popular movement in Greece in the mid-sixties, repressed by the fascist junta from 1967-1974, but re-emerging at the beginning of the eighties; intermittent economic and political instability in Turkey, especially alarming to the U.S. after the downfall of the Shah of Iran; the 1978 expulsion of the British from the naval base in Malta after three hundred years; and, not least, the collapse of the fascist dictatorships in Portugal and then Spain during the seventies.

This short list emphasizes the constant problems posed to the U.S. by the Mediterranean region. At the time of writing, the only two apparently stable countries have been Tunisia and Albania! U.S. foreign policy makers' anxieties are exacerbated beyond measure by the developing Soviet presence in the Mediterranean. This has to be understood on the following levels: naval-military, economic, and political.[2]

The naval-military presence is first of all to be understood in the light of Soviet problems in access to the oceans. Soviet ships can get out through the Arctic Ocean north of Norway; through the Baltic Sea; from Vladivostock to the far East; and from the Black Sea through the slender Bosphorus Straits at Istanbul, out through the Mediterranean. The USSR's naval bases at the time of writing no longer include Egypt, where the loss of the Alexandria port and three major airfields constituted a major blow. While the Soviet Union has negotiated ship-maintenance facilities in Libya, its main drive throughout the late seventies was to try to acquire more considerable port-facilities in Yugoslavia. (The British departure from Malta has not as yet opened that port to the Soviet military fleet.) Thus, much of the re-provisioning of the Soviet military fleet in the Mediterranean has to be done through its merchant fleet, which is allowed into practically all ports.

In addition the USSR has supplied considerable arms to Syria and Libya, and some to Algeria. These range from jet fighters to guided missiles to conventional submarines. Soviet military training advisers are also present, in varying degrees, in these countries.

On the economic plane, the USSR has become closely involved with several Mediterranean countries. Spain is one, dating from the fifties; more recently the USSR has signed agreements with Turkey (for aluminum extraction), with Greece (for the construction of aluminum factories), and with Morocco in 1978 for a thirty year phosphate deal, scheduled when in full effect to deliver ten million tons of phosphate a year to the Soviet Union (its biggest Third World contract ever signed). That these countries should have this relationship with the USSR may be quite surprising to anyone who has not followed the course of Soviet foreign policy, especially since the sixties. But it does mean that the USSR is building up a major economic presence in the Mediterranean, parallel to its major trading relationship with Germany further north.

As regards its political presence, we have to take into account the popular support for various communist parties in Portugal, Spain, Italy, Greece and Cyprus—Italy and Cyprus having the largest support proportional to their population. This is not a simple matter, however: the Spanish and Italian communist parties have both declared themselves in favor of NATO membership for their repective countries, and the Yugoslav League of Communists has been been fiercely independent from the USSR since 1948. The communist parties of France, Portugal and Greece have been much more reliable allies of the Soviet Union, but none is close to significant power.[3] And the Cyprus Communist party is hardly in a position to determine Mediterranean policy.

Nonetheless—and this can hardly be overemphasized—
these communist parties represent the *only* analogy to U.S.
cultural-political penetration of major layers of the population
in various countires around the world. By and large, the U.S.
has succeeded in communicating its way of life as desirable, at
least to bourgeois and petit bourgeois classes, in a way the
USSR has never succeeded in doing. In many countries,
workers and peasants are as unimpressed by the Soviet model
as their rulers, albeit often for different reasons; but in the
northern Mediterranean there *are* sections of subordinate
classes highly sympathetic to the Soviet Union, and hostile to
the U.S. Furthermore, in the southern Mediterranean, there are
a number of Arab regimes whose rapproachement with the
USSR is governed by their hostility to the U.S. for its support of
Israeli colonialism in the Middle East.

Thus, the Mediterranean is a major and complex region of
confrontation and maneuver by the two superpowers. This is
actually visible in the waters of the Mediterranean, where U.S.
and Soviet naval fleets regularly follow each other around. But
the maneuvers extend well beyond this. For example, U.S.
military aid to Spain quadrupled in 1975-1980, compared with
1970-1975, in the face of the overthrow of fascism in Portugal in
1974, and the subsequent demise of Franco and his regime.[4]
When it looked as though the Italian Communist party might
become the main parliamentary party in the 1976 general
elections, U.S. Secretary of State Henry Kissinger warned that
the U.S. would not tolerate such a development. Following the
Turkish invasion and partition of Cyprus in 1974, accomplished with the connivance of Britain and the U.S., the latter began
to plan to station its Rapid Deployment Force on the Turkish
occupied northern sector of the island.

Among these maneuvers must be included the efforts of
southern European communist parties to wipe out all political
movements to their left, so as to have undisputed hegemony
over all socialist opposition forces. This strategy has been
particularly visible in Italy and Portugal, where popular
movements outside Communist party control made very considerable headway during the seventies. There is a determination by these parties to force an alignment with one
superpower against the other, which means that those movements, which reject both of the superpower models for future
world society, had not one but two major opponents. Until this

political fact of life is grasped, the full range of problems encountered by political movements in Italy and Portugal in the 1970s cannot be accurately assessed. In turn, the self-managed media these movements brought into being cannot be understood outside of this context.

Footnotes

1. Cited in R. Hofstadter (ed.), *Great Issues in American History: From Reconstruction to the Present Day*, New York: Vintage 1969, p. 414.
2. For what follows, see S. Silvestri and M. Cremasco, *Il Fianco Sud Della NATO* (NATO's Southern Flank), Milan: Feltrinelli Editore 1980.
3. That is, the Exterior Communist Party of Greece, at the time of writing the larger of the two Greek Communist Parties.
4. R. Hadian, "United States Policy Towards Spain 1953-1975", *Iberian Studies* VII.1 (Spring 1978), pp. 3-13.

12

THE
PORTUGUESE EXPLOSION

The General Background

From May 28, 1926 to April 25, 1974, Portugal was ruled by the most stable fascist regime in history (despite a number of attempted revolts against it). Antonio Salazar, dictator of the "New State" until his death in 1968, was succeeded by Marcello Caetano for just six years. They ran a country where poverty and illiteracy were the highest in Europe, and whose economic development was the most backward.[1] Portugal was also, however, an international colonial power, controlling most significantly Angola and Mozambique, but also Guinea-Bissau, the Cape Verde islands of São Tomé and Príncipe, East Timor and Macao, as well as Madeira and the Azores in the North Atlantic. (The Azores were a major refuelling stop for U.S. planes, especially in the 1973 Israeli-Arab war.)

The contradiction between Portugal's international role and its internal misery was a striking one. By 1971, 49 percent of its budget was tied to fighting the liberation movements in its African colonies, while compulsory military service was for four years: a staggering economic and social drain, but one actively supported by Britain and the U.S. because of their strategic and economic interests in southern Africa. Furthermore, over a million Portuguese workers were in France, and others were working elsewhere in the world, from Massachusetts to Melbourne.

Within the country, the proportion of the workforce industrially employed had outstripped those agriculturally employed for the first time in 1970. Many Portuguese workers worked directly for foreign concerns, with the U.S. taking over

167

from Britain as Portugal's main external investor by 1969. French, Belgian, West German and Swedish capital were also significantly involved in Portugal. Wages were exceptionally low, hours were extremely long and industrial discipline harshly enforced by the "New State."

Health and housing were both appalling for large numbers of Portuguese. In rural areas there was about one doctor per six thousand people. Medical maternity care was only available for the rich. Fifty-eight children in a thousand died at birth. Thirteen percent of children born suffered from some deformity. Rural housing very often lacked water or sanitation, let alone electricity. On the outskirts of Lisbon, at least thirty thousand *families*—almost two hundred thousand people, in a population of eight million—were living in shanty towns. Huge numbers more lived in substandard, grossly overcrowded housing. Women usually bore the full brunt of this situation, experiencing multiple pregnancies (birth control devices were only available for the wealthy) and the acute hazards of bringing up children in these conditions. In the countryside, women regularly worked at backbreaking physical labor for very long hours.

As is predictable in a fascist state, organized and individual opposition were brutally repressed. Workers' "unions" were state-run, with censorship omnipresent. The major instrument in this repression was the PIDE (International and State Defense Police), who spied on, harassed, tortured or assassinated people opposing the regime. Indeed, de Figueireido has presented a case that economic and political conditions for the mass of the population in the metropolis were as bad as they were for colonized Africans—a unique instance in the history of colonialism![1]

This is not to say that there was no resistance. Significant opposition inside the military, albeit divided into anti-colonialist and neo-colonialist wings, dated back to 1959; two radio stations broadcast into Portugal from Algiers and Prague; workers and peasants maintained clandestine forms of labor organization.[2] The church was overwhelmingly pro-regime, but had a much weaker popular base than in neighboring Spain.[3]

It was against this background that the revolt of April 25, 1974, took place. The character of the popular movement which then erupted is dealt with below, but let us note some critically important dates in this process. The revolt of April 25—29 years to the day that Mussolini was executed by the Italian resistance—was itself led by the Armed Forces Movement (its Portuguese initials are MFA). The MFA represented for the most part the middle-ranking and junior officers. The coup deposing Caetano met with no resistance. General Spinola, veteran of numerous savage campaigns against African liberation movements, accepted the role of President of the Junta of National Salvation.

There were two failed attempts at countercoups, on September 28, 1974, and March 11, 1975. These were directed at trying to halt the sharp leftward trend in the country at large. After the first failed coup, Spinola left Portugal and joined Caetano in exile in Brazil. The Junta of National Salvation was replaced by the Council of the Revolution. After the second coup attempt, both the government and the people began to embrace more radical policies, from bank nationalization to farmland seizures. A period of extremely hectic transformation ensued, toward the end of which various counter-revolutionary forces inside the country (the Catholic Church, the party-political right, the Socialist Party) attempted to portray the left as planning a coup. It was barely two years since the Pinochet coup against the Popular Unity government in Chile, and on October 1 a document was leaked to the press (*O Século*) which set out the main objectives of a further coup from the right: purging the left, reconstructing the army and police as loyal instruments of repression, military occupations of radio and TV. Rádio Renascenca and *República* were specifically named.) This was what eventually took place on November 25, 1975, but its publication generated a great deal of public agitation about the armed defense of the revolution, which was then taken as pretext for a massive clampdown. Radical units within the army, such as COPCON, were demobilized; radical senior officers, such as COPCON commander, Otelo de Carvalho, were cashiered; most media were silenced and then reopened under new management. An absolute halt was called by the new conservative coalition majority in the government to any further socialist measures in Portugal.

The international capitalist media were jubilant at this reassertion of the right. A *Time* cover in December 1975 was headed: "At Last The Good Guys Seem To Have Won." Then, naturally, the saturation coverage of Portugal that had emerged over the previous nineteen months declined to its former trickle. No longer were landowners being expropriated from their land, or capitalists from their factories, the main concern of the international media when reviewing Portugal during those months. The country had not, after all, been "lost to the West" (Kissinger's anxious conviction at one stage). No one would have guessed, from reading these media, the wide extent of revolutionary opposition to Soviet imperialism inside Portugal.

Let us now turn to two specific aspects of the Portuguese situation with a direct bearing on self-managed mass media in 1974-75: the context of official mass media, and the general character of the political movements in Portugal.

The Context of Official Mass Media

Up to April 25, 1974, the established mass media had a relatively simple status. They were under the direct supervision of the state censor's office, which had been in operation in various forms ever since 1926. By 1936, all media had effectively been brought under the control of the New State; and as radio, and later on television, developed in Portugal, they too were subjected to this censorship, together with records, books, magazines and all other communication media.

The rules for the press, first systematically codified in 1932, read at certain points like such regulations anywhere else, though at other moments the character of Catholic rural Portugal also makes itself obvious:

> The following are forbidden: a) insulting references to the Head of State, the senior State authorities, foreign Heads of State, and their representatives in Portugal; b) disrespectful references to official authorities and bodies; c) references to topics with a direct bearing on public order; d) news of violence of a political nature; e) detailed news of political court sentences; f) news which creates alarm and public unrest...; i) letters, news or articles referring to political deportees or emigres, which involve questions of national policy... k) systematic criticism of the actions of the Military Dictatorship, revealing less the intention to enlighten and be constructive then the desire to disorganize and to destroy; l) suicides, with the exception of those committed by known criminals, and presented as such to the public; m) infanticides, when not accompanied by news of the punishment meted out by the tribunal's sentences to the authors of the crime; n) predictions by astrologers, witches, seers and others; immoral love

letters...occupations of suspect morality and any occupation whose presentation clearly might encourage
the dissolution of traditional customs...
q) allusion to the Censorship services; r) white spaces,
erasures or other marks from which, even if in error,
the Censorship's activity might be deduced...
u) the promulgation of political doctrines considered
dangerous to the state...[4]

The conjunction of Catholic morality and political stability in
the minds of the framers of these regulations is obvious, and
demonstrates all too clearly the deep involvement of the
Catholic hierarchy in Salazar's consolidation of power over
Portugal. The regulations cited here have been reproduced in
one of the series of documentations on the fascist regime
sponsored by the Presidency of the Council of Ministers since
1974.The same volume gives further insight into the minute
workings of the Portuguese censorship system, reproducing
lists of records seized (114 of *Up To The Neck*, 6 of *Songs of
the Cuban Revolutionaries*), and lists of banned books and
magazines in not only Portuguese, but also Spanish, French,
German and English, mostly about marxism, or sex, or
pornography. It reproduces the special 1965 directive, forbid-
ding all references to the PIDE (the secret police), and a letter
from the head of Portuguese broadcasting to Caetano in 1972,
lamenting the problems he was having in finding "reliable"
journalists for TV current affairs work!

This censorship background is very important, to understand what followed later. Its immediate effects however were
twofold. One was that journalism came to have an exceptionally low prestige as an occupation in the minds of many
Portuguese. One of the more amusing stories of the Salazar
regime concerns having formally congratulated Portuguese
journalists in 1961 for their sense of responsibility to the New
State. "Today," he said, "our journalists have no need of
censorship because they operate not only within legal boundaries, but according to an ethic of moderation and equilibrium
according with the national interest."[5] This, claimed Salazar,
made the censorship "services" scarcely necessary, and thus
the Portuguese press one of the freest in the world! (Note
Mussalini's similar claim for the Italian press, in the Introduction to Italy section of this book.) However, the other effect
of censorship was that a whole array of clandestine papers,

bulletins, posters and flyers made their appearance, especially in the ten years preceeding the Revolution. In the press, a number of codewords became commonly known to the leaders.[6] Benfica, the leading football team, became known to stand for the Communist Party, because of its red shirts. This clandestine communication was most important in building up people's revolutionary hopes.

However, the press was less significant in Portugal than broadcasting, given Portugal's astronomical illitaracy rates: as late as 1971, over a third of the population could not read. This meant that with state broadcasting, the nominally Catholic Rádio Renascenca and the Francoist Rádio Clube Português played a significant part in attempting to stabilize the increasingly unstable Portugal of the late 60s and early 70s.

After April 25, 1974, with censorship lifted, there quickly emerged in the media both a substantial shift in ownership, and a furious battle for control. The shift in ownership came about simply as a result of the nationalization of Portuguese banks in March 1975. Since, in turn, the banks owned the great majority of the press, the State immediately found itself owning nearly all newspapers as well as most radio and all TV.[7] In the context of 1974-75 this was not disturbing, for to most Portuguese the basic issue seemed to be that the state was never again to be in fascist hands. By 1980, the pattern of ownership looked much more disquieting, with the director of Portuguese broadcasting publicly contending in *Diário de Notícias*, the leading newspaper, that since the media were part of the country's power structure, it was reasonable for the government to expect them to be responsive to its own outlook.

What most people found much more significant at the time was who actually controlled the media. Essentially, all the major political parties took the same view, that whoever controlled the media would be in command of the direction of events. They were extremely cautious—who could not be?—of the heady effect of open media after 48 years of censorship. Their view was a completely manipulative one, however, regarding the media as targets in their own battle for competitive colonization of the power structure. *None* of them believed in popular democracy.

In this particular area of party-political competition, the general consensus was that by summer 1975 the Portuguese Communist Party had enjoyed the most success. It was widely reckoned to have its members or sympathizers in control of four Lisbon dailies, including *Diário de Notícias*. This was not as spectacular a coup as it might appear because of the greater importance of radio and TV, but it nonetheless represented more "success" than was achieved by any other single party. (We shall see the significance of this when considering the case of *República* and Rádio Clube Português.)

This book covers the major cases of media where battle for control was won by the workers themselves, at least until November 1975. (There are other cases not covered here, such as the *Jornal do Comercio*, which was taken over by its workers in September 1974, together with a number of weekly political magazines such as *O Jornal, Tempo*.) In *República*, Rádio Renascenca and Rádio Clube Português, as in the factory bulletins and newspapers, very different conceptions reigned of the politics of information than those current in the main political parties of right and left.

In general, however, one of the most striking features of the Portuguese upheaval was the explosion in communication following the stifling silences of the New State. From major news media to spray-cans—the walls of Lisbon's center in particular were so covered with messages and slogans that at one point there was no room left for any more—the Portuguese were speaking openly at last on all issues. Phil Mailer cites, as an extreme index of this eruption of speech, the solemn printing by some newspapers in the first days of the upheaval of an offer to charge half-price to soldiers below the rank of lieutanant— by a group of prostitutes.[8]

This communication explosion is especially common in countries where an old regime has been overthrown that dominated news diffusion, such as in Czechoslovakia in 1968-1969, or in countries with a strong popular movement such as Chile. Its first exhilaration is bound to pass, though; as a workers' leaflet from an electronics factory in Setúbal put it: "We have passed from a situation of hunger to a situation where we can say we are hungry."

For the established politicians, the autonomy of this upsurge was very far from welcome. Admittedly, they moved at once to close down the old Propaganda Ministry, and replaced it with a Ministry of Social Communication. This post was regarded with such seriousness however, that Vasco Gonçalves, Prime Minister of three provisional governments, personally took over that ministry for most of his tenure in office. These politicians' hostility to the old censorship did not arise from their commitment to worker-managed media! This was made plain in a number of ways. The Socialist Party made great international play with accusations of media censorship against both *República* and Rádio Renascença, joining unashamedly with the Catholic Church in the later case. The Communist Party was never to be found defending these self-managed media. The views of the Popular Social Democrats (right of center reformers from the old regime) and the Center Social Democrats (functionaries of the old regime under a new name), can both be imagined. The only soil in which such media flourished was the massive popular movement in Portugal. By 1980, when this movement had subsided to some extent, even the official media were being subjected to a whole series of reforms and purges designed to sanitize them of any revolutionary content. The publicly expressed views of the director of state broadcasting were noted above.

The Character of the Popular Movement in Portugal

The single most striking feature of the situation in Portugal from 1974 onwards was the chasm between the realities of the vast popular movement and their transmutation through official party politics. Throughout these years, right up to 1980, it continued to be the case that the mass of voters tried to do the best they could for themselves at elections, given the available choice and established political structure. The ferocious tug-of-war between the Socialist Party and the Communist Party over the leadership of the unions—the PCP dominated Intersindical, the major union federation, while the PSP campaigned vigorously against a single federation—was a classic example of the infighting that occurred, which was quite contrary to workers' interests. Simultaneously, operating as citizens and political actors, these same voters were often to be found both expressing their contempt for party-political intrigue and infighting, and their yearning for a wider political vision in harmony with their own.

Depending on the observer's stance, either the one of the other of these realities has customarily been stressed in interpreting Portuguese politics in this period. Essentially,

socialist commentators have stressed the huge political demonstrations: as late as 1980, in the space of a few weeks, there
was a demonstration of one hundred thousand at Évora, a
small town at the center of the land-seizures of 1974-1975, in
their defense; and a demonstration of three hundred thousand
in Lisbon. (The equivalent numbers of demonstrators for size
of population would be seven hundred thousand and over two
million in Britain, or three million and eight million in the
U.S.)

Conservative commentators by contrast, have stressed the
increasing "maturity" of the Portuguese electorate in moving
steadily away from marxist propaganda toward a right-of-
center alternative. This rather flatulent interpretation of the
situation is supported by actual shifts in voting patterns,
particularly in favor of the Popular Social Democrats (PSD,
initially known as the PPD). What this view omits however, is
that with the exception of the tiny monarchist party, every
party in Portugal has had to assume a socialist title: the most
conservative party called itself the Center Social Democrats,
the PSD has been mentioned, and the other two main parties
are the Socialist and Communist parties. Even the monarchist
party calls itself the *Popular* Monarchist Party!

This process of naming indicates the need to accomodate
on some level to public political awareness and feelings. The
conservative interpretation also lumps together marxism as
such with the actual behavior of Socialist and Communist
parties in Portugal. Thus it evades the widespread disillusionment felt with the Socialist Party as it claimed on the one
hand—internally—to be a marxist party, yet at the same time
actively encouraged the western powers to identify its own
political ascendancy with liberalism, its own failure with
imminent totalitarianism. The conservative view also takes no
account of people's disillusionment with the Communist Party's continuing attempts to blot out the rest of the left, or of the
PCP's undoubted bases of strength among trade unionists and
southern agricultural workers. For such commentators, marxism is marxism, and the Portuguese, after an early infatuation
with "it" were astute enough to reject it.

I am arguing here for a different interpretation, namely
that the Portuguese population is strongly politicized, and in
many areas of the country highly radicalized, but that the
contradiction between their radical consciousness and their

continued political dependence on the given parliamentary parties has yet to be overcome. This initial assessment of Portuguese political realities is the key, I would claim, to understanding the strengths and limitations of the political movements in Portugal during 1974-1975.

For most of the army captains who planned the revolt, for the liberal capitalists who recognized the economic strangulation of Portugal by its antique colonial-fascist structure, April 25 was the opportunity to get rid of the drain of the colonial wars, and to jerk Portugal into a productive relation with the EEC. The MFA's document announcing its progam began:

> In view of the fact that after thirteen years of struggle
> in the overseas provinces, the political system has not
> suceeded in defining concretely and objectively poli-
> cies which might lead to peace between Portuguese
> people of all races and creeds..."9

The successes of the African liberation movements are cheek-by-jowl here with the continuing definition of Angola, Mozambique and other colonies as "overseas provinces," and of the colonized as "Portuguese people." A neo-colonial relationship was clearly the one envisaged for the future. The MFA document did promise also to develop economic policies to benefit the working class, but as a very small part of the entire program, and in entirely declaratory terms. The abolition of censorship and the independence of the judiciary were the two concrete pledges made. Resolving the colonial issue dominated the document.

Yet this lifting of the lid by General Spinola—whose reactionary political commitments have already been noted—was the signal for the eruption of a gigantic popular movement, not merely against the war, but against landlords, the desperate housing shortage, employers, mass media controllers, the Catholic hierarchy, Franco's regime, NATO and the EEC. The parliamentary parties fought each other savagely to lead (the left) or to stifle (the right) this movement, but the momentum never passed securely into their hands until after November 25, 1975. Then, the absence of any organized resistance to the demobilization of radical military units, or to the dismissal of the army's most radical officers, proved to the parliamentary parties that for the time being the stage was theirs. The mass of the Portuguese people had not sloughed off their radical convictions, but were stymied as to what to do about them.

Let us recall some actual events to underpin this conclusion. By September 1975, nearly 400,000 hectares of private farmland had been seized by nearly 11,000 agricultural workers. Two months later, in November 1975, the area seized had risen to a million hectares. Numerous factories were under self-management. Most factories had Workers' Committees, whose function varied from place to place, but which were often a major power center in the factory. Empty dwellings had been occupied at a very fast rate, shanty-town inhabitants were actively organizing against their conditions, and rents had been frozen as a result of working class tenants' pressure. In the armed forces, there were numerous revolutionary bulletins circulating, frequent cases of soldiers disobeying their officers if they considered the latters' directives counter-revolutionary, numerous instances of soldiers joining demonstrations rather then controlling them.[10] And late in 1975 there was the development of the SUV (Soldiers United Will Win), whose manifesto called for soldiers' committees, the sacking of reactionary officers, stronger links with workers and peasants, the destruction of the bourgeois army and its replacement by a people's revolutionary army. SUV held a demonstration of over a hundred thousand in Lisbon on September 26, 1975. Finally, a number of mass media (essentially those discussed in this book) were also under popular control.

These are the major indices of the autonomous revolutionary momentum in Portugal, which was developing especially in late 1975—but completely without centralization, and always subjected to attempts to capture its particular thrusts by one or many political groupings. The movement was national in scope, embracing all ages, both sexes, and people from every class background—though obviously the majority were working class or peasant by origin. This distinguishes it from the Italian movement of 1977-1978, which was far more concentrated on young people, and in the northern part of Italy. In Portugal the involvement of the mass of the population was patent.

However, this is not to say that the movement was not flawed politically, over and above its difficulties with central organization and the cut-throat competition for its soul by the parliamentary parties (not to mention a number of others to their left). Its flaws centered, arguably, around its position on the colonial war, its understanding of Portugal's post-colonial future, the place of women in the movement, the problem of the rural North, and also to some extent a generational problem.

The movement tended to be absolutely anti-war, but not to the same extent anti-colonial. In this sense, the MFA document accurately reflected public opinion. It was a major surprise, not to say shock, to many Portuguese to see a million settlers returning from Angola and Mozambique; up until then they had assumed those people would stay in harmoniously re-structured southern Africa. What decolonization meant for the national self-understanding of many Portuguese people, espec-ially the *retornados*, was never seriously addressed by the movement. This allowed the Socialist Party freedom to re-peatedly mobilize the *retornados* against the left. Similarly, the movement tended to define imperialism in somewhat oversimplified terms, and very much in relation to particular scandals, such as the donation of CIA money to the Socialist Party via the British Labor Party and the Social Democratic parties of West Germany and Sweden; or the role of trans-national firms in exploiting Portuguese workers; or the USSR's overwhelming interest in Angola. This meant that other issues were left rather unexamined: the future of Portugal as a dependent neo-colony, supplying cheap labor for northern Europe and traditional know-how for transnational invest-ment in Angola and Mozambique, while in turn utilizing the cheap labor of 300,000 Cape Verdeans, a group occupying the most menial and despised position in Portuguese society (though not the only black people in Portugal). The questions of colonialism, neo-colonialism and racism were rarely posed in their full dimensions.

As regards women's involvement in the movement, we must begin by recalling how women have been subjected to some of the most acute oppression in Portuguese society. When one group of ten women echoed a number of demands of the international women's movement—against domestic op-pression, against sex-role stereotyping—in a tiny Lisbon de-monstration in January 1975, they were treated as a joke by the press, denounced by the Communist Party's women's organi-zation, and were physically threatened by male onlookers, escaping unhurt only with difficulty.[11] While women were active and vocal in the squatters' movements and as factory

workers, all other dimensions of their existence were completely downplayed in the movement at large.

The political problem of the Northern countryside, with its
tiny farms, mostly rented for just a year at a time, has often
been remarked on in discussions of Portugal. The militancy of
the southern farmworkers, who mostly worked on the vast
estates of absentee landlords, was never to be seen in the
North. Indeed, the ideological grip of the Catholic hierarchy in
the North, coupled with the aggressive character of Communist
activity there, seem to have led many rural people to become
disenchanted with the revolution. The result was that the
Northern rural population constituted a large base for conservative parties such as the CSD and PSD. Indeed, shortly before
November 25, leaders of conservative opinion were poised to
lead a near-secession of the North by blocking all rail and road
links between North and South—"to cut the country in half,"
as they put it. There is little question, at least initially, but that
they would have had enough support from the rural North to
carry out their plans.

The last problems of the movement which have to be
recognized are the related issues of age and political outlook.
Older workers tended to be much more cautious than the
younger ones, less likely to push conflicts to their breaking
point. At the same time, the militancy of younger workers was
sometimes based on enthusiasm, rather than on a sober
assessment of the scope for meaningful revoltuionary action.
Not surprisingly, each generation was more at ease in pointing
out the other's deficiencies to confirm its own sense of political
virtue, than in dealing with its own problems. This rift had
none of the depth of the generational chasm in Italian politics
in 1977-1978, but it was present nonetheless.

Like all major social movements, the Portuguese upheaval
exhibited contradictory and even negative aspects. Glorifying
it, or discounting it as a temporary aberration from conservative good sense, both evade its real dimensions. It is only in
the context of this intense and turbulent revolutionary period
that it is possible to understand the emergence, significance
and degree of success of a self-managed *República*, Rádio
Renascenca and Rádio Clube Português.

Footnotes

1. See A. de Figueiredo, *Portugal: Fifty Years of Dictatorship*, Harmondsworth: Penguin Books 1975; P. Mailer, *Portugal: The Impossible Revolution?*, London: Solidarity 1977; W. Minter, *Portuguese Africa and the West*, Harmondsworth: Penguin Books 1972; B. D'Arthuys, *As Mulheres Portuguesas e o 25 de Abril* (Portuguese Women and the 25th of April), Oporto: Affrontamento 1976.

2. A. Rodrigues, C. Borga, M. Cardoso, *O Movimento dos Capitães e o 25 de Abril* (The Captains' Movement and April 25th), Lisbon: Moraes Editores 1974, chs. 3 and 5A.

3. G. Grohs, "The Church in Portugal after the coup of 1974", *Iberian Studies* V.1 (Spring 1976), pp. 34-40.

4. Commissão do Livro Negro sobre o Fascismo, *A Política de Informação no Regime Fascista* (Information Policy in the Fascist Regime), Sintra: Grafica-Europam 1980, pp. 51-52.

5. Cited from J.C. Pires, "Técnica do golpe de Censura" (Censorship coup technique), in *E Agora José?* Lisbon: Moraes 1977, p. 212.

6. M. Braga da Cruz, "Résistance et dissidence populaires à l'Information officiell salaoriste au Portugal", paper given to the Conference on Popular Alternatives to Mass Communication, Cambrils/Barcelona May 25-30 1978.

7. For the media in Portugal before and after 1974, useful accounts can be found in J. Seaton and B. Pimlott, "Media and the Portuguese Revolution", in A. Smith (ed.), *Newspapers and Democracy,* Cambridge: The MIT Press 1980, pp. 174-199, and in F. Perrone & International Mass Media Research Center (eds.), *Portugal: Political Struggle and the Mass Media*, New York/Bagnolet, International General/IMMRC, 1984. Seaton and Pimlott broadly represent a viewpoint favorable to the Socialist Party; Perrone offers a viewpoint favorable to the Communist Party. My perspective is different again, but I have not troubled to specify points of divergence as such in the text. I am very grateful to all three for allowing me to see their work before publication.

8. Mailer, *op. cit.*, p. 81.

9. Cited in Mailer, *op. cit.*, p. 357.

10. A. Rodrigues, C. Borga, M. Cardoso, *Abril nos Quartéis de Novembro* (April in the November Barracks), Amadora: Livraria Bertrand 1979, pp. 87-95.

11. Mailer, *op. cit.*, pp. 218-220.

13

RÁDIO RENASCENÇA

Rádio Renascença (Radio Renaissance) was the Lisbon radio station whose revolutionary career was cut short by an army unit that blew up its transmitter in November 1975, about two weeks before an abrupt halt was called to the revolution's progress. Before the April revolution it had been a Catholic station; and after November 1975 it reverted to its previous ownership. Along with *República*, it was used as a scandalous case of leftwing censorship by the Socialist Party (PSP) in its attempt to bring international pressure to bear against its own opponents inside Portugal. Interference with the freedom of religion was added to interference with press freedom in this instance. But what was the real story of these nineteen months of self-managed communication?

The Build-up To Self-management

The story has to begin with the character of Rádio Renascença before the 1974 revolution. Only in name was it a Catholic station. Its output included a single half-hour on religion each day, usually a broadcast mass or a broadcast rosary. Its ownership, as the radio collective discovered later in 1974 when they had taken control, was in the hands of an obscure property company with an address in the Algarve (the southern coast of Portugal), which nonetheless had no known involvement in real estate in that region.

181

Its financial affairs were handled by an advertising agency called Intervoz, one of whose leading board members had had the doubtful distinction of leading the attempted naval invasion of Conakry, Guinea, in 1970 (as an attempt to deter Guinean support for the liberation struggle in neighboring Guinea-Bissau, against Portuguese colonial rule). Thus the station was to all intents and purposes on the far right in its managerial politics, and only technically a Catholic institution.

A clear illustration of what this meant in practice is the way its journalists used to be regularly censored before the April revolution if they were even to refer to the so-called "social doctrines" of the Second Vatican Council. These represented rather vaguely defined positons on elementary social justice, but were obviously considered dangerously close to dynamite by the management.

There was discreet opposition within Renascenca to this censorship, though clearly nothing much was possible by way of effectively defying it before April 1974. To some extent the Cardinal of Lisbon was not only aware of this opposition within the station, but quietly tolerated it, seeing it as his role to maintain a balance between the Portuguese bishops' conference, unashamedly reactionary in character, and the emerging liberalized Catholicism increasingly popular among lay Catholic intellectuals. His ambivalent position would prove to be very important in shaping the station's future during its period of self-management.

Two issues, above and beyond the events of April 25 itself, were turning points in the shift to self-management in Renascenca. The first was censorship, the second was hiring policy. (It is essential to understand from the outset, that self-management developed only in the Lisbon station; the other main station in Oporto remained under the old regime wihtout a break. This fact also proved to be very important.)

The censorship issue arose in the very first days after April 25 in the Lisbon station. Initially the management took the line that the political crisis would blow over, that nothing of substance was changing, and that the station should continue to operate as usual. But then the exiled leaders of the official left began to return: Soares (Socialist Party), Cunhal (Communist Party), and others. A Communist Party member in Rádio Renascenca took the initiative of recording an interview with Cunhal. Its news value was indisputable, since it would have been the first time Cunhal's voice would have been heard from a radio station inside Portugal!

Given the organization of the news division in the station at the time, this journalist would have been able, had he so chosen, to include the interview in the next news bulletin before the senior management could have intervened to stop it. Instead, he decided formally to ask their permission to broadcast the interview, precisely in order to force the censorship issue. Not surprisingly, they refused him permission outright. The long simmering issue of censorship burst instantly to the surface, and the radio workers went on strike.

The strike lasted only a few hours, but by the end of those few hours the radio workers had added to the demand to end censorship a further demand to have their poor physical working conditions improved. They also elected their own workers' committee.

The management, true to its political colors, refused point blank to recognize or negotiate with the committee. Undeterred, the committee contacted the Armed Forces Movement (MFA) to acquaint it with the situation that had arisen. The MFA responded by first contacting the administration, and then, once it was clear that this would be fruitless as a way of settling the dispute, proceeded to send in its nominee to act as intermediary between the workers' committee and the management. Before April 25, such a concession of legitimacy to the workers' grievances would have been unimaginable. Under these circumstances, the radio workers could only take heart from the MFA's response to the situation.

The second confrontation on hiring policy came shortly afterwards. The management proposed to set a new precedent by requiring would-be employees to take psychological tests,

Once again the MFA was called in, and sent in a new person to act as intermediary. The mangement, by now throughly enraged by the MFA's alliance with "its" subordinate workers, simply withdrew from the station. Intersindical (the Communist Party dominated trade union federation) took over the payment of the seven trainees' wages, and shortly after this, the management discontinued payment of all wages (except to a number of "trusties," who stayed comfortably home until after November 1975, on full salary, and then smoothly resumed their duties as though nothing had ever happened). "So," as one of Renascenca's former journalists put it, "we simply got on with it ourselves." This simple statement, however, does less than justice to the enormous external hazards they faced during their period of self-management—though unlike *República*, the station's internal life was remarkably peaceful.

External Pressure—and Support

The major issue confronting Rádio Renascença was its relation with the Catholic hierarchy. For a long period, the radio collective bent over backwards to be accommodating, letting it be known in public and in private that it was not hostile to the Church, but only to the former management of the station. It stressed that it did not wish to seize the Church's property away from its owner, but simply to broadcast the new realities of Portuguese life without the reactionary control of the previous administration. The collective, to underline its position, actually offered the Church more air-time than it had ever had before. A number of priests publicly supported the moves to make the station independent, which earned them the fury of the Catholic hierarchy. In 1975 the Bishops' Conference denounced "all who present themselves as priests or religious or simple christians, and are taking advantage of the irresponsible climate of freedom reigning in certain sectors of the media to publicize ideas contrary to the church's thinking."[1]

The hierarchy's reaction was to tell its clergy to refuse all cooperation with Renascenca so that when broadcasting units turned up at churches to tape or broadcast services live, they would be told they were unwelcome. Negotiations dragged on meanwhile for nearly a year, though the Cardinal of Lisbon gradually became more inclined to accept the station's new broadcasting policies. Eventually, Renascença's workers succeeded in hammering out a new constitution for the station, to which the Cardinal agreed verbally as being fully in accordance with the social doctrines of Vatican II. The workers also offered to try to compromise on a management council whose personnel were acceptable to the Cardinal.

Never, however, was the Cardinal's verbal consent ratified in writing. At the formal meeting in which he indicated his consent, the workers' representatives signed the constitution document, and he promised to countersign it that night so they could have the agreed text the next day. As one of the workers' representatives put it wryly in 1980: "I am still waiting to receive that document." It seems likely that he was headed off by one of the most aggressively rightist members of the Portuguese bishops' conference, namely its president, the archbishop of Aveiro, who probably intimidated him with the threat of isolation from his episcopal brethren if he were to countersign the constitution.

Throughout these long negotiations there were also other skirmishes. The former management, doubtless with the Church's connivance, tried to get the essential services cut off, ranging from electricity and water to the Reuter telex machine. They also sabotaged Renascença by removing some crucial crystals from the transmitter.

The supply of electricity and water was never actually interrupted, due to prompt solidarity action by the workers' commissions in those services, who refused to interfere with the new Renascenca. The affair of the crystals was much more damaging because without them the transmitter was useless. At this point emerged some effective international solidarity with Portugal: the French section of the trotskyist fourth international managed to get hold of the precise replacements and handed them over to Renascença. Both episodes indiated that Renascença had crucial support, which was particularly important for the workers in their beleagered situation.

The episode of the Reuter telex turned out a little differently. Reuter's position was that it could only deal with the properly constituted legal management, and that under the new circumstances they could not even be sure their existing bills would be paid. Thus, they argued, they had no alternative but to cut off their telex to Renascença.

The Renascença workers, however, managed to persuade Reuter's Lisbon representative to come to discuss the matter with them. He arrived, put Reuter's view to them, and was at the point of leaving, when they urged him to listen for a moment to their own position. They began to explain to him the modern history of Portugal, its results in the wretched conditions under which many Portuguese lived, and the consequent significance of the April revolution. The Reuter's representative listened, thanked them politely, and began to rise to his feet. One or two restraining hands were placed on his shoulders, and he was urged to sit down and hear more. He sat down for a while, then once more rose with the intention of leaving. Again restraining hands were placed on his shoulders. He asked, in apprehension mixed with irritation, whether he was being detained against his will. He was assured this was not the case, and was then presented with a further detailed exposure of the relation between the old Portugal and the new Renascenca. To their surprise, in the end he agreed to recommend to Reuter's that they re-connect the telex, and to assure them of his own confidence that all the telex bills would be paid. Unlike the Cardinal, he kept his word.

Other media, such as Rádio Club Português, had been allowing Renascenca to use their Reuter machines, but it was obviously a victory for Renascenca to get its own machines in operation once more.

These were not the only external hazards faced by Renascenca. The former management's next card to was to pay the workers in the Oporto station to travel down to a general assembly of all Renascenca workers. This—from a management never previously known for its interest in worker democracy!—was in the hope it could engineer an overall majority for itself, with the Lisbon workers outnumbered. The Oporto station had been expanded immediately following the Lisbon switch to self-management, with more staff, and new equipment that could broadcast to most of the country, including Lisbon itself.

However, the Lisbon workers met the Oporto workers as they got off the train, and asked them to talk with them first, so they could explain their own point of view in taking over the station. The Oporto workers agreed, and the end-result was that the assembly adopted a united resolution which deprived the old management of any authority to move against the Lisbon station.

These were the management ploys. Their pressure was experienced in concert with the hostility of the Socialist Party (PSP) and the Popular Democratic Party (PPD—later to retitle themselves the Popular Social Democrats). As soon as the radio workers organized themselves autonomously, these political parties accused them of being hostile to the Catholic Church, of seizing its property, and of interference with its right to broadcast. They pursued this line with special energy abroad, where the image of Portugal fostered by the foreign media was one of a country rapidly lurching from an archaic fascism to an authoritarian "communism." In turn, these accounts in the foreign media were regularly used as a lever inside Portugal to try to dislodge the socialist direction of the revolution.

A further accusation of these two political parties against the Renascenca was that it was dominated by the Communist Party (PCP). The charge was absurd, since there was only one PCP member in Renascenca. A PPD/PSD member who had played an exceptionally active role in most of the committees before and after the switch to self-management himself dismissed the charge as ridiculous to this writer. Indeed, a distinctive feature of the radio collective's operation was that despite its constant shortage of funds, and the drying-up of advertising revenue following the move to self-management, it consistently refused advertisements with either sexist or party-political content. Autonomy was a reality in Renascenca.

Indeed, the true position vis-a-vis the PCP was a good deal different from these claims from the right. To understand it, we have to recount a major clash between Renascenca and the Church, which was instantly seized upon inside and outside the country by Renascenca's enemies. In turn, this clash produced a further alienation between the PCP and Renascenca.

The event which catalyzed these reactions was a demonstration, mostly by elderly women and schoolgirls, outside the Cardinal's house in June, 1975. The demonstration had been called to appeal for the return of the Lisbon Renascenca studios to the Catholic Church's control. One of the far left parties, Popular Democratic Unity (UDP), with a particularly strong commitment to revolutionary media democracy as a foundation of socialist development, arrived a couple of hours later at the cardinal's house and staged a counter-demonstration. Faced with this new contingent of "atheistic communists," the Church demonstrators nervously sought refuge in the cardinal's mansion.

The cardinal telephoned the MFA and demanded army protection for the pro-Church demonstrators. A military detachment turned up, but instead of placing themselves between the rival groups, or telling the UDP group it had made its point and should move on, it told the pro-Church contingent it had to get into the army vans and be driven away. The elderly women had a very difficult time getting into and out of the vans, and some of the soldiers took the opportunity to sexually harass the older school girls as they bundled them into the vans.

This handling of the situation by the military detachment gave Renascenca's opponents a perfect propaganda victory. For it was the fifth provisional government, headed by General Vasco Goncalves (well known to have been in close sympathy with the PCP for many years), which had sent the troops. Their apparent partiality was laid at the door of the presumed partiality of Goncalves himself, and of the PCP, toward Renascenca, and their enmity both to the Church and broadcasting freedom. On June 22, Pope Paul VI sent a note to the Cardinal expressing his "concern" at conflicts involving the Church in Portugal.

The pressure became so intense at that pont that the PPD member interviewed had resigned from the station. Paradoxically in view of the accusations from the right, it had been the station's only PCP member who had argued, unsuccessfully, that the counter-demonstration should be held at the head office of the old management, rather than outside the Cardinal's residence, in order to make it fully clear whom Renascenca was attacking. On June 20 the PCP issued a statement describing the UDP demonstration as having played into the hands of "the enemies of the revolutionary forces."

Once the PSP and PPD campaigns around this incident were in full swing, however, it became rapidly apparent to both the PCP and to the Goncalves administration that in the international arena Renascenca was now (with *República*) the major symbol of their alleged authoritarian tendencies. They came to the conclusion that it would be better to deprive their opponents of this symbolic weapon. Thus on July 1, Goncalves and his Minister of Social Communication, publicly urged the Lisbon Renascenca workers to return the station to its former owners. He also called in some of them privately, and frankly told them of his own dilemma, of being perfectly agreeable to what they were doing, but of wanting to safeguard the revolution as a whole.

The reaction of quite a large number of Renascenca workers to his appeal was to dismiss it as part of a general PCP drive to assert its hegemony over the Portuguese revolution. The tone of many Renascenca broadcasts on the PCP became very hostile as a result, to the point where Intersindical refused to pay the seven trainees' salaries any further, and the PCP member resigned his seat on the workers' commission (though he remained at work in the station). Thus the relation of the PCP to Rádio Renascenca was very far from the one ascribed to it by the PSP, the PPD, and their international media echoes.

The experience of self-management in Rádio Renascenca was not only one of constant threats to its existence, however.

This book is centrally concerned with a realistic appraisal of the problems of media self-management, but it should not be thought that the station only experienced hostile criticism from the outside. Renascenca enjoyed powerful support from the political movement in Portugal. We have already seen how the electricity and water supply workers came to their aid, and there are plenty of other examples beyond these. This support was most evident during those periods, especially in 1975, when it looked as though Renascenca might be physically attacked. Instantly, masses of people flooded into the streets around the station in central Lisbon in order to defend "their" station. The atmosphere was electric, with some people playing guitars and other instruments most of the night to keep the defenders' spirits up. Several Renascenca workers described these experiences of human warmth and solidarity as unforgettable, the living proof of their work's significance to the mass movement in Portugal. People stayed day after day. One former Renascenca worker described how another time someone none of them knew turned up one evening, announced he had come to help defend them against attack, stayed up by the main door most of the night, fell asleep in an armchair mid-morning, and was gone by late afternoon. They never knew his name and never saw him again. Spontaneous support was frequent on every level. Even while relations with the PCP were strained almost to the breaking point, many PCP members told Renascenca workers during a tour they made through Alentejo (a southern rural PCP stronghold) how much they appreciated Renascenca's broadcasts. Following Goncalves' appeal, the station asked Lisbon's Industrial Belt workers and others how they felt. Their answer was a demonstration of many thousands of workers who marched past the station in orderly lines in their work clothes, singing the Internationale with clenched fists. (The Council of the Revolution rescinded the directive.)

In assessing Renascenca's experience of self-management, therefore, it is absolutely impossible to divorce this experience from its relation with these various outside forces, from the Catholic Church and the PSP through to the mass movement of which it was an integral part. Self-management is not a blissful celebration of socialist nirvana, but a way of organizing production, and in this case, of organizing mass communication. The true nature of self-management does not emerge only when social struggles have died away; rather, self-management is a form of involvement with those struggles, *inside them*.

Let us turn now to examine some main features of the internal organization of Rádio Renascenca as it developed during its period of autonomy.

The Internal Processes of Rádio Renascenca

As in many other firms and businesses, Rádio Renascenca elected its workers' commission of eight people in the first weeks after April 25. One of the key internal decisions taken by the commission was to equalize all salaries, an action which contributed greatly both to the cohesion and unity of the collective, and to the avoidance of entrenched new hierarchies inside it. Neither *República* nor Rádio Clube Português ever took this step.

However, the activity of this commission was concerned almost exclusively with external relations: negotiating with the MFA, with the Council of the Revolution, with the Catholic Church, with the political parties, with Intersindical, and with foreign countries. Knowledge of the heavy external pressures faced by the station renders this concentration on external relations entirely understandable. The constant threats from outside had a powerful unifying effect on the Renasçenca workers, who were also fortunate under the circumstances in having had no major blocs among themselves aligned with existing political parties.

Thus the daily work of the radio station was largely unsupervised and remarkably conflict-free. The content was utterly different from what it had previously been, but the basic areas of responsibility remained much what they had been before the changeover. General assemblies of workers could be and were called to discuss major issues and problems, and there was a general readiness to collaborate in view of the external hazards that perpetually threatened to overwhelm the station.

The combination of these hazards with the incredible pace of events in 1974-1975 had other effects on the station's internal life. Arguably, it may have led to too facile a unity at certain points. Some individuals working quite happily and unquestioningly in Renascenca before April 25 instantly transformed themselves into red-hot revolutionaries once it became clear which way the wind was blowing. Their motivation was never really queried.

Perhaps worse, one worker at the station was almost certainly an ex-member of PIDE (the fascist secret police), and another a priest who probably acted as the cardinal's spy throughout the long negotiations with the Church. Practiclly no one would countenance sending either of them packing from the station. About the alleged ex-PIDE agent, a typical reaction was, "Well, he has a wife and a family, how can we strip him of his job?" This last reaction was particularly surprising, given that even the normally pacific Portuguese came close on many occasions to killing PIDE agents who were recognized after April 25.

The PCP member of Rádio Renascenca was of the view that the station badly lacked a coherent policy line, and therefore any basis on which to hammer out policy for the future. Without taking the further step of agreeing with him that the appropriate line for the station would have been the PCP line, his criticism seems nonetheless to be grounded. There were never any workers' assemblies on, for example, how to broadcast, or what a revolutionary broadcasting policy would be, or the role of imaginative material in broadcasting or the role of women in mass communication. And while it might be argued that such discussion would have been a luxury in view of the November 1975 bomb, and that events were far too hectic to allow for long-term reflection, such arguments are short-sighted. They discourage preparation, thus putting people completely at the mercy of events. Further, they encourage a dangerous complacency about existing communication policy, resting on the laurels of the obvious support Renascenca enjoyed rather than seeking to deepen it. The internal organization of Lisbon Renascenca seems to have experienced a possibly deceptive honeymoon, which would have been certain to change had not the course of the Portuguese revolution been abruptly halted. This recognition is important in the service of revolutionary realism, for otherwise there is a tendency to view Renascenca as more successful than, say, *República*, with its violent internal clashes. Clashes in themselves do not indicate progress, but a harmony constructed mainly by outside pressure is not to be confused with principled socialist unity, especially when history shows how much harder it is for socialists to handle their internal divisions than external attacks.

In retrospect Renascenca's virtual burial in the immediate was recognized by some of its former workers as having led to problems. Early on, the workers decided to broadcast only Portuguese music or foreign revolutionary music, and to discard American or American-style popular music, which was dismissed as a manifestation of cultural imperialism, pure and simple. Very early in the morning they would broadcast traditional rural songs for the peasants getting up to start work in the countryside. This programming was appreciated, but the musical diet soon became extremely thin. The policy was never changed, however.

On another level, Renascenca became a "politicos" radio. News bulletins were often an hour in length, and while it was easy to find material for them from the rush of events, and people did listen to them all the way through, the output was pitched at one level only, that of immediate political struggles and developments. As one former Renascenca worker said dryly, "Imagination was not in power in Renascenca!"

For another Renascenca ex-worker, the key error had been not to endeavour to achieve workers' control at the Oporto station as well. This failure had left the much more con-servatively inclined north of the country without a committed revolutionary paper or radio station (illiteracy was high, and *República's* distribution was often interfered with). Leaving the Oporto station under its previous management had also, as we saw, made it much easier for the latter to buy new equipment to extend their broadcasting into the south of the country. It is hard to know how feasible it would have been to extend workers' democracy to the Oporto station, but it is significant that no concerted attempt to bring it about was ever made.

We must examine again, however, the crucial question of the relation between the Lisbon station and the political movement. "We always saw the people as our employers," said one former Renascenca worker, and it is clear that this was the hallmark of the station's relation to the Portuguese people, as well as to representatives of colonized Mozambique, Angola and Guinea-Bissau. Predictably enough they learned fairly quickly that this relation could not be defined in a purely instantaneous way; that if a worker turned up expressing a factory grievance, for instance, it was always sensible to check first with the workers' commission there in case it was just a purely individual complaint. In cases where different groups of workers had opposing positions, Renascenca's line was "plural-istic," namely to give each viewpoint access to the airwaves.

The only political organization within the movement to which they refused this access was the MRPP (Movement for the Reorganization of the Party of the Proletariat, one of the pro-Chinese groups). This refusal was based on two considera-tions. First, the MRPP always insisted on broadcasting its own bulletins itself, whereas other groups and organizations trust-ed the Renascenca workers to read their statements for them. Secondly, its bulletins were always saturated with empty and strident slogans such as "Death to imperialism!" or "Death to Social-fascism!", which harangued listeners rather than com-municating with them.

Aside from this, Renascenca believed in allowing open access to all tendencies and currents in the movement. Indeed, it was both striking and moving, according to one of its former workers, how people politically mute for forty-eight years under fascism transformed themselves at a stroke into elo-quent and fully coherent speakers, evincing no microphone nerves or communicative incompetence. Workers, housewives and peasants alike spoke fluently and effectively without rehearsal, let alone training. Women were extremely active in the squatters' movement, as noted already, and in that capacity in particular spoke vividly over the radio on many occasions. Indeed the opposition Renascenca encountered was always from the official parties, left and right, and from the Catholic Church. Portuguese workers and peasants never attacked Renascenca.

One group on the left with which Renascenca had what might be called a pleasant problem was the UDP, a group which as we saw earlier, took the line that a self-managed Renascenca and *República* were critical to the success of the revolution in Portugal. The UDP set up permanent defense pickets outside the Lisbon studios, wearing UDP armbands, and at one point went so far as to check people going into the building. The Renascenca workers were displeased at this unsolicited action, especially as it gave a wide impression, still current in 1980, that the UPD was running Renascenca. They asked them to desist, which they agreed to do. At the same time their support was valuable, despite its occasional over-enthusiasm.

Renascenca also had good relations with both Frelimo and the MPLA, whose Lisbon representatives had full access to the airwaves to communicate their independence demands for Mozambique and Angola to the Portuguese public. The implications of decolonization for Portugal, however, either in terms of its national self-understanding or in terms of re-emigration to Portugal (the *retornados*) from the ex-colonies, were as little examined by Renascenca as by other revolutionary media.

The last point to make in relation to Renascenca and its links with the political movement, is to emphasize the most striking dimension of its great strength, namely its immediacy. There is no question but that the voices of the movement were heard and the movement's critical moments communicated vividly, as a result of Renascenca's "immersion" in the ongoing struggles and developments of the period.

One person to whom I spoke recalled vividly, as if it had been the previous day, the voice of one of Renascenca's workers phoning an on-the-spot account of a pitched battle between demonstrators and the police. He himself had been beaten by police with a nightstick on his head, the police were massing for another charge and he was saying over the phone: "There's blood running over my face, and I can scarcely stand, but this is what's happening now..." On another occasion my respondent had phoned in and played a song about Sacco and Vanzetti, the Italian revolutionaries executed in the U.S. on trumped-up charges in the 1920s, from his record collection. This went out over the airwaves, and a long discussion on the air followed with people phoning in their views and arguments. Quite a change from before April 25, 1974!

In this sense, Renascenca's achievement was a centerpiece of the movement—not seeking to impose its views on the movement, but assisting the movement's self-development. Like the other Portuguese media we are surveying, its early demise robbed the Portuguese movement, and socialists in general, of a valuable development in the experience of revolutionary communication.

Footnotes

1. Cited in Perrone, *op. cit.*, chapter on Renascenca.
2. A. Rodrigues, C. Borga, M. Cardoso, *Portugal Depois De Abril*, Lisbon: Intervoz Publicidade Lda 1976, p. 217

14
REPÚBLICA

República was the second international *cause célèbre* of the Portuguese media during 1974-1975. It began that period under Socialist Party (PSP) management, and ended as a self-managed daily newspaper, without party affiliation. Its career was an exceptionally stormy one, and there are bitterly contested accounts of what happened in those years. Its shift to self-management was publicly criticized not only by the conservatives, but by the PSP, and also by the French and Italian Communist Parties.[1] Along with Rádio Renascenca, therefore, its internal organization was a long way from being purely an internal affair.

Before April 25, 1974, *República* was the only tolerated daily opposition paper in Portugal. Inevitably, however, its opposition was a rather muted affair, given the state censor's office. For example, when *República* sent its journalists to the conference of the Socialist Party, held by necessity outside Portugal, in Grenoble, France, in 1973, the paper was forbidden to print any of the proceedings, including a lengthy interview with the PSP leader, Mario Soares. It lost the money spent and the interview. Soares himself used to write regular articles for it from Paris, under the pseudonym Clain d'Estaigne, a play on words never picked up by the censors!

Only in the brief two week run-up to national elections, when an official period of grace permitted the press to be a little more candid than it was normally allowed to be, could *República* express any significant opposition to the regime. It was a symbol of resistance, rather than resistance itself, depending largely on its regular subscribers' support. In turn, this support was an expression of their commitment to its symbolic value.

From 1971 the PSP took a majority shareholding in the paper, and proceeded to put in its own editors, Raúl Rêgo and Vitor Direito. The PSP also had had some of its members among the journalists and the printers. According to Rêgo, the printers were among the best paid in Lisbon, because of the PSP's commitment to the working class. In these years, according to one PCP (Communist Party) member, formerly a *República* journalist, relations inside the paper were very good, with a general sense of unity in opposition to the old regime. Everyone to whom I spoke agreed that hostilities broke out remarkably shortly, however, after April 25.

While it would not be accurate to attribute this to some kind of inevitable confusion because of Portuguese inexperience with democratic politics, this was the view put forcefully to me by Raúl Rêgo, who compared Portugal in 1974 with a person bedridden for forty-eight years (under fascism) who suddenly had to learn to walk. Rêgo argued that this was the only light in which the *República* events made any sense. The evidence, however, shows that *República*'s career was determined by less atmospheric, and rather more tangible processes and events than Rêgo claimed.

The growing clashes inside República: April 1974—May 1975

The struggles inside the paper in the first year of the revolution can only be understood against the (already noted) background of Socialist Party and Communist Party rivalry for hegemony over the revolution, and their shared assumption—shared, moreover, by all other major political parties—that control of the media would mean control of the revolution itself. Thus, as the first twelve months proceeded, the PCP became the dominant force in mass information, controlling the Lisbon dailies, one of which was the "quality" newspaper *Diário de Notícias* (Daily News). The PSP found itself with only *República*, because it was its majority shareholder. From the PSP point of view, to "have" one paper in this overall context was not asking too much, especially if it owned it financially.

Rêgo insisted to me, however, that *República* was never simply a party newspaper. There is, despite his insistence, considerable evidence of actions which indicate PSP determination to use the paper that way; and in turn, these actions were at the root of the strife inside the paper. For example, Soares himself used to telephone the paper repeatedly, insisting it cover particular stories. On one occasion, another leading PSP figure was interviewed about a NATO visit to Portugal, and then *demanded* he be shown the journalist's article on the interview to okay it before publication. Editorial policy at certain points indicated the PSP affiliation with great clarity. An example was the relegation of a huge Intersindical (the PCP-dominated union federation) demonstration to the inside pages, while a tiny PSP picket was given front page coverage with a photograph. Another instance was the repeated hiring of new, pro-PSP journalists to try to weight the paper's writers in favor of the PSP. Those journalists who balked at writing what seemed to be purely PSP communication projects were often refused any assignments at all by the editors, and were simply left to cool their heels.

The reaction of the PCP journalists on *República* was to leave *en bloc*, albeit accompanied by some others, in April 1975. The PCP journalists gravitated, naturally enough, to the four Lisbon dailies with a strong PCP presence. Many felt, beyond their frustrations, that some kind of explosion was likely within the paper after they had left, but at the same time none would have predicted the actual course of events. Indeed one PCP journalist said that in retrospect he regretted they had all left when they had because in his view if the PCP group had stayed it could have limited the conflict to the issue of editorial interference with journalists' writing, and so have forced the editors into resigning over censorship. As it was, he concluded, the PSP lost the battle for control of the newspaper, but won the international propaganda war against the leftward trend of the Portuguese revolution by drawing to western attention a supposedly growing encroachment on press freedom in Portugal—with themselves cast in the role of the embattled heroes! They, and the PPD/PSD, actually gave this as their reason for leaving the government in July, 1975.

A number of things pointed to a change in *República's* significance for the PSP at the time. The newspaper became a "case" from which to squeeze political advantage rather than a mass medium valued for itself. For example, the paper's format was very shoddy, reflecting the antique machinery on which it was printed. Although the money to install new presses was available—as the later founding of *A Luta* demonstrated (see below)—the PSP never bothered to do so. The PSP used the smear of PCP control to its advantage in its own international circles, though in other circles the smear had no impact: *Libération* and *Lotta Continua*, neither known for its sympathy with the Communist Party, both sent support messages to the *República* workers. When eventually the Council of the Revolution handed back the keys of the press building to representatives of the management and workers in July (see below), the workers' representative was Luis Porto, a PSP activist. Finally, for all its public talk about media "freedom," "objectivity" and "pluralism," it would be the PSP that approved the dynamiting of Rádio Renascenca's transmitter, which decreed the nationalization of Rádio Clube Português, and which after November 25, 1975 moved, in conjunction with other parties in government, to begin to rein in dissonant voices in the media.[2]

May 2, 1975: the printers' strike

"It was as though my secretary here in Parliament refused to type my letters!" expostulated Raúl Rêgo to me in April 1980, his fury still unabated. His words convey the ideology of ownership very precisely. What had originally provoked his anger was the printers' strike which erupted the day after May Day, 1975. He and the PSP consistently interpreted the strike as a PCP plot among the arrogant *República* printers to wrench control of the paper from the PSP. The PSP leadership insisted, and does to this day insist, that the printers also wanted to write the paper themselves: "the madness that took over *República*," as Rêgo put it.

The strike lasted several days. The printers' initial demand was for an internal reorganization, and a ban on hiring new journalists unless this was negotiated and approved by the workers on the paper. This was clearly designed to choke off the "packing" of *República* with PSP nominees.

They elected a Workers' Co-ordinating Committee (CCT) from the Workers' General Assembly. This Committee was elected by occupational sections, with one representative per fifteen workers in each section. The committee was mandated to negotiate a statute of independence for the paper's political line. On May 6th, the Committee approved a working document which proposed dialogue with the management on the issues of how the different sections of the paper should be re-organized.[3] It also demanded financial and party-political independence—especially the latter—for the paper. It further urged regular reviews of the paper's management structure. The continuing thread, however, was the demand for a non-sectarian paper of the left: "All the progressive parties must be treated in the same manner," said the May 6 document. It added, finally, that the arbiters of the paper's non-sectarian policy were to be its workers, through their democratic insitutions such as the General Assembly and the CCT.

This demand for an open paper was certainly not a demand for the exclusion of the PSP perspective, or for hegemony of the PCP perspective. Yet, it proved to be a demand that was quite impossible for *República*'s management to contemplate. Like all the other major parties, the PSP management was trapped in the manipulative—and deterministic— assumption that media control granted control of the revolution's direction. On May 14, Belo Marques, finance director of the newspaper and very close to the PCP, submitted his resignation. The CCT asked him to remain, but called for the resignation of the rest of the management. In an action which demonstrated the printers' degree of determination, the CCT also organized a picket of the newspaper in case of a management attempt to seize the presses.

On May 19, most of the journalists refused to write for the paper anymore, taking as their pretext the CCT's refusal to print management's account of the paper's internal crisis in the forthcoming issue of the paper. The CCT responded by suspending the management, with the support of ninety-three out of the one hundred forty present at the assembly meeting (the paper's full strength being about one hundred ninety). It then brought the paper out for one day with Belo Marques' name on the masthead. That day the PSP mounted a demonstration outside the newspaper. Soares headed it, and in an exchange with the workers, told them they were "objectively playing the game of reaction." One replied: "This is not the PS headquarters. You and your colleague Cunhal must recognize the strength of the workers. You have to stop playing games with the people. Both of you, go back to where you used to live!"⁴ The reference to Cunhal, PCP leader, is indicative of the true state of feelings in the paper. COPCON (the crack military unit) promptly intervened in the situation. A night of fruitless negotiations followed with the government's Information Minister in the chair, but openly supporting the management. (In an interview on May 23 in the weekly *Expresso* he said he was "convinced" the workers were wrong.)⁵ At six o'clock in the morning, the *República* offices were evacuated and sealed off. The paper was not on the streets again until July 10 when it was re-opened with an official military director, but actually under workers' control. (A little later, Belo Marques left the paper after his plan for *República* was turned down, despite his almost irreplaceable grip on the paper's administration and finances.)

Thus the printers' strike was about control of the paper's political line, or rather against its sectarian adhesion to the PSP, but was never a demand that they should write it themselves. On the contrary, they expressed, in the context of *República*, the general Portuguese public's growing sense of total alienation and impotence at the destruction of the revolution's impulse by vicious feuding between leftist political parties. Their demand was simple, and in one sense negative: that *República* should not be dragged down to that level. The more positive notion of a newspaper "of the mass base," which dominated the period of self-management, was a notion which only surfaced well after the strike, not before it. As the printers put it in their manifesto:

> We the workers of *República* are conscious of being in a society lacking science and education, in which especially there is absent a politics of information which, instead of disabling the poor and exploited working classes, gives them intellectual and economic power... We declare that in information it is the workers who have the power to decide that the fruit of their labor—the newspaper—should be devoted to activities concerned with the transformation of mankind and of life, and not with the aggressive objectives of political leaders, not with privileges of corrupt minorities, or with party-political exhibitionism.⁶

The period of self-management

The period of self-management in *República* was thus extremely short, lasting only from July 10 till November 25, when *República*, like all other media, was forcibly closed by government decree. Both Rádio Clube Português and Rádio Renascenca enjoyed a much longer experience of self-management. Nonetheless, the five months were important for the Portuguese movement, despite November 25. At a Lisbon political rally on April 25, 1980, when I was carrying a special copy of *República* brought out as a commemorative issue by the PSP, some people asked to see the paper in the hope that it might be reappearing. At the time, I was standing on the edge of the large PCP contingent. One worker actually took the PCP's news-sheet handout and made as if to hang on to *República* and throw the news-sheet away! *República* had clearly lodged itself in Portuguese workers' minds as a demonstration of what workers had achieved for themselves, and could achieve by themselves.

The first change in *República*'s organization was the influx of new journalists to replace the old PSP members who had left. (Most of these latter were re-hired on the short-lived daily *A Luta*—The Struggle—published by the PSP.) Many of the new people on the paper were students, with no previous journalistic experience of any kind, and joined the paper purely out of political commitment to its struggle. *República*'s funds were critically low, since anything which could be sequestered from its finances by the former PSP owners was removed. Advertising revenue dried up, then resumed, but only at a trickle.

Thus wages were difficult to pay, as were all of the paper's bills. Its newsprint bill, for instance, was enormous, and the government refused to help it to pay it. Eventully the workers decided in their Assembly to ask for public support, and held a mass demonstration on the April 25 bridge (formerly the Salazar bridge—a suspension bridge which straddles the wide Tagus estuary to Lisbon harbor). This appeal realized no less than 700,000 escudos, a tangible index of the popular support *República* enjoyed. All the same, it was practically impossible to send journalists anywhere to report on events because of the paper's financial morass. And there was no decision, unlike in Rádio Renascenca, that everyone should receive the same wage. Lastly, the printers were less than enthusiastic about having a large body of volunteer collaborators on the paper, because they felt this could open it to a fresh wave of party-political colonization.

This complex of factors quickly dictated the kind of paper that the new *República* could be. Under self-management it rapidly transformed itself into a newspaper of the base, dependent to a large extent on information given to it, rather than ferreted out by its journalists. It was as a result a highly combative newspaper, giving almost all its attention to immediate popular struggles. Its coverage of two types of struggle was especially strong: the squatters' movement, led largely by women; and the political conflicts inside the armed forces' barracks, mostly between the politicized soldiers and their reactionary officers. It is hardly surprising that conservative and centrist forces inside Portugal were dismayed and angry at this trend in the paper.

As was predictable from the May printers' strike, the new *República* gave voice to the reaction against the official political parties of the left, and to the desire for people's power over the revolution's direction. In the words of its own new statutes, published in the issue of August 1, 1975.

> The newspaper *República* is oriented on marxist principles and takes it as given that the workers' emancipation and liberation are the activity of the workers themselves. It is involved in an uncompromising defense of a line of National Independence against the superpowers' hegemony, and moreover fights all forms of class collaboration...The working class and other exploited classes must intervene critically in the content of the newspaper *República* through their independent organs of popular will...So that the newspaper *República* may fulfil the specific mission of this constitution, it must be controlled by all the workers through their executive organ the CCT...The final organ of decision is the workers' Plenary...We recognize as its legitimate source of information, communications from the commissions of workers, squatters, unemployed, soldiers, sailors, and all the base organs representing the Portuguese workers.[7]

Like Rádio Renascença workers, *República*'s workers also

saw the revolutionary movement in Portugal as their ultimate employer and authority. As anyone might suppose, this was not always a straightforward matter to realize in practice. Relations with the other workers' commissions did not assume a stable form, but were only realized in the context of particular struggles, and for the duration of those struggles. In that sense, any notion of regular and continuing intervention by the paper's readership proved extremely problematic. The commission might present highly localized and fragmented accounts of the problems they encountered, or might themselves be divided along party lines. Often the commissions themselves looked to *República* for guidance, rather then the reverse; and this guidance was rarely forthcoming. Thus the movement itself was not sufficiently unified or organized to be able to govern the newspaper's output in any consistently meaningful way. As in other instances reported in this book (Radio Popolare, the women's section of *Lotta Continua*, Controradio), the collective found itself forced to make its own decisions.

Internally, however, the paper did not move to cancel the division between intellectual and manual labor (as would have been predicted from PSP claims about the printers' arrogance). Admittedly the official military director played a purely formal role. But the printers themselves were content simply to act as custodians of the paper's party-political independence and openness—its conscience, not its censors. The journalists continued to write *República*, with only occasional contributions from its administrative staff or its printers. The other contributors were, as noted, the commissions. There was plenty of discussion between printers and journalists, and a number of ideas certainly originated with the printers, but the paper's overall content was and remained in the journalists' hands.

Beyond this, there existed the simple fact of diversity among both journalists and printers. Not all the journalists had the same skills or experience, so that invariably there emerged an informal hierarchy among them. Among the printers, there were some still locked into a purely trade union consciousness, others were mainly preoccupied with maintaining their jobs, and yet others, often the younger printers, were evincing a very rapid growth toward political maturity and activism. Those with the most active say in the paper's running were those who were politically active, whether journalists or printers.

The printers, however, were resigned to the continuing fact of the division between intellectual and manual labor. They found it easier than did some slightly guilt-ridden *República* journalists, to accept the sheer fact of the journalists' educational experience, wider perspective, writing experience, and grasp of the emerging political system in Portugal.

It is in the light of these practical realities that we should interpret the election in September 1975 by the workers' plenary, of a political commission to review the paper's content each day before it "went to bed." The commission was composed of four people. All four were printers concerned with lay-out, for the simple reason that when the paper was being written, the lay-out printers were the only ones with the time to work on its contents with the editorial co-ordinating committee (of four journalists). The whole CCT (Workers' Co-ordinating Committee) was too large a body to do this, as even more obviously was the workers' General Assembly. Thus in the everyday running of the paper, these eight people, with varying political perspectives, were effectively in control of the detail. The political commission rarely objected to anything of any magnitude, intervening rather on the level of appropriate headlines and such practical matters.

For more basic questions, either the CCT was invoked, or the plenary if the CCT felt unable to resolve the issue itself. Anyone was free to approach any of these committees at any time. An example of a decision refered to a plenary was when a series of articles politically slandering Mario Soares was before the CCT for consideration. The plenary refused to publish them. On another occasion, the plenary was called to approve or reject publication of an interview with Captain Fernandes (one of the original planners of April 25 who had distributed 1500 guns to revolutionary activists). It did approve this interview.

In the end, the fundamental problem facing *República* under self-management was not its penniless condition, nor the collective's political or journalistic experience, but the huge gap between the politics of the movement and official party politics, a chasm which still existed in Portugal in 1980. At the grassroots, there were numerous independent creative initiatives, but these had no accurate reflection in official politics. None of the major political parties took up any of these moves.

Consequently, people began to stop bothering about overall political realities. While the parties, even the tiny ones, were talking non-stop about the problem of state power, the people were talking about their immediate struggles—and hoping things would turn out all right overall. People quite often even combined their own local initiatives with a continuing reliance on one or another of the existing left parties at the national level.

There was no apparent resolution of this crushing problem. Jorge Almeida Fernandes cites a foreign revolutionary, actively engaged in the Portuguese events, who proposed through the pages of *República* that the paper should become the directing center of the non-party political movement. He observes dryly: "The utopia inside the newspaper was always a more realistic one."[8] The paper backed the popular movement, but always hoped for time, for a period of grace in which the movement could coalesce—as though the tensions in Portugal between the forces at odds with each other could continue without some resolution. Fernandes quotes from *República's* report of the paratroopers' dynamiting of Radio Renascenca:

> ...the only alternative to counter-revolution...is to rein-force mass mobilization, and organization, in order to reinforce the centralization of popular power and the worker-peasant alliance, and to reinforce the soldiers' and workers' ability to respond and take the political initiative...

The analysis was flawless; but the means were unavailable. November 25 followed swiftly.

When the *República* collective met to discuss its reaction to the events of November 25, there was a prompt split, essentially between the older and younger members. The younger ones wanted to bring out *República* as quickly as possible to help to rally popular resistance. The older ones wanted to keep their heads down and save their jobs if they possibly could. But only about thirty people were there, arguing for hours into the night. The paper did come out again in spite of the older workers' fears, on November 30, but by that time the new government had effective overall control. In January 1976, *República* was closed by the government.

Despite its short period of self-management, *República*'s experience is instructive. Not only does its history demonstrate the practical viability of media self-management, it demonstrates that this is possible even with very limited funds and journalistic experience. The key to its success was its living relationship to the ongoing political movement in Portugal. For example, a former *República* journalist told the writer how at one stage in late 1975, when the PCP was extremely hostile to all strikes, and was expressing this daily through its control of much of the Lisbon press, she was the only newspaper journalist to whom the Lisbon metro workers would speak while they were on strike. The success of *República's* public appeal on the April 25 bridge is another instance of this close relation between the paper and the movement at large. This bond with workers, with squatters, with the barracks, with African liberation movement spokespeople in Lisbon, was the foundation of *República's* viability. The official attacks by the Socialist Party, and the Communist Party's disapproval, both bounced harmlessly off *República*, given this mass support. (The most effective attack the PSP contrived was to get distributors in the north of Portugal outside Oporto to refuse to handle *República*, and to distribute *A Luta* instead.)

At the same time, the problems of the movement were also *República's* problems, as we have seen. Additionally, as in the case of Rádio Renascenca, the sheer pressure of events each day meant that a number of deeply important issues tended never to surface: the place of imaginative material in the paper's communication, the implications of de-colonization for Portugal's self-understanding, the position of women in Portugal. In this last instance, it must be said in fairness that women often intervened in the paper as squatters or as strikers and that the four women journalists on the paper, according to one of them, were treated without any form of discrimination. Finally, another major social problem in Portugal, illiteracy, meant that *República* was essentially a workers' paper, read only in the main industrial towns and cities.

In the final analysis, however, *República's* strength lay in the dedication of its collective to the movement's right to self-determination, a political position which always echoed the everyday practice of direct democracy inside the paper. The bond between these two aspects of the revolutionary process was never snapped, even though *República* could not single-handedly support the momentum of the revolution against the events of November 25. *República* stands, nonetheless, as a compelling testimony to the extraordinary potential of self-activity by the working class even in the face of crushing difficulties.

Footnotes

1. *France Nouvelle* (September 1, 1975), p. 20 and *L'Unità* (June 11, 1975), cited in Alex Macleod, "The French and Italian Communist Parties and the Portuguese Revolution," paper presented to the second international meeting on modern Portugal, Durham, NH, June 21-24, 1979.

2. See for this later development *Gazeta da Semana* (Lisbon), issues 6 (p. 6), 7 (p. 5), 16 (p. 6), 19 (p. 5) which appeared respectively May 6-13, 13-20, July 15-22. August 5-12, 1976.

3. "Breve Nota Sobre 'O Caso'," (Brief Note on "the case") *Gazeta do Mês* 1 (May 1980), p. 14.

4. Cited in A. Rodrigues, C. Borga, M. Cardoso, *Portugal Depois De Abril,* (Portugal from April) Lisbon: Intervoz Publicidade Lda 1976, p. 203.

5. Perrone, *op. cit.*, chapter on *República*.

6. Cited in "Breve Nota," n. 3.

6. Cited in Jorge Almeida Fernandes, "Duas ou tres coisas que eu sei do *"República"* (Two or three things I know about *República), Gazeta do Mês* I (May 1980), pp. 14-15.

8. *Ibid.*

9. *Ibid.*

15

RADIO CLUBE PORTUGÛES

Rádio Clube Português (RCP) was the most financially successful of the three self-managed Portuguese media during 1974-1975. And whereas Rádio Renascenca was closed by dynamite, and *República* by decree, RCP was actually nationalized, and this by the post-November 25 government whose watchword was "No more nationalization!" What lay behind this curious turn of events?

For forty-three years up to April 25, 1974, RCP had been owned by a company with direct links to the Franco regime in Spain. In that sense, RCP was a second Francoist embassy in Portuagal. Thus, like Renascenca, it had an extremely reactionary political orientation. Its studios were to be found in Lisbon and Oporto, but also in Luanda, Angola (under the name of "Freedom Station" radio!). It also owned a record company, a cinema under construction when the MFA took over, and some very valuable real estate. It was however over its transmitters that the popular song "Grandola" was broadcast at 12:29 am on April 25, 1974, as the signal for the armed forces to seize power.

After April 25, RCP's workers met together at the Telecommunications Union office, and decided to press for the
director's resignation. On May 3, one of the captains who had
taken command of the station was nominated by General
Spinola as the new junta's delegate to RCP. Three days later,
the directors handed over all their powers to him. The consequence was, as in so many Portuguese enterprises in those
days, that the delegate was then instructed by the government
to find either a member of management, or someone elected by
the firm's workers, to run RCP's affairs jointly with him.

However, at this point the workers in the station chose to
push the issue further. They decided to press for an Administrative Commission, composed of four members elected by secret
ballot, and one representative of state power. In support of this
demand, they noted how RCP's previous directors had been
totally identified with "the corrupt and oppressive methods of
the deposed regime."[1] On May 6 the government agreed, in the
person of its Minister of Social Communication, none other
than Raúl Rêgo. Rádio Club Português, of all places, was under
revolutionary self-management; all 290 of its workers in Portugal were behind the switch in power (unlike the unfortunate
division between Oporto and Lisbon studios of Renascenca).

This structure remained more or less intact throughout the
eighteen months of the revolutionary phase in Portuguese
politics. On March 11, 1975, the Administrative Commission
was expanded to six people, responsible as before for both the
Lisbon and Oporto studios, medium wave and FM broadcasting. Inside each section or department there was also a democratic structure, with heads being elected from inside their
departments, and reporting to the Administrative Commission. There was, in addition, a Workers' General Assembly,
which met either on demand, or at least every six months. At
such meetings, members of the Administrative Commission
could be asked for their resignation.

On one occasion this did happen. The Commission's delegate from the government was a Socialist Party member, like
Rêgo, but with a strong drive toward financial success. He
strenuously urged on RCP workers the need to diversify the
enterprise into holiday centers, construction projects, and the
like (so exemplifying perhaps the strange split soul of the
Portuguese Socialist Party). Eventually the mood of hostility
among RCP workers grew to such proportions against this
vision of the station's future that he was asked to resign. He did

so without attempting to contest the situation further. His successor delegate from the government made it quite clear from the outset that he neither could nor wished to play any part in broadcasting policy, but was happy simply to represent RCP's workers to the government if occasion arose. It was another success story for RCP, both in the smooth working of its democratic processes, and in the good fortune of its replacement delegate from the government.

Financially, the station had no problems at all, unlike virtually every other case-study in this book. Advertisers not only continued to place advertisements, but actually stepped up their advertising. Thus in 1973, RCP's advertising revenue stood at 44, 635,000 escudos; in 1974, at 47,758,000; and in 1975, at 69,174,000. The 1975 figure would probably have stood at 80 million escudos, had it not been for the station's closure from November 25 through to the beginning of 1976. Jaíme Fernandes, who had been elected chair of the Administrative Commission during 1975, also told me how RCP had been in a very tight spot financially for three days on one occasion because of a problem synchronizing the monthly payment date for salaries with the usual date for receiving advertisers' checks. RCP's bank manager agreed without the slightest demur to provide 1.8 million escudos to pay the RCP workers on the date they expected to be paid, but even went further, and made no charge for the loan!

In retrospect, Jaíme Fernandes concluded that the station's financial success probably had a good deal to do with the fact that its output was less inflammatory than either Renascenca's or *República*'s. The programming continued basically as before, with the addition of one new weekly slot for Intersindical. For the entire eighteen months, however, news and current affairs programs were "balanced" in the accurate sense of the word. That is to say, that interviews were sought with all sides to a dispute in a major struggle—not simply with the representatives of power, as is usually the case in establishment media, nor simply with the exploited or oppressed, as was the practice of Renascenca or later of *República*.

This balance was a radical departure both from pre-April 25 Portugal, and for the RCP, where such attention to a dispute had been previously out of the question. Nevertheless, it marked a considerably less revolutionary policy than in Renascenca or *República*, and a much less politically defined stance than that taken by the four Lisbon dailies under PCP control in 1975, which became transmission belts for the PCP's positions in most instances. Even those hostile to the new RCP used to listen to its news and current affairs because they felt them to be reliable. Thus, from the advertisers' perspective, knowing this continuing audience for RCP programming, and knowing the audience was not just composed of penniless squatters or striking workers, RCP must presumably have offered a desirable marketing outlet—especially given the "loss" of Rádio Renascenca.

This is not to say, however, that the political forces within the country were uniformly happy with RCP. The Lisbon studios were occupied by the military on Spinola's orders on September 28, 1974; on March 11, 1975 there were machine gun attacks on the Porto Alto transmitters; on November 11 the same year there was a joint demonstration in Oporto against the station by the Socialist Party, the Popular Democratic Party, the Center Social Democrats and the Popular Monarchist Party. And on November 25, the station was shut down.

Initially, there were also heavy threats from the government of penalties for broadcasting news about Franco's Spain. The station faced a complete embargo of news about the Portuguese island colonies of São Tomé and Príncipe because of an earlier RCP broadcast interview with an officially disfavored opposition group in those territories. The interview was smuggled into Portugal in defiance of government policy. Despite the completely legal status of RCP's self-management, unlike the more confused situation in *República* and Renascenca, the right wing continued to decry its existence and operation almost continously, searching for any scraps of information that might discredit it. For instance, a public accusation was made in a newspaper that RCP had been supplying arms to COPCON, the special military unit under Otelo de Carvalho which came to play a significant role in supporting a number of progressive struggles during the revolutionary period. The arms in question turned out to be relics from the Spanish Civil War that had been unearthed on RCP premises following the takeover of power, and which had been passed on to COPCON to be deposited in the Army Museum!

RCP was also attacked from the left, mostly for its alleged bias in favor of the Communist Party. This is worth a little investigation. The workers in news and current affairs were divided into three broad political categories: those to the left of the PCP, those in a whole variety of positions to its right, and those in or close to PCP. These last were never in the majority. In terms of the 15 people responsible for news bulletins, only three belonged to the pro-PCP group.

However, the structure of the news division meant that it was possible at times for the station's bulletins to be run for eighteen hours with a continuous PCP "slant." While there were weekly meetings for everyone in news and current affairs to discuss the forthcoming events, the actual programming was left entirely to these 15 individuals, operating on a 6 hour continuous shift system. The impression could easily gain currency—and did—that the station was run by the PCP, especially in the atmosphere of extreme suspicion between political groups (including those on the left), and in the context of the PCP's 1975 ascendancy in four Lisbon dailies.

Indeed, at one point, these internal divisions erupted into RCP's own news bulletins. [3] The occassion was a speech by the MRPP leader, Arnaldo Matos—the MRPP was one of the most vocal pro-Chinese groups—in which he attacked the political arguments for a single trade union federation. This was a direct assault on the policy of the Intersindical to have all unions formally inscribed in its own ranks and beyond this a direct attack on the PCP's hegemony over the Intersindical leadership. The Telecommunications Union put out a communique attacking the RCP's news division for giving space to "extremist groups...attacking the revolution and encouraging...reaction."

This communique was broadcast by a PCP member of the RCP news division. Twelve other members of the RCP news division promptly read out their own communique on the 1:00 pm news, in which they condemned any attempt to exclude non-PCP political views from RCP news. They pledged themselves to "struggle for a information (service) open to all political currents, except fascism," and to give pride of place "to Portuguese workers' struggles against capitalist exploitation and for the end of exploitation..."

In turn at 3:00 pm this communique was followed, respecting the right of reply, by another response to it. This rejected any intention of interference with the news, and then went on to describe as ridiculous the pledge to end exploitation, "given some of the twelve signatories." In the 8:00 pm news a joint communique was broadcast announcing that while both sides reserved their positions, the matter would from then on be taken up in the union local. (The eventual outcome was an editorial statute expressing the position of the twelve.)

Apart from this sudden eruption on November 18, 1974, the internal politics of the station seem to have been peaceful enough. When Jaíme Fernandes was elected chair of the Administrative Commission, before he would take the job, he expressed the view that the RCP should strive to be professionally excellent in broadcasting, and not politically partisan. This was overwhelmingly accepted by RCP workers, probably feeling like other Portuguese workers at the time that the political parties, large or small, were engaged in playing games with their own destinies. Thus the PCP and its sympathizers were effectively dominated by the majority in RCP, despite some external appearances to the contrary.

The end of RCP came quite soon after the workers voted in favor of Fernandes' economic plan for the station (devised as a substitute for the grandiose schemes of the former government delegate to the Administrative Commission). After the station was closed down, Fernandes was called in by the new Minister for Social Communication who lectured him severely on RCP's supposed failings and misdeeds, but promised that he would strive with all his might to prevent threatening its independence. The very next day he nationalized it.

The nationalization was met with a curious silence, seemingly indicating consent. It was curious because the move satisfied not only the left political parties, who were generally in favor of nationalization, but also the right. The left quite plainly did not grasp that nationalization was a way of controlling RCP with less offense to international opinion than the dynamiting of Rádio Renascenca. However, the new government's intentions were clarified when eight workers were promptly sacked, and another sixty suspended, including the entire journalistic staff. These last stayed under suspension without any formal charge or hearing for fourteen months.

The government publicly defended its actions as creating a structure of broadcasting similar to most Western European countries. It solemnly asserted the importance of having a radio station with "the characteristics of a public service to serve the public and the Revolution." There had been too much passion and too much partiality, read the government statement, and these had distanced people both from the radio and the Revolution.[4] What, or whose, revolution, was discreetly left undefined.

It is indicative of the political character of the new government and the forces behind it, that the relatively sober and entirely legal Rádio Clube Português demanded such treatment. Of all the cases under examination in Portugal and Italy, RCP was easily the least "revolutionary," in objective terms. However, for the Portuguese counter-revolution, such abstract generalizations weighed less than dust.

Footnotes

1. Cited in Adelino Gomes, "RCP em autogestão do 25 de Abril ao 25 de Novembro" (RCP under self-management from April 25 to November 25), *Gazeta do Mês* 1 (May 1980), pp. 18-19.
2. On the myth of balance in British Broadcasting, see my *The Media Machine,* London: Pluto Press, 1980, chs. 2, 4, 6.
3. *Gomes, art. cit.*
4. *Ibid.*

16

THE ITALIAN FERMENT

Four Dimensions of Italian Politics

In what follows, I have selected four features of present-day Italy which are essential to understanding the social framework of the political movements of the sixties and seventies, and the self-managed media which were such a visible feature of those movements. The four features are: the sharp division between North and South, the experience of fascism from 1920 to 1945, the continuing weight of the Catholic Church, and the emergence of the Italian Communist Party as the largest such organization in western Europe.

Regional divisions play a significant role in many societies, yet the split between North and South in Italy must be among the most striking. It has forced itself on every analyst of Italy, native or foreign. The unification of the country in 1870 was passionately resented in the South as a Northern coup. The South is still much more rural than the North, and its traditions much more stable. The two major northern industrial cities, Milan and Turin, are both only a short distance from the Swiss and French frontiers, and have a northern European ambiance, whereas Naples and Palermo and the more southern countryside are much closer in feel to the Third World. An extreme example of the northern culture is to be found in German-speaking areas on the Swiss and Austrian borders, where Italian speakers are actually met with cold hostility and contempt. An extreme example of the southern culture is the continued operation of the mafia.

215

The South still operates with severe economic disadvantages as compared to the North. A shocking revelation of what this means in crisis conditions was provided by the virtual lack of response of the Italian government to the southern earthquake which occurred in 1981. Aid for the survivors reached the scene from the U.S. and Britain before there was aid from the central government. Many died of exposure, trapped in rubble for days because the Italian Army was not mobilized in time to deal with the emergency. Contemptuous attitudes towards southerners are frequently encountered in the North, and this official inaction perfectly reflects the usual dismissive disregard for the generally wretched condition of southern peasants. The fact that the patriarchal extended family still holds sway in much of the South, that old-style Catholicism still has a firm grip there, that the mafia operates with virtual impunity from state interference (especially in Sicily, Calabria, and Naples), that poverty is widespread, are taken to represent the stupidity of the Southerners, their preference for a cultural mire, rather than their dereliction by the forces of economic development in Italy. The arrival of new industries in the South during the seventies in search of cheap and docile laborpower, has not yet happened on a scale to alter the South's patterns to any marked extent.

The notion that somehow southerners are happy with the mafia, or that it is an organization with no ties to the national government, is one which dies hard. Let us examine briefly an instance of the mafia at work in order to clarify the oppressive conditions in whch ordinary southerners have to live out their struggles. In Calabria in June 1980 the secretary of a local Communist Party branch, Giuseppe Valeriotti, was murdered. A few days later, hours after his funeral, two workers who had been bold enough to walk in the funeral cortege, were gunned down on their way back home. Valeriotti had been threatening to release evidence that the mafia had begun actively penetrating newly formed rural organizations, such as farmers' cooperatives, and also the local Socialist Party branches, in order to head off any possible challenges to its control from these quarters. Till then, only the Christian Democrats, the party which has governed Italy since 1948, had mafia members.

The newspaper *Repubblica* (June 13, 1980) included a part of their reporter's interview with the local deputy mayor, a Socialist Party member acting as second string to the Christian

Democrat mayor. The tenor of the interview strongly suggests that this man was himself a part of the infiltration that Valeriotti had been threatening to expose.

How, *Repubblica* asked the deputy mayor, is the killing of Valeriotti to be explained?

I don't know, but I exclude a political motive and also the mafia. We are all friends here.

But, asked *Repubblica*, the mafia is present in this area isn't it?

I have heard so. But I am in no position to say.

How, *Repubblica* persisted, could a whole crop of recent incidents be explained, such as the burning of the Calabrian Communist Party leader's car a few days before the murder, the fire-bombing of the local Communist Party office, threats made against the local borough surveyor?

It's not my job to find out. Behind all this there must have been personal issues, resentments. You will see that they will eventually find out that perhaps even behind the murder, it was some dispute about women.

Repubblica cited to him the report of the local *carabinieri* (the senior police forces in Italy) that every single business in the area paid a heavy levy to the mafia.

I don't know anything about this. I have never been asked to do so.

said the socialist deputy mayor...

This was not 1880, but 1980. And despite *everyone's* knowing the truth of the situation, these terror-actions went unpunished. Some writers have gone so far as to say Italy is actually two separate countries, and would cite this kind of situation as an example of the sharp differences between South and North. The plausibility of this argument declines, however, as soon as the deep bonds between the two parts of the country are recognized.[1] These bonds are principally twofold: the fact that the South continues to provide an exceptionally cheap labor-pool for northern industries and for northern firms operating in the South; and the fact that the continuous place of the Christian Democrats in government since World War II has been assured by their southern base. *Thus the condition of the South is also a fundamental condition for the basic economics and politics of the whole country.* No agency of the state would effectively prosecute the organization behind the murder of Valeriotti and his two fellow workers. In this Italy is indisputably a single nation.

The second major dimension of contemporary Italy is the imprint of fascism, first Mussolini's, then Hitler's. Perhaps its most signal effect has been on the political consciousness of Italian workers, who, whatever their other views, are solidly and viscerally anti-fascist. In Italy it is almost impossible to imagine anything similar to the penetration by the KKK into the northern U.S. working class, or by British neo-Nazi groups into the working class there. Italy has a fascist parliamentary party, the MSI (Italian Social Movement), which by 1980 was trying to launch a new mass-based politics, especially among the youth. (Its Rome radio station was called "Alternative Radio"!) Its only impact, however, was among middle class youth. In Naples, its only urban power-base, the MSI's sole success in the 1980 municipal elections consisted of splitting the right wing vote and so allowing the left into power by a whisker. In terms of mass politics, therefore, fascism remains a marginal force in Italy, even though it is well represented at certain key points in the state.

This instinctive anti-fascism is also one of the strongest planks of the Communist Party (PCI) within the working class and in turn is central to the PCI's self-understanding. The republic and the constitution, as bulwarks against any revival of fascism, are the habitual watchwords of the PCI, in posters, at meetings, in its media. It should never be forgotten that the PCI's roots in Italian society developed during and because of the huge popular movement of resistance to Mussolini and the Nazi axis in World War II. Thus to speak of fascism's imprint on Italy is first and foremost to speak of the extraordinary culture of political resistance that fascism first provoked, and then was swallowed up by in 1944-45. It was the Italians, not the Allied Forces, who captured and executed Mussolini. Only now is a generation emerging whose parents have had no direct experience of fascism.

On another level, however, fascism is still a force to be reckoned with in Italy. Personnel in many key government departments were not changed following the defeat of Mussolini and Hitler, and so have been able not merely to continue as individuals, but to wield power and recruit like-minded people to swell their presence. Almirante, head of the Italian secret service until 1976, became leader of the fascist MSI immediately afterwards. Appalling bomb-explosions in public places in the 60s, 70s and 80s were not only instigated by fascists, but people in high places undoubtedly knew about them in advance. Links were forged between these circles and the fascist colonels in control of Greece from 1967-74, in the hope that Greece would prove an ideal base for their own activities in Italy. They were unsuccessful in their wilder dreams, but they have by no means departed the scene. It is unclear at the time of writing whether the shadowy organization P2, whose existence was revealed, in 1981, to include key members of the judiciary, the military, the government, the civil service and the media in Italy, was itself a fascist nest, or whether it was content to enjoy a working relation with fascist circles. At all events, fascism and anti-fascism are not dead issues in Italy.

The third aspect of Italian society which must be assessed is the continuing weight of the Catholic Church. Although it is sometimes said that new Catholic converts should be discouraged from visiting Rome, lest the experience wither their religious enthusiasm, the Church still functions in Italy on a mass level. Its base is at its strongest in the South, and among the more traditionally minded middle and upper classes. Historically, the Church hierarchy actively supported Mussolini, especially while Achille Ratti (Pius XI) was pope during the 20s and 30s. After the second world war, the Catholic hierarchy switched its commitment to the Christian Democrats with equal fervor, usually intervening before major elections to remind Italian Catholics of their duty to oppose the PCI's godless atheism.

At the same time, the PCI has worked hard to neutralize the Church's opposition. Its degree of success was first publicly visible in the 1965 funeral procession of Palmiro Togliatti, the leader of the PCI since the death of Gramsci in 1937. At the procession were to be seen some cardinals and bishops in their official robes. Symbolically, too, the wife of the present PCI leader, Berlinguer, is known to be a practicing Catholic. On occasion in working class areas priests are to be found who vote PCI. As in all such negotiations between powerful institutions, it is unclear in the short term who is gaining and who is losing, but for the time being it is patently clear that the Catholic Church is far from having lost its influential role in Italy.

This leads us to the fourth dimension of our selectively condensed introduction to Italian politics: the famous "historic compromise" between the PCI and the Christian Democrats in the mid-70s. At that point, its major expression was the decision of the PCI not to oppose the Christian Democrats in parliament—to be, therefore, an implicit support to CD policies, without tying its own hands to the extent of formally allying itself to CD. The first policy the PCI shed was its position in favor of women's abortion rights.

The roots of the "historic compromise" go back much further than this, however. Arguably they originate from the point when Togliatti publicly called on the Italian Resistance, overwhelmingly supportive of the PCI, to lay down its arms and allow the Allied Forces to chase out the Nazis, rather than holding onto their arms for a revolutionary struggle. The "historic compromise" developed in economic terms during the fifties and sixties in northern regions of Italy, especially Emilia province, whose capital is Bologna, where from very early on the PCI was in a permanent majority on the city council. During these years, the PCI gradually worked out a stable relationship between itself, the unions it sponsored, and local employers both large and small. What it offered the employers was the unions' and its own helpfulness in assisting with labor discipline. What it provided its supporters with in return was stable jobs in the area. This was the initial economic core of the historic compromise policy, involving a form of local capitalist state planning with the PCI at the helm of the local state machinery. By the 1970s, Bologna was the PCI showcase of what "good government" looked like—the words are one of the PCI's favorite slogans.

At the national level, the PCI's parliamentary record had mainly been one of supporting CD in its various legislative measures, right from the 40s to the present day. The choice of the term "historic compromise" was only new in the sense that it distilled the PCI's response to the murderous coup in Chile in September 1973. Berlinguer and the PCI Central Committee argued that so far from proving that once marxists attain parliamentary power and do something with it they will be crushed by the military, the Chilean coup's real message was the opposite. The true lesson of Chile, said the PCI, was that the Popular Unity government there had gone too far, too fast, and had not taken a sufficient majority with them, particularly in terms of the centers of bourgeois power such as the armed forces, the media, and so on. Hence, in Italy, the "historic compromise" with CD.

However, this proclamation was made at the same period that the 1974-75 international recession began to bite. In western Europe, Italy and Britain were the two major countries hardest hit. Once half-in government, the PCI could not fail to take a position on the crisis. What it did, was to once more line up solidly with CD in calling for cuts in government spending, and for pay-restraint by the working class. Through its direct control of the CGIL, one of the three union federations in Italy, it was able to exert very considerable influence over the level and militancy of wage-demands. Thus the PCI found itself nationally, as it had been for so many years in localities like Emilia, in the position of controller of labor, rather than being labor's advocate.

In the developing dialectic of Italian society, this crystallization of the PCI's direction helped, in turn, to provoke profound challenges to Italian capitalism throughout the late 60s and most of the 70s. We shall examine the major social and political movements of this era below; but let us first recall that the characterization of Italian society so far is only of certain basic elements which are necessary to understand the *continuities* of Italian society, in a sense, its stability despite its flux. Since our main focus is on political movements and self-managed media, it would be dangerously easy to neglect these dimensions, just as it would be to neglect the position of Italy in the Mediterranean theatre of superpower rivalry. That way we could quickly get caught up in a triumphalist analysis of what were certainly profound political challenges to the rule of capital, but were never on the brink of socialist revolution.

2) The Context of Official Mass Media

Postwar Italy's established media offer a rather different picture from Portugal's before 1974. During the fascist era, the state's sole major concern with broadcasting had been news bulletins, with entertainment defined as largely harmless within certain limits acceptable to itself and the Catholic Church. Mussolini's position on the press had been remarkably similar to Salazar's, boasting that

> the freest press in the entire world is the Italian press. Elsewhere the newspapers are at the command of plutocratic groups, of parties, of individuals...Italian journalism is free because it serves but one cause and one Regime.[2]

Like other power structures in postwar Italy, the major mass media kept the majority of their staff intact from the fascist era. They were no more open to mass influence than before, and effectively switched their allegiance to the permanent Christian Democrat government without any significant changes in their mode of operation. Let us briefly examine the press, and then broadcasting (television was introduced in 1954).

Throughout this period the Italian press had some characteristics which marked it out from the press in many other countries. Firstly, although there are at least 13 daily morning sold nationally, no paper is *read* nationally to any meaningful extent, with the exceptions of the PCI daily *L'Unità*, and the two minority papers which are part of the focus of this study, *Lotta Continua* and *Il Manifesto*. For example, *La Stampa* (The Press), despite being the second biggest daily, sells relatively few copies outside Turin and the far North of the country.

Secondly, Italy has one of the lowest commercial newspaper sales per head (excluding the political party press which accounts for 11 percent of the total), and one of the highest magazine sales per head in Europe. The possible reasons need not detain us here, but the figures in Bechelloni[3] indicate that in the late 60s only Albania, Portugal and Yugoslavia had lower newspaper sales per head. Within Italy itself the rates varied sharply, from one paper to every nine people in the Northwest of the country down to one paper to twenty-nine in the South, and one to a hundred and six in Sicily.[4] Only one southern paper sold over 100,000 copies.[5]

The "quality" press, with the partial exception of the new arrival of the 70s, *Repubblica*, makes no attempt to communicate with the general public. The sensationalist press, for its part, makes no attempt to communicate serious, political information. There are some signs that the trend toward concentration of press ownership and ownership by industrial conglomerates may begin to shake up some of these patterns in the interests of expanding sales, but it still cannot be said that the Italian press as a whole is a factor of major distinction in the country. Indeed by 1980, most newspapers were losing money fast, and were only still afloat because of a long-heralded government bill which would subsidize newsprint (see further the discussions of *Il Manifesto* and *Lotta Continua* below).

Broadcasting continued to be a state monopoly in Italy after the fall of fascism. CD controlled the state, and thus put its nominees into RAI (Radio Reception Italy), the broadcasting corporation, at every level that mattered. Macali has graphically described what this CD stranglehold meant in practice:

> for thirty years (RAI) has been the trusty mouthpiece for the ideas of the Christian Democrats and the bosses...For thirty years, the opinions, the wishes, the threats, even the internal rifts of CD have been the only yardstick to measure governments, heads of state, unions, singers, popular movements, laws and decrees, news of the day, inflation, civil wars, foreign statesmen, sports events, popes, student struggles, Sanremo festival, battles for civil rights, and every other happening. For years millions of Italians have had the sole freedom to decide whether to listen to channel one on the radio (CD) or channel two (CD), almost always produced in Rome, far from their own towns, and equally far from the problems, language, customs, and needs of local town and country communities in different regions of Italy.[6]

The first tiny cracks in this monolith began to appear in 1968 when the Socialist Party (PSI) was admitted for the first time as a government coalition partner with CD. Part of the horse-trading was a little share in authority in RAI, which from then on became a major arena for "competitive colonization" by the parliamentary parties, constantly vying with each other for positions of influence inside it. Meanwhile RAI itself had been in the process of drastic internal reorganization under its director general, Bernabei.[8] Without venturing into detail, the structure of RAI now became so centralized that journalists and producers often felt pushed into a category not very far removed from technicians and manual workers in the organization. In turn, this stimulated a certain radicalism among the journalists which developed in a whole series of protests and strikes from the late 60s onwards. Sometimes these actions embraced technicians and manual workers as well, and were usually directed against the CD monopoly in broadcasting. Thus external and internal pressures combined to change the RAI-CD monolith.

The changes which occurred during the 70s were the addition of representatives of still other political parties, including the PCI, to the RAI board of governors, and the development in the late 70s of a third experimental channel. This last rapidly bacame something of a home for dissident TV journalists and producers, and began to show fairly radical and well-produced programs of a kind never seen on the first two channels. There were large areas of the country where the third channel could not be received, but it did represent a new move. Whether it will continue, expand, or be more strictly controlled still remains to be seen. It is important to note, however, that it was very successful in drawing away people who had been working in independent socialist radio stations such as Radio Città Futura (Radio City of the Future)[9] in Rome, through being able to offer a stable income and the chance of working in TV on moderately radical programs. In that sense, it represented the most sensitive outreach of the Italian establishment to the explosion of new energy in media communication on the far left—the people to the left of the PCI—at the time.

The main changes which took place in Italian broadcasting did so *outside* RAI. They can be pinpointed to two years, 1974 (the legalization of cable TV) and 1976 (the lifting of direct controls over local broadcasting). This latter decree was brought about by the independent action of private TV companies and illegal broadcasting by a growing number of radio stations, including independent socialist stations. The legal situation became so chaotic and fell into such disrepute that, effectively, the state gave way to a situation outside its control.

The result was an estimated 2278 non-state radio stations and over 500 non-state TV stations by mid-1978.[10] In Milan, alone, by 1980 over a hundred radio stations were advertising their existence. Most TV stations showed old films much of the time; a few were purely pornographic. Many radio stations broadcast music of various kinds for much of the day. But the development which was of the greatest significance for socialist practice was the emergence of self-managed revolutionary radio stations, spread over the country as a whole, but more concentrated in the North.

We shall be examining two of these in detail below, and I have already written elsewhere about a third (Radio Città Futura, Rome). In 1978-79 there were nearly a hundred of these stations in Italy, and there even emerged a short-lived Federation of Democratic Radio Stations (FRED in its Italian inititials), which held conferences attracting representatives from most of them. FRED eventually collapsed in 1978 over the issue of whether it should set up an advertising agency to channel advertising revenue to its member-stations.

The survey above of the conditions of broadcasting and the press in Italy leaves little doubt that these media developments were urgently needed by the socialist movement in Italy. A classic instance of the problems of the socialist movement without its own media, and of the widespread demand for a media revolution, is provided by Baldelli[11] in his detailed account of how the main media (including *L'Unita*), handled the notorious Pinelli-Valpreda case from 1969 onwards. The case revolved around the almost successful attempt of the police in Milan to pin the blame for a bomb-atrocity in a Milan bank that year, killing over thirty and wounding another ninety, on two Milan anarchists—Pinelli and Valpreda. The explosion was several years later proved to have been the work of fascists. But in the course of interrogation, the police dropped Pinelli from a window, causing his death. They claimed, and they were overwhelmingly supported by the media, that he had leapt to his death in an agony of guilt and remorse. Those media which discounted the story refused nonetheless to conduct any campaign for an inquiry into the death, or into Valpreda's continued imprisonment.

It was only the then bi-monthly newspaper *Lotta Continua* which kept the matter continuously alive, together with groups of people who put up posters and called meetings. A book was written from inside the left taking the details of the police story of Pinelli's death apart piece by piece, and quickly went through five editions, contributing greatly to public awareness of the issue. It was translated into French and Swedish.[12] Three other books were eventually published on the case as well.

Finally, two years after the bomb-explosion and Pinelli's death, and with Valpreda still in jail, *Corriere della Sera,* the leading Italian newspaper, called for action on Valpreda's trial, as the case was bringing Italian justice into national and international disrepute. (The remarks above may be recalled about the "quality" Italian press being mainly a vehicle for internal communication within the ruling class.) *Corriere* insisted, however:

> The Milanese are demanding that light be shed on the massacre...and request it firmly after twenty-four months of silence...But they wish to seek it democrati-cally, without entrusting their demands to the adven-

turism of minorities who do not represent them...Are
the extremists the voice of the public's conscience? Not
even in a dream...(December 11, 1971)[13]

Corriere made no reference to its own 24 months' silence or to
the fact that without the patient work of "the extremists"
silence would never have been broken. It was not until April
1972 that *Avanti!*, the Socialist Party paper, truly broke the
silence and actually accused the police of murdering Pinelli
and covering it up. (How easy it continues to be for anarchists
to be disowned by the rest of the left!)

This episode reveals both the character of established
Italian media (including the PCI's *L'Unità*), and the growing
tradition of organizing effective counter-information which
culminated in socialist free radio later in the decade. However,
following the mass political arrests of April 7 and December 21,
1979 and January 24 and March 11, 1980,[14] which jailed large
numbers of people on the far left accused of organizing
terrorism (see the following section on political movements),
there was almost a complete replay of the official media
handling of the Pinelli-Valpreda affair. The media arraigned
and defined those arrested as incontrovertibly guilty of terrorist activity, even though the evidence against them was
completely of a circumstantial characater, and even though
the state prosecutors kept dropping the original charges and
evidence in favor of new accusations, which were often
dropped in their turn. This time it was to be *Il Manifesto* in the
autumn of 1980 which had the honor of beginning to query the
state's case—a case energetically supported, let it be said, by
the PCI through its judges, its media, and on still other levels.

The need for lateral mass communication in Italy—outside
the ruling class and the PCI—had in no way disappeared.

3) Political Movements in Italy

Nineteen sixty-eight was marked in Italy, as across much
of the planet, by major social tumults. There was upheaval in
the universities, though on a far lesser scale than in France.
What distinguished Italy from most other cases was that, with
peaks and lulls, the movement of social rebellion spread and
continued practically throughout the 70s. As Bobbio put it in
his history of the revolutionary organization Lotta Continua
(Permanent Struggle):

while in other European countries '68 underwent a
sharp decline, in Italy it persisted in a "long wave"

which travelled through factories, schools, neighborhoods and institutions in a capillary and diffuse
fashion, giving birth to processes of mass organization and politicization, and provoking growing
disorganization in the power structure in terms of
political instability and disturbance of production.[15]

The first instance of this "long wave" was the so-called Hot
Autumn of 1969.[16] Immigrant workers from the South, who
had been brought up to the Fiat motor plants in Turin and
elsewhere as inexperienced, docile labor suddenly erupted in
anger at the continual speed-ups and at the low pay. Moreover,
their anger was not contained within the normal, established
collective bargaining processes. The union leaders were as
powerless as the management to control the strikes and factory
occupations that flared up and down without warning.

Some groups on the left quickly read this as evidence of a
new working class, uncontaminated by union compromises,
and out to do face-to-face battle with capital. Later, other
groups, such as women, young people, gays, the unemployed,
were added to this analysis and collectively termed the *emarginati*, those pushed out to the margins of society and hence with
no commitment to capitalism.) Certainly the immigrant
workers' dismissal of orderly negotiating procedures was
impossible for the management to handle, and certainly the
laborious rituals of official union bargaining were part of the
control process which these workers rightly challenged. It is
not nearly so clear, however, that their powerful insubord-
ination contained the conscious challenge to capital *as a whole*
which was ascribed to it by some leftist groups, however
strategic Fiat was and is for Italian capitalism.

This was, nonetheless, a turning point and a high point in
Italian workers' struggles. They were joined at once by student
supporters, especially from Lotta Continua,[17] who picketed
with them, printed leaflets for them, and engaged in demonstrations and street battles side by side with them. There was
not the intense social distance between workers and students
in Italy that characterized this relationship in other countries
(though the PCI in Turin did its best to foster this distance). To
some extent the comparable age of students and immigrant
workers was a help. Furthermore, university students in Italy
rarely get financial aid, and quite normally combine their
studies with part-time and full-time work, often in the underground economy. This lengthens their period as students, and
makes the whole category of "student" much more fluid than in

countries where one is a student for three or four years full-time before joining some career-ladder immediately upon graduation.

Nineteen sixty-nine also saw the birth of a major split inside the PCI, namely the expulsion of a whole group on its left called the Manifesto group after the name of the newspaper they produced, *Il Manifesto*. The organization Lotta Continua also coalesced into an effective political force in 1969. In terms of political seismography, then, 1969 was indeed a crucial year in Italy. It ended with the counter-attempt by fascist circles to foment an atmosphere of panic and chaos by exploding the bomb in the Milan bank, with the tragic consequences already mentioned.

The years from 1970 through to the end of 1976 were amazingly fast-moving, but are exceptionally hard to characterize without a mass of detail.[18] How does one summarize the struggles over divorce and abortion, the 1970 semi-insurrection in Reggio Calabria in the far South, the explosive strikes at Fiat's Mirafiori plant in 1973, the first emergence of so-called red terrorism in 1974, the intermittent bomb-nightmares by the ultra-right, the movements for "self-reduction of prices" in 1975, the failed attempts at far left unity, and, in 1976, the self-dissolution of Lotta Continua, the emergence of socialist free radio-stations and the eruption of the women's movement in a strongly separatist form, each charged with significance in relation to the others—how can these be condensed into anything approaching an explanation?

Suffice it to say that these were years of constant political turmoil both inside and outside the country. They were years in which it began to seem as though the PCI and PSI, along with some of the smaller parties (the Social Democrats, the Republicans, the Radicals[19]) were about to topple CD for the first time in 30 years, and that the far left might even, collectively, achieve three percent of the vote in the 1976 general election, and so become a pacemaker for a government of the established left parties (along the lines of the Movement of the Revolutionary Left (MIR) in Chile during 1970-73).[20]

None of these hopes was fulfilled. CD did not collapse, though its share of the vote sagged to a new low; the PCI promptly went into semi-support of it (its "historic compromise" policy); and the far left achieved well below three percent of the vote. At the same time, the far left's hopes had not been based on simple fantasy, and it is their partial reflection of the spirit of the period which is used here to convey something of its atmosphere. Readers accustomed to stable societies will have to do their best to imagine the constant flux of these political movements, and should read some of the material cited on them in this book. Just as in the Portuguese elections, so the parliamentary results of 1976 were only a partial reflection of the prevailing public mood, even though they were taken by the far left with such deadly seriousness that they helped to cause the self-dissolution of Lotta Continua later the same year! The logics of political movements and parliamentary elections do not regularly coincide. This election was a case in point (compare the "parallel reality" typical of eastern European societies and regimes).[21]

In the year following, 1977, there were two major insurrectionary movements, first in Rome (February-April) and then in—of all places—"showcase" Bologna (March).[22] Both were sparked by the police, shooting to disrupt demonstrations against violence from the ultra-right on campus. In Rome there were numerous demonstrations of thirty to a hundred thousand and daily assemblies at Rome university involving many thousands. Their most distinguishing characteristic was their violent rejection of the "historic compromise." Lama, general secretary of the PCI's union federation, was literally chased out of Rome university, reportedly weeping tears of impotent rage, following his attempt to justify wage-restraint and budget cuts to the assembly. The Bologna insurrection occurred in the very city where the historic compromise had been a fact of life for two or more decades, where everyone was supposedly happily settled at work under "good government," but where as a matter of fact, one hundred thousand students found housing hard to find, and meals prohibitively expensive.

These movements were a gut rejection of the whole future mapped out for Italian society by the main alternative to the CD, namely the PCI. Stability, security of employment, the virtues of hard work and discipline, the merits of a degree of austerity "for the national good": these objectives were derisively referred to as a strategy for the "Germanization" of Italy. These movements also took up the attacking slogans of the previous eight years' struggles, such as "We want everything!", "More pay, less work!", and improved on them. When Lama arrived at Rome university, he was greeted with one chant playing on his name: "Lama Sutra: a hundred ways to shaft the working class!", and "Workers' Gastronomy! Cannibalization! Knives! Forks! Let's Eat the Bosses !" "What's all

this crap about liberation? PCI, give us more oppression!"
"Free radio is a provocation! All power to TV!"[23] Graffiti
appeared everywhere, appealing to the imagination in power:
"After Marx, April"; "After April, mai" (the French May);
"After Mao, June." A whole movement sprang up, albeit short-
lived, of "metropolitan Indians," whose slogans were particularly imaginative and provocative, who painted their faces and
paraded in the streets. Rather than argue point by point
against the status quo, they used wit, irony and the bizarre as
their weapons.

The PCI never forgave the leaders or the movements for
the ridicule and hostility which both heaped upon the party.
Their fury was especially intense when Lama was chased
ignominiously from Rome university, and then when Bologna
was "chosen" as the site of the other upheaval. Their emperors
were stripped naked in public.

In Bologna, the event which actually triggered the uprising was the cold-blooded shooting of a student, Francesco
LoRusso, by a *carabiniere*. This was just about blotted out in
L'Unità,[24] which instead gave massive coverage to the breaking of shop windows in the city, the looting of one or two
restaurants and the looting of a gun-shop. The actions against
the shops and restaurants were taken *after* and because of the
slaying of LoRusso, but anyone not there at the time and
dependent on *L'Unità* for information could be forgiven for
being unaware that anyone had been killed. The gun-shop
incident was probably a right wing provocation: the first news
of it was in a local far right daily, *Resto del Carlino,* which
appeared on a Saturday morning announcing the looting of a
gun-shop the previous evening. The looting actually took place
the same Saturday evening. The attitude of *L'Unità* (and of
Resto del Carlino) was extended in *Società,* a PCI monthly,
which claimed that the Bologna events were masterminded by
an international conspiracy of (CIA-trained) exchange students from Johns Hopkins University, in an unholy alliance
with the so-called Autonomists. (This was the name for an
exceptionally diffuse far left tendency of the late 70s, but the
favorite villain of the PCI.) Even in 1980, *L'Unità* was still
trying to ram home their condemnation of these upsurges
whenever possible, for instance printing a three-year-old photo
of someone in the Lama demonstration in Rome, who had just
been arrested as a terrorist. The PCI media coverage of the 1977
upsurges was unremittingly hostile.

It is not surprising that this reaction emerged across the entire spectrum of established politics, for these movements— although confined to these two cities, and to young people— went much further outside the pale of the historic compromise than had earlier ones. The new socialist radio stations, especially Radio Alice in Bologna[25] and Radio Città Futura in Rome, played major roles in amplifying debates during the insurrectionary period, and in the former case in co-ordinating demonstrators against the police. (See the section on Radio Popolare for a further discussion.) For the first time, too, these movements included a major critique, not just of factory despotism or educational politics, but of the character of left wing political activity and of the nature of the family. Geographically and socially isolated as these explosions were, they still raised some of the critical issues of three-dimensional politics: power and domination in left wing political structures, and in the sexual hierarchy of the family. Of course these movements were deeply offensive! They challenged everything—and did so with a levity which was extremely serious, which twisted the nerves of bourgeois society *and* of the staid, organized "socialist" alternative, with its public claim to be communism with a human face.

In the midst of these movements, however, was also growing a minority tendency which would eventually be used by the state to stifle their political gains. It was the tendency which already regarded physical violence as a proper method to settle political disputes between comrades (the Rome Autonomists had a particularly thuggish reputation in this context). Increasingly, these people left the open debate and confrontation of the movements in favor of secret organization for armed confrontations with the state. They joined the Red Brigades, or formed Prima Linea (Front Line), the other main "red" terrorist group. Their strategy became more and more to liquidate the most humane and reasonable representatives of the power structure in order to help create a more violent and unscrupulous battle between capitalists and workers. In 1980 they shot, amongst others, a Naples judge who was trying to expose and bring to trial the mafia and a Milan journalist who was well known as an anti-fascist and honest writer. Some older PCI members were initially sympathetic, wishing they could turn the clock back to before Togliatti's call to the Resistance to lay down its arms. Before very long, however, even their feeling became dampened by the wave of killings and kneecappings.

The most publicized of all these actions was the 1978 kidnapping and subsequent assassination of the Italian prime minister, Aldo Moro. Moro had been the supreme symbol of the elements within CD willing to engage in the "historic compromise" with the PCI. It was on the very morning he was due to go to the Italian parliament to ratify a major public agreement providing the PCI with a greater share in government that the Red Brigades killed his five bodyguards and took him prisoner. His body was eventually dumped by them, again symbolically, half-way between the CD head office and the PCI head office, in the center of Rome.

The effect of these clandestine terrorist groups on movement politics, on open political debate, on the *continuation* of the upsurges of the previous decade, was catastrophic. It took many groups, such as the *Lotta Continua* newspaper collective, a long time to decide that any temporizing with terrorism in conditions neither fascist nor colonial was a betrayal of mass-based politics. While they were still working this out, the state had already moved against the independent left. This was done with the active support of the PCI leadership, which saw itself both as having to prove its anti-terrorist credentials, and as having at last the power to clear the ground to its left, to its own advantage. This is a consistent strategy of southern European Communist parties, and must be viewed within the context of superpower rivalry within the Mediterranean. Only a party able to claim undisputed hegemony on the left can "deal," such parties feel, with the problem of the state. Like their eastern European cousins, the spectre of a progressive political movement or movements outside their control is something to exorcise, not support. The Spanish Civil War was certainly not the last case in point; and as then, the exorcism is never merely ideological.

The state's movement against the independent left was referred to already at the end of the previous section. In the mass arrests of 1979 and 1980, one of which was the largest peacetime action ever by the Italian army since World War II, many well-known marxist activists and intellectuals were rounded up and imprisoned on charges which dated from the 1929 fascist penal code, and which deprived prisoners of the right to a trial for four years. (Toni Negri of Padua University, and Oreste Scalzone, a former student leader, were the best known, but there were numerous others.) They were accused of planning and executing the liquidation of Aldo Moro, of organizing the Red Brigades and Prima Linea, and were charged with numerous other offenses. The fact that both these organizations continued their mayhem unabated counted for nothing; their existence was used as an excuse to wipe out a whole mass of inventive marxist thinkers and doers, all beyond the pale of the historic compromise. In turn, these repressions had a powerful deterrent effect on others from even showing support for those arrested. While I was in Italy from May-August 1980, no one was prepared to talk on the phone about anything connected with these arrests, in Italian or English. Meanwhile, the Italian state had sharpened its teeth still further, for example by lengthening to *twelve years before trial* the period in which "suspects" could be held prisoner if charged with "subversion" against the state.

Thus there was no public space left for the movements of the previous decade to grow. They were caught in a vise between the state authorities, including the Italian Communist Party, and Prima Linea and the Red Brigades. Debate and discussion continued, but mostly in small gatherings or in the pages of journals and magazines of the left.

One tragic aftermath of the movements in 1979-80 was a sudden and widespread growth of heroin use by a number of ex-activists. During 1980, heroin-dependence, in a country where it had never previously been a phenomenon, mushroomed to the point where between one and two young people a week were dying from its use or from related causes (hepatitis, septicemia, etc.) It would be more comfortable to end an analysis of these movements and this decade on another note, but honesty demands this discussion. There are two issues involved: the sources of this sudden explosion (and it is difficult to dismiss the mafia); and the reasons why political activists switched from the adrenalin of the movement to the artificial prolongation of this intensity via heroin. Despite the fact that this switch was far from being a transition by the majority of activists, it is clear that a part of the commitment to the 1977 movements was ephemeral, and incapable of sustained energy. The aftermath is only one aspect of the movements, but it is undeniably a significant one.

During this period of slightly more than a decade, therefore, Italy was shaken by more profound political upheavals than perhaps any other Mediterranean country during the 60s and 70s, if the criterion is the duration of the upheavals or the extent to which they radically challenged basic political, economic and cultural structures. If the involvement of the whole mass of the population is the measure, then Portugal, not Italy, would have to stand first. In neither case did the movement maintain its momentum, albeit for different reasons (though maintaining momentum is generally exceedingly difficult for political movements). The lasting contribution of these events to the socialist movement internationally, however, includes as one of its major elements a detailed experience of the possibilities and problems of self-managed media as agents of revolutionary transformation. It is to them that we must now turn.

Footnotes

1. L. Ferrari Bravo and A. Serafini, *Stato e Sottosviluppo: il caso del Mezzogiorno italiano* (State and Underdevelopment: the case of the Italian south), Milan: Feltrinelli 1972.
2. Cited in V. Cappecchi and M. Livolsi, *La Stampa Quotidiana in Italia* (The Italian Daily Press), Milan: Bompiani Editore 1971, p. 113.
3. G. Bechelloni, *Informazione e Potere* (Information and Power), Rome: Oficina Editore 1974, Table I, p. 131.
4. Bechelloni, Table 2, p. 132
5. Bechelloni, p. 140.
6. G. Macali, *Meglio Tardi Che RAI* (Better Late Than RAI), Rome: Savelli Editore 1977, p. 60.
7. For the detailed version of the story that follows, see F. Siliato, *L'Antenna Dei Padroni* (The Bosses' Aerial), Milan: Mazzotta Editore 1977, pp. 52-127.
8. This dimension of the story is best explained in F. Pinto, *Il Modello Televisivo: professionalità e politica da Bernabei alla terza rete* (The Pattern of Television: professionalism and politics from Bernabei to the third channel), Milan: Feltrinelli Editore 1980.

9. See J. Downing, *The Media Machine,* London: Pluto Press 1980, ch. 9, for an account of Radio Cittá Futura up to fall 1979.

10. G. Richeri, "Radiotelevisione: verso un monopolio imperfetto?" (Broadcasting: towards an imperfect monopoly?), *Ikon* 1-2 (September 1978), pp. 124-145. The situation remained similar in 1981: see Alessandro Silj's forthcoming contribution to *Les Radios Libres* (The Free Radios), Paris 1983.

11. P. Baldelli, *Informazione e Controinformazione* (Information and Counterinformation), Milan: Mazzotta Editore 1972, pp. 127-208.

12. *La Strage di Stato* (The State Plot), Savelli, 1970. One of the best known plays of Dario Fó also bases itself on the Pinelli case, *The Accidental Death of an Anarchist.*

13. Cited in Baldelli, p. 182.

14. See "A dossier on the arrests of 1979," in *Working Class Autonomy and the Crisis,* London: Red Notes/CSE Books 1979, pp. 139-166; and *Italy 1980-81—"After Marx, Jail!"* London: Red Notes 1981. See also the article by G. Soulier, "Le procés du 7 avril en Italie," *Le Monde Diplomatique* 345 (December 1982), p. 5.

15. L. Bobbio, *Lotta Continua, storia di una organizzazione rivoluzionaria* (Lotta Continua, history of a revolutionary organization), Rome: Savelli 1979, p. 114.

16. "The struggle at Fiat," in *Working Class Autonomy and The Crisis* (n. 14), pp. 167-95.

17. L. Bobbio, *op. cit.,* pp. 27-40.

18. The two Red Notes texts cited above are a mine of information. See also another Red Notes publication, *Italy 1977-8: Living with an Earthquake* (London 1978); B. Ramirez, "The working class struggle against the crisis: self-reduction of prices in Italy," *Zerowork 1* (1975), pp. 142-50. See also L. Bobbio, *op. cit.*

19. The political positions of these parties were as follows: the Republicans were like a left wing splinter from the Christian Democrats, strongly in favor of the historic compromise; the Radical Party came back into major prominence in the latter part of the 70s, campaigning as an open party for a variety of radical reforms (against new repressive legislation, courts martial, nuclear power, for abortion rights and the legalization of marijuana). For the Social Democrats, see my comments in the section of *Il Manifesto,* under the heading "The Newspaper's Finance."

20. L. Bobbio, *op. cit.*, pp. 124-28

21. See Part III on eastern Europe, and n. 6 in the section on Czechoslovakia.

22. See *Italy 1977-78: Living With an Earthquake* (n. 18); *semiotext(e) III.3 (1980), Italy: Autonomia;* F. Calvi, *Italie 77, le "Mouvement," les intellectuals,* Paris:Editions du Seuil 1977; M. Macciocchi, *Doppo Marx, Apile* (After Marx, April), Milan: I Libri del Espresso (1978); P. Bernocchi (and others), *Movimento Settantasette: storia di una lotta* (The movement of 77: history of a struggle), Turin: Rosenberg & Sellier 1979; autori molti compagni (authors many comrades): *bologna marzo 1977...fatti nostri...*(Bologna March 1977...our events), Verona: Bertani Editore 1977; V. De Matteis and A. Turchini, *Machina: osservazioni sul rapporto tra movimento, istituzioni, potere a Bologna* (Machine: observations on the relation between movement, institutions and power in Bologna), Bari: Dedalo Libri 1979; M. Morcellini, "Modi di formazione della coscienza politica" (Modes of formation of political awareness) in F. Faccioli (and others), *I Nuovi Giovani* (The New Youth), Cosenza: Edizioni Lerici 1979, pp. 111-69.

17

IL MANIFESTO

History and Character

The original *Il Manifesto* group was the first major organizational rupture with established Italian politics in the postwar period. Members of the group were expelled from the PCI in the "hot year" of 1969, essentially for their role as a coherent voice within the PCI against its growing accommodation with the Christian Democrats. The *Manifesto* line was also much more sympathetic toward China than toward the USSR in the Sino-Soviet conflict, though not for the familiar reasons elsewhere in the world (loyalty to the Stalin era). It was rather the militant anti-imperialism and radical internal democracy associated with China at the time which constituted its attraction for the *Manifesto* group. Indeed, a unique feature of the *Manifesto* split was that despite its members' decades of experience inside the PCI (in some instances), its members did not lapse then or later into Cold War anti-communism, unlike so many prominent ex-Communist Party figures.

Five or six members of the group had substantial journalistic experience in newspapers and magazines. On April 28, 1971, they launched a daily newspaper, *Il Manifesto*, selling for the absurdly low price of 50 lire. The first issue had only four pages, no advertisements, and began the paper's uncompromising tradition of serious marxist journalism. Its first three or four days were astonishing: 200,000 copies were sold each day. Then for its first year it settled down to a steady thirty or forty thousand a day. Given that all Italian dailies taken together sell only about four million a day and that *Il Manifesto* set out to be far more than just a conventional bourgeois newspaper, its one per cent share of national readership indicated a much more significant contribution to Italian political life than one per cent. Those who read it were not politically passive consumers.

In 1972, however, the national elections failed to return any *Manifesto* group deputies to parliament. This reverse had a bad effect on the paper, and its sales fell, not really recovering till 1974. The paper's fortunes began to revive with its resolute position in favor of the legalization of divorce during the 1974 divorce referendum. From 1974-76, when it seemed that the socialist movement in general, from the PSI and PCI leftwards, was gaining daily in strength, and gathering enough force finally to defeat the seemingly collapsing Christian Democrats, *Il Manifesto* was in the center of political debates and struggles. It continued to benefit from a whole string of prestigious contributors from abroad, such as Fernando Claudin, Daniel Singer and K.S. Karol. Its sales rose once more to 30,000 a day.

With the 1976 general election results, in which CD was returned to power yet again, and where the combined far left's hope of achieving 3% of the vote was also dashed, a period of political disillusion set in. Many people left the *Manifesto* group. Then emerged the movements of 1977-78, and *Il Manifesto* found itself in the paradoxical situation of being judged part of the old political order, and thus an enemy, by some of the newer political currents. (Compare this to the gulf that opened up between some of the women working on *Lotta Continua*.) This view had some plausibility, since the paper did attack certain features of these movements. At the same time, the journalists working on the paper found their position increasingly frustrating because of the tight organizational bond between it and the parent organization, now entitled PdUP (Party of Proletarian Unity). Often the paper's position reflected PdUP's much more than its writers'.

Then the Red Brigades and Moro affair erupted. *Il Manifesto*, the PSI and *Lotta Continua* were the only political voices to argue for negotiating with the Red Brigades for the release of Moro. As the state began to arm itself with more and more draconian laws, giving its various police forces far greater license, and encouraging a public media image of the heroic security forces battling against dedicated destructionists, *Il Manifesto* took the dissident position that the menace of terrorism was being utilized to turn the clock back politically to the old established order of pre-1968. For these courageous stands, it became the butt of a campaign waged by four Italian dailies (especially during 1979) to present the paper as the concealed voice of terrorism!

Perhaps it is the penalty likely to befall any newspaper which argues, as *Il Manifesto* consistently did, that political solutions, not military might, are required to defeat terrorism. Beyond this, it was an index of the destructive impact the Red Brigades had on revolutionary politics and the movements in Italy, that the *first* voice of organized dissent in postwar Italy to the left of the establishment, and itself critical of the 1977-78 movements, could be seen as the only remaining major obstacle to a reconstruction of the old settled order—and thus as a major target for these rightist media.

It is hardly surprising that under the pressure of all these events, a major struggle occurred between the newspaper and PdUP. Its journalists had, as already noted, been quietly chafing for years at the restrictions imposed on them by being a party organ (the "transmission belt" model of revolutionary media). As the hectic events of 1977-78 unfolded, they had an immediate effect on the PdUP, then engaged in unification negotiations with Avanguardia Operaia (Workers' Vanguard).[1] The situation in both political organizations became increasingly confused under the pressure of the negotiations and the external situation. Yet *Il Manifesto's* journalists found themselves, day after day, having to issue the majority line within PdUP, even though it was a small political party whose internal dissent meant its line was capable of being reversed at any moment. At the same time, PdUP was losing members very fast to the new women's movement. This made it more peculiar than ever that the journalists in *Il Manifesto* were allowed to express their political judgments on a whole range of issues—just so long as they did not criticize PdUP!

The crisis of the Moro kidnapping brought matters to a head. *Il Manifesto*, as we have noted, came out in favor of negotiations with the Red Brigades. PdUP however, after a long discussion, sided with the PCI in refusing to negotiate. The strains this imposed came to a head in the Viareggio congress of PdUP in October 1978. Rossana Rossanda, *Il Manifesto's* editor from the beginning, made a spirited attack on PdUP's strangulation of the paper's life, and argued for complete independence from PdUP. Her demand was that the paper should function as an "open party," not as the public voice of PdUP's political executive. She urged abstention on the congress delegates when her resolution was voted, a tactically astute move. Forty per cent abstained, and this was sufficient to legitimate the paper's declaration of independence.

The decision had two immediate effects. The PdUP *compagni*[2] left the paper, but its sales picked up almost at once. From that time on, the basic drive within *Il Manifesto* toward an independent paper, open to a variety of positions on the left, was realized. In 1980, those working for the paper included people with a long history inside the PCI, "sixty-eightists" (the New Left), Third Worldists, "scientific" marxists, "humanist" marxists, socialist feminists, people involved with the ecological and nuclear movements. Thus the paper internally reflected most of the debates within the left at large. Not only had *Il Manifesto* managed to break loose from a number of the straitjackets for revolutionary mass media, including the role of "external fraction of the PCI" (a kind of thorn in the PCI's side), envisaged for it by some influential PdUP members. It had become, as its journalists wished it to be, a forum for the left.

Externally, this function was realized in a number of ways. The paper was very open to contributions from outside its own ranks. These might come from individuals, like the man who phoned in one day out of the blue from Sicily, his name totally unknown to the journalists, to report some large scale protest attacks on political party offices in his small town, which had not been picked up by any other paper. Or they might come from some specialists in North American studies at Turin University, who were able to cross the Atlantic frequently, and so to write up-to-date accounts of U.S. political developments. Additionally, the paper organized *Manifesto*-leagues, members' groups in the major cities, which were free in principle to include PCI members or campaigners for the Radical Party, or to be involved in any political activity that would be likely for a regular reader of *Il Manifesto*. Once a year, the paper also organized a major open conference, such as the 1977 Venice conference on power and opposition in soviet societies, or the 1980 Turin conference on new developments in the labor process. By these various means, the paper tried strenuously to avoid being a closed clique of journalists, or simply another newspaper (however far to the left). It attempted to create a living relation with its readers, and to lodge itself as a political force over and above its existence as a daily. Naturally, these attempts could not be guaranteed success; but to understand the nature of the paper, the fact that they were consistently made requires recognition.

For its first ten years *Il Manifesto* made few concessions to its readership. A level of intelligence and political knowledge is required which is far higher than for any other Italian daily, including the most elite publications such as *Corriere della Sera*, *Repubblica* or *La Stampa*. Although the position changed in 1981, for a long time there were no cartoons, no graphics, no photos, no sports reports. Indeed, inside the paper there are not infrequently articles on some of the most complex writers in contemporary socialist culture, as in the issue of July 4, 1980, which carried a full page with three articles on the relations between feminism and the revision of Freudian psychoanalytic theory by the French analyst Jacques Lacan. Even Lacan's most ardent admirers would never claim that he was an easy read!

The language used in the paper is never, or rarely, perversely obscure in the academic manner, but it often makes stiff demands on its readers. In that sense 'the imaginative' is not a major dimension of *Il Manifesto*. However, comparing it with even *Libération* or *Tageszeitung,* the other European dailies in the same mold, *Il Manifesto* is a remarkable force for critical socialist analysis on the highest level, combining as it does the realms of national and international politics with an alertness to a whole series of current intellectual developments. Inevitably, its emphasis on the latter has exposed *Il Manifesto* to accusations of elitism, of being removed from everyday struggles. Within the paper itself in 1980, there were several journalists wishing to be transferred into either the culture section or the foreign section, out of more humdrum work such as trade union affairs.

The paper's format did begin to change, however, in the autumn of 1981. First,it expanded from six to eight pages, with the inner pages being devoted to international news (p. 2), national news (p. 3), general cultural issues (pp. 4-5), and the arts (pp. 6-7). Page one provided news and page eight analysis of the previous day's news.

In early 1982, after often intense and heated discussions over a period of months, a commission was formed to present the various viewpoints within the collective on still further changes. This time, the change was inspired by the recognition that socialist political thinking in Italy was in a maze, and by the conviction that *Il Manifesto* has a unique opportunity to act as a forum for fresh ideas and perspectives on the left. As one journalist put it to me: "We certainly did not want to find ourselves being like the last Japanese soldier to leave the forest!"

The masthead was reduced in size, the columns expanded from six to seven, and international and Italian news were given two pages each (pp. 2-5). Page five, however, was new in concept, being addressed to everyday issues and problems outside the conventional categories of marxist politics: crime, drugs, the young, the handicapped, house-hunting, how Italians spend their holiday time (or don't have holidays). Page six was run by much younger additions to the collective, and focused on popular arts as well as conventional arts. Its reviews did not seek simply to lambast Hollywood film, in the established tradition of Italian left journalism, but to try to penetrate through to the reasons for their mass cultural appeal.

Page seven handled more traditional intellectual concerns, carrying debates with well-known writers such as Gunder Frank, Althusser, Rawls, Enzensberger, and others. (The people working on this page saw page six as rather frivolous; those who worked on page six, in turn, saw page seven as old-fashioned and dull!) The back page had an uncertain identity, but tried to pinpoint and analyze emerging cultural trends. Its themes had included material on new Arab and Jewish thinkers, racism in Italy, the significance of rock concerts, the music of "The Clash," the impact of western music on soviet youth, the annual Notting Hill Carnival in London.

On top of these format changes, the collective also began to bring out a special Thursday supplement called *The Thursday Mole* (costing an extra 500 lire). This carried a cartoon of an old mole with huge glasses. It would mostly be given over to a predetermined theme. Themes included Palestine, the Falklands, the conditions of the PCI, the nuclear issue. Some articles were specially written, others were translated from other countries.

Insofar as the socialist movement must have space for sharp-witted exchange on some of the most complex issues of the day, papers such as *Il Manifesto* have a valid and valuable role to play. If *Il Manifesto* were the single organ of the revolutionary left in Italy, some of the standard criticisms of its intellectual level might have a stronger basis. But this is not the case, and it should never be socialists who indulge in the tired conservative equation of the egalitarian spirit with homogeneity. Intellectual production needs democratizing just as much as factory production, but *not* so as to reduce either thought or products to their lowest imaginable level.

Internal Organization

The internal structure of the newspaper, as it had evolved by 1980, resembled that of a conventional paper in some respects, but diverged sharply in others. Deadlines and departments, each with its section-head—domestic politics, foreign affairs, unions and labor, mass culture, marxism—operated as elsewhere, even though the headings differed noticeably. There were two co-editors, Rossana Rossanda, the ex-PCI deputy who had led the *Manifesto* group from the beginning, and Luigi Pintor. In 1981 a third was added,Mauro Paissan, to represent the younger generation of journalists. These co-editors in turn shared executive authority with two chief sub-editors (*editori capi*). There was an administration and service department, including the switchboard operator and the paper's administrative director. (I will comment on the printers below.)

So much for the general parallels: now for the contrasts. First, the switchboard operator, Rossana Rossanda, and everyone else, were paid 500,000 lire a month (1981). The only people sometimes paid more were those aged 35 and over with dependents, who were paid 50,000 lire a month extra for each dependent. This pay policy had been in force from the very beginning of the paper, when everyone was paid 145,000 lire each. It is also worth noting that these pay rates were far lower than were paid in the bourgeois press, where journalists could easily earn twice to ten times as much. Luigi Pintor, admittedly a leading political figure and a very able writer, had been offered four million lire a *month* by *Repubblica* for just four articles a month. The pay policy and the pay level at *Il Manifesto* thus demonstrated how radically its political commitment and strategy differed from those of the established media.

Secondly, the structure of authority at *Il Manifesto* differed sharply from the usual apparatus of editors, sub-editors, and the frequent dominance of the advertising department. Although it was hierarchical, there were also democratic structures. The six times the paper was produced each week were marked by a daily meeting beginning between 12:30 and 1:00 and lasting between an hour and an hour and a half. Its discussion-themes were open to be decided by anyone in *Il Manifesto*, and anyone was free to intervene. Usually they ranged over one or more subjects directly relevant to the next issue of the paper. Examples over one three-day period included the PCI's performance in local government elections; the death of Giorgio Amendola, supreme symbol of the PCI's "historic compromise" strategy; and the growing abstention rates in Italian elections (still miniscule by most standards, but significant in a post-fascist country). During 1980 other regular topics had been European social democracy, China after Mao, and the Iranian revolution. In conventional media, this opportunity for the 'specialists' to be challenged on their articles and views by their fellow-workers in the paper *before* their views are printed does not exist.

In terms of the newspaper's content, the results of these daily meetings naturally enough varied from day to day. One of the chief sub-editors, Gianni Riotta, told me how an article he had written on terrorism had been sharply criticized at one of these sessions, and that he had consequently rewritten the entire article, trying to represent people's different viewpoints within it. He cited another instance, where his position on the links between Donat Cattin, a leading CD politician, and members of Prima Linea, the terrorist group in which Cattin's son was active, had been rejected outright by the daily meeting. (Although, he added with a wry smile, his own position was eventually vindicated by subsequent events!) It is hard to imagine a chief editor in a bourgeois paper being overruled from below, or if it actually were to happen, not reacting with fury—witness Raúl Rêgo's reaction to the same experience as editor of *República*.

As far as Rossana Rossanda's editorial authority went, everyone to whom I spoke underlined that she enjoyed a more personal, than an official authority. Her own dynamism, her vast political experience, and, in certain ways, her lack of commitment to journalistic norms, were a crucial ingredient in the paper's organization. We shall see the same factor at work in *Lotta Continua*, as well as in Radio Popolare; some of the U.S. examples (*Akwesasne Notes* positively, *Union Wage* negatively) evinced the same pattern.

As well as this daily meeting, there were also meetings every three to four weeks to discuss more general issues. There was also an annual general meeting. In terms of the daily schedule, however, there was a more production-oriented meeting each evening at about 7:30 between editors, section-heads and chief sub-editors, to finalize headlines and last minute changes. (The chief sub-editors were, as elsewhere, responsible for the paper's lay-out.) This evening meeting, though fairly casual in atmosphere, was an important one, and from time to time crystallized certain power-relations inside the paper, as will be seen in the discussion below on women's roles in *Il Manifesto*.

Thus, taking this internal democracy together with the attempts to construct an external democracy by readers' groups, voluntary correspondents and public conferences, it can easily be seen how much *Il Manifesto's* structure differed from a conventional newspaper's. Perhaps a critical instance of this in terms of the eventual product, the newspaper itself, was the degree to which conflicting positions were expressed in the same issue: there was no stifling uniformity of line.

The fact remains, however, that there were problems. No more than any of the other cases in this survey did *Il Manifesto* operate in a utopian situation.

One very obvious problem lay in the relation between the printers and the rest of the staff. The printshop was three floors below in the same building, and was organized as an independent collective whose main work consisted in printing *Il Manifesto*, and *Quotidiano Donna* (the feminist newspaper). In fact people in *Il Manifesto* had been directly instrumental in advising them how to set up such a collective while they were still working as individuals for a printing firm so relations on a day-to-day basis were perfectly friendly, just as at *Lotta Continua*. The problem lay in the fact that as a union the printers were mostly in the PCI, and thus inevitably at odds with the political lines of the journalists in the newspaper. It would have posed intractable problems for the paper to admit them as a voting bloc into the daily discussions of content. So, thanks to existing political configurations in Italy, the division of labor on the paper proved insurmountable.

However, there was also a certain division of labor still operational within *Il Manifesto's* own staff. For a long time a number of the non-journalistic staff did not play any great role (through their own choice, it should be said) in the daily meetings, perhaps partly because of the high level of political information required to participate meaningfully in a number of these meetings. By 1982, however, this was changing as a result of active encouragement from the leadership. There were some complaints, for instance by the switchboard operator, that she was treated very dismissively by some members of staff; by another, that he was spoken to as an employee, not as a *compagno*, by a number of people. Still other members of the journalistic staff were very conscious of these problems, recognizing that they were hard to discuss because they were so close to "home," but that they demanded attention because they created a degree of alienation within the collective. In practical terms, this alienation meant less discussion than was needed between the people responsible for the paper's distribution and its writers.

In conclusion, however, everyone to whom I spoke recognized that the degree of exchange and communal activity in *Il Manifesto* were quite inconceivable in any bourgeois newspaper. Problems remained, and were not to be dismissed, but the quality of life was utterly different from elsewhere in the established media world. Some who had left because they could not afford to live on the pay enormously regretted the personal cost of working in a conventional set-up, as opposed to *Il Manifesto*.

Finances

Finances were, and would remain, a critical problem for the paper. In August 1980, its price had to be sharply raised to 500 lire, compared to every other daily's price of 300 lire. At the same time, for two months in the summer of 1980 none of the *compani* could be paid. This situation was unfortunately not unique to 1980, and there was a well developed mechanism for assigning any funds which were available to those in the most desperate need (i.e. those without any possibility of family support, there being no social security payments in Italy).

The origins of this recurrent financial crisis were several: the politics of newsprint paper costs, the politics of press advertising revenue, the costs of distribution, and the vicious circle of not having enough funds to compete with other dailies in assigning squads of journalists to a whole range of issues. This last problem meant *Il Manifesto* was always a second newspaper, bought by fewer people than would otherwise be the case. While this last point is self-explanatory, let us clarify the first three.

Since 1976 the Italian parliament had been discussing a newsprint finance bill to subsidize newspapers' costs in purchasing newsprint out of national tax revenue. This bill was of great interest to the Italian monopoly newsprint firm, Fratelli Fabbri, and to the 'big three' Italian publishers (Rizzoli, Mondadori and Caracciolo), as well as to the press in general, which was in most cases saddled with financial crisis. All stood to gain from the bill's passage into law, especially as its provisions would be retroactive, but had been forced to wait literally for years while the characteristic delays of Italian parliamentary life ran their course. However, whereas major publishers and newspapers had bankers happy enough to wait, the smaller fish such as *Il Manifesto* and *Lotta Continua* were in desperate straits through having to pay unsubsidized and constantly rising newsprint bills. As far ago as 1976, the press in general was in debt to the tune of 120 billion lire.[3]

In March 1981 bankruptcy seemed inevitable. *Il Manifesto* decided to make an all out effort to pressure the Italian parliament to pass the bill. Luigi Pintor called a major news conference attended by the leading TV, radio and press, at which he announced that the paper would be forced to close on April 28, its tenth anniversary, unless the newsprint bill were ratified. Articles appeared internationally in *Le Monde, El País*, and the UK and West Germany. As fortune would have it, the deputy then chairing the Italian parliament was none other than the widow of Togliatti, who took a direct personal interest in the matter. Many city mayors—from Venice, Florence, Turin, Milan—wrote public letters of support, but due to her efforts in particular, the bill finally passed through parliament in May 1981, and then through the Senate in July. *Il*

Manifesto was now due to receive about one billion lire.

However, the paper once again ran afoul of its enemies, since the question of exactly how much money each paper was entitled to receive in back payments for its paper costs was handed over to a committee headed by an inactive near octagenarian. This new tactic effectively blocked further progress, and *Il Manifesto* then took the unprecedented step of taking the Italian state to court to force it to pay up its debts. To their astonishment, the judge in the lower court (the *pretura*) found in their favor. He ordered the state to pay up by March 31, 1983. On April 1, a senior member of the paper's staff went to collect the check, only to find that a higher court judge had taken the also legally unprecedented step of suspending the particular kind of court order issued from the *pretura*.

At this point, *Il Manifesto* once again appealed to the public for support. The response was overwhelming. The President wrote to say the paper should not be closed. The Radical Party leader, emphasizing his differences with them, gave them a 60-day loan of up to 60 million lire. PdUP gave 75 million. The greatest surprise was that the PCI gave 150 million, without conditions, and Berlinguer asked the PCI in general to offer its support. In many places, people selling *L'Unità* also sold *Il Manifesto*. The three trade union federations offered their real estate as collateral for bank loans. The paper was flooded with letters of support. At the time of this writing, its future was not certain, but brighter than for some time.

A second source of the endemic financial problems faced by the paper was its relatively small advertising revenue. The advertisements it ran came via the state SIPRA agency in Turin. Up until 1976, SIPRA had been a state agency under complete Christian Democratic control. With the flowering of the PCI's "historic compromise" strategy, a number of tangible concessions were made to the PCI, including the presidency of SIPRA. The new head, though a PCI member, was favorably inclined toward *Il Manifesto*, and immediately questioned the existing SIPRA policy of refusing to place advertisements in the paper. As a result *Il Manifesto* began to receive advertising worth 100 million lire a year. Nonetheless, this was a paltry sum compared with *L'Umanità*, the subscription only newspaper of the small Social Democratic Party (PSDI), which received 600 million in advertising each year. (PSDI is widely acknowledged in Italy to have been set up as, and to act as, the "labor" mouthpiece of U.S. interests in the country.)

Advertising revenue was never such as to guarantee *Il Manifesto's* finances. Gianni Riotta remarked with some amusement that around election times the paper always had a sudden rush of "instant food" ads. He had long been puzzled by this, until he concluded that it was because the manufacturers calculated that political activists would be especially hard-pressed for time during election periods.

Distribution costs were also substantial. Italian papers are strongly regional, based in many caes on a single city and its suburbs. The geography of Italy makes distribution (from Turin to Brindisi and Palermo) especially difficult. *Il Manifesto* and *Lotta Continua* were, with the PCI's *L'Unità*, the only papers which seriously set out to reach all parts of the country. Yet the cost of sending two or three copies each to a whole series of remote newstands far outweighed the price paid for the paper at the newstand. This was the other major problem of *Il Manifesto's* finances.

Thus the decision to raise the price to 500 lire an issue was taken pending the enactment of the newsprint subsidy bill. Whether in practice the pressure of the other costs, including printers' wages, could be absorbed by the backdated funds that would accrue following the bill's enactment, or whether 500 lire would have to remain the price, remained to be seen. The situation inside the paper was, naturally, rendered acutely difficult by its financial pressures. Working conditions were very cramped, with two or even three people working in very small rooms. Foreign visits for the international specialists were extremely rare, with the result that only crises were reported on the spot, and not the ongoing life of other countries which would make the crises much more readily understandable. This in-depth reporting can sometimes be found in "quality" bourgeois newspapers, but is even more of a requirement for serious marxist journalism.

Worse still, as has been noted already, was the fact that during May and June 1980 there had been no salaries paid to anyone, with the single exception of the printers. People were living on their families, any savings, or bank overdrafts. This was one of the pressures leading to the price-increase, but the hardship and uncertainty it produced, both for the workers on the paper and for their dependents, had a predictably souring effect on some relations within the paper. People found it much harder to disagree with each other—the variety of political positions inside the collective was, it will be recalled, con-siderable—and still get on well with each other personally.

Nonetheless, the paper still came out regular as clockwork every day, and I could find no one who did not volunteer that, notwithstanding these problems, the quality of collective life still scored incomparably better than in the normal journal-istic career. The practice of self-management, in other words, was fully strong enough in *Il Manifesto* to ride out these storms, even when, as in the case of finance, they threatened to engulf the paper altogether.

In 1982 *Il Manifesto* decided to offer shares in the news-paper (at 200,000 lire each) in order to help finance it. Each share or group of shares gave one vote at public meetings, and would give an actual share in ownership ten years later. At the time of this writing it is too early to see how or whether this new structure will operate, but those at the paper were already astonished at the response. Even people who disagreed with them wrote in to say they were buying a share "because you are an important voice to disagree with in Italy." Another wrote in and said "*Il Manifesto* gives voice to a *good* Italy." Many journalists contributed as well. To the first public meeting came people of all ages, many political views, and from a variety of locations. The paper clearly fulfilled a major need.

Women in the newspaper

Il Manifesto is unique among its peers in or out of Italy in having women as forty percent of its staff right from the outset, as well as a woman editor. Apart from strictly feminist newspapers, this proportion is virtually unparalleled in the male chauvinist world of journalism. (Some of the U.S. in-stances in this book, such as *The Guardian* and *Akwesasne Notes*, are to be counted in the tiny group of media where this does not apply.) As one of the women members of the news-paper said, a proportion that high would probably seriously subvert the existing patterns of running a conventional male-dominated newspaper. How did problems in the relation between men and women work out in the collective?

The first, sober recognition must be that *Il Manifesto* offered no real scope for liberated women, only for emancipated women (striking though this advance is). What did this distinction mean? Most obviously, there were no funds (and no space at all in the cramped premises) for a nursery. Women with children were given freedom to pop out to check on them, or to make sure they had got home from school, unlike in a conventional newspaper. But in this process, they inevitably "lost power" in decision-making. The main point at which women with children lost power was in the meeting at 7:30 p.m. which finalized the next day's edition. By then, women with children were very likely to be at home with them. Only women without that tie could be present. And there was, realistically, no other way of running the paper. As one woman in *Il Manifesto* put it: "We tried once or twice to adapt the paper's organization to our needs, but it simply would not tolerate it. It was a machine with its own dynamic, and it resisted any effort to restructure it."

However, and complementarily, women were in a variety of positions on the paper: editor, sub-editor, head of the trade union affairs section, head of the mass culture section, the person in charge of subscriptions, and the "terrorism" specialist (a crucial job in Italy in the period from 1978). Women were proportionately a little more present in the administrative section than in the journalistic section, but it is clear that they did exercise considerable authority inside the collective. They never operated as a unified bloc within the paper, however, unlike the experience for a time of *Lotta Continua* and some of the Italian far left radio stations. One of the male journalists argued that for the paper *not* to have what he termed "professional feminists" concentrating on women's issues was more progressive and constructive than the apparently more radical practice of having women to focus on those issues alone.

One of the *compagne* said that in everyday life in the project, women—especially if they were new to the paper—quite often found themselves intimidated by the axiomatic assumption of authority by some at least of the men in it. They also tended to define issues differently as journalists. Male journalists would typically analyze unions in terms of their internal political struggles. Women journalists would typically analyze them as bastions of male privilege inside the working class. Male journalists might well be interested in Freud and later developments in Freudian theory, whereas women journalists would be more interested in women's "everyday madness."

Another *compagna* felt that although *Il Manifesto* was far in advance of other papers in its proportion of women, their presence had made little difference to the perspectives of most of the men working in it. As an admittedly extreme instance of what she meant, she cited one of the men as having remarked, "Rossana Rossanda is really too brilliant to be a woman!" Another person cited to me her own experience of having gone through a difficult personal period when she felt extremely depressed, but of having to work just as though nothing unusual was going on in her life.

In truth, *Il Manifesto* seems to have represented a kind of middle case for women in revolutionary media. No woman ever left it for feminist reasons, although they had left the parent body PdUP in droves for these reasons. Rossana Rossanda's own political career had been in the world of male-dominated left politics, and the concerns of that politics dominated the paper's origins. As she describes in her introduction to her published radio interviews with women (*Le Altre*),[4] the 1976 eruption of the new women's movement in Italy at one and the same time alienated her, yet forcibly reminded her of long-repressed truths. Furthermore, the involvement of *Il Manifesto* in reporting, for instance, Italian establishment politics, meant that women who covered that area had to exist in some kind of working relation with their hard-bitten, cynical, aggressive counterparts in the established press. To combine that "self" with the non-"masculine" sensibility of a conscious feminist created problems for women reporters in their work outside the office, in addition to their problems, in perhaps a less harsh form, inside it.

Il Manifesto represented a substantial breakthrough in women's media involvement, therefore, although at the same time it was a long way from a solution to the contradictions of sexism. It remained to be seen how far the *compagni* and *compagne* would succeed in forging a radically revised gender culture inside the collective's daily operation.

The Newspaper as a Training School

Finally, it is in order to comment briefly on *Il Manifesto's* extraordinary role in training journalists. Journalism colleges in Italy are few and dreadful. A substantial number of people have passed through *Il Manifesto* (and *Lotta Continua*), and learned their trade as journalists from scratch in these papers. On the one hand, it is a "contribution to democracy," as one of the *Il Manifesto compagni* put it (just as is the similar training function in the use of radio we shall see in the radio-stations Controradio and Radio Popolare). However, it is also a tribute to the continuing financial pressures on people with dependents, that people's enlargement of their communicative competence ended up so often at the service of the capitalist press, hamstrung as to what they could write about, and when, and how.

Training procedures were straightforward in *Il Manifesto*. New workers would be sent out on small assignments to test out their capacity to prioritize issues in their reporting, and to grasp the political relevance of what they described. Otherwise, the main pressures were for a plain, non-rhetorical style, with clarity as the basic goal. If the new entrants managed to absorb these principles successfully, with mostly friendly advice and criticism from the other members of the collective, then they would in time be assigned more significant events and issues to report.

Largely absent were the myths of bourgeois journalism concerning the journalist's professional career, the necessity for "balance" or the propriety of the writer's prejudices, the obligation to defer all the time to senior colleagues, and in general the assumptions of the acceptability of capitalist social structures. Professionalism in the sense of accurate, good writing was highly valued, and the whole question of a "new" professionalism for socialist journalists was very much under discussion during 1980 (we shall return to this theme in the conclusion). But the training was remarkably free of the usual baggage of the ethos of conventional journalism.

A decision taken early on, however, was to encourage the journalists of *Il Manifesto* to get themselves admitted to the National Journalists' Order, the official professional association. Most people in the collective felt that this body should be abolished, and it was often attacked in the paper's columns for its elitism. To enter the order normally required eighteen months of work on a paper, yet obtaining work on a paper normally required prior membership! By law the editor of any Italian newspaper had to be a member. Despite its hostility to the Order, the collective considered it a protection to its members to be enrolled in case the paper should ever cease publication.

In 1982-83, *Il Manifesto* was also beginning to work out a policy with the city council of Rome to begin a new training school for Italian journalists, of a kind hitherto unknown in Italy (comment has been made in the introduction to this section on the generally poor quality of Italian newspaper journalism). Thus despite its many trials, the paper continues to play a major role in the democratic development of Italian society.

Footnotes
1. See R. Pellegrini and G. Pepe, *Unire É Difficile*, Rome: Savelli Editore, 1977.
2. In Italian, the word *compagno* means both personal friend and political comrade, without the external undertones of the word "comrade" in English (compare *compañero* in Spanish for a parallel to the Italian term). Ending in *o* it means a man; in *e*, women; in *i*, men, or men and women combined. I shall use it untranslated because it conveys something important about the "feel" of the left in Italy.
3. P. Murialdi, "I partiti hanno paura dell' informazione" (the parties are afraid of information), *aut aut* 163 (Jan-Feb 1978), pp. 110-114.
4. Rossana Rossanda, *Le Autre*, Milan: Bompiani Editore 1980.

18
LOTTA CONTINUA

An Outline History

The case of *Lotta Continua* presents parallels and contrasts with *Il Manifesto*. As we saw in the account earlier of political movements in Italy, the political organization Lotta Continua (Permanent Struggle)[1] also came into being in 1969, based in two different communities: Pisa university students and young immigrant workers from the South at the Fiat plant in Turin. The very first issue, when *Lotta Continua* was a bi-weekly, focused on student clashes with the authorities, and had as its main headline: "Pisa Is Just The Beginning." As the next ten years would demonstrate, this was no empty prediction.

At that time, Lotta Continua (from now on the letters LC will be used for the organization) represented a sharp break with many of the traditions of Italian left politics, and of European leftism in general. The simplest summary of LC's political stance is to say that it attempted to work out a number of the stated principles of the Chinese Cultural Revolution of the 60s, but within the specific conditions of Italy. This completely marked it off from the Union of Marxist-Leninists, the leading pro-China group in Italy at that time, which like so many other similar groups in other countries was happy endlessly to

255

mouth then-current Chinese political catchphrases, from "paper tigers" to "revisionist cliques." Also, LC never held back from criticizing Chinese policies when it considered they merited it. LC's stance also marked it off politically from a whole gamut of other groups, who were either organized primarily in relation to the PCI (such as *Il Manifesto* at that time), or were organized essentially as marxist intellectuals (e.g., Potere Operaio—Workers' Power). LC emphasized very heavily the importance of mass-based politics, revolutionary militancy, and internal party democracy. The paper recommended Argentinian urban guerillas to its readers, for instance, as a model of determination and organization, unfettered by any fetishism of the electoral process. The paper regularly had a strong emphasis on Vietnam, China, the conflict in Northern Ireland, and on factory struggles, especially by young workers outside the official unions.

In 1972 *Lotta Continua* became a daily, and for the next four years would sell about ten thousand a day. During those years the international events which most dominated it were in Chile and Portugal. LC saw itself as roughly akin to the Chilean MIR, and the Portuguese explosion as representing exactly the mass-based libertarian movement that was the hallmark of genuine revolution. The paper was available in most parts of Italy, including the South, since the organization had a policy of sending a number of its militants down South as political organizers in southern factories. (At the same time, the fact that it was very often the (leninist) political organizer's link with his or her party, meant that relatively few people outside LC or its fringes would normally see it or read it.)

Then came the 1976 Rimini congress of LC, at which the organization liquidated itself as a national political formation, convinced it no longer had the answers, and that no revolutionary organization should continue to exist from inertia. Its local units and branches continued however in many cases to operate from where they were, and within the broad confines of LC's political stance.

The reaction of many of those who had worked on the newspaper was similar to that of these local groups. The core was convinced that the paper should continue, parent organization or not. About fifty people on the paper therefore continued to produce it as an independent revolutionary project. This marked its break with its previous existence as the articulation of the LC organizational line. By 1980, about half these original fifty were still working on the paper.

Perhaps the most decisive moment in *Lotta Continua*'s history followed shortly afterwards, namely the eruption of the movements of 1977-78. *Lotta Continua* in most essentials moved from defining itself as the newspaper expressing the *movement* to its activists (not a vanguard role, unlike *The Guardian* in 1967). It was *the* platform of movement activists, and the most accurate source of information about the movement's directions. To be seen carrying it was equivalent to wearing a lapel-button proclaiming movement involvement.

In fact at that time there emerged an extraordinary crossover sequence between the established media and *Lotta Continua*. To begin with, the only national daily to take the movement seriously was *Lotta Continua*. It began to sell about six thousand a day in Rome alone—half, that is, the Rome sale of Italy's premier quality daily, *Corriere della Sera*—and for a while became Rome's fifth largest paper. Nationally during this peak period, it ws selling thirty to thirty-five thousand copies a day. What is more, the official media, which initially had no access to the movement at all, used it as their basic information source about what was going on.

Once the establishment journalists began to recognize the political significance of what was happening, and to report it themselves, they came to report the events with more accuracy than *Lotta Continua*. This was because *Lotta Continua compagni* had become so closely identified with the movement in their own minds that they refused to expose, let alone to criticize, its excesses and failings. They were acting as a transmission belt, no longer for a political party, but for the movement. Their operational model up to 1976 was effectively revived.

Towards the end of the movement's period of vitality, this position began to become less and less tenable. The turning point proved to be a vote of 2000 present at a Rome movement assembly to go ahead with a demonstration, despite the absence from the assembly of the other 30,000 or so who had previously been active. The absurdity of this situation finally forced *Lotta Continua* to take a much more critical and detached position within the movement, as it had been forced to do once before in 1976.

The next decisive turn of events came hard on the heels of

the movement's decline, with the eruption of so-called "red" terrorism. The only occasion LC had ever actually supported such activity was in 1972 when an Alfa-Romeo executive was briefly kidnapped and then released unscathed (the factory's work force applauded for the most part). However, it took a long time for the newspaper to clarify its attitude. Some used to want the paper to use the term "killing" (*uccisione*) rather than "murder" (*assassinio*), and to employ circumlocutions rather than the word "terrorist." This wing of opinion felt the Red Brigades were comrades committing gross political errors, rather than criminals to be condemned out of hand.

With the kidnapping of Aldo Moro, the debate moved into a new phase. *Lotta Continua* joined the PSI and *Il Manifesto* in arguing for negotiations with the Red Brigades. It launched a public appeal, signed by many bishops (some, incredibly, took out subscriptions to the paper). Following Moro's murder, the mists began to clear. The Red Brigades' strategy of liquidating, not Mafia bosses or neo-fascists, but the most humane and reform-minded members of the ruling class in order to eliminate the conciliators, came to be seen for what it was: a viciously destructive elitism, the exact counterpart of the repressive state it was sworn to overthrow.

It was a very confused and confusing time for the paper, because its internal structure was very open. Anyone who wished to join in writing for it was free to do so, and to join in the daily assembly which decided on the next day's contents. In 1978, about 110 people were involved in producing the paper. At the end of the day each temporary worker would be paid 5000 lire, the same amount as the permanent journalistic staff. Apart from the fact that some people used to turn up and stay all day without really contributing, simply in order to collect this payment, the structure led to endless complications in terms of a coherent editorial line. Some of those involved in the assembly were drifting toward the left wing of the PCI; others might be ambivalent toward the Red Brigades. Those within the area of *Lotta Continua* politics were constantly being undercut by these different currents, through the paper's ultra-democratic internal structure.

These experiences, of the problems of being an organization paper, then of being a paper so open that it could not define itself coherently to its readers, culminated in 1979 in a resolution to reorganize *Lotta Continua* drastically. The decision was also taken under heavy financial pressures, since the paper was losing subscribers extremely fast. At this watershed point, not only was it resolved to stick to an independent political line, but also to change the structure of authority inside the paper. From that point on, the paper was run under the absolute control of a seven member editorial board, elected only from among the permanent workers, but subject to their recall at any time.

The new internal structure was designed to put an end to the problems engendered in the newspaper by its ultra-democratic practice. Yet the change was not designed to cancel out democracy inside the paper, nor did it have the effect of doing so. Every two weeks there was an assembly of all the *compagni,* and in between, such assemblies could be, and were, called by two or three members at a moment's notice. Nor did the new structure lead to any kind of censorship power operated by the editorial board. As one *compagna* observed, the power structure inside the paper had simply become "a *known* power," rather than a diffuse but nonetheless real power. Another *compagno* observed that during a trip he had taken to Iran, every one of his articles on the Iranian situation had been printed just as he wrote it, and he was not the paper's foremost (or Farsi-speaking) writer on Iran.

On any given day, moreover, a considerable proportion of the paper was written by friends, sympathizers, and members of former LC branches, who would send in articles and news stories on a whole range of issues. Thus the paper did not become simply the private property of a mini-elite. Also, because of financial pressures there was space for people who did not expect payment to join the paper so long as they were able to demonstrate their commitment and competence. They would, rather like in *Il Manifesto,* observe what was done for a couple of weeks, and then begin to try their hand at short pieces, with comradely criticism for their training. The paper had begun to organize gatherings of readers' groups in different parts of Italy in order to comment on the contents, but postponed this project until a later time becaue of the financial morass in which it found itself.

The direction in which *Lotta Continua*'s internal organization developed is an important indicator of the difficulty of defining effective popular control by any single democratic mechanism out of its particular political context. A superficial analysis could easily conclude that the "iron law of oligarchy" had reasserted itself in *Lotta Continua,* transforming the most democratic structure gradually but inexorably into a conventional power structure. The reality was far more complex.

One of its complexities was—just as in the case of *Il Manifesto* and to some extent in the case of Radio Popolare—that the personality and skills of the editor were of the greatest importance to the continued running of the paper. Everyone to whom I spoke who had knowledge of *Lotta Continua*'s organization agreed on this point. Thus the grasp and style—"charisma" is at once too flamboyant and too superficial a term—of this one person were crucial ingredients in its success. The notion that socialism must be dedicated to gray purges of individual talent is demonstrably absurd, not least in these instances of revolutionary media.

A different aspect of *Lotta Continua*'s structure in 1980 was its organization of departments. To some extent this paralleled that of the conventional press, with people concentrating on foreign news, unions, courts, women, and so on. However, one particular problem at the time was the division between journalists and administrative workers. Of all the "areas" in Italian far left politics, *Lotta Continua* was the least likely to harbor anyone who had a self-image as a bureaucrat. Indeed, to be a financial administrator, an accountant, an advertising executive, was an anathema to anyone in that area, similar to becoming a senior state official or a capitalist. Yet *Lotta Continua* needed administration if it were to continue in existence.

During the summer of 1980, the problem was that the editorial board pressured those who worked on the paper, but did not have the same writing skills that others enjoyed, to transfer themselves into these tasks. It was an unenviable situation, because it meant bluntly telling certain people they had less communicative skill than others, while hoping to retain their loyalty. A compromise was in the process of being hammered out while I was present, which involved such *compagni* accepting this rotation for six months, after which the situation would be reviewed. But in the paper's financial straits, where no one was being paid in 1980, this too demanded a high degree of loyalty on the part of those relegated to these unglamorous and frankly stigmatized roles. The experience of most of the media already surveyed also underlines this problem of finding politically committed people who know their way around administration.

The other dimension of the paper's organization which requires comment was its printers, who worked on the ground floor, while the rest of the paper's producers worked on the floors above. Just as in the case of *Il Manifesto*, the relation between the two sets of people functioned well. The printers were, and always had been, paid full union rates, far more than any journalist on the paper: in 1981, two million lire a month for only six-hour days, Monday through Saturday (the best rates in Rome). This was for obvious reasons of political principle on the part of the *Lotta Continua compagni*. However, none were LC members and they reconciled their own politics with working for *Lotta Continua* in the same way as they would have reconciled them with working for a capitalist. There seemed to be no attempt by the *compagni* on the paper to draw them into the project, nor did the printers make any effort to enter it. In both newspapers, Italian political realities appeared to make impossible any attempt to overcome this aspect of the capitalist division of labor. Personal relationships between journalists and printers were very good, however.

Thus the crude category of the iron law of oligarchy cannot handle the specific complexities of this case: it would be eagerly applied by its proponents to the position of the printers, but could not begin to explain the political cross-currents which were part and parcel of their non-involvement in the newspaper's running. And it would predict that the administrative staff would have dominated the journalists, rather than the situation which actually obtained. Finally, it would collapse altogether in the face of the various strategies adopted by the *compagni* to maintain the democratic character of the newspaper. *Lotta Continua*'s history is important for this reason alone.

The Newspaper's Finances

In 1980, the financial situation of *Lotta Continua* was at least as desperate as *Il Manifesto*'s. The decline in sales from the high point of the 1977-78 movement was one crucial cause. The maximum copies sold in any one day amounted to 25,000, while the paper needed 30,000 assured sales to finance itself via subscriptions. There were other elements in the paper's financial difficulties. Advertisers were simply uninterested in the paper, partly because of its politics, and partly because its regular readers were mostly low-income young people. Although the state-run SIPRA agency had come under a degree of

PCI control since 1976, as we saw in examining *Il Manifesto,* neither its PCI president nor the rest of SIPRA's political sympathies extended as far to the left of the PCI as *Lotta Continua.* This second potential source of advertising was therefore closed to the newspaper.

The whole question of newsprint finance and the continually delayed parliamentary legislation (with retroactive clauses) was explained in describing the financial problems of *Il Manifesto.* At *Lotta Continua* the *compagni* had calculated that by summer 1980, the state already owed them 300 million lire. Despite this rather solid security (for no one doubted the bill would eventually become law, because of its massive advantages to Fratelli Fabbri and the major publishers and newspapers), no bank could be found to lend any money to the paper to tide it over. Less revolutionary projects naturally fared better. Thus the paper was in the frustrating position of having sums of money just out of reach, which would have done much to underpin its solvency.

At the same time certain of its costs were constantly rising. The distribution costs had reached the point where to get one copy to a small town or railway station newsvendor cost 3000 lire in many cases—ten time the paper's price. Printers' costs were also constantly rising in line with nationally negotiated rates. *Il Manifesto* nearly doubled its price, but *Lotta Continua* was fortunate in obtaining one loan from the Radical Party. Even so, no one had been paid properly (aside from the printers) since July 1979. Everyone in the summer of 1980 was owed about a million to a million and a half lire by the paper.

In the absence of any social welfare provision in Italy, this forced some people to leave the paper altogether, and others to work part-time while doing the variety of "underground economy" jobs especially characteristic of the Italian labor market. Still others depended on their close friends and family to keep them above the breadline: the "granny-state," as opposed to the welfare state, as some people described it. However, the consequence was a great deal of instability in the production of the paper. One *compagno* frankly confessed that he was regularly surprised when the paper actually came out at the end of each day. The working conditions were atrociously cramped. The financial situation also made it hard to think and plan ahead realistically, hard, too, not simply to be engulfed in gloom to the exclusion of the drive and energy required to maintain the project's momentum.

It is not surprising then that some outside observers felt that *Lotta Continua* was in danger of losing its coherence and was perpetually reporting events without any overall strategy. The *compagni* found this situation extremely frustrating, since they could see only too clearly the major political opportunity provided for *Lotta Continua* by the dismal quality and small readership level of the Italian press—but could do nothing effective to fill the vacuum. For example, only two foreign trips were made by the paper's international staff from September 1979 to June 1980, and each was done at the individual's own expense. Under these circumstances, there was no way that *Lotta Continua* could rival the main press and cease to be just a second paper for the politically committed, even given the fact that on principle it would always have stayed away from the official diplomatic circles that are the staple news source of regular foreign correspondents.

The critical nature of the situation was not lost on the banks who refused to lend to the paper. The most innovative and revolutionary project cannot survive, let alone flourish, on thin air. In 1980 it remained to be seen how far *Lotta Continua* could succeed in emerging out of its financial ordeal and, in fact, on January 14, 1981 the last issue was printed. From then until the time of writing, negotiations were attempted with various quarters, including the PSI, but without success. They printed some special single-issue pamphlets on topics like Poland, Iran, and the Italian earthquake of November 1980, but that was all.

The Changing Roles of Women in the Newspaper

Up to the 1976 Rimini congress when LC dissolved itself, the position of women inside the paper was as a minority, and essentially as political activists in the masculine style, fully acceptable on those terms. The congress changed this dramatically, since women's issues were one major source of the divisions on which LC foundered. This almost at once rebounded onto the paper, with some women insisting on creating their own separate section under their complete control. The male *compagni* would only know from day to day how much space the *compagne* wanted—usually one to two pages—but never what was going to be in it until the women presented it to them by the daily deadline. (Similar restructuring by autonomous women's groups was going on at this time in Radio Città Futura, Rome, and in Controradio, Florence.)

The women's demand that the paper be organized this way was accepted without demur by the men who numerically dominated the paper. Some men left, however, even though they did not resist the demand. Some women also left the paper on the ground that revolutionary politics demanded that women and men revolutionaries work together to overcome sexism. Others left on the ground that this separate structure should be taken to its own logical conclusions, and that women should get right out of any project with males in it. A year later, the foundation of *Quotidiano Donna* (Woman's Daily) crystallized this move.

What happened in *Lotta Continua* was an exact replica of major trends within the newly emerging women's movement in Italy. This movement began, as we saw earlier, with a powerful separatist current, predictable enough given the saliency of patriarchal structures and ideologies in Italy. The experience for the women inside the movement was, as almost everywhere else, one of release and delight—suddenly and at last—in finding themselves able to speak confidently with other women about the myriad levels of their oppression, about the experiences repressed inside themselves as individuals for the confirmation of common recognition. "It was like a flower unfolding" one *compagna* put it.

Inside the women's autonomous section of the paper, there was a fierce determination to organize neither as males nor as journalists, but as feminists. They refused to sign articles so as not to elevate themselves individually (with one result being that some *compagni* were always nosing around asking "who wrote this piece?"). They opened their pages to every tendency within the women's movement, including non-marxist feminists (there could be no more telling commentary on the gap between U.S. and Italian political culture than the implication of this decision). They defined their role at the beginning as constituting "a postbox for the feminist movement," as enablers of a transmission of the realities of women's lives. They insisted on their equal ability to write, on their absolute unity as women, on their personal warmth and openness to each other, on their refusal of power as a patriarchal distortion of social relations. They were hostile to chiefs, competitivenes, geniuses, narcissism—the whole bag and baggage of masculine journalism. At the same time they rejected the purist-separatist argument. "The paper is our formal dialogue with the *compagni*," they argued, "and that is at once the most and the least we can achieve at the present time."

It was an extremely intense and explosive period in Italian politics at many levels. But just as we have already seen for *Lotta Continua* in general, so this "transmission belt" self-definition began to run into problems for the *compagne*. Some *did* write better than others, and having *compagni* single out particular pieces for comment, when everyone inside the women's section knew who had written them, added to problems inside the section. Even within the section's consciousness-raising sessions, some people were more adept at self-expression than were others. Yet there was a kind of competition for the lowliest place, as opposed to the typical competitiveness of men.

Eventually, they began signing their articles, on the ground that to refuse to do so was to pretend they had not chosen to say one thing, or to adopt one line, as against others. It was to abdicate their own responsibility for what they said, to hide behind an impersonal mask.

A different issue emerged in the women's section as new currents began to appear in the women's movement as a whole. One new dimension was the way that generational and age alignments between mothers and aunts on the one hand, and their daughters and nieces on the other, came to cross-cut sisterhood simply defined. The family is still a more embracing institution in Italy than in some other societies, and generational power is still very strongly buttressed by common practice and ideology, independently of religious affiliation. If the realities of women's lives demanded urgent exploration by feminists, this reality could not be denied.

To the outsider, an extraordinary double-take of the issue posed itself during the 1977-78 movement. The teenage high school and college students involved in that movement found feminist separatism both incomprehensible and passé. They looked with incredulity at the *compagne* in *Lotta Continua*, aged for the most part in their early twenties, and told them: 'We are new, the movement has transcended your hang-ups about men, and men's about women; we *can* live together. Your attitude seems as remote from us as our mothers' does." Superficial as this judgment may have been, the intensity of the movement meant that the *Lotta Continua* feminists' sense of being outflanked on the left was real enough, and contributed to their gradual development of a different position.

Above all, however, it was the kidnapping and assassination of Moro which forced a re-evaluation of their initial strategy as feminists. Until then, terrorism had been in their eyes a topic for "male politics," but they could not brush aside as irrelevant to women the profound implications of defeat or victory *under these conditions* for the "historic compromise" policy. The event was certain to affect the entire society, men and women alike. Very slowly and tentatively, after not having discussed anything with the *compagni* for over a year, the *compagne* began to discuss the Moro affair and its aftermath with them. It was the beginning of a new phase, a recognition that dialogue is possible, desirable and even necessary, given certain conditions (such as abandonment of overt or impervious sexism).

Their gradual shift had not eliminated many problems, to be sure. Some *compagne* were much more confident in verbal exchanges with the men on the paper that were others. This, and the question of different writing skills, continued to create difficulties for the feminists' unity. They were utterly determined that these differences not crystallize into power-positions. The women developed certain tactical skills in dealing with sexism on various levels. They continued to discuss all the issues in the women's section, either collectively or in spontaneous twos and threes, before any assembly meeting. The problem resolved itself on one level into the question: how to be "professional" without being "a journalist"? We saw the same question surfacing in *Il Manifesto*, and we will see it again in both Controradio and Radio Popolare. "Professionalism" was partly an issue of a necessary political independence for a revolutionary newspaper (or radio station), and also partly an issue of the sheer capacity to communicate effectively. Neither feminist nor marxist commitment, nor their combination, could automatically realize the former or generate the latter.

The Labor Movement and Lotta Continua

For reasons outlined earlier in the analysis of Italian political movements, *Lotta Continua*'s relation with the official labor movement was weak. To be sure, workers' struggles had always been actively supported and written up in its pages, and *Lotta Continua* never aspired to the intellectual plane of *Il Manifesto*. Its base was the young *emarginati*, half-in and half-out of employment and study, and to some extent groups of younger workers. But the PCI-dominated unions, for instance, simply operated on a different plane, valuing organization and stability over movement and change. The division was in part a generational question, and reflected to a great extent the extreme youthfulness of the 1977-78 movement. As we saw earlier on, one major reason for the failure of this movement to spread to other sections of Italian society was its arrogant age-ist dismissiveness toward the older generation. The episodes in the women's section of *Lotta Continua* illustrate this point more than adequately, where first after the Rimini congress women aged 25-35 left the paper (opposed to feminist separatism) and then those in their early twenties shortly afterwards found themselves defined as an older generation by the teenagers of the 1977-78 movement.

Yet there seemed no more will to bridge this chasm between movement activists and the official labor movement in *Lotta Continua* than anywhere else in the young left in Italy (with the possible exeption of Democrazia Proletaria).[2] It was not that the chasm was denied to exist, simply that it ws taken fatalistically to be unbridgeable. One of the very few *compagni* trying to build bridges between these sectors admitted that his was a lonely furrow to plough inside the paper. He argued that there were small but significant openings to be worked within, such as the growing demand from the factory floor for unpaid leaves of absence, or for absence partly paid from future pension entitlements. These represented tiny but significant invasions of the principle of political refusal of capitalist work, and not surprisingly were most popular in factories with a youthful labor-force. Yet no one else on *Lotta Continua* was even interested in using these shifts in consciousness to build bridges into the official world of labor.

The most serious political, as opposed to financial, hazard facing the paper was, arguably, its degree of encapsulation within youth politics. As a newspaper, *Lotta Continua* was in the potential position of being able to help generations of the Italian left to comunicate with one another, *outside* the confines of the PCI and other entrenched political establishments. This could only act to everyone's advantage in strengthening the general revolutionary movement in Italy. The initiative would otherwise only come from the established parties in the shape of their regular organization of youth sections—the selection mechanisms to enable gifted *enfants terribles* to be talent-spotted and hopefully weaned into eventual *responsible* commitment to the party's professed goals (or purged altogether). That was the kind of politics that the movement of 1977-78 had kicked into the drain, in its entirely positive rejection of the old political models. *Lotta Continua* seemed less concerned to move into the future in this respect, than to content itself with denouncing the past.

Imagination and Language

On these scores, *Lotta Continua* had an excellent record. Its photos, for example, especially its front-page photos, were often exceptionally striking and original, impossible as it is to convey their impact in words. Their quality was widely recognized, including by people from outside the left. Cartoons were also given considerable prominence, and especially in the earliest phase of the paper were very imaginative. *Lotta Continua* also utilized the standard comic-strip characters of the bourgeois press, such as Superman, but with completely altered stories and dialogue. Superman, for example, became the representative of U.S. imperialism.

The single most significant criterion of a revolutionary newspaper's communicative capacity has to be its language. Radio enables people to debate directly, whereas a newspaper cannot even rephrase what it says in response to a question. It is a single utterance. Its freshness and clarity of language are therefore even more important to it than to radio.

Now, as noted already, in the overview of the Italian revolutionary movement of the 60s and 70s, several groups on the left were usually recognizable by their deliberate construction of particular jargons peculiar to themselves, which then acted both as beacons to outsiders, and as reaffirmation rituals for insiders.[3] The one newspaper and organization which broke out of this mold was *Lotta Continua*. Its language in its earlier days was studied systematically by Patrizia Violi, an outside observer, who also updated some of her earlier observations in the journal *Ombre Rosse* in 1979.[4]

In its earliest phase, *Lotta Continua* was notable for the immediacy of its language. Perhaps the sharpest example was its use of southern dialect in reporting the views and struggles of southern workers, and of migrant workers from the South in northern factories. This practice issued naturally enough from LC's political involvement in these sections of the working class, but it also offered a clear contrast with the regular use of "proper" language by the media in general. For LC it was especially a way of bolstering southern workers against the hostility or contempt they regularly encountered in the North. *Lotta Continua* continually used standard working class expressions, difficult to translate directly, but which helped make the paper instantly understandable, de-intellectualizing without talking down.

Much of its contents were written as if being spoken, with short sentences, and frequent use of the dramatic present tense. For instance:

The morning after, about 200 police swoop on the place, smash in the gate, race up the stairs, beat up the comrades they meet, chuck them outside, arrest two, but come to a halt in front of the women and children gathered in the corridor.

The use was frequent of rhetorical questions, of repetition for effect, of accumulated statements. Here are some examples:

Comrades, let's ask ourselves plainly, was there ever a slave who loved his chains?

Each of us can become an activist and organizer of this struggle for housing, against rents, against price-robbery, against disgusting living conditions, against the destruction of health, against privilege and inequality, against the split between those who give orders and those who carry them out.

The factory is the heart of this society; the towns, the houses, the streets, the schools, the hospitals, the prisons, the barracks and the shops are made so that people eat, live, think, obey, travel, fall ill, are cured, and move with the discipline and inhumanity of capitalist production.

Lotta Continua also often used irony to good effect:

The reformists are at best like the soldier in the story who was heard yelling 'Help, help, I've taken this guy prisoner, but he's holding on to me and won't let go!

This vivid directness was not to be found throughout the paper though. Its economic analyses, for instance, tended to be much more conventionally framed:

The PCI's alternative economic growth strategy, contrasting with the monopolies' strategy, is often a merely nominal expedient to justify electoral contests, above all where monopolistic economic growth is irreversible and given, so great is the competitive and productive capacity of capitalist agricultural enterprises, and such is the importance of capitalist industries for national production.

Explanatory articles tended at that time to be pitched at this level, whereas news stories were much more graphic.

Also, it must be admitted that *Lotta Continua* did suffer at that period from some more standard vices of far left communication. Some terms were used so intensively that they became ciphers rather than communicative instruments; opportunist, creativity, political growth, authentic, contradiction, struggle, consciousness, clash, (proletarian) violence, (proletarian) anger. *Lotta Continua* did tend to define itself as the sole bearer of the truth, denying all other currents on the left any but a confusing role in the revolutionary process. And it was triumphalist:

> ...a really packed demonstration, of over a thousand workers and students, marches in the city, behind the Lotta Continua placard. It is a combative march, with a fine political thrust. It is a march which forcefully launches the concrete campaign against bourgeois elections, and consolidates the organization and unification of the proletariat. It is a bitter defeat for revisionism.

Or in 1979:

> Iran is not an 'Islamic republic,' its backbone being Shiite organization, a capillary and informal structure which has gathered up a thousand years of tradition of opposing the power structure and has announced its rebirth—with millions of people in the squares.[5]

Notwithstanding these defects, *Lotta Continua* played a remarkable national political role in a number of instances, precisely through its imaginative use of language and even layout. The expression *"fanfascismo"*—a fusion of "fascism" with the then Presidential candidate's surname, Fanfani—was repeatedly in its pages, and moved into general political discussion as a summarization of the political trend of Christian Democracy at that point. Similarly, the murder of the anarchist Pinelli inside police headquarters by a Milan police chief, Calabresi, was taken up by the paper and became a continuous theme. Calabresi's photograph was rarely absent from the paper, often without caption or news story being attached; it was just *there,* all the time reminding people of what had happened, prodding them to consciousness of the state's capabilities, urging them to call for exposure of police violence. (So widespread became this campaign that the expert liquidation of Calabresi in a Milan street in 1972 was rumored to be the work of the Italian secret sevice, who wished to get rid of this symbol of Italian state repression.)

In the later 70s, according to Gad Lerner[6], himself for a long time a writer for *Lotta Continua*, the paper's style changed somewhat from the earlier phase analyzed by Violi. By the later 70s it had adopted a rather more traditionally left wing vocabulary with a strong "Chinese" imprint. Following the eruption of separatist feminism in the 1977-78 movement, its language changed yet again to some extent in response to the then current vocabulary of Italian feminism. Both he, and Violi (in her later retrospective article), agreed that in both political language and political line, the paper had become pretty confused in the 1977-80 years. The major example for both of them was the ambivalence toward terrorism which characterized the paper up to 1979.

Violi cited the paper's treatment of the Red Brigades' assassination of Guido Rossa, a PCI activist and shop steward, who had given names of possible Red Brigade activists to the police, and had publicly urged others to do the same. *Lotta Continua*'s headline ran: "Guido Rossa, PCI worker, delegate, 'model citizen,' assassinated by Red Brigades." The sub-head was: "'The Red Brigades' iron logic ends by killing a worker, for spying." The illustration provides a good example of what Lerner more generally referred to as the way the paper provided "a chronicle of repression...in which guilty and innocent, known clandestine activists and comrades mistaken for clandestine activists, victims of judicial excesses and deeply sick individuals, get mixed up with each other."[7] Although by the time I arrived at *Lotta Continua* this period was definitely over, I have discussed it here so as to dispel any notion of automatic illumination and progress in revolutionary communication. The upturns, downswings, and cross-currents of the revolutionary movement probably have much more impact on revolutionary *media*—if they are open, and not little sectarian ghettoes—than even on political organizations.

It still remains the case that *Lotta Continua*'s style is unusually fresh and imaginative. In 1980, the paper included a regular weekly science fiction story, as well as poetry at frequent intervals. Music features were contributed by groups half-in and half-out of the regular staff and there was an increase planned in sports coverage.

For me a good illustration of the difference between *Lotta Continua* at its best and many other left newspapers was a piece in March 1980 by a member of the Radio Popolare collective in Milan on the funeral of a gypsy king in northern Italy. If most revolutionary papers had covered the event—and many would not have done so—they would have commented no doubt on gypsies' bad living conditions, their education problems, their harassment by the police. The *Lotta Continua* article wrote with sympathy and respect of the cultural traditions of Romany people; and of the fact that a Romany king is elected, and has no army or police to force obedience to his will. It described the funeral ceremonies as a dignified reaffirmation of this culture. This *openness* constituted the hallmark of *Lotta Continua* at its best.

Footnotes

1. See L. Bobbio, *Lotta Continua,* Rome: Savelli Editore 1979, for an excellent account of the organization and its milieu. I have used it extensively in this section.
2. For this political group, see Radio Popolare, n. 5.
3. A. Caronia and E. Pellegrini, "Oltre la communicazione acefala" (Beyond acephalous communication), *aut aut* 163 (Jan-Feb 1978), pp. 6-17.
4. P. Violi, *I Giornali dell'Estrema Sinistra: i tranelli e le ambiguità della lingua e dell'ideologia* (The Newspapers of the Far Left: pitfalls and ambiguities of language and ideology), Milan: Aldo Garzanti Editore 1977; P. Violi, contribution to debate on communication and movements in *Ombre Rosse* (red shadows) 29 (June 1979), pp. 16-21. Pages 69-168 of her book were devoted to *Lotta Continua's* language, and with the exception noted, all quotations from the paper are drawn from her text.
5. Cited from Violi's *Ombre Rosse* article.
6. G. Lerner, contribution to the debate on communication and movements in the *Ombre Rosse* issue noted above, pp. 21-34.
7. Lerner, *art. cit.*

19

CONTRORADIO, FLORENCE

History and self-definition

Up until the end of 1980, Controradio (Counter-radio) was located in a narrow street quite a distance away from the centers of tourist attraction and expensive shops that are the visitor's image of Florence. Entrance to the radio station was through a bare hallway and up some well-used stairs. The station occupied three rooms, none of them large. Decor and furnishings were at a minimum, and the studio itself was sound-proofed with sheets of black plastic and eggboxes nailed into the wall.

Controradio began its life in 1975. Initially it was directly tied to the organization Lotta Continua, seeing itself as a local radio equivalent of the newspaper. The Florence Lotta Continua group continued, even after the self-dissolution of the national organization in 1976, to use the newspaper *Lotta Continua* as its central reference point, reading directly from it in news bulletins as though it was the most authoritative news source and political commentary in Italy. However, it became increasingly difficult to maintain this relation with the newspaper alone, and all the more so, given the paper's relative weakness as a news source on issues outside youth movements, women's movements and student movements in Italy. But perhaps the final push toward a independent development path for Controradio was *Lotta Continua*'s own move toward a pluralism of the left after the organization's collapse in 1976.

In 1977 the station hit the national news in Italy, accused by the rightwing daily *La Nazione* of being the "GHQ" of

273

urban guerrilla warfare in Florence. The accusation was made during the period of media paranoia about the political movements in Rome and Bologna. Police swooped down on the station and made off with some supposedly incriminating tapes, but nothing eventually came of the whole affair. It was very dramatic, but not at all revealing of the actual political role played by the station then or since.

By 1980, the station no longer saw itself as one link in a national revolutionary strategy co-ordinated from any central point. Its politics were still revolutionary, but it had re-defined its place in the revolutionary process—and indeed had re-defined that process itself at certain points, as will be seen.

One of its members defined three established routes for former movement activists in Italy: joining the left wing of the PCI; joining a terrorist group; and political apathy. Controradio, he said, was struggling to create a fourth path—a path without existing models, except the negative models of American "free" radio stations, and of northern European social democracy. This fourth path involved the attempt to link the immediate reality of operating as a *local* radio station in Florence—a city with highly specific characteristics—with a much longer term revolutionary strategy than had characterized the far left in Italy since 1968. The core of this longer view was the recognition that revolution had to be based on the political self-development of the working population; that this self-development could not be achieved in hothouse conditions overnight, but had to emerge from many localities, each with their particular experiences; and that the PCI's long view of political change was a long view for the benefit of its leadership, not its "infantry."

Within this setting, the Controradio collective did not see itself as a party or a group, but defined its task as a facilitator, putting the radio at the disposal of Florence's socialist public to express itself of itself (compare the similar views of Radio Città Futura.[1]) At the same time, however, Controradio has also been marked by the same shift toward a new "professionalism" that we have seen in other media of the Italian revolutionary left. Back at the height of the 1977-78 movements, Controradio policy had been to open the microphone to anyone on the left who wanted to say anything. This had led to a serious degree of disorganization on the radio, particularly when the decline of those movements and the end of the novelty of democratic radio stations meant that fewer people were anxious to communicate by radio. The result had been that music had come to dominate the station's output, simply because it was the easiest way to run the station on an *ad hoc* basis. If a yawning gap opened up, they could always put on a record. And then another, and then another.

This drift began to provoke long and intense discussion within the Controradio collective on the practical implications of their policy. The eventual outcome of these discussions was that the collective decided to maintain its own firm grip on all broadcasting, no longer allowing anyone instant access to the microphone. Effectively they had hammered out a distinction between open access and instant access, as had Milan's Radio Popolare. It meant that they had rejected once and for all the notion that the radio was simply an empty box to be filled with anything or everything. It also meant that once having defined themselves as workers in the field of information, they were bound to make decisions about whether they agreed with the political perspectives and practical abilities of the people who came to them with a project for broadcast communication. Both were important, for the project might be excellent, but the necessary experience to realize it successfully might well be lacking.

The description of this shift in policy could lead to the judgement that the collective was establishing itself as a little clique, no doubt democratically organized on the inside, but effectively proof against mass control from below. The undoubtedly important fact that its members had a long history of working together in the station, could also be cited as a factor predisposing the collective in this direction.

In actuality, however, this interpretation of the shift in policy would be facile, as three instances of Controradio's practice indicate. The first consideration is that while the collective had a core of ten full-timers, and fifteen part-timers, there was also a considerable number of other people who worked with them on a whole variety of short-term and long-term projects. A second consideration is that each morning was given over to the "Open Microphone" phone-in program, where listeners could and did express their views spontaneously.

The other consideration is that the collective took considerable time and trouble to help people use the medium effectively. Massimo Smuraglia, the person chiefly responsible for this training process, mentioned two cases. One was of two young men who started broadcasting their particular program, but without experience. Literally dozens of times he talked with them, explaining to them how to use the equipment, what mistakes they were making, how to avoid them. Their broadcasts, which had begun by being nearly disastrous, ended by being very popular, with many people phoning in during them.

The counter-example he cited was of a person who had wished to present a regular slot on blues music, but who was frankly hopeless in learning how to do it, and had eventually to be told to discontinue his project.

These examples show that what was at stake for the Controradio collective was not its own status as a little local elite, but its determination that the radio's output should be as good as it could be made. Their shift in broadcasting policy has to be interpreted in this light.

Controradio's evolution as a radio collective had also led it to get involved in a number of activities beyond just broadcasting. Thus they were active in Florence in summer 1980 in promoting certain cultural events, for example organizing sales of tickets for a major reggae concert by Bob Marley in Milan (which eventually drew a hundred thousand people). During 1980, they anticipated a move to a new location in the autumn, which would function not merely as a radio station but also as a center for theater, video, poetry (many young Italians write and listen to poetry), and food. Again, this could be taken to indicate the station's "institutionalization," but in fact the new project had much more to do with the collective's recognition that the revolutionary process does not and cannot simply engage people on the level of political militancy and eyeball-to-eyeball confrontations. The collective was itself acutely conscious that it might be playing with social-democratic fire and might wind up as a purely social center, rather than as a revolutionary socialist center. While this awareness would not magically preserve the project from doing just that, it is still clear that their shift in policy was not for them a denial of their revolutionary commitment.

Controradio and the established political parties

This is an appropriate point at which to assess Controradio's developing relation with established political parties of the left. With the PCI, relations were, not surprisingly, bad. From the station's origin, direct and aggressive opposition to the PCI's line had been normal. Locally, the clash between them had centered more than anything else on the housing question. In Florence, housing was a political hot potato, because apart from luxury accomodation, new dwellings were few and far between. Controradio had consistently supported the squatters' groups which had predictably mushroomed in the city; and as consistently it had attacked local PCI policy, which was to downplay the issue. This was in order to avoid antagonizing the very considerable number of local shop-keepers, who preferred Florence to be kept "touristic" at the price of not building new housing estates. (Only at elections, when the PCI needed mass votes, did it make any issue of the housing problem.)

Other points of contention between Controradio and the PCI existed. The station had been an early advocate of the legalization of heroin as a means of removing it from organized crime. This was violently opposed for a long time by the PCI as though it were a concession to drug abuse (though by 1980 its opposition was beginning to soften a little). The 1979 Soviet invasion of Afghanistan was condemned outright by Contror-adio, even though the local PCI—against its national leader-ship!—was in favor of it. A third continuing point of contention was in the PCI's local radio station, Radio Cento Fiori (Radio Hundred Flowers), which broadcast music carefully aimed at attracting teenage listeners—perhaps in order to detach them from the longer established, but less well financed Controradio, with its much stronger emphasis on information. This could be perceived as a peaceful form of socialist competition, except that if Controradio's unyielding independence were to disap-pear from the Florence scene, Radio Cento Fiori would un-doubtedly act to cement PCI power over the city. Which would not, it seemed, help to solve even its housing problem.

Relations with the PSI were more mixed, being quite warm at the time this research was conducted, at least with the libertarian and leftwing social democratic members of the Florence branch of the party. In general, Florence was a stronghold of the PSI's left wing. Since the PSI had gained two percent more votes in the 1980 local elections than the PCI, these links promised to be of some importance in the station's viability in the early 1980s. Relations with the Radical Party were also good, both operating as thorns in the side of the body politic. (Also, Controradio's *direttore responsabile*[2] was a Radical Party member, a marxist of many years' standing.) However, as one of the Controradio *compagni* put it, this warm relation could easily change were the Radical Party to get any closer to power in government.

The issue of concern to some members of the collective, as noted above, was whether they were involuntarily becoming part of the "Germanization" (the northern European social-democratization) of Italian politics. Receiving small grants from Florence city council for particular projects, the prospective move to a new address, and the expansion of the station's activities to be a kind of socialist cultural center, were all activities which would make them dependent at certain points on the political establishment. Would compromises lead subtly to integration, to co-optation? These were some of the questions, inevitably unanswered, as they contemplated their immediate future.

Internal Democracy and Organization

As we have seen throughout these studies, internal democracy cannot be separated from external relations which media have with social movements and with subordinate classes. As self-managed reactionary radio station is perfectly conceivable; indeed, the right wing political weekly *Tempo* in Portugal is a journal organized pretty much along these lines. Nonetheless, internal democracy remains central to revolutionary media. How did Controradio address the practical problems of realizing it?

Formally, the core collective of ten full-time radio workers made all major decisions at weekly Monday night meetings, or at specially convened meetings. Certain individuals were entrusted by the collective with particular tasks, such as training in use of the equipment and the medium for those unfamiliar with either, or assessing new program proposals from outside the collective. However, a crucial basis of the Controradio collective's style of work was its common history and development over the three years since its members got together in 1977, to raise 200,000 lire to buy the transmitter from the previous group in charge. Over these years, most issues had been thrashed out in great detail, so that if there were to be a Red Brigades' incident in Italy, or if the problem of heroin-dependence came up, there would be no need for fresh discussion to decide on the collective's position.

On new issues there would automatically be discussion, both formal and informal. When a relatively small group of people meet each other most days in a radio station, month in and month out, the significance of spontaneous discussion becomes at least as great as that of formal policy debates. This cohesive aspect of the collective's operation was emphasized to me in terms very similar to those of the Radio Popolare collective, when I asked about the mechanism of democratic recall of, say, the collective's chair. The *compagni* insisted that the station simply did not operate on that plane; that relationships inside it were of a kind that would make that type of formal control either irrelevant, or so relevant that the project would already be falling apart and in ruins anyway! Mutual trust, developed in relation to a series of political struggles inside and outside the collective over a period of years, was a key factor in the Controradio station.

The two other dimensions of the station's internal democracy which demand attention concern its relation to women and its emphasis on youth. As alway, the role of women in revolutionary media is an acid test of those media, perhaps especially in a "frontally" patriarchal society such as Italy. The history of women's involvement in Controradio paralleled in some respects their involvement in *Lotta Continua*, and in Radio Città Futura. For a period of six months in 1976, the station was reorganized into two independent sections, one being organized separately by women. This situation came to an end when the transmitter was sold to the present collective. Women continued to be involved, but in the overall project, not separately.

Until 1979, the main women's collective making programs was named Donna-Informazione (Woman-Information). (I did not make contact with former members of this collective.) In the view of Controradio, Donna-Informazione had not been seriously interested in the business of communicating, and they cited in support of their view the low number of telephone calls that ever came through during Donna-Informazione transmissions.

Other forms of women's involvement were that three members of the Controradio collective were women. With one specializing in cinema, another in rock music, and the third on the heroin problem, none seemed to be engaged in "women's issues" as such. Nonetheless, the station was entirely open to approaches from other women's groups, and had a history of various groups making programs for periods of three to five months at a time (a very standard period for these occasional projects). Most recently, for example, there had been a women's health advice center which had started up nearby, and had regular weekly slots on Controradio to make its existence known. Another group, focusing on women and film, was also engaged in putting out regular programs.

Thus, as regards women's involvement in the station, Controradio had ceased trying to perform the probably impossible task of operating with both separatist-feminist and revolutionary socialist perspectives. It operated with considerable openness to other feminist perspectives, but the net result of this experience was the presence in the station's output of a variety of more or less compatible socialist and feminist positions, rather than any worked out feminist-socialist position.

As regards the question of youth, Controradio was like the other Italian cases with the exception of *Il Manifesto*: the age-range of those involved was from about nineteen to thirty-two. Only one older person, a fifty year old bank clerk, was regularly involved in the station. His task was to prepare the weekly Friday evening hour of economic news and analysis. Many older listeners were in the habit of calling up the station, but the collective had made no other attempt to involve older people in its operation.

It is important to recognize, however, that hardly anything exists for young people to do in Florence. Consequently, Controradio's youthful bias, and its expansion into cultural activities of direct interest to young people (such as helping to promote the Bob Marley concert), filled a major gap in Florence life. Its focus on youth did represent in certain ways, though, that self-same *distance* from the older sections of the population that plagued the political movements of 1977-78 in Italy.

The last matter to be dealt with here is the question of finance. As members of the collective constantly pointed out, it is always a problem to raise the five million lire a month necessary to run the station. They had come to reject making public appeals through the microphone or in other ways, because they felt it gave a public image of the station as perpetually tottering to its collapse. However nearly true that might have been at certain points, it was unlikely to inspire involvement in supporting the station among the public at large; indeed it could prompt people to think they would just be throwing good money in after bad.

Thus the station came to rely on advertising and financial support from friends and friendly backers. A third source of income was the standard mixture of part-time or occasional work, with family support, which characterized the lives of so mny younger Italians during the seventies and into the eighties.

At one stage advertising had been rejected on political grounds, but eventually had been adopted as a source of revenue, though with keen misgivings as to its possible tarnishing of Controradio's revolutionary credentials. In practice these misgivings had not been realized, in part perhaps because there had been an absolute policy from the outset of refusing sexist material. Most advertisers, too, defined Controradio as pre-eminently a young person's station, and so the advertisements were in areas of direct interest to most of its listeners: musical instruments, books, clothes, cafes, crafts and travel.

Controradio also tried to develop relations with advertising agencies. One such was a complete disaster, having promised the collective forty million lire a year in revenue, and having produced just six million. One member of the collective was working almost full-time on trying to get more advertising for the station, and he had manged to gather in about another two million lire a month. The collective was actively trying to get more revenue through a Milan agency, Mediottanta, and was also canvassing a new, rather pushy Rome-based agency, SPER, in the hope of more still. The tragedy of the collapse of FRED (Federation of Democratic Radio Stations) in 1978, over precisely this issue of whether or not to create a central advertising agency to handle advertising for socialist radio stations, was never more apparent than in observing this chain of financial worries in Controradio. (The role of SIPRA in relation to *Lotta Continua* and *Il Manifesto* underlines the same point still further.)

Friends' financial help was important, and would be especially so in the move to new premises. The other source—the family and occasional employment—was, as noted, just as critical for Controradio as for all the other far left media in Italy at the time. The only paid person in the station was the one who was trying to organize advertising, because people recognized this as a particularly uninspiring, yet very demanding activity. Nine other full-timers had to get money from somewhere; and so although some worked part-time, it is clear that the station's finances were founded on the basic assumption of family support. Whether these parents involved approved fully of their adult sons' and daughters' involvement is not clear, but parental support is a material reality which must be recognized if the nature of these stations is to be fully grasped.

Footnotes

1. See John Downing, *The Media Machine,* London: Pluto Press 1980, pp. 208-217.
2. This post is required by Italian law in all media. It denotes the person responsible in the sense of "liable" for any infringements of the law. In court, this person would be the one to answer for the collective, and the one to be fined (or even imprisoned) if judgment were found against it.

20

RADIO POPOLARE, MILAN

Introduction

Of all the radio-stations of the Italian independent left in 1980, Radio Popolare (People's Radio) had the best image. Activists in other socialist radio stations, even while sometimes disagreeing with its policy, nonetheless saw it as the most efficiently organized and successful project in their own ranks. Journalists from conventional papers or weeklies regularly mentioned Radio Popolare when writing about what was going on in Milan. (Though this habit, one of Radio Popolare's members commented, said as much about the journalists' own distance from the general life of Milan, as about Radio Popolare.)

Milan, sometimes called the capital of the North in Italy, is a city with the wide range of economic activities that characterize the average metropolis. It is neither a cultural center such as Venice and Florence, nor a city dominated by a single industry such as Turin. Factory and office labor, professionals and businesses, the university, fashionable and spacious neighborhoods, greyer and tougher quarters, air pollution during the winter months leading to heavy fogs, all combine to make Milan a city very similar in its ambience to a large number of northern European cities. Its political culture is definitely to the left of many of those cities however, with a city council run by a "red committee" (giunta rossa) of PSI and PCI members in the main plus one or two councillors further to their left. The PCI dominated but the mayor was from the PSI.

Radio Popolare was situated not far from Piazza le Loreta where in 1945 the body of Mussolini was displayed by the Italian resistance to Milan and the world. It was in a side-street in a row house, which it occupied entirely. Inside furnishings were functional at best. Soundproofing in the studios was home-made, consisting of cheap curtain material draped around the walls and ceilings. The premises were distinctly crowded, with members of the collective having to edge past each other in the tiny studios as one program drew to a close and the next program's producers came to take up their places by the microphones.

Basic Self-Definition

The unique feature of Radio Popolare from the very outset was its members' determination to develop a new type of mass information and communication, sharply distinguished from existing models, while recognizing that for Italy as a whole there were several valid ways of operating a radio station. Their objective was to enable all the ordinary members of the socialist public to communicate with one another—not the leaders of political organizations, let alone the leaders of a single political group, nor simply the section of the public actually involved in a particular political movement. As their elected director, Biagio Longo, had put it in an article in the journal *aut aut* in 1978:

> (for us, what is crucial is) the recognition that the class, the proletarian masses, are never the same thing as the organizations and even the movements in which they express themselves from time to time. We refuse to reduce the multiplicity, the richness, the diversity of people's perspectives...(not) flattening them into a monolanguage, and without dispersing them into ghettoized or colonized spaces.[1]

(The problem of the different mini-jargons of particular revolutionary groups in Italy was an issue we have already had cause to mention.)

Federico Pedrocchi, the radio collective's chairperson, emphasized the point by contrasting their policy with that of Rome's Radio Città Futura (Radio City of the Future) at the height of the 1977 movement. At that point, he stated, Città Futura set out to be the voice of the movement. Leading figures in the radio station would organize assemblies of the movement on the air, in which people were allowed to speak exactly as they felt, but would begin these sessions by discoursing for forty-five minutes to an hour non-stop to establish the boundaries of the ensuing debate. Conversely, an ordinary PCI member who phoned in would be allowed to speak on the air, but would be told by the *compagno* at the microphone: "We know the reason you're saying this, it's because you're in the PCI!" The objective of Radio Popolare, he argued, was to bring together the PCI worker and the young movement activist, not to help maintain their distance from each other. Conversely, he queried, what type of politics encourages anyone to think they have the right to talk for 45 minutes to an hour non-stop?

Whether this was an altogether fair characterization of Radio Città Futura at that time is not at issue.[2] The two comments show clearly the distinctive character of Radio Popolare as a project: its attempt to encourage and develop a lateral communication outside the existing channels of communication which regularly separate people into social categories of sex, age, party membership, political activism, educational background and the rest. To develop people's capacity to communicate on a mass level, across these barriers, neither accepting the barriers as inevitable nor denying their existence, is indeed a fundamental condition for the growth of a mass-based socialist movement.

The usual criticisms levelled by the revolutionary left against Radio Popolare were twofold. The first was that it had no coherent political edge, no antagonistic potential against the power structure, including the PSI/PCI city government, because of its desire to get the maximum number of people to listen to it. To win their consent and commitment as participants in the communication exercise required an approach which did not alienate PSI and PCI members. The second objection was that RP was gradually becoming a little institution, developing its own professional journalists in the bourgeois mold, who could then claim the right to interpret reality for the rest of us: "to choose what slice of reality to put first, to decide which protagonists to consider," as Longo put it in summarizing this accusation.[3]

Over and above RP's existing critique of socialist mass information practice, the reactions in Radio Popolare to these charges were that they were preconceived and schematic. As to RP's supposed lack of political bite, they pointed to its involvement in numerous Milan struggles, around abortion, compulsory military service, and in factories. The clarity their critics professed to enjoy on which the key struggles were and who was leading them, or on what was the next phase of the revolutionary movement, was bogus. Who could claim unerring insight into these matters? Yet, if RP were to become simply the voice of one or more group in struggle, it would effectively be claiming this bogus clarity for itself.

As to the charge of becoming "professionals," this raises a number of issues already mentioned in other case studies in this book, which have been widely discussed and written about inside the Italian revolutionary movement. For Radio Popolare, the accusation of careerist professionalism could sound plausible, for it had a paid full-time staff at its core, quite unlike most such stations on the far left, and quite unlike the floating job experience of large numbers of younger people in Italy in the late seventies. The RP *compagni* insisted, however, that the charge of "professionalism" blurred certain distinct and vital issues. While rejecting the journalistic profession as organized in bourgeois media, they nonetheless asserted that a certain kind of professionalism is indispensable for revolutionary information projects to work. Their argument was as follows.

Firstly, it is a hollow pretense to claim that radio workers should or can be exactly the same people as those involved in struggles in the community or at work—in the terms used in Italy at the time, that the "subjects of information" and the "subjects of struggle" must become the same individuals. The only way to approach the real distinction betweeen people who operate a radio station and those active in particular campaigns, they argued, is to be honest about it: "to make this contradiction clear as a means of controlling it," as Longo put it in his article (p. 20). To claim this distinction does or should magically vanish in movement radio leads to a denial of certain practical realities, and often by a subtle process, to precisely the opposite effects of those desired.

Secondly, constant instant access to the airwaves for those involved in particular struggles means the station becomes identified as only concerned with those particular issues or sections of the public. The station ceases to be a forum for the widest possible spectrum, and so transforms itself into an internal affair, communicating only to the select. Furthermore, not to recognize that unpaid people at the core of a radio station are always those with the time, energy and interest to be involved—and perhaps even a certain level of financial support from their families, thus introducing a class division into their self-recruitment into the station—leads inexorably to the position that radio activists automatically represent the bulk of the people who listen to the station, or who might do so. Yet again and again in its early days, RP found it was recruiting its activists from the same pool: young people and students. In no way did immediacy guarantee representativeness.

Thirdly, the practical results of pure immediacy, spontaneity and lack of professionalism were a habit of muddling through the day's programming, confusion and ignorance about how to program, and an ever tighter circle of people involved, despite an avowed commitment to open access. A good example of what the refusal to be dominated by immediacy meant in practice was the 1981 decision to open up a weekly slot to program in Arabic for Milan's thirty thousand strong Arab community.[4] This was a policy of conscious outreach. Thus, the RP *compagni* came to the conclusion: "Why should this structure be informal, precarious, disjointed, and not at a decent technical and organizational level instead, in order to respond to the needs of our own listeners?" The parallel with Controradio's experience is striking.

At the same time, their decision to "professionalize" their activity did not mean taking on the bag and baggage of conventional journalism. A crucial case in point is their development of networks of correspondents in factories, neighborhoods, and schools, so as not to be dependent entirely on bourgeois news-agencies. These networks, and the assemblies RP organized area by area, were a long way from perfect, but did indicate RP's position in the essential divide between conventional and revolutionary mass communication: the possibility of the base's control over information. Bourgeois media survey their "consumers" for their own purposes, and print some of their letters or allow some of them to speak on phone-ins. They do not try to develop any alternative information network of this kind, and only allow legitimacy to certain of their consumers' critiques. A further dimension of RP's reformulated professionalism was their recognition of the dialectic between media and movement. On the one hand, Radio Popolare was used by movements of struggle as an instrument of information and organization. On the other hand, the information actually produced through the mediation of the RP *compagni* had its own further impact on the movement. Movements did more than simply express themselves when they spoke through Radio Popolare: the process often stimulated fresh processes of reflection, debate and action within the movements themselves.

The specifics of Radio Popolare's self-definition were, then, a commitment to developing lateral communication inside the general public (always recalling that the public, in the case of Milan, largely takes a number of socialist positions for granted); and to organizing this communication as "professionally" as possible. Let us turn to the history and organization of the station to understand how these objectives materialized.

History and organization

Radio Popolare was started in 1976 by a group of five people then working in one of Milan's first socialist stations, Radio Milano Centrale. Characteristically for RP, they worked carefully on preparing the project for practically a year before setting it in motion. The five had grown increasingly restive at the continual encroachment of PCI domination over Milano Centrale. They were committed from the start to enabling all the people of the left to communicate with each other—hence the station's name, Radio Popolare.

Their preparation had involved discussions with both the PCI and the PSI as the two major parties in Milan's city council. Only the PSI's left-wing seemed interested, however, and even that faded after a time. However, in the formal structure of the station, each of the parties had representatives on the Council of Administration. This early determination to have a satisfactory relationship with the immediate realities of official politics in Milan undoubtedly contributed to the station's positive image in the eyes of many people in the city. "Their" parties were not attacking it as a juvenile ultra-leftist project, and indeed were officially part of its political sponsorship. Very fortunately, too, for RP, the parties never made any attempt at its "competitive colonization" after the pattern of RAI.

Also noticeable was the degree of stability of personnel in the station. Although the five original organizers had all left by 1980, nine out of the eleven full-timers in summer 1980 had been involved from the moment the station had actually gone on the air. Possibly the regular payment of salaries had something to do with this: in summer 1980 every full-timer, including the technician, received 350,000 lire a month. Hardly a princely sum—especially if its quite frequent non-arrival two months out of twelve is taken into account—but all the same quite uncharacteristic of the other independent left stations. Also, the collective's method of handling wages during these recurrent financial difficulties was to pay those most in need first, the degree of need being established as best as could be by collective discussion. Solidarity in the collective (which predictably enough had to co-exist with particular personal dislikes) was arguably strengthened by this method of facing financial problems, just as it was by the single pay-level during less troubled times.

The resolve to organize a fixed, paid core of radio workers did produce a fresh set of problems. As Longo remarked in his article, they suddenly found the question of finance had come to absorb much of their energy. Until they had developed a certain administrative know-how, including accounting, raising advertising revenue, and similar practicalities, this continued to be the case, and even then the problem never disappeared. For example, in 1980 the station needed 120 million lire a year. Of this, about 50 million were raised by advertising, 22 million in individual subscriptions, 10-12 million from organizational contributions, 15 million from fund-raising events, and 8 million from an annual lottery run by the station. These approximate figures show clearly enough the constant battle to keep financially afloat: 15 million lire remained to be found.

Radio Popolare had faced two major political, rather than financial, crises up to 1980 (though the second had arisen directly from the financial issue). The first crisis was directly over broadcasting policy, led to the resignation of the first editor, and arose at the end of 1977. To simplify the issues, it boiled down to a clash over whether the station should concentrate more on youth, or more on the solid core of the working class. Representatives of *Lotta Continua* and of Democrazia Proletaria[5] were active in arguing for the second position. The then-editor adopted a policy of staying neutral but ended by being accused by some people on either side of not wanting to resolve the dispute. He found this an impossible situation, and resigned. Since then, tempers have cooled, and there was hope among the *compagni* in 1980 that he might become involved in their projected expansion into television.

But while the argument raged, it ws a time of extreme bitterness and rancor.

Nonetheless, the clash resolved itself in two ways. Firstly, the strength of the student and feminist movements in 1977-78 in Bologna and Rome, finally hammered home to everyone the political significance of sectors outside the traditional factory working class. At the same time, the collective gradually formed their own view, that it was absurd for a radio collective to keep such a discussion confined within their own ranks. Since the relation between organized labor and these newer movements was a general problem, an area of mutual suspicion and even outright hostility, the role of Radio Popolare was to encourage maximum public discussion of the issues. By spring 1978, this resolution of the argument had finally crystallized into the station's broadcasting policy. As an approach to handling contradictions among the oppressed, it was fully in line with the radio collective's self-understanding. In turn, this was a conspicuously different approach from, say, leninist democratic centralism, where divergences are allowed to be unleashed until a majority decision is taken, after which a single "line" prevails (at least till the next vote). That model makes sense for a clandestine party operating in what amount to civil war conditions; for a revolutionary radio station working inside a liberal democracy, it does not. (Compare the experience of Third World Newsreel.) To break out of the leninist model seems to be commonsense in these conditions; one suspects Lenin would have found it obvious, unlike latter-day leninists.

The second crisis was with the main political parties in 1979. The conflict arose within the Council of Administration, which met two or three times a month with three or four members of the radio collective in attendance. (As noted already, this Council is important in assuring the general legitimacy of Radio Popolare.) Formally subordinate to it, the collective nonetheless found infuriating the Council's habit of perpetually talking about the station's financial problems without ever organizing anything concrete to deal with them. Organizationally, fund-raising was not supposed to be the collective's responsibility, and it found this position increasingly perilous for the station's survival. The argument raged for three months, with the collective saying to the Council: "If you are too busy, we will raise funds; but if you are anxious that we will use this to pry ourselves loose from your oversight, then you had better start fund-raising quickly yourselves." The Council, in turn, defined the clash very much in terms of the collective demanding independence from its tutelage, but still could not develop its own fund-raising activities. This forced it to concede the collective's right to get on and raise funds.

The crisis in relations did not worsen, and indeed weathered this shift in power quite easily. But the issue at stake for the collective was their commitment to maintaining public legitimacy for their project, which meant they could not afford to alienate the Council too far.

These, then, were the two major points of conflict in the station's history. The *compagni* who lived through these storms undoubtedly strengthened their social identity as the Radio Popolare collective in the process. As Pedrocchi put it, while he as chair of the collective or Longo as radio editor could be democratically recalled at any time, the likelihood of this happening was nil. It would be the sign that the project was in collapse, that relations had disintegrated inside it beyond salvage. (The parallel with Controradio is clear.) Naturally enough, personal likes and dislikes continued, sharpened a little around the time I was there by the fact that the premises were too small, and everyone was on top of everyone else. But the *compagni* were able to appreciate the pressures this involved, and the prospect of a move around the corner to larger premises was doing much to make these problems bearable.

To understand this cohesiveness, it also needs to be realized that RP collective meetings were regular and frequent. Once a week there was a meeting of the full-time core to discuss ongoing problems. Part-timers, paid and unpaid, were not invited to this meeting, as their absence enabled the regular staff to discuss and assess the contributions of inexperienced new contributors more freely, with less abrasive impact (and less tendency to half-state the truth) than if they were present. Also once a week there was a meeting of everyone involved in the radio to discuss the week's programing, essentially of news. Usually a particular theme would be chosen for discussion, from the Iranian revolution to the problems created by uncontrolled dogs on Milan's streets, from the significance of local and regional election results (the evening I was present) to the issues of personal politics. Attendance was expected, and forthcoming, with the meetings lasting from 9:00 p.m. often until midnight.

The collective had also evolved, through experience, a mechanism to assist in the smooth functioning of working relationships. The collective's chairperson, after the resignation of the station's second editor, was no longer editor as well. The chair's job was to talk to people, sometimes to interpret them to each other, to get them if necessary to speak to each other, in order to avoid personal frictions becoming unmanageable and threatening the station's work. It had been found that to combine this job with that of editor was practically impossible, and so the collective had elected as chair the *compagno* generally recognized as having the most adequate personal skills to fulfill this task.

The final point which must be made about the collective's cohesiveness is that most of the working day was spent in doing extremely general tasks, which were shared out quite evenly. The specific and more exciting activity of broadcasting through a microphone took up quite a small proportion of the day's activity. Hence, the collective had avoided a potentially dangerous division of labor between broadcasters and also-rans. In this context, it is important to note that the full-time technician and his three part-time assistants had also joined Radio Popolare out of commitment to its political objectives, not just as a way to earn a living or to pass the time.

In general, it would be accurate to say that the collective's evolution had led to a fresh style in socialist organization. Pedrocchi recalled how in the early days, in 1977 for instance, the collective's meetings were rather like the central committee of a revolutionary political party, with people always presenting prepared positions on whatever was being discussed. Three years later people had gradually learned to be more open and flexible in their discussions with each other. This may have been helped by the fact that in 1980, only two of the collective's members had a working relationship with existing political parties (the PCI youth section, and PdUP), and that there had been no attempt at competitive colonization of the station by the left parties. Nonetheless, Pedrocchi expressed the view that it would now be very hard for the collective's members to involve themselves in the culture of normal left parties.

The process had not always been an easy one: the political tension can be imagined, for instance, at the expression of arguments for and against the "historic compromise" policy of the PCI. Yet they had achieved it through patiently working it through—in a sense, their strong conviction of the constructive potential of patient, open discussion within the left (as distinct from within its formal committees and by its official leaders), was the *leitmotif* of Radio Popolare's self-definition and experience. What they had themselves achieved inside the collective, they argued, could be achieved outside it and was the task of the radio station to promote. If their work is to be assigned its full value, it must be assessed within the context of political parties' deep penetration into Italian social life and postwar history, as within the context of the chasm between the pre- and post- "sixty-eightists."

However, let us examine more closely what their evolution meant in four practical areas: the role of women within the station, the kind of language used in broadcasting, the place of imaginative material in the station's output and the relation between the station's permanent core and people who turned up with material to broadcast, or people whose material the collective wanted to broadcast. These are direct elements of media democracy in the real world. Formal structures and intentions are important, but inevitably the acid test is how they operate in practice.

Women's roles within the station

This issue seemed to have been much less a problem inside RP than it might have been, particularly in view of the experiences of Radio Città Futura, *Lotta Continua* and Controradio. This was not necessarily a good feature of the station, for perhaps certain issues posed by the feminist movement might have been bypassed rather than addressed. But certainly by 1980, although there were women involved full-time and part-time in Radio Popolare, they did not constitute a "coherent group" as one of them put it. In that sense, they did not operate as a power bloc inside the radio station, but participated as individuals. There had been many more women involved during 1977-78, with numerous programs on women and work, women and culture, women and health, and other themes, most of which had been organized by a separate women's collective within the station. More recently, the numbers of women involved had shrunk for a range of reasons. These include practical personal problems or switching to better paid media work or just plain exhaustion. Also separatism had disappeared as a major feature of the Italian women's movement by the early 80s. The pattern of women's regular involvement inside the station by 1980 was that two women worked full-time, two part-time, with a larger number of voluntary women workers. There was however a tendency for them to be involved more in administration and advertising than in political communication.[6]

One of those involved part-time said that the men inside RP had time by 1980 to adjust themselves to feminist perspectives, and that the real difference in political perspective among the *compagni* was between those more committed to personal politics, and those more committed to external politics, rather than between men and women as such. In the collective's discussions on personal politics, there was often much more tension in the air than on the "external" realm.

As regards the other forms of women's participation, the mid-morning "open microphone" program each day attracted mny telephone contributions from women, mostly young, usually housewives or teachers. Women factory workers involved themselves much more rarely. The other point at which the classic issues of feminist politics tended to surface was during the night-time music and phone-ins, when the station was at its most spontaneous.

Feminist politics was not then a burning issue inside the collective in 1980. There were no policy discussions on women, whereas there were frequent policy discussions on youth. By 1981, however, with two national referenda being organized on the question of abortion, one being by Catholic activists against abortion rights, the other representing a moderately pro-abortion position by the Radical Party, the matter was opened up in a major way. Radio Popolare declared itself against both positions, though naturally more so against the Catholic "Movement for Life." It constituted a prominent topic in phone-ins, and in programming.

The use of language

We have already seen how the newspaper *Lotta Continua* in particular succeeded in breaking out of the traditional stereotyped jargon of the left in Italy, but how nonetheless many currents on the Italian left insisted on defining themselves by their own internal jargon. What was RP's position?

Fortunately, there has been independent comment on Radio Popolare's language by one Italian writer. Fofi, also writing in the journal *aut aut*[7], contrasted RP's language with that of Radio Alice, the famous station at the heart of the Bologna movement (to which I made reference earlier).

His basic point was that the Radio Alice collective could easily identify the "subject of struggle" with the "subject of information," exactly because in their case the contributors and the listeners came from precisely the same narrow social band. As he put it, the strength of Alice's language was that it could be "richer and fresher, because it is the language of a particular cultural and social stratum, which is created and invented every day."[8] He proceeded however, to identify the problem in this approach:

> Politically, the risk is of inventing a ghetto communication and culture, which is not concerned to speak with 'the others,' but only with its peers. But which does have the advantage of freedom of methods and of open-minded elaboration.[9]

His comments on Radio Popolare are lengthy, but very informative. They are cited almost in full:

> [Radio Popolare's] network of "informers," contacts, listening points, while not perfect, has guaranteed an interchange between informers and informed, between transmitters and receivers, which has no equivalent in any communication initiative in post war Italy...It is clear that Radio Popolare's language is less innovative, given its problems of mediating, that it does not require liberated invention and creativity, but the discovery of a median language, because the ordinary person and the worker do not, or do not yet, speak the same language as the kids in the clubs, or the student, or the feminist. But this "median"-ness is certainly very different from the many transmissions which the State radio has put out in imitation of the free radio stations, often using new left *compagni* as guides. What is taking place is the fruit of a process of cultural exchange, following on the class redefinitions which we are part of; an exchange constructed inside the class, where the stably employed and the unstably employed have the possibility of speaking and listening to each other in turn."[10]

There is no way of proving that RP had consistently achieved these targets, but the fact that this could be written by an observer in early 1978, and that the RP *compagni* still considered language as a fundamental concern in their development of radio, suggests that some major steps forward had been taken. Emerging from the inner jargon of left wing ghettoes is a basic condition of socialists' communication with the wider public. Or more accurately, *helping us to express ourselves across our internal divisions*—themselves often revitalized each day by bourgeois media—is a basic condition for the growth of a revolutionary movement. This is a *leitmotif* of this book.

The imaginative dimensions

A revolutionary movement, however, cannot construct itself simply on the basis of common, rationally expressed political analyses and programs. The left wing ghetto typically denies, explicitly or in implicit practice, any significance to imaginative or symbolic communication. Hard politics, tough-minded economics, unmasking bourgeois ideology: this is the steel-and-concrete world proposed as satisfying living, with sex and alcohol as permissible short holidays. A signal contribution of the women's movement has been to deride and condemn, usually from outside left wing groups, this cramped, alienating vision of a socialist altenative. Within the left, too often, the only opposing perspective has been of a marxist cultural intelligentsia, exquisitely and—let it be said—sometimes brilliantly, dissecting the nuances of literature, art and film, but still incapable of communicating in imaginative or any other terms to people outside the intelligentsia.

Whereas Radio Alice was probably never dull, this was only within its own terms. Radio Popolare made the attempt to comunicate outside the left wing ghetto in imaginative terms as well, and was in the process of expanding this further during the writer's visit. As one *compagno* put it, using a common Italian expression: "You always have to flip the omelette." (In other words, if you carry on too long on one track, you'll get stuck.)

One area in which RP had developed this dimension for quite some time was in its broadcasts after 11:00 p.m., when, as Pedrocchi put it, "we used to discuss many things: the family, sex, death, what the future holds." One device they used for some time late at night was to watch tv with the listeners, and to ask them what they thought of what they were watching. Or to watch a tv film with the sound off, and substitute RP's own spontaneous commentary. Pedrocchi explained how they had even done this with a Channel Five film (the main pornographic tv station in Milan).

A different format they had developed was to ask a woman and a man to phone in and then to ask them to role-play: "You've been living together for ten years, but things are going badly between you now. What would you say to each other if you were talking about this together?" Often there would be as many as five or six different "takes" of this conversation between different people.

Pedrocchi gave a further example of a major new departure RP had recently undertaken in its broadcasting practice. In February 1980, a man in his late twenties had gone armed into an office in central Milan at 5:00 p.m., and had held up the staff of ten. The siege lasted two or three days, and ended with him shooting dead one woman, then himself. He was insane, but had begun by announcing himself as a member of the Red Brigades, and then of the "Communist Proletarians." Outside, the streets were like an Olympic stadium, with journalists everywhere, and people spending long periods of time simply waiting. When the bodies were finally brought out, the crowd surged forward to see them, including two old women who had been there almost continuously for two days.

Radio Popolare assigned four of its people to this event, on a rotation. They had many phone calls from men and women on the left, ringing in to say "Why are you covering this grim little affair when there is Iran and all these other major questions to talk about?" Pedrocchi recalled how they had tried to expose the assumptions in these callers' objections. They would ask them, "All right, what have you got say that's new about Iran?" (The callers would tend in response to drift into discussing Korea or Vietnam instead.)

For RP itself, it was an occasion to question certain underlying issues. One was many people's fascination with death and violence, as evidenced in the street outside the hold-up. Another was the question of terrorism. "What do you think of his claim to be in the Red Brigades?" they asked people. Some said, "He's just crazy." Then some would say, "But then again so are the Red Brigades, if it comes to that." "Why do you think, in his insanity, he chooses to proclaim himself as a member of the Red Brigades?" was a further question RP put to its callers. RP also used the occasion to try to encourage people to talk about what they thought insanity actually is.

The event and RP's relation to it, generated other conflicts, such as when one member of PdUP rang in to attack the significance Radio Popolare was assigning to the event, only to be instantly contradicted by another member of PdUP on the telephone!

These are just some examples of the exploratory work undertaken in imaginative communication by RP. Any discussion of socialist democracy in communication which omits this dimension, omits the fact that the democratic subjects themselves are flesh-and-blood, not concrete-and-steel; that they have feelings, fantasies and fears, humor and pain; and that a major reason for the success of bourgeois media, as Dieter Prokop has pointed out [11], is their ability to play upon and exploit precisely these aspects of people's everyday existence. The "imaginative dimension," as it is titled here, is that area in which socialist communication has to move, yet in a non-exploitative and anti-elitist fashion. Radio Popolare was acting as a more constructive pioneer in this regard, for these reasons, than Radio Alice.

How RP teaches compagni to use radio

At its outset the RP collective was trained to use the radio by its director, a man with twenty years' experience in working for RAI. They had political experience as young movement activists, but nothing more. He taught them how to make programs. The director would review the day's events, analyse them, assign them priorities, and explain how they could be presented on radio. The account of this event should be followed by a commentary; on that event, by an interview, usually with the public, rather than with "names"; another event, he would point out, was insufficiently clear to be covered right away and required further research.

Then after the program had been transmitted, there would be an assessment meeting, when the director would point out its inadequacies: this news item was too long, and was read too fast; that interview could have been conducted more bluntly, what was in it was hardly worth the bother of recording it; using honorific titles when referring to public figures was out of place in "People's Radio." Thus, the procedures for gathering and selecting information, giving it the station's particular "stamp," and communicating it as clearly as possible to listeners, were learned on the spot, as were techniques for using the mixer, how to speak through the microphone, the tone of voice to be adopted in telephone interviews, methods of putting together a montage, and all the rest. These latter elements took longer to learn than some of the others. As Longo put it to me, "When you're learning to swim by being thrown in the deep end, you have to brace yourself for people commenting as they watch you drowning, that your strokes are rather inelegant!"

The core group learned a great deal in those early days about how to join political insight and experience with a good level of technical and professional quality. They, in turn, instructed newcomers, although their knowledge of other areas, such as programming music or radio drama, was much sketchier, and they left these to part-time collaborators. Of these, some were content just to put out their own programs, where others opted for a more active involvement with the collective. The daily Youth Program acted as a major source of new talent, with five out of eight new members of the collective in one year coming up through it. At moments of staff turnover, this replenishment was very opportune, except that it posed a constant problem of sustaining the original vision of the station. There was a tendency for the station to become more and more youth-oriented, which seriously restricted its functioning.

The Scylla to this Charybdis was ensuring that existing collective members were paid, before taking on new financial burdens in the shape of extra members. This had the effect of closing off the station to fresh ideas, except—once again—those emanating from the youth-student sector which had the time, energy and financial support to work voluntarily, or nearly so. Neither qualified journalists nor factory workers were likely to be much in evidence.

The other major difficulty experienced by RP was that a number of people used it strategically as a training school for the 18 months' experience legally required for entry into journalism, and then left for more stable and better paid work elsewhere, leaving a vacuum of experience where they had been. We have seen the same pattern to some degree in both *Il Manifesto* and *Lotta Continua*, and it was also evident in Radio Città Futura.

To try to tackle these problems, RP began an open three-month course in radio, for 20 people at a time, selected from the list of applicants by the collective. They succeeded in getting involvement by local bodies, the journalists' association, and the mayor. Students were allowed to take part in programs on an experimental basis, and were introduced to all major technical and programming matters. The classes also examined issues such as the structure of Italian media, the overdue publishing reform, the conventional canons of journalism, the problems of censorship and self-censorship, and "the miseries and splendors of free radio" (Longo). Journalists, media critics and representatives of the journalists' union took part in teaching. At the conclusion, some students became voluntary collaborators in the station. The training helped to ensure both a continued flow of fresh program ideas into RP, and from people drawn from a wider spectrum than before.

Conclusions

Radio Popolare offers an extremely instructive experience in organizing independent lateral communication *inside* our own ranks as the general public. Naturally, its Milanese location enables it to function in ways quite different from those obtaining in a small town in southern Italy, let alone inside the U.S., with its weak socialist traditions. However, the careful collective thinking and planning that went on inside the collective offers many suggestions for how certain headings—the relation between the station and its listeners, the mechanisms of internal democracy, the role of the imaginative and of language, to name only a few—indicate standard issues to be tackled by any autonomous mass medium. In that sense, it is a particularly important case to examine.

Footnotes

1. B. Longo, "I limiti della communicazione 'interna'," (The limits of 'internal' communication) *aut aut* (Milan) 163 (January-February 1978), pp. 18-26. This quotation comes from pp. 24-25.
2. See my *The Media Machine*, London: Pluto Press 1980, ch. 9.
3. Longo, p. 19.
4. This information comes from Kathy Lowe, *Opening Eyes and Ears,* Geneva: World Council of Churches 1983, who also studied the station in 1982. I am very grateful to her for making her text available to me before publication.
5. Democrazia Proletaria (Proletarian Democracy) was a merger group for electoral purposes in the 1976 general election, between PdUP, Lotta Continua, Avanguardia Operaia (Workers' Vanguard) and Movimento dei Lavoratori per il Socialismo (Workers' Movement for Socialism), the last two being *approximately* trotskyist and maoist in perspective. The merger lasted beyond the election up to the time of writing.
6. See Kathy Lowe, *op. cit.*
7. G. Fofi, "Lottare su due fronti" (Struggling on two fronts"), *aut aut* 163, pp. 46-52.
8. Fofi, p. 48.
9. *Ibid.*
10. *Ibid.*, pp. 48-49.
11. D. Prokop, *Massenkultur und Spontaneität* (Mass Culture and Spontaneity), Frankfurt: Suhrkamp Verlag 1979.

21
CONCLUSIONS

Democratic media in Portugal and Italy have played a much larger part in national life than their counterparts in the U.S. Especially in Portugal, they were at the earthquake's epicenter. The political cultures of the two European countries are very different from the U.S., except in areas where radical media have flourished in the latter, namely at its stress points—labor, state repression, racial minorities, women, the Third World, ecology, the nuclear crisis. But where these struggles seem often to be at the periphery of mainstream national life in the U.S., in Portugal and Italy they have equally often been at the core. The dialectic between their political movements and their alternative media has been a richly informative one for the present study.

Whereas Portugal represents the high water mark of these media's impact on national politics in western Europe, and served to direct the attention of large sectors on the European left to the question of media in revolutionary processes, Italy offers a whole debate on the character and future of such media. There have been books, journal articles, newspaper features, all focussing on their problems and prospects. Some have been referred to already in the course of analyzing the case-studies[1] (need to avoid jargon, repetitive cliches, evasive phrasing of awkward problems within movements); professionalism in a non-career context; and the relation between these media and large-scale media (including the widely circulating Communist Party media). They explore the links between developing a small-scale counter-information activity and the later growth of regularly produced media, as well as how such media handle the ebbing away of mass political upsurges.

All these questions have been addressed in the previous pages, but it must be recalled that only four cases have been thoroughly analyzed. Even though they are amongst the leading instances, they occupy a certain stretch of ground in the spectrum of Italian left politics and media. They belong neither to the weary phrase-mongering of traditional sectarian journalism, nor to the dizzy intellectual soaring of Radio Alice, nor to the ideology of continuous street confrontation, nor yet to the struggling media voices of the South. Given that Italian political culture is generally well to the left of U.S. political culture (not a difficult achievement), it could be said that despite their differences one from another the four examples I have discussed belong to the center of the non-Communist left. As such, they offer the strongest experiences of avoiding the duopoly of Western and Eastern models of media communication, and of doing so as a positive, continuing exercise, not as a purely negative exercise in avoidance. The Portuguese examples were infused with a rather similar spirit.

In the section that follows, I shall examine what has been achieved by two countries in eastern Europe by way of challenging the media straitjacket of the soviet model. For the twenty-first century, these varying strategies and experiences in media communication are of signal importance.

Footnotes

1. See the texts cited in the footnotes to the introduction to Italy (n. 6, 7, 11, 25); to *Lotta Continua* (n. 4); in general the issue of *aut aut* 163 (Jan-Feb 1968) devoted to mass information and class communication; and the excellent articles in *Ombre Rosse* issues 20 (March 1977), 29 (June 1979) and 30 (September 1979).

SECTION III
EASTERN EUROPE

CZECHOSLOVAKIA
AND POLAND

22

INTRODUCTION

Question to the Polish reader: "Do you believe anyone
in the West can understand what it is to write a book in
secret?"
Miklós Haraszti[1]

This section of the study is necessarily shorter than the
others. This is for reasons of my linguistic competence and
completeness of access to the people involved.[2] Politically
speaking it is a vital component of the book. It reaffirms the
refusal of the duopoly of East and West stated in the Introduction, but goes further. It makes overwhelmingly obvious the
growing forces demanding alternative communication channels and structures throughout the industrially developed
world—and the emergence of a politically committed Third
World cinema makes the same point for the majority of
humanity. What could be achieved without repression, without
censorship, outside the safe conventions of communication, is
only intimated by these examples—but how powerfully intimated! These accounts from eastern Europe, specific as is
their experience, are testimony to an almost universally thwarted yearning for lateral communication.

Some very brief remarks about eastern Europe are necessary to introduce these final studies. First, the six Soviet bloc
countries of eastern Europe are very diverse. Poland, Czechoslovakia, and Hungary, have particularly rich cultural traditions. Bulgaria and Roumania are still stamped with a
strongly agrarian culture, even though a majority in both
countries now works outside farming. Roumania has an
independent foreign policy and refuses Warsaw Pact maneuvers on its soil. The German Democratic Republic has an
economic standard of living higher than that of Britain. In
Poland the Catholic Church is still a major cultural and
political presence, but not elsewhere. Czechoslovakia is two
nations, Bohemia and Slovakia—the latter a part of Hungary

till 1919. Hungary has a substantial, and oppressed, Romany population. Large elements of the Communist Party were a leading force in the Prague spring whereas in Poland, a huge number of Party members threw away their cards in 1980-1981. Especially in Czechoslovakia, Poland and Hungary, resistance to Soviet control is not only anti-imperialist, but is based on the historical differences between Russian cultural traditions and the cultural traditions native to those lands.

Secondly, it is vital to understand how politically significant is autonomous cultural expression in these countries. In the West, few may be like Goering who instinctively reached for his gun at the mention of the word "culture," but many regard it as a kind of luxury for the irrelevant intellectual, to be counterposed to the mass culture of TV and sport. In the East, to develop any substantial cultural activity outside Party control of film, literature, art, theater, is exceptionally difficult and sometimes dangerous. Furthermore, once "politics" in any normal sense comes to be banned, it resurfaces in other areas, culture being a major outlet. The arguments and debates which people wish to conduct in one realm are forced out into the other, albeit usually in veiled forms.

The institution of censorship, which has taken different forms in different countries and at different times is designed to halt this resurfacing of political debate.[3] Censorship's universal presence in some form or other renders the power structure much more obvious than it is in the often subtler processes in liberal democracies (which by their subtlety are often forced to allow certain communications to take place). In both Czechoslovakia and Poland, the suppressed desire for communication exploded once the censor's controls were evaded or lifted, demonstrating the intensity of people's feelings concerning that repression.

It is in these circumstances that much more occasional and small circulation and clumsily produced media than have been our focus so far, are of direct political significance. Books, irregularly appearing periodicals, almost illegible newsheets, retyped lectures, "public" gatherings of 80 people squashed inside a single apartment, "public" lectures attended by 120 people: these are potent reconstructions of an oppositional public realm. They are treated as such both by those of the many potential sympathizers who are lucky enough to get to hear them, or even to hear about them, as well as by the guardians of "socialism": a word spoken only with irony or bitterness by people in whom western radicals would normally recognize themselves.

For as in the other countries examined, these small and apparently insignificant media communications have usually been at the roots of the social rebellions that have erupted, as of the larger scale media that have emerged during the later phases of those revolts. In their own interests, the power structure—whether via the FBI, the PIDE in Portugal up to 1974, the carabinieri in Italy, the political police in the East—is undoubtedly correct in trying to squelch these media as early in their lives as possible. Maybe true detente between East and West will begin with cultural exchanges between their police forces: Vice-President George Bush and premier Yuri Andopov should undoubtedly set the organizations they at one time headed to work on it.

Footnotes

1. Adapted slightly from Miklós Haraszti, "Avant-propos", in his *Opposition = 0.1%: extraits du samizdat hongrois* (Opposition= 0.1%: Extracts from Hungarian Samizdat), Paris: Seuil 1979, p. 17.

2. My sources were those involved in producing or distributing these media who had managed to escape jail by taking refuge in the West.

3. Jane Leftwich Curry, "Media control in eastern Europe: holding the tide on opposition", in J.L. Curry and J. Dassin (eds), *Press Control Around the World*, New York: Praeger 1982, ch. 5.

23

CZECHOSLOVAKIA THE PRAGUE SPRING

"It is also thanks to the press, radio and television that the Czechoslovak spring was able to mark up another major success to its credit: the re-establishment of horizontal linkages. The Stalinist pyramid does not know, does not admit, does not support, any form of horizontal organization. Every direct contact between the various parts of the pyramid is immediately considered suspect and dangerous, and thus is expressly forbidden."[1]

A.J. Liehm

Detailed material on the media in Czechoslovakia during 1968 and in the period leading up to the "Prague spring" is hard to come by, and there is, as in the other cases from eastern Europe cited in this section, no study which raises precisely the questions of the rest of this book. Nonetheless, there is sufficient information, and the issues are sufficiently important, to warrant this summary account. The story separates fairly naturally into three parts: the antecedents to the Prague spring; the concentrated events of 1968 up to the Soviet invasion of August 21; and the extraordinary week that followed (the "Seven Glorious Days").

Antecedents to the Prague spring

What happened in Czechoslovakia in 1968 is often defined as simply the culmination of long-suppressed intellectual outrage at censorship, combined with national outrage at

Soviet domination. The truth encompasses both these dimensions, but is much richer and more complex than this reduction. For example, on the question of censorship: it was from meetings of *farmers and workers* that support for having abolished censorship poured in during 1968. This was not just an intellectuals' issue, therefore, nor were the resolutions the conventional stage-managed flurry of formal Party resolutions. As regards Soviet domination, Czechoslovak attitudes to the USSR up to August 1968 were a great deal more positive than in many other eastern European countries. There had been no Soviet armies on their soil since 1948, and until the early 60s the country had been something of an economic showcase within the Soviet bloc, due to its earlier history of advanced industrial performance as contrasted with all the other territories annexed after the Second World War. Overwhelmingly, too, change was desired by people[2] at all levels in the Communist Party itself.

The Czechs and the Slovaks[3] saw themselves, in fact, as simply taking a series of pragmatic steps to redistribute power away from the apex: "The readaptation of socialism to the specific conditions of Czechoslovakia"[4]; "a renaissance of socialism."[5] Western liberal commentators gave them hesitant support, hoping to have their own myths confirmed; western leftists subjected them to suspicious scrutiny, in case they really were restoring capitalism; and the soviet bloc oligarchs regarded them with genuine panic, hearing the tocsin of their own demise.[6] Czechoslovakians found it increasingly incomprehensible and frustrating that their perfectly reasonable activities should be given such loaded interpretations, particularly when their own consensus was for organizing a self-managed socialist order.

The ground had been gradually prepared well before 1968. The ultimate "ground" of the Czechoslovak experiment, however, was undoubtedly the historical character of Czech culture itself, which from the fifteenth century revolt of Jan Hus and his followers against established religious and political authority, had represented an island of commitment to religious tolerance and to some degree even democracy, in a Europe of sectarian strife and absolutist monarchs. Setting it totally apart from the other eastern European countries is the fact that the Czechoslovak Communist Party gained over 35% of the votes in the open election of 1946, and together with the Social

Democratic Party won an absolute majority in parliament. These powerful democratic and pluralistic traditions, although repressed under the Nazis from 1938-45 and under stalinism from 1948, were very far from having been annihilated. The country's emergence from the crudest version of stalinist repression was a slow and painful one, but was pioneered in the main by people working in certain magazines, in film, and by economists and sociologists.[7] In particular, the Writers' Union played a very significant part in the struggle for a different society. It had its own publishing house, not owned directly by the state, and it also administered the Literary Fund. This latter drew its revenue from receipts on its published books and magazines, and especially from its editions of classical texts. In turn this enabled the Fund to pay writers, to give them stipends or advances, and allowed the Writers' Union an autonomy which, though inevitably limited, gave this institution considerable political weight within the country.

The Writers' Union's first signal victory was one which seems tragicomic from a distance. It was the decision of their conference in 1963 to rehabilitate Franz Kafka as a national writer of eminence. Given his enduring mark on world literature and political vision, the decision was ludicrous. But given his meticulous dissection of the procedures of unaccountable state power in *The Trial* and *The Castle*, the vote was vital.

The printed focus of the resistance was twofold, namely the Czech weekly *Literární noviny* and the Slovak weekly *Kulturny zivot*. Although subject to censorship, for the reason noted above writers for both enjoyed rather more space to express themselves than other journalists. In practical terms, *Literární noviny* came to be under virtual self-management during 1967, as a result of disputes between the Communist Party leadership and the Writers' Union about who should fill its leading posts. This left a formal vacuum of power at its head, and so eased the situation of its writers still further. Relations between the center and the magazine had been strained for a considerable period. Hamsik[8] cites one particularly striking example of how the magazine was denied permission to reprint an excerpt from the technical magazine *T67*, which had run an article on the astronomical costs incurred in mistakes made while planning the construction of Prague's new underground railroad. These extra costs had been equivalent to the costs of constructing 6000 new apartments. In any given week, up to a third of the material in *Literární noviny* would be confiscated—an index of the restive mood of its writers, continually bucking against censorship. (And naturally, without the censor's stamp, no printer would dare to run the presses.)

Matters came to a head in the fourth Writers' Union Congress of June 1967. Without any prior planning (because of the ingrained fear of political police interventions against "anti-party groups"), speaker after speaker, using independently prepared materials, rose to attack the censorship system and the state's muzzling of writers and communicators. The powers-that-be were enraged, banned *Literární noviny*, threatened to abolish the Writers' Union and seize the Literary Fund, and put an army colonel in charge of a new, safe weekly, also entitled *Literární noviny*. No one was deceived: all the familiar names had disappeared from the magazine, which was very dull. And the Slovak Writers' Congress denounced the change-over publicly.

This was the most dramatic confrontation to date between communicators and the power center. It significantly influenced the decision of the Communist Party central committee in January 1968 to vote for the termination in office of Antonín Novotný, first secretary of the Party since the mid-50s. The charged nature of the confrontation was due in no small part to the intense attention that the power center bestowed on the press, as against broadcasting or even film. There was a profound fear at that level that an overspill might take place from the weekly magazine into the daily newspapers. And indeed there were stirrings taking place inside all the mass media. A particularly significant practice had gathered momentum in the period leading up to 1968, of having journalists tour the country and engage in question-and-answer sessions to face-to-face meetings. Such lateral communication was unprecedented, and in these informal verbal encounters, the journalists were often a great deal more forthcoming about the true situation and their feelings concerning it, than they ever felt free to be on the air or on the printed page.

The appetite for change was therefore being whetted, but at that point its stimulation consisted of largely separate and mutually insulated endeavors, with no one circle usually being aware of the similar perspectives or even the existence of the others. The quotation at the head of this section explains the origins of this problem by reference to the very structure of stalinist hierarchies, which adamantly refuse people the chance of lateral communication. The result is that individuals and groups become atomized, incapable of mustering their collective forces for autonomous activity. (The critique of soviet definitions of communication in the General Introduction to this book has already raised a number of these issues.) Censorship was only one of the two critical aspects of this control, therefore, the other being the vertical flow of information. Havlicek commented:

> In conditions of strictly secret reports flowing from below to the central bureaucratic apparat, which then released selected and manipulated information in little doses, a horizontal understanding of this kind had been impossible.[9]

The period of the Spring

With Novotný's imminent removal, the efforts of individual journalists and of minority media such as *Literární noviny*—although it had grown to a circulation of 120,000 in a country of 14 million—began to be taken up by the major media.

The impact was, and continued to be, astonishing. At once, many isolated groups and individuals started to discover their commonality of feelings, frustrations and aspirations. Perhaps the media productions with the most impact in the early months were a live television broadcast of a several-hour-long youth meeting, and of a similar type of open discussion meeting in an agricultural cooperative. In March, a large meeting of 17,000 people was held in Fucik Park Congress Palace in Prague, and broadcast live by radio to the whole country. It went on for six hours, and contained many moving pleas for justice for those wrongly imprisoned and executed in the 40s and 50s; for a democratized socialism; and ended by voting overwhelmingly for Novotný's resignation from all posts in the Party and the government.

These were major media occurrences, but not isolated ones. Journalists began for the first time to be allowed behind the scenes at district and regional party conferences, and were given immediate reports of *debates* within the Presidium (even White House arguments are leaked, rather than presented). Very rapidly, broadcasting switched to searching out the general public and asking people live what they thought about the issues of the day. The readers' columns of the press expanded to handle the flood of correspondence that arrived from masses of people hitherto mute. None of the Novotný regime's idols was sacred: his own son, appointed director of Artia, the foreign languages publishing house, was publicly interviewed because of widespread disbelief in his qualifications for the post. He claimed in his defense to have completed his postgraduate economics course at the Prague School of Economics. The station was immediately afterwards telephoned by the School's rector, who set the record right on the air by pointing out that Novotný's son had dropped out of school after two years.

This instance mirrored many others. Leading regime figures were telephoned on the air and asked questions about public policy; after they had finished speaking, the lines were opened for critical comment from listeners. One semi-weekly radio program, "Songs With a Telephone," became especially well known for its work in this realm. The impact of the media on the power structure was formidable in certain cases. Lomsky, then Defense Minister, gave a particularly low-level performance on TV. Soon afterwards, he resigned, embarrassed out of office. The trade union newspaper, *Pracé*, wrote an editorial on the art of knowing when to resign. Not many days later, this was followed by the resignation of the head of the trade union federation.

Perhaps the tensest broadcasting encounters were radio interviews with people who had been tortured in the 40s and 50s, or with former prison guards in such institutions. One TV program actually brought together some of those who had been tortured with their former tormentors. Of all issues, this was the most sensitive, and had been the most absolutely censored, for it laid bare the pretensions of the post-1948 regime to speak in the name of socialism or for the people. Justice for those deeply or irrevocably wronged in that period was a major preoccupation of political debate in the Prague spring.

The public's reaction was extraordinary. People were buying six or seven newspapers a day, and some of them were listening to the radio till three in the morning. There were homes where both radio and TV would be on in the same room, with the listeners attending first to one and then to the other, depending on what was being said. The comparison with Portugal after the end of fascism is irresistible.

Regime figures were not, in the main, so enthusiastic. We have already seen the acute embarrassment caused them by the adverse media coverage. Many were exceedingly nervous about speaking to the media, being totally unaccustomed to any form of accountability or public contact in relation to their decisions. (At least they had not developed the slick and smarmy newspeak of western politicians.) Even major reform politicians such as Josef Smrkovsky took the view that the media had run ahead of themselves. In a press interview in Moscow, possibly tailored for Soviet Politburo consumption, he nonetheless bluntly affirmed that once the journalists had talked themselves out, it would be necessary to clip their wings.[10] The view was common at the top that journalists now thought themselves to be the natural organizers of the country, though this arrogance was only to be found amongst a miniscule number of them in actuality. Thus, even reform-minded politicians were still strongly stamped by the secretive traditions of the past, and found media openness unnerving rather than exhilarating. Their reaction was not shared by most people, who for the first time found they were being empowered to act as citizens rather than as cogs.

It should be said, though, that there were far-reaching changes in the official definition of the media underway even between April and August 1968. The April manifesto of the new Communist Party direction, the Action Program, described the media as "state institutions". The media policy document prepared for the Communist Party's 14th Congress, scheduled for September, had revised this to "social institutions", and asserted that "it is only natural that their activity should be kept under review by the representative organs of the people"[11]— i.e. parliament, not the permanent officials of the state.

Journalists themselves changed rapidly during 1968. Some were encouraged to vacate their posts by financial inducements such as early retirement. A number of older, even fairly conservative journalists welcomed the change in media direction, not so much out of deep desire for change, but because they felt less anxious about getting into trouble from above for what they wrote. Others became suddenly and quite unpredictably radicalized. In *Rudé Právo,* the party newspaper, the conservative editor was regularly outvoted at editorial meetings.

Most importantly, many of the directing figures left, for one reason or another. This meant that new appointments had to be made with Party approval; and since no one on the side of reform wished them to be made until the personnel in power in the Party had been changed at the forthcoming 14th Party Congress, no one was in a hurry to urge the vacancies be filled. Thus, in the absence of the former controllers, media workers simply got on with their jobs. In this sense, the media were self-managed, to a surprising extent.

> The exceptional character of the situation explains why the independently acting editors and journalists took over increased responsibility and why they became, to a certain extent, an "independent" political group (or several groups).[12]

Regrettably, there is far more information about the practicalities of workers' self-management in action during this period than there is about media self-management. For the time being, therefore, many questions about how it operated on a daily basis must go unanswered. However, it is clear that new figures of authority were chosen democratically:

> Gradually...personnel changes were occurring all over, as the adherents of the new course were being appointed—in an entirely democratic manner, by the decision of their editorial councils and with the concurrence of trade unions and even of their basic party organizations.[13]

There were cases where journalists wrote contrary to their instructions from above. In most such cases, Jezdinsky reported,

> there was no punishment or even reprimand, since any tampering with an author's text would be considered a violation of the proclaimed freedom of the press.[14]

In other cases, when journalists were forbidden by a superior to write about certain issues, they went straight into writing stories about how and why they were being censored. The journalists also reformed their own organization, the Journalists' Association, which previously had been packed with hacks and nonentities. In April 1968 they formed the Prague City Organization of the Journalists' Association (more journalists worked in Prague than anywhere else), which would be responsive to their needs and wishes.

In general, once journalists began managing their own production, they became active in demystifying the past and in preparing people to take an active share in public decision making. This demystification, as well as clarifying what had really happened since 1948, also meant debunking the political codewords prevalent in the previous discourse of politics. Phrases were held up for scrutiny, such as "the readjustment of prices" (price increases), "love of truth" (readiness to denounce one's neighbor), "love of humanity" (relentless repression of dissent). Preparing people to act responsibly in the present was widely defined by journalists as developing "critical distrust of the government" in the period when it was unclear whether the reformers would go as far and as fast as the mass of the public wished. When it later became clear that a Soviet invasion was on the list of possibilities, this definition changed to one of "critical cooperation" with the government.

One final, but crucial dimension of the Prague Spring must be underlined. It is quite clear that the activists in the cause of reform were initially students and intellectuals. Workers, long accustomed to being refused their own rights to organize autonomously, and to perpetually bearing the brunt of mistaken policy changes from above, were initially suspicious and slow to be closely involved. As the weeks went by, however, the long-dormant political and union consciousness still present within the working class began to revive and to impinge ever more forcefully on the situation. So much so, that self-management structures in industry outlasted the Soviet invasion for well over a year before the Husák regime could reassert its control over them. The speed with which this change to involvement took place within the Czechoslovak working class is deeply encouraging, given its deprivation of political engagement for a whole generation. No organizations such as the Writers' Union existed within the factory working class to act as spaces for argument and debate during the long winter of the Novotný regime.

August 21st-28th 1968

The story of the media in resisting the Soviet occupation is an extraordinary one. Jezdinsky writes of it that the media

helped to destroy the original Soviet plans—quick formation of a pro-occupation government, and liquidation of Reform leaders.[15]

How did they do this? Firstly, there was massive cooperation by people in official quarters with media workers—in the post office and the army, as well as non-journalistic staff of the media themselves. Secondly, there was a whole network of radio transmitters which had originally been installed in the country to act as an alternative communications network in the event of a NATO attack. In August 1968 this network was mobilized to defend the country against the Warsaw Pact forces.

Stations broadcast 24 hours a day during that week, giving news of the Soviet occupation, urging people to stay calm, dispelling the credibility of Soviet claims, announcing the number-plates of secret police cars, and even giving weather reports to farmers. A number of large enterprises had their own transmitters which were used both to broadcast and to jam Soviet broadcasts. There were frequent reassertions of unity between the Czech and Slovak nations, to avoid any divide-and-rule tactics then or later by the occupying power. Programs were also broadcast in minority languages: Czechoslovakia's quarter of a million gypsies were addressed in Romany, and other broadcasts were made in Polish, Hungarian, Ruthenian and Russian. After five days there were four different TV channels operating secretly, as against the normal two.

Wechsburg has described the situation in graphic terms:

Old ladies brought the (media) workers flowers and cookies, telling a Soviet patrol to look for them in the opposite direction. There were stations that stayed in one place, and also mobile ones, many, it seemed, under control of the Czechoslovak army...[16]

Havlicek also describes how

all major features, good and bad, of a partisan way of fighting were present: personal initiative coupled with personal responsibility, self-controlled work in small autonomous teams which kept establishing and re-establishing contact with each other, while being guided by framework instructions; setting up of joint staffs "from below"; self-imposed discipline, etc.[17]

The end of this week is well known. Yet the importance of the media in providing something approaching a legitimate governing body in that chaotic turmoil, can hardly be overstated. Had the Soviet occupation been able to move more quickly, the 14th Congress of the Communist Party could never have taken place clandestinely in the labyrinthine factory at Vysocany; it would not have been able to crystallize, as it succeeded in doing, a self-management model for the whole of the society; and the results of the constructive ferment of years would never have been brought to any summation. When the threads of that Congress are taken up once again in Czechoslovakia, the aspirations of its people will once more be heard and debated through its mass media. Until then, the final announcement of the last major radio station to survive can serve to close this account of the media in the Prague spring:

> We want to assure you that we will never betray you. We've become a living part of the nation and of the Communist Party. You gave us a mandate and we fulfilled it, day and night...[18]

Footnotes

1. Antonin Liehm, *Il Passato Presente,* Bologna: Cappelli Editore 1977, p. 92. In preparing this section I have drawn heavily on this book, regrettably never published in English, and also on an unpublished manuscript by P. Bernstein and M. White, *The Overlooked Alternative,* 1973. I should like to thank Paul Bernstein for allowing me to read the manuscript and use it here.

2. See the illuminating account by a highly placed insider, Z. Mlynar, *Nightfrost in Prague,* New York: Karz Publishers 1980.

3. Historically, there has often been considerable tension between the two nations, Slovakia being to the east and much more rural than Bohemia/Moravia. The languages are, however, extremely close to each other.

4. Liehm, *op cit.*, p. 86.

5. Dusan Hamsik, *Writers Against Rulers,* London: Hutchinson 1971, p. 161.

6. Western conservatives may well have responded like a British high court judge of impeccably reactionary credentials who remarked to a barrister of my acquaintance how pleased he was at the Soviet intervention in Czechoslovakia. Upon being asked in surprise why he took such a view, he delivered himself of the verdict that "something has to be done about all these students!"

7. The reasons vary. Film was organized in small workshops, especially animated film production, which made it hard for the power center to exercise close supervision over all of them all the time. Economists' views had to be taken with some seriousness because of the disastrous performance of the economy, despite its earlier relative pre-eminence in the soviet bloc, under the absurd "planning" structures of stalinism. Sociologists, studying actual life under stalinism as opposed to the official rhetoric, became willy-nilly spokespeople for what Liehm has called the "parallel reality" (*op. cit.,* p. 50) ic. everyday experience, as contrasted to government definitions of reality.

8. *Op. cit.,* p. 126.

9. D. Havlicek, "Mass media and their impact on Czechoslovak politics in 1968," in V.V. Kusin (ed.), *The Czechoslovak Reform Movement 1968,* Santa Barbara: ABC Clio Press 1973, p. 251.

10. K. Jezdinsky, "Mass media and their impact on Czechoslovak politics in 1968," in Kusin, *op. cit.,* p. 265.

11. Havlicek, *op. cit.,* p. 250.

12. *Ibid.,* p. 249.

13. Jezdinsky, *op. cit.,* p. 265.

14. *Ibid.,* p. 267.

15. *Ibid.,* p. 275.

16. J. Wechsburg, *The Voices,* New York: Doubleday 1969, p. 32.

17. Havlicek, *op. cit.,* p. 255.

18. Wechsburg, *op. cit.,* p. 110.

24

POLAND 1976-1980

You can find a government program in the newspaper kiosks for overcoming the crisis and stabilizing the economy...But what does it connect up with? Nothing. It is a letter addresed to no one; or rather, a letter which does not reach its addressee...

The power structure has no means to elaborate this program with society. It did not have them previously, but it could exercise its authority based on its monopoly of organizations, information and decisions. Now we have broken these three monopolies, and the system of exercizing power has, by the same token, collapsed...

...[but] we need to remind ourselves of what Zbysek Bujak said at the Warsaw conference: "If we are a union, then it's a union of sailors whose ship is sinking."

So what is to be done?..it is necessary to construct a new organism to govern. This must not be a party, but a self-management movement which would organize the management of the economy, firms and regions. The struggle for self-management must become our principal struggle.

Jacek Kuron, KOR co-founder
and Solidarity Adviser, 7/25/81[1]

The Poles' aspirations for freedom and democracy are often identified with supposed anarchist tendencies... Polish society in 1980-81 was not anarchist. The '81 Poles were rejecting blind obedience to the authorities, but they understood the need for a freely acepted social discipline...before everything, they were refusing force as a solution to social conflicts.

Krzysztof Jasiewicz[2]

Introduction

If liberated media are the subject of discussion, there was a decisive difference between the Polish experience of 1976-81 and the Prague spring. In Poland, with a few notable exceptions, the media which expressed mass consciousness and debate were organized independently of the government and the party, and survived despite sustained efforts to crush them by the authorities. Rather than a reform sponsored by many leading elements within the regime, the Polish experiment consisted of an endeavor to solve the nation's chronic problems in economy, politics, culture, public ethics and social morale by developing a carefully bounded opposition movement, deeply conscious of the limits set upon its freedom of maneuver by the Soviet invasions of Hungary and Czechoslovakia. Solidarity, despite its internal divisions, was agreed upon this; so, overwhelmingly, were the organizers of underground media.

The story of these years has been told in so many books and articles that it would be pointless to recount it here.[3] Instead, to explain the huge hunger for underground publications and their critical influence within the upsurges that culminated in Solidarity, I shall focus on the pre-existing official media system.

Simply to use the term "censored" to describe Polish media fails to capture the reality, at least for a readership accustomed to the more complex mechanisms of ideological hegemony in western countries. To begin with the absurd: at one point in the 70s, a satirical Warsaw nightclub called "Cellar" was closed by the authorities, and the censors instructed the press to avoid references to "Cellar." The very word disappeared for seven months with peculiar rephrasings of coal cellar or storage cellar bemusing Polish readers.[4] A much more serious instance was when TV crews were told to adopt camera-angles for the Pope's 1979 visit which would cut out the crowds around him.[5]

By way of contrast, let us consider two actions taken by one of the rare examples of critical state media, during its period of experimentation in 1980-81 (the *Gazeta Krakowska*). In February 1981, the then Party leader, Kania, publicly promised in Moscow that all anti-socialist elements in Solidarity would be crushed on behalf of the people of Poland. The paper reminded him he had the right to speak for the three million Poles then members of the Communist Party, but not for all Poles. In March, the paper sent its own correspondent to investigate the police mayhem in Bydgoszcz, when Solidarity members were savagely beaten up, rather than simply taking the reports of the official news agency. These actions were unprecedented for Polish media.[6]

In general, censorship became particularly harsh during the second half of the 70s following the Helsinki Agreement provisions for free communication, with the state trying to pre-empt any attempt by Poles to make use of the new "rights." Thus, even though Poland has a very long history of underground publications, the explosion of unofficial media from 1976 onwards was a response to this official clampdown.

In 1977, one of the Polish censors fled to Sweden, taking with him seven hundred pages of documents from the censor's office dating from August 1975 to March 1977.[7] The texts included the following gems:

> All information about the direct threat of industry and the use of chemicals in agriculture to human life and health must be expunged.
>
> All publications presenting general statistics with regard to conditions of safety and hygiene at work or to occupational diseases must be withheld.
>
> Figures illustrating the state and growth of alcoholism on a national scale are not to appear in the mass media.
>
> There should be no criticism of decisions made about wages or of social policies currently pursued.
>
> No information is to be released about the bribery affair in Sandomierz.

And on a different plane:

> It is forbidden to publish information relating to meetings and rallies held by young people and students from Arab and African countries temporarily resident in Poland, if Arab and African regimes are attacked during the course of such demonstrations.
>
> No information should be published concerning possible trade with Rhodesia and South Africa, or contacts between Polish institutions and South Africa.

Socialism in full spate...

Apart from clarifying immediately why Solidarity's third demand out of 21 in 1980 was for the end of censorship, these documents revealed even to the mistrustful Polish populace the extraordinary level of government intervention in public information. (The contents were communicated internally by the organization KOR, on which more below.)

Subsequent to this revelation, and to the imposition of martial law in December 1981, another document was smuggled abroad, consisting of a clandestine taping of an official meeting in April 1982 to review the artistic merits of a film (Bugajski's *The Interrogation*).[8] The film, which may well have been physically destroyed by now, focussed on the use of torture by the Polish secret police in the Stalinist period. Some of the committee defended the film; most, like the following speaker, insisted it should not be seen:

> ...a mass audience will react to this film unequivocally as, how shall I say, the breaking of human beings by people in Polish uniforms...The breaking of human beings that took place in history, which is incomprehensible to the *masses*. But we can understand it, provided that we are deeply convinced that this was happening in the name of socialism. *They* would not make distinctions between Stalinist non-socialism and the socialism of the state of war (i.e. martial law)... (my emphasis)

I have included this further example because it goes to the heart of what Polish censorship has meant for public communication in the country. The controls have not simply blotted out a series of scattered political topics from public debate. They have eviscerated mass awareness of Polish history from 1939 in particular, and have come close to stifling Polish mass culture, including the vitality of its language. When an atheist from a Jewish family tells you that she used to attend mass because it was the only public event in Poland where the language was not formal and lifeless, it is hard to believe this stifling is overstated. The taped discussion on the film is evidence of this: the word "Stalinist" was only used once, "torture" twice, Instead, "methods," "those times," a "painful period" were the only terms the group's members, unaware they were being recorded, could bring themselves to use. One of them distinguished himself by his capacity to defend the utterly indefensible in ringingly hypocritical tones:

> Let us make films a hundred times more trenchant...but let's show what was at stake in those times. There was a collision of two world-concepts, of life and of Poland,

above all...I don't know whether Bugajski ever heard
of the existence of a special department that spied and
checked on police functionaries. A functionary could
not allow himself *to do too much when his actions
weren't directed against the enemy*.[9] (my emphasis)

This evacuation of public morality, the reflex justification
of the state's grimmest deeds, the bankruptcy of the offical
language, the credibility chasm, the reasons why "socialism"
and "marxism" are dirty words in Poland, can all be deduced
from this fleeting but significant illustration of the system in
action. When the state archives of the 1956 Poznan workers'
uprising and the harsh repression it occasioned no longer
contain the court records but instead a note from the political
police in the file stating "materials with no historical value"[10];
when the 1940 Soviet army massacre of thousands of unarmed
Polish officers at Katyń is systematically dated by the authorities in 1941, while the Nazis held the territory ("it is necessary," wrote the censor in 1975, "to stress the undesirability of
an exhaustive treatment of the Katyń affair in either historical
or, more particularly, in journalistic works")[11] ; when such
deformations are common and consistent and condoned, then
a whole people's culture, language, historical awareness and
sense of public ethics are seriously undermined.

These factors go a long way toward explaining the widespread scepticism of media in Poland, the fierce hunger for
reliable information. Scepticism of official media has been
perfectly summed up for a western readership by the Polish
writer Adam Szcypiorski:

Foreigners thus sometimes find Poland to be a country
of bizarre reactionaries who refuse to believe the
crimes of the Chilean junta, are sceptical about the
problems of terrorism in Italy, reject as untrue reports
of racial segregation in South Africa, approve of the
Berufsverbot in West Germany, and so on. A mind fed
on garbage becomes poisoned.[12]

The corresponding yearning for reliable information was
the motor which drove the unofficial media that began to
blossom from 1976 onwards, but to an extent which even took
their organizers by surprise. *Puls* (Pulse), a literary magazine,
cost ten times the price of the official literary periodicals, but
only the problems in producing it held its run at 2000. *Gazeta
Krakowska*, already referred to, had a cover price of 1 zloty, but

an unofficial Warsaw price of 300 zlotys. It printed half a million copies, but its editor estimated that without the endemic paper shortages it could have sold three million.[13] Even a year after martial law was imposed, the deputy chief of the political police said his squads had seized over a million leaflets, silenced eleven radio transmitters, found 380 printing shops, and confiscated nearly 500 typewriters.[14] Needless to say, independent media work still flourishes despite police repression. Its rationale was cogently set out in *Information Bulletin* 8 (February 1977), put out by KOR:

> The information (this) contains serves the cause of openness in public life and constitutes a chronicle of reprisals both against its culture and its heritage. By disseminating this bulletin you are acting within your rights, and playing a part in their defense. Read it, copy it, and pass it on. Expose cases of violation of civil rights. Remember—by destroying this bulletin you are sealing your own lips, and those of others.[15]

Thus far, the situation is fairly clear. But what of the Catholic Church, whose place in Polish life was the most confusing element in the situation for western spectators? Film of hard-bitten shipyard workers confessing to priests, kneeling to receive communion, singing to the Virgin Mary, while in the midst of the most politically significant strike in postwar Poland, undoubtedly mystified many outside observers, including myself. The rather conservative stance of the Polish Catholic hierarchy on doctrine and personal ethics, compared to say the Dutch or even the American Church authorities in the 80s, served to make the problem even more intractable.

It is important first of all to divide the question of contemporary issues in personal morality from the question of Polish national politics.[16] A hierarchy conservative in one respect is not automatically so in the other.

Secondly, an explanation of the place of the Catholic Church in Polish life must take account of the Church's history. Rarely did the Catholic Church identify with movements for independence (Ireland and Biafra being the only other instances). This is important, even though the romanticized version of that history neglects to mention many self-protective equivocations with political authority by the Catholic hierarchy over the years and centuries, or its dismaying concessions to anti-semitism in the interwar years. However, during the Nazi occupation, the clergy were almost entirely identified with the resistance, playing a significant role within the Warsaw uprising and elsewhere. By 1945, the Church was closely in tune with Polish aspirations, and its claim to national allegiance had been eased by the near-disappearance of all non-Catholic minorities (by reason of Nazi extermination, Soviet-sponsored frontier changes, or emigration).

Thirdly, in contemporary Poland it is precisely the Church's role in providing *an alternative public space* which has been decisive in sustaining its vital place in Polish national life. In the final analysis, too, it is the people who make up the Church, not just its hierarchy. It is then *their* definition of what Church membership means which must be taken seriously in any sociological explanation. Faced with the erosion of a meaningful public sphere and with the collapse of public morality, only the Church existed as organized guarantor of certain key values and possibilities for Polish society. Only there was any idealism possible. Furthermore, only by hierarchical organization was the institution protected from the State, as Stanislawa Grabska, a woman theologian, explained:

> Take the situation of a parish. If the parish priest tries to democratize the parish, by involving lay people, or organizing a commission to oversee economic matters, then, very soon, a proportion of those lay people will turn out to be members of the political police. And how is he to detect them? How is he to involve people without immediately coming under the influence of the government?[17]

We have here, ironically, an analysis of the situation of the Church in Poland almost exactly parallel to Lenin's arguments for the necessary centralist form of party organization to survive the Tsarist secret police in his *What Is To Be Done?* The irony subverts Polish government pretensions, not Stanislawa Grabska's analysis.

We see then a society voided of authentic public communication except within the confines of the Catholic Church. It is a society with a protracted history of national suppression from east and west, and even from the south as well in the days of the Austro-Hungarian empire. Within this history, and especially under Nazi occupation, underground media were constantly being organized. Since the establishment of Soviet-backed rule in Poland, the aspirations of the Poles have repeatedly forced themselves to the surface: in 1956 in workers' demonstrations in Poznan; in 1968 in student demonstrations; in 1970 in Gdańsk, when unknown numbers of workers— estimated in hundreds—were shot down; in 1976 in Radom and the Ursus plant near Warsaw when again workers struck; and in 1980-81 with the formation of Solidarity. Our task in the remainder of this chapter is to record how the explosion of underground media took place from 1976, and their vital role in the development of the political struggle. Let us begin with the latter issue.

The media struggle 1976-81

The struggle over media formed a major strand throughout the conflicts of those years. The first of the new wave of underground media were the signed *Communiques* of KOR (Committee for Workers' Self-Defense), and *U Pragu* (On the Verge). KOR has been mentioned twice already. What is it?[18] In 1976, after many of the striking workers at Radom and the Ursus plant had been arrested, badly beaten up in many cases, imprisoned, and blacklisted from work, a group of intelligentsia decided to set up KOR. Its members included people with a long background as dissonant marxist theorists, a distinguished abbot, and a large component of unaffiliated humanitarian individuals. There were two noteworthy features of KOR in particular. First, its members signed their names— "going public" was a very courageous action, which for the first time opened up the possibility of an open countersphere. Second, KOR set out to publicize the details of individual workers and their families victimized by the police, and to collect funds to support them financially, legally and medically. The *Communiques* concerned themselves almost exclusively with these cases. Whereas in 1968 the student intellectuals had protested alone, and in 1970 the workers alone, for the first time a tiny attempt was underway to join forces. No glimmer was available however to any of the people involved of the dramatic impact these sometimes barely legible typed sheets were about to have. They were like the proverbial flower cracking through concrete.

The power structure reacted quite sharply, though not instantly, and jailed a number of KOR's members. However, they and the 1976 strikers were all freed in an amnesty on July

22, 1977. The stage was now set for the next confrontation. KOR expanded its name to Social Self-Defense Committee. Several new publications emerged, such as the *Information Bulletin* (after the paper by the same name from the Warsaw Uprising in 1944), *Glos* (Voice), *Robotnik* (Worker), *Spotkania*, *Opinia* and others. KOR and ROPCiO (Movement in Support of Human Rights) generally supported this activity. The only official expression of KOR remained the *Communiques*. ROPCiO was closely tied to the monthly *Opinia*. Several of KOR's members emerged among crucial advisors to Solidarity in 1980.

In between 1977 and 1980 there emerged a stream, then a torrent, finally a flood of underground publications,[19] representing a huge range of viewpoints on how to deal with the Polish crisis. Initially reproduced by the most primitive methods (the classical Soviet *samizdat* method of typing and retyping with carbon paper), the technology gradually became more and more sophisticated—and correspondingly subject to stiffer and stiffer fines and sentences if you were caught. The central node in this publication system, though not its only outlet, was the publishing house NOWA (Niezalezna Oficyna Wydawnicza, Independent Publishing House). At its peak, NOWA was using no less than five tons of paper a month, and had printed more than 200 pamphlets, journals and books: an incredible achievement for a venture defined as illegal by the authorities, if not by the Polish Constitution.

The underground press became more and more visible over time, in the sense that people would begin to display its titles and those of the emigre press openly on their bookshelves. Then, people started to read this material openly on the buses and trains and in other public spaces. Finally, it became extremely chic to have read a wide range of underground publications. There came to be very well known distribution points for this literature, which were intensively patronized.

Thus, by the time Solidarity emerged there was already an amazing volume of independently produced print media, covering national and foreign literary classics to modern novels and poetry, from political journals on a high theoretical level to single-issue flyers and posters. As noted previously, the third demand of the Inter-Factory Strike Committee (the embryo of Solidarity) in August 1980 was for an end to censorship except for state and economic secrets, pornography and the protection of the rights of atheists and believers alike.[20] The tempestuous months between August 1980 and December 1981 were to see repeated struggles over the right to independent media communication.

The State, having almost no journalists of talent to defend itself, and with most of its broadcasting crews and printers belonging to or sympathetic to Solidarity, was reduced to pathetically crude attempts at disinformation which nobody believed, to news blackouts on key events (these, inevitably, had more impact), and to sporadic repression of independent communication projects. By the late summer of 1981, with the economy in deeper and deeper crisis, the authorities opted to try to place the blame on Solidarity, and this became the main thrust of their media strategy in the short term. In August 1981, five leading members of the Polish Journalists' Association, journalists on state papers, issued the following press release:

> We feel it our duty to draw attention to the fact that the most recent propaganda campaign is helping create the mood of confrontation...(The media) are condemning a partner who is not allowed to speak for himself... A whole series of interventions by the censorship have served to promote a version of events that is out of keeping with the truth.[21]

Only the Solidarity newspaper reprinted this statement; its publication, however, was bitterly denounced by government spokespeople.

Meanwhile, the State was moving into action on two other fronts. The political police began arresting increasing numbers of distributors, usually in major public places at the busiest time of the day, as though they were trying to spark a clash.[22] Secretly, from the end of 1980,

> Security and police officers collected the names of all Solidarity followers who were holding important jobs in communications. All regional broadcasting was subject to strict central control from Warsaw, without which nothing could be broadcast. Technical breakdowns in communication were arranged in order to block undesirable broadcasts. Only specially vetted technical staff approved by the police were to work in an emergency and all broadcasting stations were carefully maintained to prevent any intrusion by "undesirable" persons.[23]

Solidarity, faced with persistent refusal to grant it the access to the airwaves it had been promised in 1980, decided to strike back. It called a newspaper strike for August 19-20, 1981, which it promised to call off were it allowed to explain its case on radio or TV. The government refused, saying that Solidarity already published a weekly paper of over half a million copies and "an avalanche of leaflets and posters." The strike itself was successful. *Trybuna Ludu*, the Party newspaper, was printed on the small presses of the Central Committee. Most newspaper stands refused to accept the papers which were printed.[24]

Following this, Solidarity refused access to any Polish TV crews to its Second Congress in the beginning of September, the government having already refused to send a crew consisting of Solidarity members. At the Congress, there was an overwhelming vote in favor of public control of the media.[25]

Once martial law was instituted, the tenuous control the Jaruzelski junta enjoyed over the minds of media personnel was illustrated by the fact that just one radio channel, one TV channel, two national dailies (belonging to the Party and the Army) and a few minor provincial papers, were allowed to continue until the new authorities felt their control was sufficiently secure. Public control of the major media was clearly off the political agenda for the while. Independent media, as we have seen, continued to burgeon, their often primitive aesthetics totally outweighed by their existence and message. One of their first major messages was a detailed set of instructions on how to make your own copy-machine...

Brief Case Histories

A book could easily be written on these experiences. In the meantime, I will present five short case histories of how new public space was organized in Polish society, both practically and politically. I will focus on *Robotnik* (Worker) and *Solidarność z Gdanskiem* (Solidarity with Gdansk, a Lodz weekly papers) as examples of mass circulation publications; on *Glos* (Voice) and *Puls* (Pulse) as examples of smaller circulation journals of political and literary debate despectively; and finally on NOWA itself, the central node in Poland's underground media.

This list is far from exhaustive. A book-length treatment would have to deal with the Solidarity weekly paper, even though it submitted itself to censorship; with *Jedność* (Unity), a weekly paper published in Szczecin without censorship; with the processes that enabled Andrej Wajda to make and exhibit *Man of Marble* and *Man of Iron*, and other film-makers to produce sometimes deeply critical films; with the making and impact of the documentary *Workers 1980* (on the Gdansk negotiations); and with the diffusion of numerous cassettes of those negotiations through Polish factories. A book would also have to address the impact of broadcasting material from all the independent publications through Radio Free Europe. What follows is based on the testimony of some of those deeply involved, and living at the time of interview in exile in the U.S.

Robotnik

Out of all the mass publications, this was the one which played the crucial role in forging an alliance between the intellectual opposition in Warsaw and the workers' opposition outside in Ursus, Gdańsk, Szczecin, Katowice, Nowa Huta and elsewhere. The process was not a magic one. Indeed, given the usual problems in this relationship, added to which were repression by the political police, it is surprising to see how successful it was. Furthermore, few people would have been more surprised than the *Robotnik* staff themselves, despite their hopes.[26]

After the initial phase of practical assistance to the Radom and Ursus workers had passed in 1976, the future *Robotnik* group started to organize workers' study groups. A number of workers came up to Warsaw and took part in the discussion. However, this project was not fruitful. The workers knew that association with Warsaw radicals could easily lead to further repression, and the study groups were not sufficiently productive of practical results to appeal to the workers involved. As one staff member put it, "Not every victim from the crowd is able to become an aware activist."

Back to the drawing board. A member of the group, Wojtek Onyskiewicz—"who is known to have visions," as one of his colleagues pleasantly put it—argued for starting a newspaper, to be the instrument and connecting link for the formation of workers' commissions. These were explicitly conceived on the analogy of the illegal unions formed in Franco's Spain, and had been the subject of discussion within KOR.

Typed on a sheet of 8 by 11 paper, single-spaced, without margins, and folded in four for discreet distribution, the first issue of 400 copies hardly looked like a conventional newspaper. Nonetheless, its very specific, down-to-earth contents and the very fact that it was not official, made it enormously attractive. From hectographic reproduction, they moved to silk-screen printing, the logic at that time being that if the police were to seize their printing technology, they would not be financially prevented from starting over. In silk-screen printing, three people were needed initially to produce in large quantities. One to pull down the press, a second to lift it up again, and a third to remove the printed sheet and replace it with a blank one. "A technical revolution," as one of them cheerfully put it, took place between issues 8 and 9: it consisted of using the elastic from a pair of briefs instead of a second crew-member. Production of issue 9 shot up to 3000 copies. By issue 16, they had moved to three columns, by about the 20th they were paying to have it printed, by the 40th they were paying several printers' teams, and issue 60—a chronicle of the August 1980 strikes—hit 70,000 copies.

A mushroom growth indeed. Distribution was organized by sending packets of the paper to fifty different locations, from where they would be individually distributed. Distribution carried less severe penalties than printing, and in certain localities it was done fairly openly. Lech Walesa was better known to most shipyard workers in Gdańsk as a *Robotnik* distributor at the gates, than as a former electrician in the yards.

This was not to say the paper was left in peace by the police. People were arrested, beaten up, continually harassed. One woman ran into an attempt to have her small daughter thrown out of pre-school. A miner lost his bonuses, was put on the lowest pay-scale, had his windows painted over, cow dung put under his front door, and his wife was told—she had distant relatives in West Germany—that there was no future for her in Poland, and that she should leave for the Federal Republic. "Socialism" in high gear.

As regards feedback from their readers, for a long while there was nothing for the editorial board to go on, beyond the rapidly mounting demand for the paper. Readers' letters were very few and far between. Thus they had to produce *Robotnik* according to their own lights. However, after a time they began to add to their usual copy on strikes, labor conditions, industrial mismanagement and corruption, and agricultural conditions, some articles with a wider focus.[27] They had begun to sense that their readers were now ready to consider larger questions than these immediate issues. Historical articles on Poland, biographical sketches of leaders of the Polish Social Democratic Party (extremely influential between the two world wars, and still a source of inspiration to many Polish activists), articles on the Pope's visit and the 60th anniversary of Polish independence, became important parts of the paper. This shift in emphasis coincided with the switch to three columns, where the first was used for issues of the moment, and the other two for more analytical pieces.

The paper's political thrust was an anti-dogmatic egalitarianism, derived in equal part from certain fundamental tenets of the socialist and christian traditions. Not that its editorial group decided on a "line"—it was simply the character of their project. The choice of "Worker" for the title was born out of the specific experiences of Polish workers in 1956, 1970 and 1976, not out of a theoretical marxist tradition. "Our concept," said Henryk Wujec, "was based on help in the creation of a workers' movement. We sought to aid in the rebirth of a workers' self-awareness." It should be added that the group was totally isolated within Warsaw's oppositional circles during its first years of activity. Most people they knew in those circles thought there were quite different priorities in opposing the regime.

At the same time, it should not be thought that they had easy communication with workers. To begin with, terms like "trade union" and "working class" had to be systematically shunned because of their debasement by the regime. But their problems went deeper than this. "To supply financial and legal aid," said Irena Wojcićka, "was relatively easy. Whereas to understand one another, to extract information, was extremely difficult." None of the Robotnik group considered themselves a writer. So they found that "with each sentence, it was necessary to ask ten questions in order that it be understood (by the readers)." Witold Luczywo added that in this kind of journalistic work, "it is not so important whether you are able to converse well, but rather if you are able to listen well and whether you are sensitive to language." (This vital issue of language also surfaced in discussions of Lotta Continua, Radio Popolare, and the National Guardian/Guardian.)

The editorial group divided their labor according to particular abilities. One person, for instance, was excellent at collecting material, but could not handle writing it up. Another specialized in programmatic and historical texts. Another was actually a very gifted writer and produced excellent copy. Yet another concerned himself with distribution and technical matters. Editing, at least to begin with, was the specific function of three women members. People were paid travel expenses but otherwise did work in their spare time. KOR helped financially, as did some union activists in the West, but not with large sums. Only in 1980 did they begin to charge for the paper.

Their relation to the workers' movement in Gdańsk, which eventually gave birth to Solidarity, was uncertain at the outset. Initially, the *Robotnik* group felt that the official unions' election procedures should be utilized to put up some reform candidates to challenge the power structure institutionally. The notion of free trade unions aroused their distrust, because they saw these as likely to be purely nominal bodies with no practical clout in working conditions. As time passed, however, and Gdańsk leaders like Lech Walesa, Anna Walentinowicz, Alina Pienkowska, began to meet with them and they saw the growing level of organized militancy in the shipyards, the *Robotnik* group came to sense that a new and explosive movement was in gestation. The communication problems they had battled with scarcely existed between the workers and engineers who comprised most of the Gdańsk leadership. They spoke an easy common language, and had successfully studied together issues in Polish history and existing labor legislation. Conditions in Warsaw, dominated like so many capital cities by a heavy concentration of intellectuals, were not nearly as conducive to the bridges they were trying to build.

Their *Charter of Workers' Rights*, published in the summer of 1979, proved to be the real turning point in attracting worker activists to come to speak with them—rather than simply "dissident workers," as Witold Luczywo put it. The *Charter* put forward a highly concrete program, many of whose elements resurfaced in the Gdańsk Agreement. It included demands for improvements in cost-of-living allowances, for a minimum wage, for the reduction of pay-differentials, and the abolition of secret privileges. It called for open allocation of bonuses, holidays and accommodation, a progressive curtailment of the working week to 40 hours, and stricter oversight by workers of their health and safety at work. The right to strike and the cessation of pressure on individuals to inform on their fellow workers, were also important elements in the *Charter*, as was the call for free trade unions.

It was at this point then that *Robotnik's* contribution to the development of the Solidarity movement finally emerged from its chrysalis. Its trajectory had not been a straightforward or an easy one, but it is most instructive. During 1981, the paper voluntarily went into liquidation, considering that it had now served its purpose, and that its members could best address themselves to new projects.

Solidarność z Gdanskiem

This was a weekly produced in Lodz after August 1980. Notwithstanding its title, its editorial board strove to achieve and succeeded in achieving a complete independence, not merely of the government and of the Party, but also of Solidarity itself. They began it independently, acquiring their own machine and materials, and then went to Solidarity for a license. Initially, the local Solidarity Board tried to insist that it would vet each issue before it went to print. The editorial group of six dug its heels in, and after a couple of weeks the Solidarity Board relented. They did not therefore find themselves in any way having to reproduce or to represent the views of the Board. Indeed, they even publicly criticized it on two occasions. One concerned a local Solidarity leader who had conducted a public meeting rather like a standard Communist Party official, basically through inexperience in conducting such gatherings democratically. The paper criticized him, and the effect, so far from souring relations, was very positive, helping the leadership to learn very quickly how to conduct itself in a way different from the usual authoritarian models in Poland.

The paper's format was a little larger than *Robotnik's*. With a reduced typeface, its contents were equivalent to a 16-page newspaper. In Lodz, with a maximum population of a million, it sold 20,000 copies a week. Its articles were quite often reprinted in other papers elsewhere in the country, and some thousands of copies were also sold in other cities.

The paper regularly included articles on union policy and on the different strands of opinion inside Solidarity. After the Bydgoszcz incident referred to above, it campaigned against continuing negotiations with the government. One of its themes was exposure of corruption in the municipal authority. Articles were written by the staff, but the paper also printed many letters representing a wide spectrum of opinion. These letters were also a major source of information on scandals of one kind or another taking place in factories. The editorial group, however, was always at pains to check allegations and complaints in person, to avoid disinformation tactics by the political police as well as concocted information from disturbed individuals.

On one occasion, the police came to confiscate their copy-machine. They demanded to know where the papers were for the machine. An editorial member demanded in response: "you have to have evidence we are in illegal possession of it. Where is your evidence?" "We do not have any." "In that case you are legally bound to return it to us until you have evidence." It didn't work of course, but it did reflect the determinedly defiant attitude of the underground press organizers toward the authorities' abuse of the Constitution. In the event, three local factories went on strike and refused to return to work until the machine was returned and the police apologized on TV. Incredibly, for a soviet bloc country, *both* demands were met!

How the staff found time and money to do the work was as follows. Here and in a number of other instances, the device used was to apply the rules governing work-release on full pay for union officials and activists to the Solidarity union. In 1980-81, that presented few if any problems. Even so, they often found themselves working twenty hours a day. As in so many other similar situations, the effect was exhilarating: "it was wonderful—people lived quite differently," said one publishing activist.

Glos

This political journal—"a monthly, issued every six weeks," as Piotr Naimsky put it—had runs of from 2000-5000 copies. It represented the wing of opinion inside and outside KOR which stuck fast to two major principles. Firstly, they insisted that Polish national independence could only be achieved by making Polish *society* (not its current State) independent. The process must consist of multiple, decentralized activities, not master-minded by themselves or anyone else. Within and between these independent movements and organizations, the debates and arguments which would take place would be the only way for a coherent future to emerge for Polish society. Secondly, they rejected any form of compromise with the Communist Party, defining it as an organization beyond recall. They were united in rejecting older models of parties and political organization, and the relevance of the old political labels (e.g. Left and Right) within contemporary Polish conditions.

No more than any other major group within Poland were they calling for a return to conventional capitalism, with its paraphernalia of private medicine and insurance, membership in NATO, aggressive advertizing, and so on, but rather for a revitalization of the culture, including the political culture, an end to economic dogma, permitting the existence of a private sector, and ultimately independence for Poland. For these targets to be achieved, they argued, the Communist Party had to be left isolated in its own cul-de-sac.

Like most other publications, the editorial board consisted of people who had known one another very well for a long time, sometimes with ties of family or friendship stretching back over decades. They were open to new members in principle; however, the bar to membership was that the journal had a well-defined position in the political spectrum to which a newcomer would need to subscribe (as well as proving to the group's satisfaction his or her lack of connection with the police).

Every copy of *Glos* printed the editor's names, and those of most of the advisors. The editorial group originally consisted of three, then later rose to five, with the named advisors numbering ten. This act of public naming was, as we have seen already, a major assertion of Polish society against the Polish State.

No one was officially editor-in-chief. The group met every Tuesday evening to discuss articles and ideas for the journal, but also wider political issues not directly linked to immediate publication policy. The agreement to publish or not was always made by consensus in *Glos*, with no vote ever being taken. (This led, naturally enough, to very long meetings on occasion.) They set out to print material primarily written for the journal, since material rejected by the censors had usually been written in a manner designed to slip past them. They wanted *Glos* to contain directly expressed opinions and perspectives, couched neither in the traditional language of politics nor in the veiled language constructed to elude the censor's eye and then to be reinterpreted correctly by the properly attuned reader. Reconstructing the language was indeed a vital element in the struggle for political regeneration.

The one difficulty which arose out of the organization of production was the relation between the printers and the editorial staff. Printing, as mentioned above, was far and away the riskiest element of the operation. The printers were the one set of people who could not afford to go public. Even too frequent personal contact between themselves and the editorial staff could easily lead to their being followed by the secret police. In addition, printing was a very exhausting and dirty activity, as we shall see in the discussion of NOWA.

So although the editors tried to maintain good communication with the printers, it was impossible for the latter to come to the editorial meetings. On occasion this led to somewhat strained relations, the editorial group getting all the kudos with minimal harassment, but the printers no recognition at all for risky and heavy labor. The result was that at times the printers would break away and form their own publishing group, focussing in most cases on books rather than journals or leaflets, and on literary and historical material rather than directly political subjects.

Thus, the impact of State repression on this division of labor was powerful. However, taken as an overall process, it actually had the effect of expanding the production of autonomous communication, despite the personal conflicts and hiatuses it produced in the short term. It ended up then as a gain rather than as a loss.

Puls

Puls and *Zapis* (Record) were the two main literary periodicals started in this period. The relation between literature and politics within the soviet bloc context has already beeen commented upon in this section and in the chapter on Czechoslovakia, so that it should not be assumed that either journal was the preserve of purely literary circles in the western sense. For purposes of clarifying the particular role of *Puls* (and not for invidious comparisons), it is instructive to compare the difference between them. *Zapis* in its first issue editorialized that it stood for the exact opposite to censorship, and proclaimed it would print what the censors refused. *Puls* went still further and sought, like *Glos*, material never written with censorship in mind at all, even including material that the official media might have printed in principle, such as some poems by Allan Ginsberg or Lawrence Ferlinghetti. Whereas *Zapis* also favored rather established authors, such as Czeslaw Milosz, and in form was rather like an anthology, and in tone rather serious, *Puls* set out to be a humorous, experimental, countercultural and controversial magazine. It certainly succeeded in arousing controversy. It published books (e.g. Vonnegut) as well as thirteen issues of the journal before martial law. It also emphasized the autonomous cultural production in eastern countries by printing people like Bierman, Erofeev, Zinoviev. Each issue had a special section headed "What's New in the East?"

Puls' readership, as might be expected, was drawn from students and the intelligentsia. Unexpectedly, however, for the West, this also included doctors, engineers and many members of the technical intelligentsia which in the West is often subculturally averse to art and literature.

The editorial board was composed and worked in ways that partly replicated the experience of *Glos*. It had six members at its core, though at one point their number rose to ten. Everyone already knew each other well, either personally or by reputation, when they began their project. Lengthy discussion was common on future articles and directions, but unlike *Glos*, an issue was sometimes resolved by majority vote. People knew each other very well, and in general the ambiance seems to have been closer to a club than that of a conventional editorial board. When, however, two of these individuals found it hard to work systematically, they switched to being occasional collaborators rather than staff members. Apart from this relatively minor hitch, the editorial group functioned very smoothly throughout.

Distributing *Puls* was organized very similarly to other underground publications. Private homes were used as selling centers, but only about twenty copies were in each home at any one time in case of police raids. The rest were spread around a variety of addresses. The *Puls* position was that since the Polish Constitution actually guaranteed the freedom to communicate, the laws preventing this were unconstitutional and should be flouted. For them it was important to remind themselves that their security measures were simply to avoid the police seizing their publication, and sometimes to cater to their customers' desire for discretion—though more so in the early days than later—much more than because they assigned those laws any legitimacy whatsoever in their own thinking.

NOWA

NOWA was the heart of autonomous media in Poland during this period, even though there were a number of other publishing ventures as well, and even though as time went on, the state publishing houses came to be used more and more for illicit printing after hours (to start with by bribing workers, later—as Solidarity grew—as an act of political commitment by many printers). NOWA marked the first step beyond the normal Polish and Soviet *samizdat* method of typing and retyping ten copies in exchange for the right to read the manuscript. As noted above, this is how KOR's *Communiques* and the *Information Bulletin* were produced initially, but their success was so huge, the enthusiasm of people for getting involved in this work so great, that underground media consumers began to transform themselves into media producers very quickly.

NOWA began with the very simplest techniques past the typewriters. They used wooden frames and silk screens, providing hundreds of pages per matrix. Very gradually they moved to spirit duplicators, then to mimeo, and finally to photocopiers and offset litho. While a few of these machines were brought in from abroad, a considerable number were models thrown out by factories and offices, and then reconditioned by NOWA activists. NOWA circles became extremely expert at making their own reprographic devices.

At its height, the NOWA operation came to involve a very considerable division of labor. Not only were there machinery experts, but people with cars who would help with transport (and who quickly became expert at knowing whether the police were on their tail), other people who would buy paper, still others who would buy powerful light bulbs for drying the ink quickly, others again who would organize the printing. Some people made their apartments or cellars or garages available for printing, for storage, for distribution. Some would volunteer to clean up after a printing run. Others would guillotine and staple. Those who needed money urgently would be paid, others would work for nothing. Yet no one knew the whole operation, as the greater the decentralization, the greater the security. Each operation would usually be set at a different place and time.

The editorial committee consisted of four people, led by a redoubtable former nuclear chemist, Miroslav Chojećki, who had been sacked from the Institute for Nuclear Research in 1976 for publicly supporting the striking workers at Radom and Ursus. In the four years between 1977 and 1980 his home was searched 17 times, and he spent in all nearly 200 days in detention of which just *five* were explicitly stated as having to do with NOWA! The pretexts offered for his repeated arrests included counterfeiting money, printing season tickets for bus-travel, a poisoning case, a murder case, and theft. No evidence, needless to say, was ever brought forward to substantiate these allegations, but the police would walk off nonetheless with books, manuscripts and a typewriter! As Chojećki said to the judge on one occasion:

> "Why has this repression come down on me, on my colleagues in the Independent Publishing Workshop NOWA? Really, the authorities should simply ignore it, since they can put up against it highly efficient printing presses, newspapers with a circulation of millions, radio and television."[26]

One wonders whether the fact that these mass media were of far less interest than NOWA's products was lost on the judge. It certainly wasn't lost on Chojećki or on NOWA.

Printing, as we have already noted in connection with *Glos*, was the riskiest and most arduous of all the tasks. It meant in practice two people living continuously for a week together in a cellar or a bedroom, eating, sleeping, working and—when they could—relaxing together. All their food went in with them, and they never left the room they were working in except to go to the bathroom. By the end of the week, they were usually exhausted, ink-stained, claustrophobic—but with an extraordinary sense of achievement.

Avoiding police interference became a major art. One leading NOWA activist recalled how the police would follow him to a certain point, and then just wait, perhaps in relays for weeks on end, for him to pass that way again in order to follow him for the next leg of his journey. Once he took a taxi over a bridge in

Warsaw, with anywhere between two and seven police cars tailing the taxi. Half way over he jumped out, ran down some steps leading off the bridge, leapt into a friend's waiting car, and sped away. They never discussed anything on the phone, or in their own apartments. Police plants—"plugs" was the word they used— also had to be avoided. Usually newcomers were accepted with references from friends, and then awarded a gradually escalating level of trust. In all, NOWA only lost a ton of paper and a couple of machines, and this as a result of carelessness with regard to the police rather than for any other reason.

Editorially, NOWA strongly adhered to the refusal to insist on any one political line for its publications. It saw itself as enabling a forum, a new public sphere for debate, to emerge and flourish, in which and through which a lost thirty or forty years of Polish culture could be recreated. Initially, NOWA looked at just three major factors when considering a proposal for publication, though these criteria became more complex over time. One was intellectual quality, the second topicality and likely demand for the text, and third but by no means last was its size, because of the logistics of production. Editorial meetings sometimes went on throughout the night, and involved major fights, with people on the board fiercely defending their own candidates. Decisions to reject for publication were sometimes reviewed later and reversed. Unlike *Glos*, but like *Puls*, NOWA operated with majority decisions after due debate.

When Solidarity was born, NOWA was largely taken up by it and practically became its publishing wing. The staff were eventually paid, the editorial board expanded its number considerably, permanent premises were found, and it switched into more trade union publishing. Until martial law it functioned as a highly professional publishing house.

Conclusions

In this final case study, self-managed media lived under more repressive conditions than most of the other instances in this book, although by comparison with their situation since martial law, this period of "semi-legality" (as it is sometimes called) seems quite halcyon. Their role, however, is directly comparable to the autonomous media described earlier, namely the creation of new spaces for public argument and debate, independent of the power structure. Their relation to the unprecedented movement of Solidarity was clearly an intimate and powerful one. What stands out about both was their incredibly rapid development from minuscule beginnings. Even before the KOR *Communiques*, there had been the Library of Forbidden Books, a distribution network set up in the aftermath of 1968, mainly to circulate products of the Kultura emigre publishing house in Paris within the country. There had been the apartment used intensively from November 1976 in Warsaw, into which 80-100 people used to cram themselves to listen to a new writer read early drafts for initial reactions before publication with NOWA. These tiny public spaces, created independently of the authorities, were vital and courageous first steps in the giant movement that was to ensue. No alternative communication channel should be written off *simply* because it is small.

The Polish experiment, as is well known, was no more popular with western banks fearful for their loans, and statesmen fearful of "their" working classes in a period of mass unemployment, than it was with the Polish or Soviet power structures. Nonetheless, the movement and its media scorched a burn-mark which will take a long time to eradicate finally— and which this brief account is intended to ensure is not quickly forgotten outside Poland either.

Footnotes

1. The two I found most useful were N. Ascherson, *The Polish August,* New York: Viking Press 1982, 2nd ed.; and K. Ruane, *The Polish Challenge,* London: BBC 1982. The double issue of *Survey* (24.4, autumn 1979 and 25.1, winter 1980) has a number of valuable articles and documents, as does A. Brumberg (ed.) *Poland: genesis of a revolution,* New York: Vintage Books 1983. Other useful texts are cited at certain points below.
2. Stewart Steven, *The Poles,* New York: MacMillan 1982, p. 259.
3. *Ibid.,* p. 258.
4. *Ibid.,* ch. 12.
5. *Survey* 24.4, pp. 173-87.

6. *The New Criterion* (October 1982), pp. 1-17. The quotation below is from p. 16.

7. *Ibid.*, p. 9.

8. S. Starski, *Class Struggle in Classless Poland*, Boston: South End Press 1982, p. 131.

9. S. Swianewicz, "The Katyn Affair," *Survey* 24.1 (Autumn 1979), pp. 188-98. The quotation from the censor comes from p. 195.

10. Stewart Steven, *op. cit.* n. 2, p. 261.

11. *Ibid.*, ch. 12.

12. Jan Nowak, "Poland's resilient underground press," *Washington Journalism Review* (April 1983, pp. 18-20, 58).

13. Cited from P. Raina, *Independent Social Movements in Poland*, London: London School of Economics/Orbis Books 1981, p. 55 n. 15.

14. C. Civic, "The Church," in A. Brumberg, *op. cit.*, n. 1, pp. 92-108.

15. Quoted in Jean-Yves Potel, *The Promise of Solidarity,* New York: Praeger Publishers, Autonomedia 1982, p. 101.

16. See Ascherson, *op. cit.*, and "The Social Self-Defense Committee KOR," *Survey* 24.1 (Autumn 1979), pp. 68-79.

17. See J. Karpinski, *Count-Down*, New York: Karz-Cohl Publishers Inc., 1982, pp. 198-201; L. Ciolkosz, "The uncensored press," *Survey* 24.1 (Autumn 1979), pp. 56-67.

18. Ascherson, *op. cit.*, pp. 174-75.

19. K. Ruane, *op. cit.*, p. 223.

20. Ruane, *op. cit.*, p. 253; L. Weschler, *Solidarity: Poland in the season of its passion,* New York: Simon & Schuster 1982, p. 121.

21. *Uncensored Poland News Bulletin,* February 19th 1982, published by the Information Centre for Polish Affairs (UK), Item 6f, pp. 31-32, "Martial law preparations in radio and TV."

22. Ruane, *op. cit.*, pp. 224-26.

23. *Ibid.*, pp. 230-32.

24. *Tygodnika Solidarnosc* (Solidarity Weekly) 3 (April 10, 1981), p. 14, "Robotnik." I am indebted to Ana Mayer for having translated this article for me , consisting of a group interview with the staff. All quotations below are from this source.

25. J.Y. Potel, *op. cit.*, pp. 6-8, 187-89.

26. P. Raina, *op. cit.*, p. 60.

25

CONCLUSION

The Czechoslovak and Polish experiences demonstrate many things, but perhaps two stand out from the rest. First, the claim of Soviet-bloc regimes to be workers' states is an utter mockery. Second, however, despite the systematic corruption of the very term "socialism," demands for socialist principles— free trade unions, open lateral communication channels, and self-management— persistently reassert themselves in these countries, as they do in the West.

This study's focus on communication is critical, however. It has revealed that the fragility of eastern power-structures is dramatically increased once the atomization of everyday life comes to be challenged. A revolution in communication inflicts a heavy trauma on the system of control. In both Poland and Czechoslovakia, the Soviet imperial machine was especially alarmed by the new public sphere being opened. They are no doubt similarly disquieted by the development of a "second circuit" in Hungary in recent years, and by the peace groups in Jena and elsewhere in the German Democratic Republic.[1]

It is inevitable that a comparison between Eastern and Western repression of lateral communication comes into play, but it is also impossible to do the theme justice here.[2] Let me just make two points. Many western radicals, very foolishly in my view, hope that something can be salvaged from the eastern rhetoric of socialism, for socialism. This is cloud-cuckoo land. These countries offer some of the most potent examples for conservative propagandists to use *against* the very idea of socialism. That is why the character of their opposition movements is so significant.

Many eastern radicals, burned by their experience, think with some relief of the relaxation of their own situation in western liberal democracies, even under rightist administrations (Reagan-Thatcher-Kohl). Yet the price of their increased individual security in those industrially advanced countries which are the liberal democracies, the very capacity of those regimes to be flexible toward them and to some homegrown oppositionists, is the condition of the Third World. Without cheap fuel, raw materials, food, labor, a certain way of life, such courtesies would be much harder to discover. The economics of civilized political behavior in western democracies is also the economics of black South African labor, of millions of migrant workers in Saudi Arabia, of Indonesian labor, of Mexican labor. It is not just a happy cultural legacy, as the degree of freedom of Blacks, Hispanics, and Native Americans demonstrates. The fact that Soviet-bloc regimes incessantly and cynically point to this fact in order to legitimize themselves, does not, unfortunately, make this untrue. Nor does it legitimize those regimes.

It seems then unavoidable that those who wish to see substantive social change must rely fundamentally upon themselves, and not upon supposed islands of socialist advancement or cases of political tolerance. Developing radical alternatives to current communication channels and structures, East and West, North and South, is a corner-stone of future progress. But the politics of this project must be global in perspective, not sectoral.

Footnotes

1. See *Index on Censorship* 12.1 (April 1983), pp. 3-15

2. The literature is enormous. See, however, the stimulating piece by Mihaly Vajda, *The State and Socialism*, London: Allison & Busby 1981, pp. 142-146 ("Is existing socialism a new variety of capitalism?") and the more comprehensive and thorough-going *Socialism Today and Tomorrow* by Michael Albert and Robin Hahnel, Boston: South End Press, which contains not only a discussion of why and how "existing socialism" is not socialist but also a description of what a true socialism might look like in an industrialized society.

26

GENERAL CONCLUSIONS

In order to pull together the extensive detail provided in the body of this study, I propose to review two symptomatic statements on radical media by socialist writers, namely Adalbert Fogarasi[1] and Hans-Magnus Enzensberger[2]. With their contrasted positions in mind, it will be easier to draw some conclusions about the implications of these varying experiences for developing future media work of a kind which outside eastern Europe it would make sense to call socialist.

Fogarasi, writing in 1919, represents the classical leftist line on organizing media. The capitalist press is defined as seeking "to preserve and promote ignorance" through its "pulverization of the social world into an incomprehensible, whirling jumble."[3] The communist press is defined in terms which simply reverse this:

> Truthfulness...and communist, that is historically-critically true evaluations of the facts are the condition of the liberation of consciousness from the ideology diffused by the capitalist press.[4]

The situation is stark: the capitalists and the communists both know the truth, though the former wish to conceal it, the latter to promulgate it. In between are "the vacillating masses ...whose interests rationally lead them to the communist camp as soon as the subjective conditions (ideological maturity) are present." It follows that a prime task of the communist press is to unmask the capitalist press, especially to persuade the petit bourgeois intelligentsia "which is so important in forming public opinion." In so persuading this strategically situated group, a "moral-psychological atmosphere (is created) which will contribute to the decomposition of the capitalist order."[5]

The communist press, so far as possible, should be written by party members rather than journalists, albeit with detailed training in economics.[6]

We see here that entrenched view of party truth, with economics at the core, which was dissected in the General Introduction—and which has been so extraordinarily effective in sparking counter-media in Czechoslavakia, Poland, and elsewhere. Although involved with Lukács and the short-lived Hungarian socialist regime of 1918-1919 at the time he wrote this article, by the 30s Fogarasi had already degenerated to a stalinist hack. The seeds of this development can be seen in his mechanistic understanding of media work. There is no sense of an emergence of experimental, provisional clarification among socialists through their media, but only of the natural, "rational" appeal of the truth the Communists are sitting on to the poor, contemptible, necessary masses. Middle-class intellectuals are a decisive component in Fogarasi's military-style campaign to "decompose" the capitalists' power—but what will be constructed positively out of the system's ashes is never debated. With twentieth century hindsight, such omissions can be seen to have been intensely dangerous, helping open the way to the savagely policed substitute for socialism that was stalinist "truth."

Enzensberger's position is very different, and has been influential in the thinking of the younger generation of media activists in Italy, West Germany, France and elsewhere. His was the first noted voice to call publicly for the socialist movement, just as it had fought for press liberty in the previous century, so now to struggle to free the airwaves in this one.[7]

It would be a disservice to his article, which brims with insight, to try to distill it all here. Instead I shall focus on certain of his major themes. He draws heavily on Benjamin's and Brecht's visions of the emancipatory potential of new communications technologies.[8] For him, electronic media are actually more progressive communications mechanisms than print because, he argues, printed communication is normally static and elitist. The new media he sees as inherently concerned with the speech of everyday, with the ongoing movement of life, and have an interactive structure—every radio receiver can be a transmitter—even if this structure is rejected by the powers that be.

Marxists are excoriated for their narrow, stick-in-the-mud approach to electronic media, tending always to see them as power-instruments manipulated against themselves, rather than as preeminently suitable vehicles for beginning to develop new forms of debate and awareness among people. In particular, Enzensberger flatly denies the possibility of Orwell's nightmare, insisting that the information demands of industrial society combine with the impossibility of totally effective censorship or phone-tapping to render the nightmare just that: a mirage. A consequence of the left's shunning of electronic media is that the only new forces to utilize them are the apolitical exponents of "counterculture" who are sitting ducks for commercial exploitation—think of the history of *Rolling Stone*. Rather than leaving the field open in this way, Enzensberger urges that socialists use the media for "mobilization". For him, this is not a military term. Quite the opposite. What he envisages is helping people to become mobile, politically energetic and demanding, the exact contrary to treating them as horses to harness to a predetermined politics.

His differences with Fogarasi could not be clearer. They are underlined by his clear rejection of the Soviet communication model as having anything to do with liberation. What would be the point, he asks, of seizing control of a giant media monopoly only to turn it over to a political party? Enzensberger, whatever might be said against his optimism concerning electronic media and the impossibility of effective censorship, or against his low view of print communication, is clearly speaking for self-organized media and against the duopoly of East and West.

He also stresses another matter: that the model of "truth-delivery" in socialist media thinking cuts out the many, many personal concerns which animate all of us. Capitalist media do not invent needs, he insists; rather, they capitalize on them. Socialist media should not be obsessed with "facts", "relevance", "exposure", economics, but should try to recognize the variety of people's needs and empower them to exchange their experiences and strategies for dealing with them.

As an agenda for radical media, Enzensberger's work represents a giant stride forward from Fogarasi's. Fifty years of experience are reperesented in his article. Nonetheless, time has moved on nearly another fifteen years from when Enzensberger first wrote his piece. What can be added now?

The first observation, which forces itself to the head of the line, is that new self-managed media have been mushrooming in country after country. Those inclined nonetheless to dismiss them as lightweight ventures by contrast with major media would do well to consider the degree of repressive attention lavished on them by governments of many different kinds. Unless these dismissive observers are inclined to define both radical media and governments as collectively crazy, the lesson is plain: *media are not to be defined as major simply by their size.* This is generally accepted of elite publications like *Foreign Affairs* or *The Economist* or *Le Monde Diplomatique*, but it is past time that it was also acknowledged to be an accurate assessment of a number, at least, of radical media. Furthermore, only such media provide any useful experience of organizing mass communication outside the straitjackets of East and West. It is precisely the recording and analysis of that experience which has been the objective of this book.

Let us begin, then, by assessing the significance of financial organization in these media. As we have seen, it has been a major problem for most of them, and in many cases it has been a nettle grasped most reluctantly. In some measure, the acute and wearing financial problems experienced in these media could have been alleviated by less distaste for the practicalities of financial control. It has to be said that this distaste is a sign of political immaturity. No aspect of the socialist transformation of society can be effectively accomplished without due attention being paid to this element of collective work, and there is something a little curious about marxist socialists (of all people) relegating this economic question to the margins of their concern. Nonetheless, it must equally be admitted that these media have confounded normal business expectations by somehow soldiering on through nerve-racking financial crises. To reduce the issues involved in creating this type of media communication to its financial nightmares, would be silly.

Much the same might be said on the question of format. Classically, the earlier wave of Polish newspapers in 1976-1978 was published typed single-spaced and without margins. Today, they have mostly returned to that. Some Italian radio stations (not the ones reviewed here) operated with very ramshackle programming. *República*'s presses were antique. The earliest issues of *Akwesasne Notes* and of the NACLA *Report* were hardly models of design. Yet in all these cases the level of demand for what they were saying negated the inadequacies of their format. At other points, the inventiveness of radical media formats even changed practices in large-scale media. An instance would be the graphic technique of "bleeding" a color over the page, which was pioneered in the U.S. by the underground press. Radio phone-ins were pioneered in Italy by democratic stations.

This is an appropriate point at which to comment on the creative and imaginative aspects of these media. As we have seen, Enzensberger rightly stressed the relation between the aesthetic and popular components of radical media work, as against its purely rational-cognitive components. In the General Introduction, E.P. Thompson was also quoted as emphasizing that people "also experience their own experience as *feeling*."[9] What we have seen is an extraordinary outpouring of energy, talent and feeling into these media. For those involved, the experience was universally described as exhilarating. Whether in Czechoslovakia or Poland, in *Akwesasne Notes* or Rádio Renascenca, in *Lotta Continua* or Puerto Rican independent film-making, the reports are the same. Not in every case did this spark and imagination flower as it might have done—readers may recall the wry comment of a former activist that "imagination was not in power in Renascenca!" Despite this, these media were generally a long way from the perspectives of a Fogarasi, who would only once bring himself to stress the importance of "living prose", which he instantly qualified as "incidentally...not identical with an impressionistic chaos of colors..."[10]

The question of aesthetics is not explored in this book anywhere nearly so thoroughly as it might be. The book's stress on organizational and political realities has tended to blot out this vital aspect of media work. If you compare the pyrotechnic poetics of Radio Alice, Bologna, with the calculated stress on contemporay rock music of the Florence Communist Party's Radio Hundred Flowers,[11] then there would clearly be a host of important issues raised about the politics of aesthetic accessibility. If you look at independent film-work in the U.S., say on the nuclear issue, and compare it with the cultural/literary flowering of the Prague spring or the Polish period examined here, the links between political ferment and aesthetic power are also posed quite dramatically.

Of all the aspects of the relation of radical media to large-scale media, perhaps the aesthetic question is the most problematic. How far do our media fail to sustain conviction or

interest, not because of repression, financial problems or distribution   difficulties, but quite simply because not enough
imagination and creative power have been involved in their
making? I would not wish to overstate this point, for as I just
noted, in any situation of high demand like Poland in the 70s or
Portugal in 1974-1975, or the U.S. at the beginning of the 60s
movement, aesthetic inventiveness is not crucial. In less pressured conditions, however, it assumes much greater significance. The attractiveness of many large-scale media, especially T.V., is a problem. Not because we should try to emulate
the slickness, the trivialization, the "whirling jumble" that
Fogarasi accurately pinpointed as characteristic of most capitalist media, but because there is more to the appeal of these
media than these facets. Not only do they capitalize on people's
real needs, but they do so in a way which is sometimes lively,
amusing, suspenseful, provocative. If the artistic energy and
talent which goes into those media, if the same energies so
terribly misdirected in the advertising industry, could harness
themselves at least in part to radical media, it would certainly
improve the latter. Think of the superb poster-art of Cuba.
Some radical media have this talent on board already, but their
number could certainly do with expansion. I would even suggest this is the present priority for radical media work in relatively settled situations.

As well as these aesthetic aspects of the interrelation
between radical media and large-scale media, there are others.
Sometimes radical media will raise issues that are later taken
up by their larger competitors. Sometimes professional journalists chafing under their editors will feed information to
radical papers to make sure it gets some airing. *Lotta Continua*'s history has examples of both these interactions. Sometimes people use radical media as a stepping stone to the bigger
media; at others, they are forced to seek this switch through
their need to realize a better livelihood for their dependents.
Last but not least, there can be a very fruitful symbiosis
between dissatisfied journalists in the established media and
radical media campaigners. Sometimes trade union issues will
bring them together, sometimes censorship issues, sometimes
a more general political crisis. It is not this book's intention to
be sectarian in spirit about the merits of radical media, as
though good media work elsewhere were somehow to be despised or declared irrelevant. On the contrary, what radical

media long for is to cease to be small scale. If their views and analyses can be more widely diffused through the larger media, who would complain? The decisive advantage of radical media is their freedom from the entrenched controls of political establishments: no *New York Times/Pravda* problems for them! And it *is* a decisive advantage, however well or badly they make use of it.

The remaining issues to be discussed are the questions of internal democracy in radical media, and their relationship to political movements. The two questions, as has repeatedly been emphasized, are intimately connected and are at the heart of this study's concerns. To repeat: internal democracy in mass media is only a step, however important, toward democratizing communications. Without an open relationship with constructive popular forces, internal democracy has a very limited utility indeed. What would be the value of an all-white male middle class media democracy in the U.S.?

Taking the experience of internal democracy first, however, two conclusions present themselves. That media democracy works; and that it takes various forms. The first conclusion is often denied outright. But we have seen in these twenty or so experiences in different countries, themselves only a fraction of the examples available, that in spite of repression, financial travail, and internal crisis, these media have gone on reproducing themselves over a period never less than a decade (in the U.S. and Italy), and in some instances for approaching four decades. The obstacles they have faced have been infinitely more threatening to their survival than the problems of running a large broadcasting network, or a major daily. And yet, they have survived, and even burgeoned. Media democracy is no mirage.

The precise forms of democracy they have adopted have varied, including over time in the same medium. This is to be expected, as the principle of democracy does not specify particular constant procedures. In quite a few cases, what has been described in the text as "ultra-democracy" has given way, with experience, to more sophisticated structures. There is no absolute right or wrong here though. The "ultra-democracy" of *Akwesasne Notes* works well because of the context in which it functions. The ultra-democracy of Rádio Renascenca worked for the period 1974-1975, though had the station not been closed by government dynamite, it would conceivably have begun to modify its arrangements. The ultra-democracy of some Polish underground media worked because of outside constraints and the close personal knowledge many editorial group members had had of one another over many years.

What increasingly did not work was the decision to adopt an ultra-democratic work-process for reasons that were abstract, namely the view that the most effective and responsive media democracy is the most absolute democracy. In *Lotta Continua*, in Radio Popolare, in the NACLA *Report on the Americas*, in *Union Wage*, in Puerto Rican film-making, the disadvantage of this position became self-evident. (Another merit of any democratic structure is that it can be changed!)

One point should be emphasised at this juncture, which goes against the ultra-democratic grain. It is this: in an extraordinary number of cases, the role of a particular individual was decisive in ensuring the project was realized, in animating it over time with a sense of direction, in enabling disparate personalities to collaborate for the common goal. The ultra-democratic assumption of the absolute equivalence of talents, and therefore of the equal claim to editorial control of all, really is highly inadequate. It is not to say that there are not many virtues in the rotation of tasks, in the avoidance of lumping the disagreeable chores just on to certain people. But the role of animator is not everyone's. And it is vital.

The relation between the media and political movements also needs discriminating treatment. It is superficially easy to say that they correlate, that as movements explode into life so do their media, and that as they ebb away, so do their voices. The plethora of underground newspapers in the U.S. in the 60s as opposed to their reduced numbers in mid-eighties; the media in the Prague spring as contrasted with their operation after the Husák-Brezhnev "normalization"; the decline in numbers of socialist radio stations in Italy during the eighties: all these seem to prove the self-evident correctness of the proposition.

Its problem, however, is that it is quantitative in its premise, and tendentially ahistorical. Bodies in the streets demonstrating are correlated with numbers of printed pages, radio programs, independent films.

This is a crass conceptualization of the relation between radical media and political movements. These movements do not spring into life like Minerva, fully formed from Jove's forehead. They mature under the dialectic of oppression *and* the lateral communication of resistance. Think of the counter-information work around the Italian police murder of the anarchist Pinelli, *before* all the radio stations began. Think of the flourishing underground leaflets circulating in fascist Portugal before 1974. Think of the slow maturation toward the 60s explosions in the U.S. Think of the patient work of members of the Czech Writers' Union in the years before the Prague spring. Think of the long history of Polish underground communication before 1976. Think of the dogged anti-nuclear communication that has worked away since 1945.

And: think of the importance of institutions like the *National Guardian/Guardian* and KPFA, Berkeley, in sustaining their activity not only before and during political tumults, but also after they had died down. The courageous work of numerous Poles since December 1981 in continuing to bring out countless publications is another case in point. If radical media did not pre-date and post-date these upheavals, established political molds would be cracked but rarely. These are the wild dandelions which split open the sidewalk, the embers which refuse to die. The bedrock of political resistance is the experience of oppression, but without lateral expression, over time, this resistance will always be atomized.

Thus the interaction between radical media and political movements is much more complex than appears at first glance. The full significance of radical media can only be grasped over the longer term. That, as I have suggested, is probably why the powers-that-be are often so anxious to make life so difficult for what seem at first sight to be such miniscule endeavors.

Radical media activists need to keep the "long haul" at the forefront of their thinking. Sometimes the very immediacy of media work, especially when combined with the kinds of pressures documented in the case-studies, makes sustained effort seem increasingly frustrating. It is to be hoped that the information in this book will lend perspective on this problem.

For, as in all political activity, there are both defensive and offensive moments in radical media work.[12] Defensively, the struggle is to reduce political atomization. In offensive strategy, the struggle is to expand political autonomy. I will conclude by expanding a little on each of these statements.

Political atomization is characteristic of both the western and Soviet models of domination. However, it takes different forms in each. In western, industrially advanced societies, it takes the form of dividing the resistance to domination into particular constituencies. In the U.S for example, women, Native Americans, workers, Puerto Ricans, Afro-Americans, generally conduct separate and competitive campaigns for their rights. Their common status either as workers, or as people of color, or as women, is very frequently over-ridden. While the established media are not the prime culprit in this process, only a support agent, for the situation to be changed lateral communication between these constituencies is needed, and lateral debate about their respective experiences. Thus media are required which enable the oppressed, as Sheila Rowbotham says, to relax their "defensive suspicions" of each other, to "nurture (their) wisdoms" and share them with each other.[12]

The integration of experiences and concerns within the *staffing* of radical media is a productive first step toward this goal. The fact of these different constituencies being represented at least to some degree in KPFA, Berkeley, *Union Wage*, *The Guardian*, California Newsreel, means that at the very crossroads of public communication there is the potential for exchange between them in a dialogue with their readers/audience. Physical co-presence is no guarantee of success, and most certainly not of harmony, but it is the first base beyond the necessary defense of any one group's rights and existence.

Within the Soviet bloc, political atomization is more individual in its effects. The control of information and the repression of anything resembling a political movement have the effect of pushing activists back into small circles of family and long-term friends. We saw in the Polish case how these were the elementary knots from which first emerged the new wave of underground publications. (There have been comparable experiences under the military dictatorship in Brazil.[14])

In this sense, Solidarity's famous letter of greetings from its first congress in 1981 "to the working people of Albania, Bulgaria, Czechoslavakia, the German Democratic Republic, Roumania, Hungary and all of the nations of the Soviet Union," which looked forward to when "our representatives meet yours to exchange experiences," was a blazing pre-emptive strike on the necessary future.[15] Whatever it lacked in short-term *realpolitik*, it was the kernel of what must be brought into being.

Political autonomy: as we saw in the section on Italy, the very word "autonomy" has been tainted in some quarters by its association with the terroristic policies of the Red Brigades. Here I propose to reclaim it for a mass-based political strategy, far removed from the elitist desperatism of slaughtering the political center. The word "independence" could be used, but it has so many associations— independence from one's parents, the independent entrepreneur, the maverick independent, Third World independence (under neo-colonial rule)—that I will stick with "autonomy": self-government, self-determination, self-management.

In both West and East, striving for mass autonomy should be the main forward strategy, and indeed there are many signs that it is emerging as such. Autonomy means creating our own spaces which we carve *out* from the political territory presently carved *up* by capital and the state. In mainly rural societies these spaces have been physically liberated zones, as in El Salvador or China or Zimbabwe. In industrially advanced societies the zones have to be in political, not geographical space.

When a hundred or so people meet together in a Warsaw apartment in the mid-70s to debate culture and politics *for themselves*, that was autonomy. When the Czech Communist Party held its 14th Congress in secret after the Soviet invasion, and debated plans for factory self-management which were actually put into practice over the succeeding months in many workplaces, that was autonomy. When the *National Guardian* was the only nationally circulating paper in the U.S. unequivocally to condemn McCarthy and defend the Rosenbergs, that was autonomy. When Portuguese radio workers took control of *Rádio Clube Português* and the rest, that was autonomy. When the Italian Left began radio broadcasting in initial defiance of the state in 1974-1975, that too was autonomy: the deliberate creation of self-governing political space in the face of the powers-that-be.

Autonomous media are peculiarly important in this process. Constructed in the ways this book has described, they are wider in scope than trade unions, and capable of being more in tune with social and cultural immediacies than most political parties of the left. I am not claiming that such media are the new red-hot hope for a confused and floundering international socialist movement, or that trade-unions and political parties belong to the dustbin of history. Far from it: trade unions will always be necessary in any presently imaginable future, and political parties can organize action in a way media can not. What I am saying is that self-managed media are capable of being responsive, of opening up the protracted debate and argument necessary to develop beyond the present impasse. They are themselves an autonomous political sphere, but are also almost constitutionally propelled to expand that sphere to embrace more people, to create a wider public realm in opposition to the hegemony of the existing order. The experience of the 20th century, West and East, is that any shortcut which skips out on that mass politics will either lead nowhere or to disaster. Autonomous media are therefore a central, continuing component in this long march.

Footnotes

1. A. Fogarasi, "The tasks of the communist press", *Radical America* III.3 (May-June 1969), pp. 68-75; also reprinted in A. Mattelart & S. Siegelaub (eds), *Communication and Class Struggle*, vol. 2, New York: International General 1983, Section F.1.
2. H.-M. Enzensberger, "Constituents of a theory of the media", in his *The Consciousness Industry*, New York: Seabury Press 1974, pp. 95-128.
3. These quotations are drawn from pp. 72 and 70 respectively of Fogarasi's article.
4. Fogarasi, *art. cit.*, p. 72.
5. The three citations in this paragraph are all from p. 73 of Fogarsi's article.
6. Fogarasi, *art. cit.*, pp. 74-75.
7. Enzensberger, *art. cit.*, p.107.
8. B. Brecht, "Radiotheorie 1927 bis 1932", *Gesammelte Werke* 18, Frankfurt: Suhrkamp Verlag 1967; W. Benjamin, "The work of art in the age of mechanical reproduction", in his *Illuminations*, London: Fontana Books 1973.
9. Cited in n. 43 to the General Introduction.
10. Fogarasi, *art. cit.*, p. 73.
11. See the section on Controradio, Florence.
12. A. Mattelart & S. Siegelaub (eds), *Communication and Class Struggle*, vol. 1, New York: International General 1979, p. 28.
13. Cited in n. 33 to the General Introduction.
14. L. Gonzaga Motta, "Cultura de Resistencia e Communicacao Alternativa no Brasil" (Culture of resistance and alternative communication in Brazil), *Communicacao e Política* 1.1 (March-May 1983), pp. 53-69.
15. L. Weschler, *Solidarity*, New York: Simon & Schuster 1982, pp. 108-113.

INDEX

abertura (democratic "opening," Brazil) 117

abortion rights 101, 220, 286, 294

access to major media 7-10, 28

Action Program (Czechoslovakia) 316

African Americans 3, 4, 5, 23, 29, 35, 42, 43, 44, 45, 48, 56, 58, 60, 68, 88, 101, 140, 143, 147-8, 154, 348

ageism 22, 63-64, 179, 205, 265-7, 280, 284, 299

Akwesasne Notes 104-14, 142, 154, 245, 250

Almirante (Italian neo-fascist) 218

alternative media
administrative and business routines 68-69, 70, 84, 103, 111, 117-8, 120, 127-8, 141, 147, 260, 352

aesthetics 24, 241-3, 352-3, 354-5

counter-information 38-42, 56-58, 59-60, 79-80, 87-88, 97-98, 104, 106-9, 113-4, 115-8, 126, 130-1, 140-43, 147-8, 150-51, 156, 168, 171-2, 173, 195-6, 225-6, 272-82, 308, 328, 329-46, 356-7

dismissal procedures 62, 102

division of labor (see also printers) 20, 60, 70, 110-11, 119, 127, 135-6, 148-9, 156, 203-4, 246, 249, 260-61, 292, 336, 342-3

editorial authority 60-61, 66-67, 80-82, 99, 109-10, 118-9, 135, 148-9, 190, 191, 192-3, 198-200, 202, 204, 209, 244-5, 258-9, 278-9, 292, 316-7, 336, 337, 339, 341, 344, 355-6

financial problems 9, 61, 62, 70, 75, 103, 149, 187, 190, 201, 246-50, 261-3, 280-2, 287, 289, 290-1, 336, 352 (contrast Rádio Clube Português 210)

imagination 24, 29, 191-2, 229-30, 241-3, 268-72, 296-8, 353-4

internal strife 62-66, 80-81, 83, 86-9, 102, 109-11, 130-33, 135-6, 196-200, 212-3, 258-9, 289-90, 340

language 55, 117, 241, 268-72, 304-6, 318, 335

major/minor media relationship 59, 74, 94, 97, 243-4, 246, 257, 263, 299, 313-4, 354-5

part-timers/external contributors 60, 70-71, 82-84, 102, 120-1, 238, 258, 275-6, 291

pay policies 61, 67, 76, 85, 109, 115, 136, 139, 243, 258, 289

political movements 58, 59-60, 63-64, 80, 85-94, 96-103, 106-9, 116-7, 119-20, 122, 126, 128-33, 150-56, 168, 171-2, 173, 177, 182-3, 189-90, 192-4, 201-5, 212-3, 237-8, 240-41, 257-8, 263-7, 271, 274-5, 284-8, 289-90, 294-8, 313-21, 329-46, 356-7

printers and technicians 60, 69, 84, 112, 119, 196, 198-200, 245-6, 261, 262, 340, 343
professionalism 61, 213, 252, 266, 274-5, 285-8
repression 37-41, 58-60, 76-77, 79-80, 112-3, 122-3, 132, 149-50, 213-4, 184-90, 211, 274, 313, 334, 338, 343-4, 352
regional structures 71-72, 79, 99-100, 121-2, 128 (see also FRED, Rádio Clube Português, Rádio Renascença)
Third World presence 68-69, 86-89, 104-14, 129-33, 140, 192, 193, 287
training 69, 84, 91-2, 112, 129, 252-3, 259, 275-6, 298-300
"transmission-belt" approach 15, 66, 238-9, 257, 264-5
ultra-democracy 17, 61, 81, 100, 109-10, 118, 127-8, 148, 258-9, 355-6
women's presence 60, 67-8, 89-92, 96-103, 111, 112, 128-30, 140, 150-51, 154, 191, 193, 206, 250-52, 263-66, 279-80, 293-4, 336
Alternative Radio (Rome) 218
anarchism 2, 16-24, 48, 110, 225-6, 322
Andropov, Yuri 309
anti-nuclear themes 4, 25, 26-7, 57, 66, 105, 151, 153, 243, 353
Armstrong, David 41-2
Arnold, Matthew 3-4
Aronson, James see *National Guardian*
atomization, political 358-9
aut aut 284, 295
Autonomists 230-231
autonomy, political 359-60
Avanguardia Operaia 239
Avanti! 226
AVCO Corporation 37
Bahro, Rudolf 19-21
Bakunin, Mikhail 19-20
Baldelli, Pio 225
Barnouw, Erik 36

BBC (British Broadcasting Corporation) 6, 75
Bechelloni, Giovanni 222
Belfrage, Cedric see *National Guardian*
Benjamin, Walter 350
Berkeley "Free Speech" movement 43
Berlinguer, Enrico (PCI) 219, 220, 248
Bernabei, Ettore (RAI) 223
Berrigan, Frances 7
Berson, Ginny (KPFA) 89-92
Black Film-Makers' Foundation 136
Black independent film 136-7
Black Panther Party 130-31
Blake, William v
Bobbio, Luigi 226
Bologna (PCI showcase city) 220, 229, 230, 290, 295
Boston v, 71, 132
Brecht, Bertolt 350
Brezhnev, Leonid 11, 356
Britain 6, 8-9, 17, 27, 162, 167, 168, 175, 178, 218, 221, 307
Buckley, William 80
Budjilawski, S. 12-15, 18, 19
Bugajski, Ryszard (film-maker) 325-6
Bush, George (US Vice-President) 309
Bydgoszcz incident 324, 337
cable television 7-8, 37, 224
Calabresi (Milan police chief) 270-71
California Newsreel 117, 139-45, 154
Canada 7-8, 27, 106
carabinieri 217, 230, 309
Cardinal of Lisbon 182, 184-5, 187-8, 191
Catholic Church 66, 111, 148, 168, 169, 171, 174, 176, 179, 181, 182, 184-5, 186, 190, 191, 187-8, 216, 219, 221, 294, 307, 325, 327-8
Cattin, Donat 244
CD see Christian Democrats

CDS (Center Social Democrats)
censorship (see also alternative media repression) 15, 28, 168, 170-71, 174, 176, 181, 182-3, 197, 204, 212-3, 300, 308-9, 310-11, 323-6, 330-1, 339-40, 341-2, 351
Center Social Democrats (Portugal) 175, 179, 211
Central America
 Bay of Pigs invasion 44
 Dominican Republic invasion 44, 116
 El Salvador 93, 116, 359
 Guatemala 104, 105, 111
 Nicaragua 88, 105, 111, 116, 117
CGIL (Italian General Confederation of Labor) 221, 229
Charter of Workers' Rights (Poland) 336-7
Chicanos 42, 88, 121
Chile v, 25, 41, 66, 169, 173, 220, 228, 256, 326
China 16, 49, 56, 65, 66, 129, 140, 237, 244, 255-6, 271, 359
Chojecki, Miroslav (NOWA) 343
Choy, Christine (Third World Newsreel) 129-30
Christian Democrats (Italy) 216, 217, 219, 220, 221-3, 228, 229, 232, 237, 238, 248, 270
Churches (Protestant) 66, 144
CLUW (Coalition of Labor Union Women) 97-8
Cold War 39, 45, 50 , 56, 57, 75, 161-2, 237 (see also McCarthyism)
Communist Party
 Cyprus 164
 Czechoslovakia 308, 311, 312, 316, 320
 Greece 161, 164, 165
 Italy (PCI) 164-5, 195, 216, 218-244 *passim*, 248, 258, 262, 269, 274, 277, 283-4, 288, 292; PCI media 225-6, 230, 302
 Poland 308, 323, 337, 339
 Portugal (PCP) 66, 164, 165, 172, 174-5, 178-9, 182-3, 187-9, 191, 196-9, 201, 206, 211-3

 Spain 164, 165
 USA (CPUSA) 49, 57, 76, 79, 101
compagni (definition) 254
competitive colonization of media 172, 202, 223, 288, 292
computers iv, 143, 153
corporations 9, 28, 37, 74, 104
Conakry, attempted invasion 182
Controradio 252, 263, 272-82, 287, 291, 293
Cooley, Mike 142
COPCON 169, 200, 211
Corriere della Sera 225-6, 241, 257
Council on Foreign Relations 3
Covert Action Information Bulletin 115
Cuba 49, 58, 65, 135, 150, 354
culture (definition) 4, 5, 19-20, 21, 24, 308
Cunhal, Alvaro (PCP) 182-3, 199, 200
Czechoslovakia 11, 15, 307, 310-21, 323, 347, 350
Danish Film Workshop 9
Democratic Party (US) 143
Democrazia Proletaria 267, 289
de Figueiredo, Antonio 168
de Tocqueville, Alexis 37
Detroit 42, 47, 65, 71, 130-31, 143
 Dodge Revolutionary Union Movement 130
 Finally Got The News 130-32
 League of Revolutionary Black Workers 130-31
Diário de Notícias (Lisbon) 172, 173, 196
DuBois, W.E.B. 48, 60, 61
duopoly of East and West v, 2, 4, 16, 28, 41, 170, 202, 232, 303, 307, 351
 Marines 116, 147
 Marshall Aid 162
 NATO 163, 176, 197, 319, 339
 Pentagon 41, 125
 Rapid Deployment Force 165
 Warsaw Pact 307, 319
 US-Soviet contention in Mediterranean 161-66 (see also Bologna, PCP, PSP)

Eastern Europe 11-15, 19-21, 229, 307-48 (see also individual countries)
Eisenhower, President 58
emarginati (see also students) 227, 266
Enzensberger, Hans-Magnus 242, 350-52, 353
established media (East) 11-15, 308, 312, 316, 323-36
established media (West) 3-10, 35-37, 108, 155, 156, 170-72, 221-6
Expresso (Lisbon) 200
fascism, neo-fascism 37, 48, 49, 162, 167-72, 186, 218-9, 221-2, 225, 228, 270, 315
Cactano, Marcello 167, 169, 171
Franco, General 165, 176, 208, 333
Goering, Herman 308
Hitler/Nazis 218, 312, 326, 328
Mussolini 168, 171, 218, 219, 221, 284
"New State" (Estado Novo) 167, 168, 171
PIDE 168, 171, 191, 309
Salazar, António 167, 171, 221
Spinola, General 169, 176, 209, 211
Fassbinder, Rainer-Werner 137
FBI 37, 41, 123, 132, 152, 309
FCC (Federal Communications Commission) 40, 79
feminism (see also women, sexism) 2, 16, 22, 23, 28, 36, 44, 66, 90, 96-103, 239, 264-66, 271, 290, 293-4, 296
Fernandes, Captain 204
Fernandes, Jaíme 210, 213
Fernandes, Jorge Almeida 205
FIAT Corporation 227-8
First Amendment (US Constitution) 3
Fofi, Goffredo 294
Fogarasi, Adalbert 349-50, 353, 354
Ford, President 42, 45, 101
Foreign Affairs 39

France 25-6, 27, 162, 163, 167, 168, 195, 350
FRED (Federation of Democratic Radio Stations, Italy) 224-5, 281 (see also alternative media, regional structures)
Freedom of Information Act (US) 40, 123
Freedom Station, Luanda, Angola 208
gays 54, 66, 154
Gazeta Krakowska 323-4, 326-7
Gdańsk 329, 334, 336
Gerima, Haile 136
German Democratic Republic (East Germany) 12, 21, 162, 307, 347 (see also Budjilawski)
"germanization" 229, 276-8
Glos 330, 338-40, 341
Godard, Jean-Luc 137
Goldman, Emma 16, 18, 39
Goldwater, Barry 39
Gonçalves, Vasco (Portuguese premier 1975) 173, 187-8
Grabska, Stanislawa 328
Gramsci, Antonio 155, 219
Greece 25, 57, 161-2, 163, 219
Guardian 55-73, 100, 102, 120-1, 128, 133, 154, 250
Gulf & Western Corporation 37
Hamšik, Dušan 312
Haraszti, Miklós 307
Havlicek, František 314, 318
Hayden, Tom 143
Heller, Celia 5
Heroin problem in Italy 233, 277
Helsinki Agreement 324
Hill, Lewis (KPFA) 75, 78, 80
Hispanic (see Latin)
"historic compromise" policy (PCI) 219-21, 228, 233, 244, 266, 292
Holocaust 48
Hungary 11, 12, 307, 308, 323, 347, 350
Hus, Jan 311
Hušak, Gustav 318, 356

imperialism 22, 43-4, 45, 105, 114,
    140-1, 146-51, 154, 167, 176,
    178, 193-4, 268, 277, 308, 310,
    326, 348
  anti-imperialism 23, 42, 43, 48,
    62, 140-1, 167, 168, 170, 176,
    182, 193, 318-21
independent film work 125-51
  distribution 126-7, 144
  exhibition 136-7, 144-5
  production 127, 129, 130-2, 134-
    5, 139-45
Inter-Factory Strike Committee
    (Poland) 330
Intersindical (Portugal) 174, 183,
    188, 190, 197, 212
In These Times 142
Iran 41, 244, 259, 263, 270, 291,
    297
"iron law of oligarchy" theory
    259-61
IRS (Internal Revenue Service,
    US) 37, 40, 123
Italy (see also Table of Contents)
    17, 25, 162, 215-303, 350
  earthquake in 1980 216, 263
  "Hot Autumn" 1969 227
  North and South 215-8, 219,
    227, 300, 303
  Resistance in World War II 220,
    284 (see also, under Catholic
    Church, fascism, mafia, PCI,
    political movements, and
    established and alternative
    media)
Jackson, Jesse 155
Jancsó, Miklós 137
Jaruzelski, General 332
Jasiewicz, Krzysztof 322
Jedność 33
Jezdinsky, K 317, 318
Jezer, Marty 48
John Paul II, Pope 323, 335
Journalists Association (Czecho-
    slovakia) 317
Kafka, Franz 312
Kania, S. (Polish premier be-
    tween Gierek and Jaruzel-
    ski) 323

Katyń massacre 326
Katznelson, Ira 45-46
Kennan, George 39, 41
Kissinger, Henry 165, 170
KOR (Committee for Workers
    Self-Defense, later Social
    Self Defense) 322, 325,
    327, 334, 336, 338
  KOR Communiques 329
  KOR Information Bulletin 327,
    330
KPFA, Berkeley 74-95, 105, 110,
    133, 154
Kultura publishing house, Paris
    345
Kulturny život, Slovakia 312
Kuron, Jacek 322
Lama, Luciano (CGIL leader)
    229, 230
Latin America (see also Central
    America, Chile, Cuba, Puerto
    Rico) 17, 88, 105, 109, 115-24,
    256, 358
Latins (in US) 5, 45, 86, 87, 97,
    101, 348
Left Index 153
Lenin, leninism 11, 15, 49, 132,
    133, 142, 290, 328
Lerner, Gad 271
lesbians 54, 66, 90, 154
Libération 28, 71, 100, 121, 198,
    241
Library of Forbidden Books (Pol-
    and) 345
Liehm, Antonin 310
Literární noviny 312, 313
Lodz 337
Longo, Biagio (Radio Popolare)
    284, 285, 286, 291, 299, 300
LoRusso, Francesco (Bologna
    student) 230
Lotta Continua (political organ-
    ization) 226, 227, 228, 229,
    255, 273
  1976 Rimini congress 256, 263,
    267
Lotta Continua (newspaper) 61,
    96, 119, 148, 198, 203, 222, 225,
    232, 239, 245, 251, 252, 255-72,
    273, 279, 289, 293

Luczywo, Witold *(Robotnik)* 335, 336
L'Umanità (PSDI) 248
L'Unità (PCI) 222, 225-6, 230, 248
A Luta (PSP) 198, 201, 206
Macali, Beppe 223
Mafia 215-8, 233, 258
Il Manifesto 222, 226, 228, 237-54, 258
Marques, Belo 199-200
Martial law (Poland) 325, 341
Marx, marxism 2, 16-23, 49, 56, 63, 134, 140, 175, 186, 264, 351
McCarthy, McCarthyism (see also Cold War) 36, 39, 48, 49, 50, 56, 58, 62-3, 75-6, 131
Media Alliance (USA) 28
MERIP *Report* 115
MFA (Armed Forces Movement, Portugal) 168-9, 176-7, 181, 183, 187-8, 190, 208
Micronesian structure of US society 42, 45-7, 154-6
Le Monde 247
Monthly Review 60, 115
Moro, Aldo (Italian premier) 232-3, 239-40, 258, 265-6
Mother Jones 123
MRPP (Portugal) 193, 212
Ms Foundation 103
MSI (Italian Social Movement, see also fascism, Mussolini) 218
Murrow, Ed 36
NACLA *Report on the Americas* 115-24, 154
Naimsky, Piotr 338
National Guardian 55-73, 100, 102, 121, 128, 133, 154, 250
Native Americans 3, 4, 35, 42, 45, 47, 87-88, 104-14, 124, 153, 348
American Indian Movement (AIM) 106, 107, 108, 111
Bureau of Indian Affairs (BIA) 107
Cheyenne nation 104
Hopi nation 106
Miskito nation (Nicaragua) 105
Mohawk nation 104, 105, 106
Raymond Yellow Thunder 107

Wounded knee 1973 occupation 108
La Nazione 273
Negri, Toni 19, 232
newsprint subsidy bill (Italy) 222, 247-8, 262
Newsreel
California Newsreel 117, 139-45, 154
London 28, 100, 131
New York 125ff.
San Francisco 130
Third World Newsreel 85, 125-34
New York Times 3, 36, 37, 58, 64, 355
Nixon, President 132, 153
Novotný, Antonin 313, 314, 315, 318
NOW (National Organization of Women) 100
NOWA (Poland) 330, 342-4
objectivity in media 3, 5, 15, 36, 37, 210-11
Old Left (USA) 44, 49, 55-62, 74-81, 101
Onyskiewićz, Wojtek (*Robotnik*) 334
Open Door (Britain) 8
Opinia (Poland) 330
Orwell, George 1, 351
Otelo de Carvalho (Portugal) 169, 211
Owen, Robert 18
P2 (Italy) 219
Pacifica Foundation 71, 74, 76, 79, 87
El Pais 247
Paul VI, Pope 188
PCI (see Communist Party, Italy)
PCP (see Communist Party, Portugal)
PdUP (Proletarian Unity Party, Italy) 238-40, 248, 252, 292, 298
Viareggio Congress 1978 240
Peace and Freedom Party (Berkeley, US) 92-3
Pedrocchi, Federico (Radio Popolare) 284, 291, 296, 297
Pentagon Papers 36

phone-in (see also Controradio, Radio Popolare, *Songs With A Telephone*) 7, 194
Pienkowska, Alína 336
Pinelli case 225, 270
Pintor, Luigi (*Il Manifesto*) 243, 247
Pius XI, Pope 219
Pius XII, Pope 58
Poland 11, 15, 93, 263, 307, 322-46, 347, 350, 353
anti-semitism between the wars 327
Polish Journalists' Association 331
political movements (see also alternative media)
Czechoslovakia 313-21
Italy 225-34, 255-72, 290
Poland 322-46
Portugal 168-214
USA 42-50, 59-60, 152-6
Popular Monarchist Party (Portugal) 175, 211
Popular Social Democrats (Portugal) 174, 175, 179, 186, 187-8, 197, 211
Porter, David 23
Portugal 17, 25, 49, 66, 96, 108, 161-214, 222, 256, 315
Northern region's significance (see also under Catholic Church, censorship, Communist Party, established media, fascism, political movements, Socialist Party) 179
Potere Operaio 256
Poznan 326, 329
PPD (see Popular Social Democrats)
Pracé 315
Prague Spring v, 173, 308, 314-8, 323, 353
Pravda 355
Presley, Elvis 50
Press Connection, Madison 28
Prokop, Dieter 298
PSD (see Popular Social Democrats)

PSDI (see Social Democrats, Italy)
PSI (see Socialist Party, Italy)
PS/PSP (see Socialist Party, Portugal)
public broadcasting 6-7, 147-8
Puerto Rico iv, 35, 42, 146-51, 154
Center for Puerto Rican Studies 134, 135
Culebra 147
Piñones 147-8
sport's political significance 150
Young Lords 131, 147
Puls 326, 340-41
Quotidiano Donna 245, 264
racism 4, 8, 22, 36, 45-46, 58, 89, 105, 114, 130, 131, 136-7, 155, 178, 242
Radical America 65
Radical Party (Italy) 228, 241, 248, 262, 277-8, 294
Radio Alice, Bologna 231, 295-6, 303, 353
Radio Cento Fiori, Florence 277, 353
Radio Città Futura, Rome (to 1979) 29, 224, 231, 263, 274, 279, 284-5, 293
Rádio Clube Português 75, 172, 173, 179, 186, 190, 201, 208-14
Radio Free Europe 26, 333
Radio Milano Centrale 288
Radio Popolare, Milan 203, 231, 249, 252, 271, 279. 283-301
Rádio Renascença 171, 173, 174, 179, 181-94, 198, 201, 202, 206, 208, 210, 211
Oporto station 182, 186
Radio Verte Fessenheim (West Germany) 26-7
Radom 329, 333, 343
RAI (Italy) 223, 224, 288
readers' letters 15, 324, 338
Reagan, President 143, 153, 348
Rêgo, Raúl (*República*) 196, 197, 198, 209, 244
Repubblica (Italy) 216-8, 222, 241, 244

República (Portugal) 119, 171, 173, 174, 179, 181, 184, 188, 190, 191, 192, 193, 208, 210
Republican Party (Italy) 228
Republican Party (USA) 5
Resto del Carlino 230
Reston, James 3-5
Reuters (Lisbon) 185-6
Riotta, Gianni (*Il Manifesto*) 244, 248
Robotnik 330, 333-7
Rolling Stone 35, 351
Romany peoples 272, 308, 319
Rome 229, 240
Roosevelt, President 43, 56, 75
ROPCiO (Poland) 340
Rosenberg case 48, 58
Rossa, Guido (murdered by Red Brigades) 271
Rossanda, Rossana (*Il Manifesto*) 240, 243, 246, 252
Rowbotham, Sheila 16, 18, 20, 21, 22, 23, 154, 358
Rudé Právo 316
Ryan, Bill (*The Guardian*) 66
Sacco and Vanzetti 194
Salniker, David (KPFA) 82-3, 92-3
samizdat 330, 342
Sandino Films 146, 147, 148, 151
Scalzone, Oreste (Italian student leader) 232
Scott, Bari (KPFA) 74, 88-9
SDS (Students for a Democratic Society, USA) 48, 49, 126
sectarian political groups 49, 65, 66, 69, 71-2, 94, 133, 134, 140, 152, 193, 271
  party-building movement (USA) 49, 121
O Século (Portugal) 169
self-censorship 12, 300, 339-40, 341-2
self-management *passim;* as a concept, iv, 2, 25-9, 67, 311, 320, 322, 347, 359-60
Sennett, Richard and Cobb, Jonathan 155-6

sexism (see also feminism, women) 4, 22, 36, 50, 90, 128-9, 187, 252, 266
Siliato, F. 9-10
Sinclair, Upton, *The Jungle* 40
SIPRA 248, 261-2, 281
Slovakia 307, 311, 312, 313, 319
Smrkovsky, Josef 316
SNCC (Student Non-Violent Co-ordinating Committee) 48
Soares, Mário (PSP) 182, 195, 196, 199, 204
Social Democrats
  Czechoslovakia 311-2
  Italy (PSDI) 228, 248 9
  Poland 335
Socialist Party
  Italy (PSI) 216, 223, 226, 228, 238, 239, 258, 263, 277, 283, 284, 288
  Portugal (PSP/PS) 169, 174, 175, 178, 181, 182, 186, 188, 195-206, 209, 211
Società (PCI Monthly) 230
Solidarity (Poland) v, 101, 323, 324, 329, 331, 337, 344, 345, 358-9
Solidarność z Gdanskiem 337-8
Songs With A Telephone (Prague Spring) 315
South East Asia (in US and Italian politics) 36, 41, 42, 43, 44, 48, 56, 58, 63, 65, 140, 147, 256, 297, 348
Southern Africa 41, 56, 66, 93, 141, 144-5, 167, 176, 192, 193, 208, 324, 326, 348, 359
Soweto 141
Southern Africa Media Center (California Newsreel) 141, 144
Southern Exposure 115
Soviet Union (see also duopoly, imperialism) 11, 12, 15, 39, 43, 49, 56, 57, 65, 66, 105, 124, 161-66, 178, 237, 277, 311, 330, 351
  anti-Semitism and *National Guardian* 58

Spain 17, 162, 164, 168, 211, 232, 333
Spotkania 330
Stalin, stalinism 13, 14, 49, 59, 76, 237, 310, 312, 313-4, 325, 350
La Stampa 222, 241
Stone, I.F. 56, 60
Strong, Anna Louise 57, 60
students in Italy 227-8, 229-31, 255, 290 (see also *emarginati,* SDS, SNCC)
Szczypiorski, Adam 326
SUV (Soldiers United Will Win, Portugal) 177
Tageszeitung 28, 71, 100, 121, 241
Teamsters Union 98
O Tempo (Lisbon) 28, 173, 278
terrorism 40, 130, 218-9, 228, 231-3, 239-40, 244, 258, 265, 271, 297, 326
Third World (see also Central America, Latin America, Puerto Rico, South East Asia, Southern Africa, Third World presence in alternative media) iv, 307, 348
Third World Newsreel 85, 125-34
Thompson, Edward 24, 156, 353
Time 169
Togliatti, Palmiro (PCI) 219, 220, 247
Transamerica Corporation 37
Truman, President 57, 161-2
Trybuna Ludu 332
Union for Democratic Communication (USA) 28
UDP (Popular Democratic Unity, Portugal) 187-8
Union of Marxist Leninists (Italy) 255
unions (see also workers, Solidarity) 9, 47, 56, 81, 84-5, 96-103, 142, 210, 245-6, 248, 256, 266
Union Wage 61, 62, 71, 96-103, 154, 245
United Farmworkers 98
Ursus factory (Poland) 329, 333, 343

USA (see also duopoly, imperialism) 3, 28, 35-166, 167, 175, 194, 218, 264, 268, 274, 300, 302
USSR (see Soviet Union)
Utne Reader 153
Valeriotti, Giuseppe (murdered by mafia) 216-8
Valpreda (see Pinelli) 225
Van Onderen (Dutch access TV program) 9
Village Voice 35, 69
Violi, Patrizia 268, 271
voting in presidential elections 153-4
Walentinowicz, Anna 336
Walesa, Lech 335, 336
Warsaw 333, 335, 336
Warsaw Uprising 328
Washington Post 36
Watergate 36, 132
Weathermen (USA) 130
Wechsburg, Joseph 319
Weinberger, Caspar 80
West Germany 13, 26-7, 57, 168, 178, 326, 334, 350
Wieck, David 18, 23
Wired World, Kitchener-Waterloo, Canada 8
Wojcićka, Irene *(Robotnik)* 335
Wolfe, Alan 153
women (see also feminism, sexism and alternative media) 3, 4, 5, 29, 35, 36, 37, 42, 45, 47, 48, 56, 96-103, 143, 150, 168, 178, 220, 228
workers (see also unions) 5, 9, 14, 35, 96-103, 141-3, 150, 167-8, 183, 185, 211, 218, 228, 256, 266-7, 268, 286, 289, 318, 324, 333-7, 347
Media At Work (California Newsreel) 143
Workers 1980 (film of Gdańsk negotiations) 333
Writers Union (Czechoslovakia) 312, 313, 318
4th Congress 1967 313
Literary Fund 312, 313
Wujec, Henryk *(Robotnik)* 335
Yugoslavia 27, 57, 162, 222
Zapis 340-41
Zionism 59, 91, 93, 165, 167, 242